RETHINKING THE
DEVELOPMENT
EXPERIENCE

RETHINKING THE DEVELOPMENT EXPERIENCE

Essays Provoked by
the Work of
Albert O. Hirschman

LLOYD RODWIN
DONALD A. SCHÖN
Editors

The Brookings Institution
Washington, D.C.
The Lincoln Institute of Land Policy
Cambridge, Massachusetts

Copyright © 1994
THE BROOKINGS INSTITUTION
1775 Massachusetts Avenue, N.W., Washington, D.C. 20036
and
THE LINCOLN INSTITUTE OF LAND
POLICY
113 Brattle Street, Cambridge, MA 02138-3400

Library of Congress Cataloging-in-Publication data:

Rethinking the development experience : essays provoked by
the work of Albert O. Hirschman / edited by Lloyd Rodwin,
Donald A. Schön.
   p. cm.
   Includes bibliographical references and index.
   ISBN 0-8157-7552-0 (cloth : alk. paper) — ISBN 0-8157-
7551-2 (pbk. : alk. paper)
   1. Economic development—Congresses. 2. Hirschman,
Albert O.—Congresses. I. Rodwin, Lloyd. II. Schön, Donald A.
   HB75.R448   1994
   338.9—dc20   94-12644
                                                  CIP

9 8 7 6 5 4 3 2 1

The paper used in this publication meets the minimum require-
ments of the American National Standard for Information
Sciences—Permanence of paper for Printed Library Materials,
ANSI Z39.48-1984

Typeset in Palatino

Composition by Graphic Composition, Inc.
Athens, Georgia

Printed by R. R. Donnelly and Sons Co.
Harrisonburg, Virginia

The Brookings Institution

The Brookings Institution is an independent, nonprofit organization devoted to nonpartisan research, education, and publication in economics, government, foreign policy, and the social sciences generally. Its principal purposes are to aid in the development of sound public policies and to promote public understanding of issues of national importance. The Institution was founded on December 8, 1927, to merge the activities of the Institute for Government Research, founded in 1916, the Institute of Economics, founded in 1922, and the Robert Brookings Graduate School of Economics, founded in 1924.

The Institution maintains a position of neutrality on issues of public policy to safeguard the intellectual freedom of the staff. Interpretations or conclusions in Brookings publications should be understood to be solely those of the authors.

Lincoln Institute of Land Policy

The Lincoln Institute of Land Policy is a nonprofit and tax-exempt educational institution established in 1974. Its mission as a school is to study and teach land policy, including land economics and land taxation. The Institute is supported by the Lincoln Foundation, established in 1947 by John C. Lincoln, a Cleveland industrialist. Mr. Lincoln drew inspiration from the ideas of Henry George, the nineteenth-century American political economist and social philosopher.

Integrating the theory and practice of land policy and understanding the forces that influence it are the major goals of the Lincoln Institute. The Institute explores the fundamental forces affecting land use and development: governments' strategies for managing change, community and individual rights and responsibilities, taxation and regulation, the functioning of markets, patterns of human settlement and economic production, and transportation systems.

Preface

ALBERT O. HIRSCHMAN has made significant contributions to the fields of development, economic theory, economic history, and the history of ideas. He has also held some of the most prestigious professorships in the U.S. academic world; and his books have been praised highly by eminent writers (such as Kenneth J. Arrow, Stanley Hoffman, Charles E. Lindblom, John K. Galbraith, Karl Deutsch, Robert Kuttner, and Joseph Kraft). So it is not too surprising that members of a faculty should decide—as ours did—to participate voluntarily in a seminar (with some specially qualified students) to explore some of Hirschman's ideas.

However, the views expressed here are not those of followers, as is evident in the ways the authors explore, extend, test, or contest Hirschman's angles of vision. This is all the more so for those who consider his contributions flawed by his failure to "model" his important insights or by the "latitude" of his policy recommendations, or because of a different way of looking at such questions as how disciplines, fields of practices, and societies grow and develop. These diverse and intense reactions are not surprising, given the differences in the participants' perspectives and fields of specialization. And since the work of Hirschman triggers such reactions, we decided to subtitle this volume *Essays Provoked by the Work of Albert O. Hirschman*. The chapters that follow provide the evidence that led to this decision.

In retrospect, it is clear that Hirschman's incisive, skeptical, ironical cast of mind commands admiration on several grounds: for his inclination to challenge doctrinaire views—not only those of the right and left, but the highly prized concepts of the economics establishment (for example, parsimony, rationality, balance, and equilibria); for his fondness for "paired opposites"—drawn from folk wisdom and literary aperçus—to serve these aims; for the broad humanism that makes him literate in many bodies of theory and suspicious in all of them, his own as well; for the anthropological eye he has cultivated that makes him avidly interested in the way the socioeconomic world works; for his historical and political perspectives coupled with his pragmatic interest in knowledge useful for action; and for the education of those who seek to play a role in helping societies and their sectoral and subnational components go where they roughly want to go.

Lloyd Rodwin
Donald A. Schön

Contents

RETHINKING THE DEVELOPMENT EXPERIENCE

Overview

One

Rethinking the Development Experience
Aims, Themes, and Theses

Lloyd Rodwin

WHEN WE , together with other members of the MIT faculty, decided to organize a colloquium on the contemporary relevance of the ideas of Albert O. Hirschman, our initial motivation was sheer intellectual curiosity. Anticipating an interesting play of ideas, we held no firm or precise intentions, such as a desire to produce this book. Most of the participants were concerned with Hirschman's approach to development—in particular, his theory of imbalanced growth (with its grounding in an elusive theory of social learning); his attitudes to the policy and practice of development economics (pragmatic, site-specific, appreciative of local knowledge and of multiple paths to development); and his empirical, historical, contrarian, and catholic social science perspectives. But we viewed these notions in markedly different ways, which reflected our special backgrounds, intellectual orientations, and dissenting positions. It was mainly the wish to sharpen our dialogue that led us to prepare papers and tapes of our discussions on selected topics and link them to some general themes.

Aims and Themes

Our agenda was tentative, modest, and open-ended. We did not try to address or solve a specific problem or set of problems. Nor—except in two instances—did we try to cover a particular territory by farming out topics to individuals for explicit coverage. The topics in those two cases were the learning assumptions in Hirschman's thinking about economic development and the reasons for the rise and fall, and possible rise again, both of Hirschman's influence among economists and of development economics in universities throughout the United States.

Our approach seemed likely to give us a great deal of autonomy, but the risk was that the choice of topics might prove uneven and limited. The approach was somewhat Hirschmanesque: sensitive to the values, preferences, and behavior patterns of the subculture and inclined to be incremental, historical, and disjunctive rather than integrated or comprehensive in style. What has emerged, not surprisingly, is a range of analyses in the papers and discussions suggesting how Hirschman's ideas on development might be adapted, extended, or critically evaluated from the special perspectives of the participants.

But there is more: the volume also presents a critical reappraisal of ideas about and attitudes toward development—first advanced by Hirschman in the political, economic and intellectual climate of the 1950s and 1960s—and it introduces some unexpectedly interrelated themes provoked by Hirschman's ideas on learning as they bear on the theory, policy, and practice of development in the 1990s. Summed up, these themes suggest ways of strengthening theory, policy, and practice in economics, when it is seen as both a discipline and a profession, and ways of coping with the broadening, and not always consistent, aims of development: these now reach beyond economic progress to include sociopolitical and cultural values such as preservation of the environment and equalization; also, the lessons we can glean from innovative projects, programs, and policies and from attempts to restructure institutions, especially the efforts to realign state and market organizations in more developed, newly developing, and former socialist countries.

We have grouped the essays in this volume around these three themes. The chapters by Paul Krugman, Lance Taylor, and Donald Schön (plus the comments of Michael Piore, given in appendix A) treat learning and development policy and the perspectives of the economic theorists. The historical analyses of Emma Rothschild, Lisa Peattie, and Bishwapriya Sanyal trace some of the changes in attitudes toward economic development and their underlying assumptions. And the essays of Elliot Marseille, Judith Tendler and Sara Freedheim, Robert Picciotto, and Charles Sabel consider the lessons that might be drawn from efforts to innovate or modify institutions, policies, programs, and projects.

We also invited Professor Hirschman to react to these essays, to the tapes we made of the seminar discussions, and to the transcribed Hirschman seminar minutes (HSM)—for an abbreviated version of them see appendix A—and to meet with the seminar participants. His response was twofold: first, a brief but valuable postscript in chapter 12 on how, over time, he has critiqued and amended his ideas; and second, his musings on his "cognitive style," his reactions to particular papers, and his responses to questions raised by the group, all of which are incorporated as appendix B. What follows are some inferences drawn from an overview of the issues raised by the papers and discussions.

Principal Issues

Underlying much of the debate is a familiar conflict: that is, between those advocates with faith in rigorous and parsimonious models of physical and social reality suggested by Occam's Razor and associated with positivist thinking, and others who value *pluralistic*, narrative, qualitative descriptions, perhaps as exemplified by Kenneth Burke's celebration of complexity and richness of the universe.

Krugman, our modeler, argues that Hirschman helped precipitate the fall of development economics because he cast his insights about the strategy for economic development in narrative, qualitative, situation-specific terms and did not formalize them in rigorous mathematical models. Krugman points, for example, to the importance of modeling economic returns to scale in the development process (specifically, in the decision to modernize production), which Hirschman and his comperes then could not or did not analyze mathematically but which Krugman says he and others can now handle. Through such incremental advances in formal modeling Krugman sees an indication of the slow but inevitable progress of economics in general and development economics in particular. He recognizes that in its present state economic theory cannot explain why one country does better than another, and that in the incremental interlacing of formal theory, some narrative insights may well be lost, at least temporarily. But he is willing to pay that price.

Taylor counters that what Krugman sees as linear progress is more really a kind of oscillation. Over the past ten to twenty years the climate of opinion has been dominated by monetary, macroeconomic, market-oriented theories of development: theories that advocate minimizing governmental intervention, establishing the institutional conditions for free markets, and concentrating on "getting the prices right." This is only *one* version of economic theory, but it is the one that has shaped thinking about development policy in the historical period from which we are only now emerging. Taylor observes that this theory's claims to usefulness and reliability as a guide to development are being increasingly questioned; and in the aftermath, he expects Hirschman's narrative, empirical, qualitative, situation-specific learning approach to rise again.

Piore goes further: he questions the market-oriented macroeconomic approach to development. It involves a model of market-price signals that must always be *interpreted*, he says, and such interpretation is a cognitive process: one that depends on contextual conditions—social, political, and cultural; and since mainstream market-oriented economic theory has nothing to say about such cognitive processes of interpretation, it is likely to be misapplied. To learn how to deal with this problem, economics should, but probably will not, welcome infusions from other disciplines. Piore, in effect, submits this explanation for the perceived failure of the market-oriented macroeconomic theories of economic development at the center of Taylor's argument.

The arguments of Taylor and Piore point up the need to *learn* from the experience of interventions aimed at promoting stabilization and development. When the market-oriented macroeconomic approach to development policy holds, there is much less need to deal with sectoral and subnational levels of social aggregation; policymakers may recognize that social learning occurs, and occurs in a way that is critical to development, but they need not worry about it. All they have to think about is the highest level of monetary, fiscal, or investment policies; the rest is presumed more or less to take care of itself. But when this idea fades—when "getting the prices right" and market-oriented policies alone are not taken as reliable guides to development policy and there is no longer a consensual theory of intervention to promote development at the macroeconomic level of policymaking, then sectoral, subnational, and even microeconomic interventions rise to prominence; and it becomes essential to know much more about policy- and decisionmakers' motivations, learning, and behavior. Schön's critical analysis details the different ways—implicit as well as explicit—by which Hirschman copes with these questions and suggests why the more traditional theorists do not address them.

Rothschild, Peattie, and Sanyal challenge still other assumptions taken for granted by mainstream economists and point again toward the importance of learning from development experience. However, their challenges come from different sources and suggest different kinds of learning.

Both Rothschild and Peattie examine contemporary economic theory and practice in the light of their formative period in the eighteenth and early nineteenth century, when economic and social thought were still intertwined.

Rothschild focuses on the oversimplified conception of "economic man" central to mainstream economic theory. She revisits the thinking of some of the founders of economics, discovering in their ideas a Hirschmanesque sensitivity to the problems of learning to economize and a far broader, more realistic, less rational conception of human nature than is contained in the contemporary notion of "economic man."

Peattie, in turn, traces the process by which social progress came to be narrowly identified with modernization and the job of promoting progress came to be appropriated by specialists in economic development. She argues that for a time discourse about development lost its connection to the larger field of social, cultural, and moral values that have once again become central to development theory. What is more, in certain contemporary movements of social protest she reads a violent rejection of this narrowing of the development agenda.

In contrast, Sanyal probes Hirschman's bias for hope: this perspective is reinforced by the diverse ways societies learn to cope with their development problems; the hidden rationalities often underlying "irrational" behavior; Hirschman's rejection of the impractical assumptions of the political left and right; and the significance he attaches to the often surprising capability of individuals, institutions, and social processes to make creative responses to the unforseen difficulties inherent in the disequilibria generated by imbalanced growth.

In short—like Taylor, Piore, and Schön—Peattie, Rothschild, and Sanyal direct our attention to lessons from development experience. But the kind of experience and learning they have in mind underscores the values—social, cultural, and moral—to which more traditional economic theory and practice give short shrift.

Not least, the analyses of Marseille, Tendler and Freedheim, Picciotto, and Sabel illustrate what may be learned from the experience of actual interventions aimed at promoting development.

Marseille tells the story of a project seeking to reduce blindness in Nepal that by all accounts ought to have failed; instead, it worked. Its unlikely success, he thinks, stems in part from the creativity displayed by local manufacturers from India who *learned* to produce cheap, high-quality intraocular lens implants, for which the project had generated an overriding demand.

Tendler and Freedheim describe the conditions under which successful efforts were made in a large-scale rural, preventive health program to get it to work well, against all odds. Drawing on existing knowledge outside of economics, and on what was learned from Hirschman about the empirical analysis of behavior, pressures, and pricing inducement mechanisms in specific development situations, they offer general heuristic prescriptions for the design of better-performing projects.

Picciotto explains how an agency that provides aid for development—namely, the World Bank—addresses the issue of policy and program evaluation. He asserts that effective development policy—national, sectoral, and subnational—depends on *learning* from the experience of development projects and programs, which is the business of evaluation. Charting the evolution of the Bank's approach to these tasks, he sees a movement from narrow economic analysis (cost-benefit studies, growth rates, comparative rates of return on investment) to the broader, messier, more qualitative, and narrative kind of evaluation practiced now by his own office. With an emphasis on the consequences of visibility and disappointment, he applauds—albeit selectively—Hirschman's "classical" treatment of project analyses, as illustrated especially by his inferences from the experience of World Bank projects recorded in *Development Projects Observed.*[1]

Sabel draws his example of intervention from Japan. He attributes the extraordinary success of the large Japanese firm not to unique cultural factors, or to game-theoretic maneuvering, but to processes conducive to continuing cooperation and trust, processes structured into the contracts that govern relations between the state and the firm, and between the firm and its subcontractors. In these contracts he finds two syntheses: first, of systematic learning to make and do things valued in markets; and then of monitoring processes by which the parties continually assess whether the gains achieved are being fairly distributed. This union of learning and monitoring, Sabel says, yields a structural solution to the fundamental political-economic tension inherent in development.

This third group of essays represents a search for useful intermediate or "middle-level" rules or criteria for improved development. The search is conducted at the level of projects and sectoral and subnational policies and programs. Valuable lessons can also be gleaned from a case-by-case study of attempts to cope with national economic problems or to promote the development of the nation, as Taylor suggests in his book, *Varieties of Stabilization Experience.*[2]

The crucial point here is the role of learning. Theories, policies, projects, and practice have intriguing familial relationships. They may be offsprings of each other. They presuppose the growth of knowledge and understanding, which are often limited and imperfect. And they are all vulnerable. But their ardently sought strengthening depends on learning, through activities such as modeling, testing, and the analysis of experience. The ordeals leave few hardy survivors.

So much for the general résumé of our efforts. Now let us mull over the specific findings to see what further insights might be drawn from them.

Specific Theses

The specific theses put forth in this book all have something to say about ways of rethinking the development experience and their implications for improving development policies and the institutions and programs serving them.

Conceptualizing Development

For most mainstream economists, as we have noted, learning does not loom as a significant problem where markets do function: if you deploy the right macropolitics and get the prices right, they argue, then you will get the right responses and behavior, as illustrated in the past few decades by the economies of Japan, Korea, Taiwan, Singapore, Thailand, and Malaysia. Development has taken place there without active intervention by the state in matters where it does not function well.

In chapter 2, however, Paul Krugman observes that "the relationship between good economic analysis and successful policy is far weaker than we like to imagine." The *learning* vital to development, he says, can be obtained from models; and it is from this perspective that he reviews the story of development economics. Despite the skill and perceptiveness of his brief, his colleagues Lance Taylor and Michael Piore register some vigorous demurrers.

KRUGMAN'S STAND ON MODELING AND ECONOMIC DEVELOPMENT THEORY.   Krugman begins his tale with what he considers the core insight of two great pioneers of development theory: Paul N. Rosenstein-Rodan and Hirschman. They recognized that promoting self-reinforcing growth in poor countries depends on the ability to create the *size of market* necessary to make possible *economies of scale*. These conditions are shown to be necessary, first, so that investments in productive activities can afford the higher wage required to draw labor from traditional to modern activities; and second, so that new markets and investments may be created (with the aid of appropriate infrastructure and other public investments), along with a variety of linkages: these make it possible to reach the minimum economic thresholds required for establishing and expanding still other activities.

Krugman quickly dismisses differences in the "details" of the ideas and policies formulated by these forerunners of development theory. The importance of the necessary conditions, he claims, was not at all obvious to the economists then "locked in their traditional models" and the noneconomists "lost in the fog that results when you have no explicit models at all"; the problem was only exacerbated, he charges, because of the discursive, nonmathematical analyses of "high development theorists" (Krugman's phrase) in the 1940s and 1950s. It was this failure to get the "rigorous proofs" incorporated into the corpus of theory in the style of presentation increasingly favored by mainstream economics methodology—that is, in the form of succinct, "buttoned-down, mathematically consistent analyses"—that led, in Krugman's judgment, to the bypassing, neglect, and ultimate decline of development theory. He does not "blame" either Hirschman or the other forerunners, because at the time no one quite knew how to introduce economies of scale into the formal models of the standard theory: all they could handle then was competitive analysis, where "firms take prices as given," and not the more relevant oligopolistic theory of price behavior of large firms with substantial market power.

Krugman is well aware of the irrelevance for policymaking of much mainstream economic theory, as well as the misuse of modeling by mainstream economists, who much too frequently overlook their simplifying and narrowing assumptions and the occasions when "more is lost than is gained" by this deliberate falsification of reality. He says he understands why Hirschman might well prefer "suggestive metaphors, institutional realism, interdisciplinary reasoning and a relaxed attitude toward internal consistency"; but he believes this was nonetheless an error, an intellectual "dead end." The reason is that the risk is great that if not "embalmed in models," the influence of ideas, however stimulating and influential, "soon decays."

Even more, Krugman said in his colloquium talk, because Hirschman abandoned "the attempt to discipline his metaphor with models," he took "high development theory off the intellectual rails," kept it from being part of a larger body of accepted knowledge, and ended up having more of an impact on people outside the field than within it.[3] Hirschman, he added, was good at liberating minds, not in giving support for how to go further. "As an economic analyst, Hirschman is an excellent novelist, valuable for his richness in observation and metaphor."[4] But the right solution, he concludes, is not to operate at the periphery or to reject modeling—which is indispensable for coping better over time with complex problems; it is, rather, to improve the models so that they become more powerful, increasingly transcend their limitations, and receive more attention and use from economists and policymakers in the field.[5]

What is intriguing is that although Krugman downgrades the use of metaphor, storytelling, and comparative interdisciplinary reasoning, he makes superb use of all three in developing his brief: particularly in the parable he recounts of geographers expanding their ignorance as they amass experience and technical knowledge in the mapping of Africa and in the tale he tells about the effectiveness of the primitive precomputer models that MIT meteorologist Dave Fultz designed to simulate the giant wobbles of air around the globe. All this Krugman uses to buttress his preference for the simple, rigorous, more sophisticated, and useful development model of market size and economies of scale: a model that requires, as he says in chapter 2, only "three pages, two equations, and one diagram," and, of course, in this instance, an acceptable falsification of reality.

What may be less persuasive, especially in nonacademic circles, is Krugman's assumption that economics is only a discipline, not a profession too, like law, medicine, or public service, with significant aims, knowledge, and norms for the guidance of practice.

TWO DISSENTING VIEWS: LANCE TAYLOR AND MICHAEL PIORE.   In Taylor's view, Krugman "gives the profession's attachment to its intellectual playthings too much weight"; nonetheless, he acknowledges in chapter 3 that as of 1993 Hirschman's influence on mainstream economics has not been too great, even though his concept of backward and forward linkages is in all the economics textbooks, as are his hypotheses about machine-paced factory production, and his ideas "on inflation as a disequilibrium process provoked by structural imbalances, and on 'external strangulation' from the balance of payments, [which] underlie the macroeconomics of the [minority] neostructuralist school." The fact is, Taylor notes, many of Hirschman's other striking ideas in *The Strategy of Economic Development* "simply vanished from sight." Among these are Hirschman's idea that development involves transitions from one sort of disequilibrium to another, his distinction between complementarity and substitution, his emphasis on the role of imports in inducing industrialization, and his interest in feasible and fruitful relationships between market- and nonmarket-oriented activities. At the same time, Taylor does not doubt that much of "this information does not look immediately useful to someone who has to make a decision about tariff T, quota Q or subsidy S for industry X today."

Nonetheless, Taylor thinks that Hirschman still has "remarkable lessons to teach students who bother to look," lessons for more developed and newly developing economies and those in the post-socialist transition. The best explanation he can suggest for the current neglect is that the strategy had stopped fitting "the spirit of the times." In the main this was because of the "neoclassical reaction against the world view of Schumpeter, Rosenstein-Rodan, Nurkse, Hirschman and company," and because "clear, simple, strong, market-friendly recommendations carried the day after 1970 in development economics." This was all the more unfortunate, in Taylor's judgment, since "setting prices to 'right values' . . . is not easy, [and] target prices are impossible to define and the economic effects of the transition toward them can be fatally destabilizing." And this is why Taylor expects renewed appreciation of Hirschman's work when the pendulum turns toward pragmatic, site-specific approaches to problems of stabilization and development.[6]

Michael Piore—who spoke at the colloquium but did not submit a chapter to this volume—suggested that it might be helpful to address problems of development from a quite different perspective: that of learning and understanding within economic theory.[7] Conventional economics, Piore observed, "rests on the price system, which reduces or converts everything to a set of problems handled by signals," that is, changes in price. To interpret these signals, people require a communicative framework that mainstream economists accept uncritically as given rather than as constructed. As a result, inquiries into how signals are developed and transmitted are "forced into theories outside of and alien to conventional economic analysis, to the way [economists] are taught to think about the world as an epistemological problem."

The logic of the argument—that "you have a framework and it has to come from someplace and can change—opens up a new dimension of understanding" of economic behavior, in which it is clear that "communication takes place within a social framework: you can't deduce it [directly] from experience itself," but only as "embedded in a social and historical context."

Piore then made a series of observations about Hirschman's relationship to the economics profession. These were based on Piore's exposure to economics as a graduate student at Harvard in the 1960s, which he called a transition point away from Keynesian "eclecticism." Hirschman was not yet at Harvard; he came soon after and was brought by people with whom Piore had studied. For that depression generation, "Keynes had created a space in economics in which everything was up for grabs, leaving room for ad hoc theories and theories borrowed from other disciplines." By way of example, Piore cites James Duesenberry, who "was prepared to draw on Karen Horney to explain the consumption function." In that "climate," Piore argues, "people were ready to entertain any theory, and also depended on practical experience rather than abstract reasoning"; this is a characteristic often ascribed to Hirschman's thinking: he put a "premium" on midlevel ideas bridging experience and theory and advocated a "catholic" approach very much in keeping with the Harvard atmosphere. Since then, however, that open, cross-disciplinary window has closed, and the field has become "less hospitable" to ideas drawn from outside its declared boundaries. Therefore, Piore says, "it may be true in retrospect that Hirschman has been operating outside the center of the profession, but not at the time in which he was developing the core body of his work."

Piore speculates that "it took the experience of living through the depression to tolerate the intellectual catholicism reigning at that time at Harvard" and that for his generation, the "tension" in the teaching of economics was "impossible" to tolerate. One response to that tension has been the continuing effort "to bring back coherence to economics"; and Hirschman, by present-day terms, is seen as "sloppy" or "lazy," because of the "lost tolerance for that intellectual eclecticism and ambiguity present in economics in the 1950s and '60s." As the discipline became more concerned with coherence and internal consistency, "the kind of people attracted to [the field] were less the kinds of people who feel at home in or turned on by the realm of practice," and so miss the dimension of experience as a "touchstone" for their work: this may explain why Hirschman has been more accessible to planners, because of "the way he speaks about the world" and "the things he uses as evidence."

HIRSCHMAN'S LEARNING THEMES: SCHÖN'S INFERENCES AND RESERVATIONS.   In Hirschman's conceptual framework, the adviser as well as the policymaker must be aware "of how at a specific time and place development activity is naturally unfolding," an awareness, Donald A. Schön points out in chapter 4, that can only be acquired through direct, on-site observation. He or she must understand the images of change held by societies in order "to anticipate how and with what consequences they are likely to change or what resistances they are likely to put up against change"; he or she must also be ever sensitive to the frequent superiority of local knowledge, which "outperforms the expert knowledge of outsiders and always relishes the 'hidden rationalities' of apparently irrational local practice." These requirements are central to Schön's analysis of Hirschman's elusive theory of development as social learning. This theory of development as learning, elusive and only partly explicit in Hirschman's early work, is directly applicable to the restructuring of institutions, systems, and political economies that now constitutes something of an international obsession.

As Schön emphasizes, Hirschman focuses on how to dispel peoples' ignorance, misconceptions, and lack of will to *learn* about the road to development; how people *learn* in various circumstances and from various pressures to experiment with policies, make decisions, undertake projects, and use available resources and latent abilities; how this *learning by doing* could be encouraged and be made cumulative through pacing devices and inducement mechanisms; how these means can be generated by some combination of market behavior and social policy plus *learning aids* such as clear aims, publicly visible and rapid feedback, measurable indices of performance, machine-based production, visible productive differences (in performance, quality, and levels of living), resort to efficient learning sequences, the pull of the image, and the like; and how, as people overcome the difficulty of taking the decisions needed "in the required number and the required speed," they acquire a more positive image of change, a sense of its possibility and desirability, of how it is brought about and how they and others benefit from it.

Many actors and institutions are involved, and there will be many problems, particularly *disequilibria and alternations*—with tensions, conflicts, setbacks, and failures; but if over time—not all at once, not in a standard way, and not subject to prerequisites, such as capital and education—countervailing forces emerge or can be generated to help people cope with the disequilibria and potentially fruitful alternations dialectically and more or less satisfactorily, even the problems will become *learning experiences*, increase their capabilities, and reinforce self-confidence.[8]

To all of this Schön—as a planner, professional practitioner, and organization theorist—nods his head; but it is all the more reason for his puzzlement that this implicit theory or metaphor of learning is never explicitly and systematically confronted (economists would say modeled) by Hirschman. Provocative examples are not enough, Schön suggests. What is needed—in a learning-based view of development—"is a better understanding of the different kinds of learning by doing" (for example, "getting practice in what is intuitively known or getting tutelage for what is not known); also, a far more systematic explanation of improvement of performance over time in terms of values, criteria, and objectives; and a way of saying what is learned in a learning sequence or episode in relation to the kinds of processes by which it is achieved; plus accounting for conditions favorable or unfavorable to improvement of performance; and confronting the question of who learns (what particular individuals, or groups of individuals or institutions)."

Schön points, also, to some problems in Hirschman's assumption that "doing" will change patterns of thinking and behaving, and that there is a core of individuals who can think, feel, do, and help others to do likewise. What evidence is there, he asks that the experience of learning by doing should "always, or mostly, influence feelings, thoughts, and beliefs to change in the same promising direction," especially considering the extraordinary range and number of individuals, groups and institutions that have to be involved?

Schön underlines, too, certain ambiguities, especially the lack of any indication in *Strategy* of the kinds and degrees of difficulty considered salutary for development. He notes, however, that this limitation is in large measure corrected in the two later books of Hirschman's trilogy: *Journeys toward Progress* (1963), which deals with three different countries' efforts over time to learn how to cope with persistent *policy* problems (connected with drought in Brazil, land reform in Colombia, and inflation in Chile);[9] and *Development Projects Observed* (1967), in which Hirschman analyzes what might be learned from eleven World Bank development projects. These analyses underline the differences between salutary and nonsalutary difficulties and the ways in which political pressures can and do promote learning from inadequate policies. They also clarify the pros and cons of projects and policies based on trait making as against trait taking and suggest why the choice of these strategies should depend on how one responds to the "wager" that new attitudes and capabilities will be *learned* within a reasonable period of time.

Ever mindful of the needs of professionals, Schön also emphasizes that Hirschman is writing not only for other academic economists but for practitioners and policymakers in developing countries; and that the inferences and "flexible" principles Hirschman draws from these analyses are designed for "selective use rather than for mechanical application." This is why, he suggests, Hirschman's views often take the form of an adviser's or coach's suggestions to help or prompt people to learn from their experiences, rather than the effort of the scientist to discover invariant relationships.

From this perspective, learners are not "empty vessels ready to be filled with externally applied wisdom"—a respectful stance by Hirschman—which, Schön teasingly observes, is offset by Hirschman's willingness to treat these learners as "manipulable by incentive effects and pacing mechanisms." Not surprisingly, Schön finds it understandable that Hirschman's pedagogy of development "is inherently an art" that "may draw on the models of economic development theory but it is just as likely to serve as a stimulus to the modification of that theory." Even more, Schön suggests, any effort to model learning from Hirschman's perspective might well require modeling "the processes as well as the effects and conditions of learning. [But] we know scarcely enough about such processes to consider modeling them" and "if we were to attempt to do so, we would be swept well beyond the bounds of prevailing conceptions of economic rationality."

Some Development Assumptions in Retrospect

Hirschman's historical interests ranged widely. Three of the more important were the biography of ideas, particularly those involved with reform and revolution and with the shifting roles of the market and society; the diversity of different paths of development, particularly as they relate to "possibilism" in behavior and social choices, and thus help, Hirschman says, "to restore a few degrees of freedom we were in danger of losing to the structuralists"; and not least, "the incredible complexity of human nature" and the variety of tensions it tries to cope with, including those between "self-interest . . . and public morality."[10] It was the sharing of these interests coupled with pronounced antireductionist inclinations that provoked Rothschild, an economic historian, to contrast the premise about "economic man" put forth by contemporary mainstream economists with Hirschman's skeptical attitudes and those of the intellectual forerunners of the discipline; and that led Lisa Peattie, an anthropologist, to explore both the ways protest movements have challenged development over time and the view that identifies economic development with rationality and progress; and that drew Bishwapriya Sanyal, a planner, to search for the roots of Hirschman's bias for hope, despite the gloomy findings and views of many of his colleagues among the economists.

THE CONCEPT OF ECONOMIC MAN: ROTHSCHILD'S HISTORICAL CRITIQUE.   In her colloquium talk, Rothschild told a story illustrating the limits of a simple, or reductionist, interpretation of price signals. It was a case in which the British government put an excise tax on leaded

gasoline, whereupon the demand for unleaded gas went up significantly. Consumers were declared price-elastic. But what this simple
analysis missed was a simultaneous campaign to reduce lead in the
environment (because of its effects on the cognitive development of
small children) and the possibility that a reaction to price changes may
reflect different kinds of communication, not just an overt response to
the price tag.[11]

One of Hirschman's strengths, Rothschild observes in chapter 5, is
that he recognizes the complexities of economic responses—in particular the diversity of economic experience across countries, across time,
across individuals and even within the life of a given individual; and
that he is skeptical of the concept of "purely economic man." He resists
the application to developing countries of reductionist theories and
uniform prescriptions for national planning (he was loath, for example,
to promote a national planning board in Colombia, thereby risking his
connection to the World Bank; and he balked at the view that the major
problems of developing countries could be solved if their national income per capita could be raised enough). In the *Strategy*, Rothschild
notes, Hirschman considered the obstacles to economic progress "reflections of contradictory drives and of the resulting confusion of the
will"; and his policy prescriptions try to take better account of the
tension between self-interest and public morality, and "the grand tension that stems from the universal desire for economic improvement
oddly combined with many resistances to change," which had to be
broken down into "smaller and more manageable tensions."

Adam Smith, however, was more "Hirschmanesque," Rothschild
suggests, than Hirschman gave him credit for being and should not be
blamed for the "oversimplified" notions of the self-interested, utility-
maximizing economic man that followed his writings; and the same
held for others in the emerging field of economics, such as Turgot and
Condorcet. Despite the skeptical views of these influential forerunners,
she draws attention to two main adaptations over time—on the part
of economists, economic historians, and others—of this assumption
of "rational" economic behavior. One is its employment of models as
heuristic devices: as deliberate simplifications, as Krugman suggests,
with recognition of their limitations. The other is their adaptation in
economic modernization policies. Essentially "prescriptive . . . it is [of-
ten] a view," Rothschild says, not only of "how people behave [but]

also of how they should behave, and also of how they should be helped to behave in more modern or more developed societies."

Rothschild concludes, however, that the really crucial question has little to do with disputes over economic technique, with being for or against Krugman's "tightly specified models," or even with whether the views of reality are oversimplified. The vital question is whether they increase understanding and what alternative assumptions or simplifications might prove more useful and provide better predictions. She then provides evidence of these arguments in sophisticated economic circles.

All of this leads her to reaffirm that theorists and theories are judged by the way they look at the world or try to explain things about the world as well as how they influence the world; and she concludes that recent development prescriptions, especially for Eastern Europe and the former Soviet Union—like the programs of the postwar bilateral and multilateral donors—still lean heavily on psychological assumptions of behavior; they tenaciously presuppose that "people have to *learn* to be modern; they have to *learn* to economize, and they also have to *learn* both the rules and the norms of economizing." But she suggests that the conflict and tension produced by the desire to achieve economic progress and yet take into account individual opinions are neither easy nor likely "to be resolved by some sort of benevolent despotism" nor to be "obedient to national sovereign powers"; and that these "were the problems with which the greatest founders of modern economics were preoccupied before the French Revolution." They are, she adds, "at the heart of Hirschman's work, and . . . are also the problem of the 1990s."

PROGRESS, RATIONALITY, AND DEVELOPMENT. Unlike most of the participants, Peattie is unwilling to make the assumption that most development is desirable. She focuses on the relationship between social life and economic institutions and on the actions that shape that relationship to remind us, as Hirschman did, that there have been in the past, and are still today, quite different ways of thinking about these institutions and development, and that there are quite different forces impinging on them. It might be fruitful, she suggests in chapter 6, to dwell not on Hirschman's contribution to economics but on his place in the tradition of trying to bring economics into the study of society.

In her remarks, Hirschman descends from "nineteenth-century grand social thought" and its concern with "progress," the process now called "development."[12] In that period, progress was a vast central organizing trend in human history, not something specialists accomplished. Even with dissent from both the left and the right, it was regarded as something in the order of nature, bound to come to pass whether you liked it or not and understood to bring with it "pain and social loss" in association with "material progress." The idea that such a process "was the outcome of skill and expertise rather than something inevitable" became the legitimating idea of development economics, and the source of its professionalization within the field of economics, much the way "doctors came to monopolize medicine."

She also reminds us that in the several different ways of thinking in the past about economic and social life, each ensured a basic role for reason in relation to interest: "this was because the pursuit of interest, however grounded in passion, involved the rational linking of means to ends." Thus, key sixteenth- and early seventeenth-century thinkers thought the pursuit of interest might help offset the arbitrary passions of rulers. And the role of reason—proclaimed by the *philosophes* of the eighteenth century—was intended, at least in part, to guide the central power in dealing with affairs of state, including the problems posed by an increasingly mobile, rootless "popular" culture. In contrast, the nineteenth-century Marxist dream of socializing the means of production was expected also to determine the superstructure, that is, to "distribute power, define roles, shape belief and meaning." And the alternative view that Peattie examines—which identified relations based on cultural traditions (*Gemeinschaft*) and relations based on rational pursuit of interest (*Gesellschaft*)—anticipated "a sense of loss around the presumed replacement of cultural tradition by economic rationality." Nor is it surprising, in her view, that twentieth-century versions of economics and development planning would draw notions of rationality from these earlier "ideological" wells and develop "a body of professional practice dominated by technocratic discourse concerning the means to a generally defined and generally accepted end."

What distinguishes the problem of our time, Peattie contends, is the evidence of erosion of the basis for faith in rationality: for example, the loss of control by the national state of economic processes within its borders, because of changes in technology and in the global economy; the hobbling of decisionmaking in bureaucracies because of their tendency to push information downward and decisionmaking upward; the widespread, distorted institutional interferences with "rational" market processes; the worldwide fears of "collective madness," expressed by many ecologists; the horror of the possible irrational unleashing of the current technological potentials of war; and not least, "the intermittent eruptions of boycotts, strikes, self-immolation, and other personal sacrifices and essays in violence by intransigent individuals and groups sworn to block hateful policies and development projects ranging from airports, highways, massports, and birth control clinics to intervention policies in Afghanistan, Iran, and San Salvador."

All of these concerns, Peattie pointed out in her colloquium talk, raise questions for which she has no answers. Indeed, the presumed rationality of certain ends claimed by the state and its institutions is what has been the target of the critique of modernism, a critique in which there is "no monopoly on the definition of rationality" but the recognition instead that such claims are based on "the power to frame." In the anti-airport campaigns, one of the movements she has studied, the opponents claimed that it was not only the proposed airport but the whole modernist project of "development" that was irrational. These conflicts were not susceptible to bargaining or compromise, since the opponents were "irrational and proud of it: . . . when you enter a world like that," Peattie said, "exit and voice take a different shape, because they assume a rational response" essentially within the same frame, an "old-fashioned notion of rational argument" to which she said Hirschman is still susceptible. Similar attitudes, according to Peattie, can be demonstrated in other protest movements, including the strategy of boycott as a hybrid of exit and voice, a way to exert control over the state and economic institutions "when you don't believe they will respond in a reasonable way."

At the end of chapter 6, Peattie observes that economic concepts and analytic techniques of development economics have been shaped so as to make it possible to keep the discipline outside all that passion and shifting meaning. The world of macroeconomics is a world of clean ideas and very generalized strategic recommendations. Given our situation, however, she wonders "what would a postmodernist development economics look like?"

HIRSCHMAN'S BIAS FOR HOPE: SANYAL'S VIEW.   Sanyal's dissection of Hirschman's bias for hope in chapter 7 brings to mind T. S. Eliot's remark that Dostoyevsky "had the gift—a sign of genius in itself—for utilizing his weaknesses."[13] Hirschman had a quite different gift, valuable but rather odd, and not at all easy to describe. This was his marvelous, disconcerting, contrarian way of seeing things. Where others saw formidable preconditions, he saw ultimate outcomes; where others noted failure, he glimpsed promise and possibility; where others sought equilibria, he worried about disequilibria; where others argued for a big push, he favored incremental change; in what others dismissed as foolish practices, he sometimes detected hidden rationalities; and when others veered to the right or left, he mined the insights at both poles. And the great merit of the wide range of examples Sanyal musters is that they do illumine these views and their roots and indicate why they may well nourish more effort and hope than frustration and failure.

As for Hirschman's place in the spectrum of development discourse from left to right, Sanyal noted in his oral presentation that Hirschman "skirts the left, with its tendency to be 'mesmerized' by the search for large structural changes and to be skeptical about small ones, which are seen as efforts (either cynical or naive) to co-opt the poor."[14] And he does not overlook Hirschman's disdain for the argument of Hayek and others of the right about the futility of "continuing state involvement in the economy." Hirschman's rejection of both views, Sanyal emphasizes, was due less to ideological distaste than to a shrewd understanding of the limited institutional ability to mount a "big push" for a "great transformation" of the European kind, coupled with an equally knowledgeable appreciation of the limited but strategic roles the state often had to play at other critical moments in the course of development.

Sanyal also compares Hirschman's pragmatism with the Marxist notion of praxis, which sets action as the basis of learning, although Hirschman stopped well short of the Marxist-Leninist faith in revolution. Hirschman's view of the state differs from the American tradition, Sanyal believes, because of his European origins; but it is far less clear whether this would account for his way of combining economics with an anthropological scrutiny at the micro-scale; and for his use of history to argue against stages, preconditions, and inflexible patterns.

When Hirschman published *A Bias for Hope* in 1971, it was a time, Sanyal observed at the colloquium, when development thinking was being severely questioned from the right and the left. "Albert Fishlow's work on Brazil showing that income distribution had worsened demonstrated that countries we thought doing well were not doing so well; Guillermo O'Donnell's work on the bureaucratic capitalist state was similarly discouraging, given that all but two Latin American countries had turned authoritarian, as well as most of Africa, and American academics, like Samuel Huntington and others, had begun to argue for political order instead of democracy—because they thought it was not important at the early stage, and that maybe democracy can come later."

Bias, Sanyal suggests, and its role in shaping development discourse, should be seen in the context of this "gloomy debate as an effort to restore purpose and direction to the field of development planning." What really stamps Hirschman's style, Sanyal concludes, is his capacity to view development from what we might term a collage perspective—namely, that of an economist and of an anthropologist, of a "here-and-now" pragmatist and a historicist, of a protagonist of change and someone avidly curious about the status quo, and having the outlook of a European-variety statist and of a libertarian North American: that melange is "what provides the intellectual sophistication to Hirschman's bias for hope."

Restructuring Institutions, Policies, Programs, and Projects

If we accept Hirschman's view of development as a process of growth in which disequilibria may, but need not, trigger the kinds of social learning that promote development, then we must become interested in examining specific situations of disequilibrium, distinguishing the features of those that are productive from those that are not. Some of the lessons of interventions aimed at promoting development are discussed in chapters 8–11. They treat such interventions as experiments from which policymakers can learn to derive better development policies and theorists better theories. They illustrate the kind of case-by-case approach to learning from development experience that is opened up by the arguments of Taylor, Piore, and Schön on the one hand and Peattie, Rothschild, and Sanyal on the other.

THE EVOLUTION OF THE NEPAL BLINDNESS PROGRAM. Eliot Marseille's account in chapter 10 of the evolution and success of the program for controlling blindness operated by the Seva Foundation in Nepal provides an initial example. This organization, founded by the veterans of a successful antismallpox campaign in India, hoped to extend to Nepal the inspired service that had been the group's shared experience in the smallpox program.

While working for the foundation, Marseille was struck by incongruities in the program: for example, the decision of the directors to focus on blindness control without making any assessment of needs or of the best place to put the organization's resources; and the erroneous assumptions that they were engaged in a technical enterprise and that the policies and program pursued were consistent with the aims and plans of the organization. His reading of Hirschman's views—about people's tendency to underestimate, to a roughly similar extent, both creative abilities and difficulties (the hiding hand thesis)—helped him understand what happened in the blindness control program.

The hiding hand, Marseille explains, operated to make blindness prevention and control look like smallpox eradication when the two were fundamentally different. It also made the success of the blindness program appear to depend on the creation of a centralized, uniformly administered nationwide program, when in fact a more complex and difficult process of research and development was needed. In addition, it hid the relatively expensive cure-oriented nature of the blindness program. And it made intraocular lenses—an expensive innovation—appear to be a problem that would undermine the public health ethos of the project, because Seva saw itself as a public health, prevention-oriented organization that promoted low-cost intervention, appropriate technology where possible, community empowerment, and village-level training. But with the treatment of cataracts, it was confronted with something quite different. Cataracts can only be cured, not prevented; and cure is also relatively expensive, requires highly trained ophthalmic personnel, and offers little scope for health education and community involvement.

More specifically, Marseille shows that although blindness prevention is similar to smallpox eradication in only a few superficial ways, reference to the successful smallpox program gave Seva enough credibility to gain support among the donor community. The rhetoric was: "We did it for smallpox; we can do it for blindness." The talk revolved around the elimination of blindness. The creation of an eye-care infrastructure—in Marseille's view, the biggest challenge—was supposed to be a by-product (an example of what Hirschman called a "pseudo imitation technique"). Had Seva tried to make a case for a research and development project with technical, administrative, and social innovation, it would have had a much harder time raising money. There was nothing cynical or planned about this: those at Seva who were pushing the program believed what they were saying. For Marseille, the experience also points up the power of models and the idea of replication: we are socialized to think that any new enterprise must be a replication of something that has been done before.

Although the hiding hand made the creation of a centralized program appear easy and useful, Marseille emphasized in his talk that it was difficult to implement and not too helpful in the Nepalese context. The familiar arguments for centralization—the need for administrative uniformity, economies of scale, increased capabilities, and equity in dealing with staff issues—did not apply at a time when blindness control was really a "voyage of discovery," and probably still is, in Marseille's judgment.[15] Unfortunately, program entrepreneurs and donors could not tolerate that level of uncertainty because it would be hard to get money for that in development work.

In any case, the effort to create a unified program failed, an event Seva lamented because it meant that there would be no one identifiable model that could be exported to other developing countries. At that time, Seva was operating on a "domino" theory, hoping to eliminate blindness first in Nepal and then in India, its real target. Nonetheless, Marseille suggests that the idea was not necessarily bad at the time: it helped capture the support of part of the donor community that wanted to participate in a coordinated planned strategy for the elimination of blindness in a developing country.

However, had Seva known the real nature of blindness in Nepal, Marseille believes, it would not have undertaken the program, since two-thirds of the problem consisted of cataracts that cannot be prevented, but only cured. By the time this became clear, Seva was already deeply involved in the program via financial costs, prestige, and personal commitment, which turned out to be a powerful motivation in the development of innovative solutions.

Equally intriguing, the prospect of treating cataracts with intraocular lenses (IOLs) initially appeared to be an expensive cure requiring inappropriately high technology, but for several reasons, it did not turn out that way. Clinical complications did not arise, and Seva worked out cheap, effective ways to do the more complicated surgery safely. Rather than being the typical story of high-quality care for the rich at the expense of the poor, Nepal's experience was just the opposite: high "inappropriate" technology turned out to be the best way to expand services for the poor. Also, the view that IOLs are not sustainable did not hold true: they generated enough financial support to make the eye-care program self-sustaining after foreign support was withdrawn.

That still leaves two critical policy questions, Marseille says. The first is how do policymakers locate the middle ground between plans that only attempt safe extrapolation from what is known and might be predicted—and thus fail to harness the engine of human ingenuity—and those that are merely fanciful optimism? Marseille's response is Hirschman's in essence: that policymakers should look for hidden opportunities, or at least accommodate them when they surface, and also be prepared both to modify plans of action in the light of new information and to raise contingency, serendipity, and the role of creativity to the status of a doctrine.

In addition, Marseille notes that managers grope because they do not know everything they need to know through strategic planning. Again, he draws from Hirschman, this time from his views on effective research and development.[16] Managers, he says, need to test their direction with small steps, detect error, be prepared to change direction, and then again proceed in small increments. Groping along is a useful notion because it recognizes that small successes are the precondition to more successes. However, while incrementalism "must be our daily bread," Marseille confesses that at times it is necessary to leap.

THE BRAZILIAN EXPERIENCE WITH PREVENTIVE HEALTH CARE.   In a quite different way, Judith Tendler and Sarah Freedheim provide still another confirmation of Hirschman's thesis that the structures of incentives are conducive to the kinds of learning that result in improved performance. Their views, spelled out in chapter 9, are intended to counteract the "lopsidedness of development thinking" that fixates on "why governments so often do badly."[17] They are interested, instead, in providing and explaining "models of good government" that are grounded in the experiences of developing countries. Their case in point is a rural preventive health program, created in 1987 by the Brazilian state of Ceará, which, among other accomplishments, helped reduce infant deaths by 36 percent, tripled vaccination coverage for measles and polio, and in four years extended preventive health services to virtually all of the state's 178 counties.

Although in a short time the state of Ceará hired 7,300 health agents and 235 nurses to supervise them, thereby creating a mass of workers whose contact with their clients was relatively unsupervised, this "large field-based bureaucracy did not become the rent-seeking nightmare of the current literature." On the contrary, the new health agents showed "intense dedication, unpaid after-hours work, and voracious learning." How was such a thing possible?

In their answer, Tendler and Freedheim combine two themes that are distinctly Hirschmanesque. They argue that the state cleverly designed its program: on the one hand, it exerted social pressures that *coerced* the workers into delivering good performance; and, on the other, it conferred on the workers so much status, prestige, ownership, and autonomy as to *elicit* good performance.

A great deal hinged on what the authors call the "drama of the hiring process." In a region of chronic unemployment—exacerbated by the drought of 1987—the hiring of 7,300 health agents was of major significance both for the "job seekers and the dozens of towns where they were to work." In the small rural towns, the number of jobs offered was "frequently the largest one-time public sector hiring"; and once hired, the uniformed health agents "became the most conspicuous and numerous public sector presence in the area." The state used the hiring event as an opportunity to educate residents in these communities, including the job applicants, about the importance of the health services they were to receive, their right to demand support for such a program from their municipal leaders, and their "responsibility" for the program's ultimate success.

Even more striking was the fact that those not hired, the rejects, were induced to become monitors of those who *were* hired. "For those who were hired as agents," Tendler and Freedheim point out, "the specter of reprisal for malfeasance and of the waiting line of eager replacements formed by the rejected applicants, translated itself into pressure to perform well." The hiring process, the advertising surrounding it, the involvement of local businesses and medical schools, enhanced the visibility of the program and built up in the workers and among the community "a sense of *collective* responsibility for it" and gave the new workers, in addition, "a feeling of protection from local politicians who might want to divert the program to their political ends."

As to the nurses who were hired through the municipalities to supervise the health agents, they experienced a dramatic rise in status and autonomy. In the clinics and hospitals where many of them had worked before, they had been subordinated to doctors and "not really able to practice nursing." Now their paraprofessional subordinates treated them as "doctors" in their own right; the nurses had considerable control over the way the program ran in their municipality, and they were able to "put into practice their ideas about how public health programs should work." Contrary to the frequent animosity of nurses (and physicians) toward the introduction of paraprofessionals in health care throughout the world, "these nurses became ardent advocates of their paraprofessional workers because they were given a more central role in planning and running the programs, and because the nurses found their jobs to be much better with the program than without."

Tendler and Freedheim argue that, for nurses and workers alike, the state created a sense of "calling" or "ministry" around a set of public jobs, which led these individuals to see their jobs and themselves differently and hence to *behave* differently: they identified themselves not with a particular agency but with the outputs of their work, the impact their work would have on the future of a community. The workers tended to take on more tasks beyond the strict definition of their jobs. They initiated "communitywide campaigns to reduce public health hazards"; they assisted mothers with "mundane tasks not directly related to health"; and they performed such curative procedures as treating wounds or removing stitches, in order to pave the way for their clients' acceptance of preventive health services and to forge relationships of trust and respect with their clients, which they seemed to need "as much as they needed to see signs of changed health practices."

Through the creation of this sense of public calling, the public visibility of the dramatic hiring process, and the three-month training period that followed the hiring event, the state was able to confer status on and engender respect for these workers: all this, in spite of the general climate of disdain for public workers that prevailed at a time "when the next president of Brazil was successfully campaigning on a promise to get rid of" so-called maharajas "who lived off the income and perquisites of their jobs without doing much work."

In view of the balance of power between the state and the heads of local municipalities, another condition crucial to the success of the preventive health program in Ceará was the state's "iron hand" on certain key elements of the program: the hiring of health agents, the supervision of the nurses, and especially the "image creation" surrounding the job and the program, and through it, the support that grew up for monitoring each community's program. "In the name of a program that partly decentralized responsibility from state to local government," the authors observe, the new program actually reduced the mayors' power, depriving them of control they normally would have had over the hiring of a large number of public employees in a program under their jurisdiction and requiring them to finance part of the program with "funds that they could have used to their political benefit in other areas without such constraints on their power." If the mayors were initially less than enthusiastic about the new program, they were nevertheless constrained by strong pressures from their communities to enter it; and ultimately, "the mayors found that when the program operated well, it was quite popular and they could take much of the credit."

Tendler and Freedheim emphasize that visibility, status, and prestige formed a double-edged tool that, on the one hand, "hemmed public employees in with pressures to be accountable" from outside their agencies, and, on the other, promoted worker satisfaction and relationships of trust and respect with clients, which had, in turn, a further positive influence on worker productivity and performance. From all of this the authors draw a hopeful lesson about the motives that shape the behavior of public employees: civil servants, they suggest, need not "act in their own interest and against the public's," even when surrounded by opportunities to do so. The authors believe that the story of the Ceará health program "helps illuminate the circumstances under which public servants will or will not act in the public interest, and what the government can do to influence those circumstances."

EVALUATING PROJECTS AND PROGRAMS AT THE WORLD BANK. In his remarks at the colloquium, Robert Picciotto, an economist—currently director general of the World Bank Operations Evaluation unit—commented on the professional behavior of evaluation specialists. They look at practice rather than theory, he said, and this role requires personal integrity, commitment to objective norms and rules, and an ability to identify best practice and provide service to all beneficiaries. The emphasis is more on utilitarian bias and the disdain of disciplinary boundaries, and on the economical search for lessons out of real-life experience.

Evaluation at the World Bank, Picciotto added, consists of monitoring its programs, comparing outcomes and plans, and learning from them. The objective is to determine what works, what does not, and why. In terms of Hirschman's metaphors, such evaluation is a pacing or pressure mechanism, a variation and amplification of "voice" and even more of loyalty. And it is a most useful tool wherever competition alone is inadequate, and "where it may help to speak truth to power." It also contributes "to the channeling of information and the encouragement of participation to convert the energy of public protest into constructive learning and reform."[18]

In chapter 10, Picciotto examines the present state of development evaluation in the light of Hirschman's ideas. To see both of these views in context, one must recall Hirschman's past association with the World Bank. More than a quarter of a century ago, Hirschman undertook an investigation of eleven Bank-financed projects. The findings were published in Hirschman's book *Development Projects Observed*. His basic hunch in this work was that "some projects and technologies have a special vocation for inducing certain types of learning, attitude change and institutional reform (and not others)."[19] He also felt that the "structural characteristics" of the projects might "go far in explaining and anticipating success and failure of projects, systemic veering from preassigned paths, propensities toward specific difficulties as well as opportunities for special payoffs."[20] In addition, given the informal but generally accepted notion at the Bank that actual decisionmaking on its projects "involves two, and only two, wholly distinct activities: ascertaining the rate of return, and, then, applying feel, instinct, 'seat of pants' judgment and the like," Hirschman suggested that his efforts could be regarded as "an attempt to reclaim at least part of this vast domain of intuitive discretion."[21]

Hirschman's unorthodox findings troubled some important Bank officials, however, and, perhaps partly for that reason, the book was not reprinted until 1994. Be that as it may, Picciotto now reports that "dissatisfaction [at the Bank] with past outcomes has given rise to a new agenda that is more appropriate but also more ambitious, and in response to it the World Bank and other development agencies have made far-reaching adjustments in their goals and practices. The new development agenda looks very much like Hirschman's old one, which is not surprising, since Hirschman has had a major impact on it. His main ideas having been vindicated, he must now find himself close to the mainstream—a bittersweet outcome for an intellectual rebel."

More specifically, in chapter 10 Picciotto focuses on two well-known ideas of Hirschman. The first is a set of interrelated characteristics of projects: visibility and disappointment. These, Hirschman mischievously suggests, can provide unanticipated pressures and other advantages in monitoring performance or reform of big or high-technology projects. The second, the thesis of the hiding hand, involves policy misjudgments, the tendency on complex projects to underestimate potential problems as well as latent and creative abilities to deal with them. These, too, he observes again with a twinkle in his eyes, often turn into pressure mechanisms with surprisingly positive effects.

Treated as generalizations, these ideas can easily provoke dissent. Aware of this danger, Hirschman stressed their "selective use" rather than "mechanical application," particularly in spotting overlooked or neglected possibilities.

What is striking in reading Picciotto is how he veers between the pros and cons of these notions. For example, he reminds us that Hirschman was surely right when he argues that small was not necessarily beautiful or better and that large, prominent, and technically advanced schemes can often restrict latitude for inferior performance. As evidence, Picciotto points to examples such as Ecuador's success, following the earthquake in 1987, in innovating streamlined design, effective contracting procedures, and efficient repair techniques and in adhering to a demanding schedule in the reconstruction of its trans-country oil pipeline. Picciotto also notes the generally higher rates of successful outcomes on World Bank loans (in excess of $150 million) in technologically demanding sectors like telecommunications, energy, and transport. Similarly, with regard to disappointment and public policy, Picciotto draws attention to the public recoil from the brutal involuntary resettlements precipitated by the construction of a major multipurpose project on the Narmada River in India and the resultant pressures and reforms designed to protect displaced people and minimize environmental spoliation.

However, World Bank experience does not always confirm Hirschman's views, Picciotto acknowledges. So he examines the experience to find out when the pressures for efficiency induced by narrow latitude,

technical complexity, and efficiency make it possible for large-scale
civil works to be more successful than small-scale, dispersed works;
and he explores situations when other factors, such as organization,
leadership, institutional frameworks, and "the salutary pressures of
'bottom-up' beneficiary involvement" explain better than scale and sophisticated technology the success of such programs as agricultural
extension, which are typically small and reliant on local skills. And
despite his admiration for Hirschman's hiding hand thesis "as a powerful and useful metaphor," Picciotto suggests that precise information
can often be critical, that "blissful ignorance . . . is not necessarily followed by timely awareness of obstacles, let alone mobilization of appropriate responses, and that much depends on who hides what to
whom." These reservations, however, do not detract from Picciotto's
recognition that Hirschman's "classic" evaluation of World Bank projects (*Development Projects Observed*) has been "an inspiration to practitioners laboring in the trenches of development." Indeed, he predicts
that the body of Hirschman's work will "in time . . . be included in the
basic tool kit of evaluators" and may yet take us into that era visualized
by Keynes, when "a new generation of social scientists . . . will join
forces in evaluation and be perceived to be as useful as dentists."

With regard to the current and future tasks of evaluation, Picciotto
emphasizes the incessant pressure to broaden development aims, to
go beyond such traditional World Bank norms as growth, rates of return, cost-benefit analysis, and the quality of public investment. Attention, he says, is already being given to a number of other goals: poverty
reduction, the equitable sharing of benefits, environmental sustainability, and the evaluation of institutions and policies. In addition, there
are efforts to encourage the reform of political and administrative processes (for example, by means of democratization, decentralization,
public participation, and debureaucratization), as well as the design of
flexible enabling environments for private enterprise, local initiative,
and social action. To be sure, the risks are greater than ever. So are
the potentials. But Picciotto thinks Hirschman's admirable examples of
intellectual trespassing plus his resistance to dispensing peremptory
advice and prescription—coupled with his adept use of stories and
"counterintuitive metaphors," and his emphasis on the centrality of
side effects, the limitations of cost-benefit analyses, and the need to
muster resources and abilities that are hidden, scattered, or badly utilized—nourish the necessary flexibility in thinking.

LEARNING AND THE JAPANESE EXPERIENCE. Sabel's study of Japanese industrial experience described in chapter 11 provides our final example of learning as a critical component of development. A political scientist and specialist on industrial planning, Sabel pursues the issue of institutional restructuring through learning in two ways: first, by shifting the focus to the relationship between learning and monitoring, and then by drawing on Japanese contract and related experience to provide pragmatic examples of Hirschman's suggestive but amended concept of learning.

In Sabel's view, a central problem of development is how to ensure that the gains from learning "to make and do things valued in markets" are "distributed according to the standards agreed" between the transacting parties. This depends, he says, on monitoring, that is, on the capacity of each party to assess whether it is getting a fair enough deal to continue dealing. Cooperation, Sabel emphasizes, is not guaranteed in a specialized environment where there is a great opportunity for one part to "hold up" the other; and he rejects—after close analysis of actual behavior and contracts—forms of cooperation allegedly explained by cultural predilection or game theory. In his view, what is needed is some procedure or institutional framework that would not require trust as a prerequisite but would produce trusting behavior over time and allow it to deepen without a requirement for blind trust—that is, without a prohibition on monitoring. Even more, he is concerned with the tension in development, in innovation at any level, between *learning* (creating new knowledge and thus change in the current situation) and *monitoring* (the need to check performance—in this case, whether partners are performing as promised).

The large Japanese firm and the Japanese state have come up with such solutions, Sabel says. The auto industry, for example, illustrates how disequilibrium may be systematically introduced into the production process with just-in-time inventory management: namely, "by stripping away buffer inventories [that] normally act as hedges against contingencies. Without inventories, synchronicity, preventive maintenance, and statistical process controls become vital, because the lack of coordination, equipment failure, and the inability to replace defective parts might completely disrupt the system."[22] These circumstances also call for a different stance toward *learning*, because the system will not be able to function without a continuous flow of information. Since some of "the vital people who can monitor and learn are the production workers and machine operators, they are brought into alignment by means of cross-training, employment security, and a merit-based ranking and bonus system whereby they benefit roughly in proportion to the increase in productivity they can muster. This creates a work-team unit with responsibility for logistics and preventive maintenance formalized as 'quality circles' and encourages more autonomy within the system. Incentives are also extended to subcontractors, who, if they meet a mutually agreed-upon standard cost for their work, will be retained, and if they can do better than the standard, will get an increment of the savings. These are deliberate ways to manage disequilibria, that is, to induce permanent disequilibrium, align interests, and assign responsibilities so people will learn [from the experience] rather than fall back on other strategies."

Japanese contracts, Sabel notes, are often detailed and complex documents about cost structures and how much cost reduction accrues to each party. They precipitate continuous discussion about performance, equity, and the interests of the parties, which are a product of jointly set goals. This is nothing "like the standard game-theoretic notion of two parties with limited information about each other signaling their intention to cooperate or not. . . . Rather, the Japanese contracts are agreements to build . . . a system for resolving disputes at whatever level required to take into account the changing mutually determined interests of the constituents."

A similar, metacontractual process of learning by monitoring guides relations between the Japanese state and the economy as a whole. There is no pretension, Sabel says, that the state has superior market knowledge. Instead its role has often been to superintend and instigate "the firms to set goals with reference to some prevailing standard so that shortfalls in performance are apparent to those with the incentives and capacity to remedy them." The firms themselves have the authority and motive to do so; and the initial goals are adjusted in the light of performance and new targets are set accordingly.

Trade associations deliberate with the state on performance standards, generating the information needed to monitor and check on both performance and the reliability of indicators. The key element in this system, Sabel asserts, is the role of the trade associations and the nature of the monitoring structure. What is more, these developmental associations are not a peculiarly Japanese phenomenon; he cites evidence of their presence in Germany, the Republic of Korea, Taiwan, and even Brazil.

In general, according to Sabel, "The great appeal of Hirschman's idea of unbalanced growth was to suggest how public authorities might be vital in economic development without presuming to know more than the economic agents about how to do business. . . . The idea of learning by monitoring . . . [shows] how in transforming exchanges into continuous discussions the actors can induce learning by perturbing the status quo, yet not make themselves hostage to fortune." Finally, he adds, "it is now fashionable to apply economic categories to political phenomena, but it is not fashionable to take economic categories and say that they do not work: for the real problem is that there is a political activity, namely, permanent conversation about equity and goal setting, and that is what is really going on and the contracts are not really about exchange: they are about establishing this political relation."

The Ideas in Retrospect

As should be clear by now, a recurrent theme in this volume is that the process of social learning is critical to development. We acknowledge that economic models, such as the elegant one on the effects of increasing returns to scale presented in Krugman's essay, are consistent with the idea that in the course of economic development agents of development—such as entrepreneurs, existing firms, and government agencies—learn to think and act in new ways. But these economic models are elliptical with respect to the learning processes whose results they may indirectly represent. The variables and relationships of the variables contained in such models have the effect of "wiping out" the learning processes that may be involved in the changing patterns of decision represented by the models. In Krugman's model, for example, the decision of entrepreneurs to invest in modern production equipment depends on judgments about labor costs and likely margins of profit. The process by which entrepreneurs learn to acquire new production machinery and realize its potential for increased efficiency has no place there.

For pluralists—in contrast to those who support conventional theory—the agents, whose decisions and actions give rise to development, and the outside observers and researchers who seek to understand and promote such local initiatives, must learn to recognize the temporally shifting patterns that, in any given case, make some policy measures appropriate and others inappropriate as spurs to development. These agents, observers, and advisers must seek to interpret the meanings of specific historical processes and draw lessons from them—especially regarding "success" and "failure"—to guide the future course of development.

If these views hold, they set a striking agenda for the kinds of competence required for the handling of development issues in the 1990s. What methods, for example, can lead to a better understanding of the processes by which projects evolve and the ways in which project managers must often handle contingency in the relationship between plans and unpredicted outcomes? And how will organizations—public, private, and nongovernmental—learn to create and shape the indispensable institutional infrastructure; or nourish the capability for undertaking continual joint problem solving between outside organizations and decisionmakers in public and private institutions, between decisionmakers and their advisers, and between sponsoring organizations, prime contractors, and their subcontractors?

If we are right in stressing the dual characteristics of economics—professional as well as disciplinary—and in stressing that this duality requires an approach to economic development that is pluralistic, narrative, and qualitative, *as well as* mathematical and quantitative, then the kind of modeling favored by mainstream economics is an inevitably imperfect means to better, but not necessarily ever more complete, understanding. It is this angle of vision, we suggest, that makes the career and the changing reputation of Hirschman—both within and outside the field of economics—so provocative an indicator. From the perspective of Krugman, a proponent of the thesis that economics is mainly a discipline, Hirschman is a "tragic hero," but from the perspective of others who advocate a more catholic and more effectively applied role for economics in our culture, Hirschman is one of the great heroes of economics: he embodies its professional as well as its disciplinary aspirations.

Part I
Conceptualizing Development

Two

The Fall and Rise of Development Economics

Paul Krugman

THIS ESSAY is not exactly about Albert Hirschman.
In the first place, I am unqualified to write such an essay. My acquaintance with Hirschman's works is very limited. In essence, the Hirschman I know is the author of *The Strategy of Economic Development* and little else. So I am in no position to write about his larger vision.

Furthermore, while I am a great admirer of *The Strategy of Economic Development,* I do not think that it was helpful to development economics. That may sound paradoxical, but I will try to explain what I mean as I go along. To put it briefly, however, I regard the intellectual strategy that Hirschman adopted in writing that book as an understandable but wrong response to what had become a crisis in the field of economic development. Perversely, the very brilliance and persuasiveness of the book made it all the more destructive.

If this chapter is not about Hirschman, what is it about? It is about two intertwined themes. One is the strange history of development economics, or more specifically, the set of ideas that I have elsewhere called "high development theory".[1] This set of ideas was and is highly persuasive as at least a partial explanation of what development is about, and for a stretch of about fifteen years in the 1940s and 1950s it exerted a deep influence on both economists and policymakers. Yet in the late 1950s high development theory rapidly unraveled, to the point where by the time I studied economics in the 1970s it seemed not so much wrong as incomprehensible. Only in the 1980s and 1990s were

economists able to look at high development theory with a fresh eye
and see that it really does make a lot of sense, after all.

The second theme is the problem of method in the social sciences.
As I will argue, the crisis of high development theory in the late 1950s
was neither empirical nor ideological: it was methodological. High development theorists were having a hard time expressing their ideas in
the kind of tightly specified models that were becoming the unique
language of discourse of economic analysis. They were faced with the
choice of either adopting that increasingly dominant intellectual style
or finding themselves pushed into the intellectual periphery. They did
not make the transition, and as a result high development theory was
by and large purged from economics, even development economics.

Hirschman's *Strategy* appeared at a critical point in this methodological crisis. It is a rich book, full of stimulating ideas. Its most important
message at that time, however, was a rejection of the drive toward
rigor. In effect, Hirschman said that both the theorist and the practical
policymaker could and should ignore the pressures to produce
buttoned-down, mathematically consistent analyses and adopt instead
a sort of muscular pragmatism in grappling with the problem of development. Along with some others, notably Gunnar Myrdal, Hirschman
did not wait for intellectual exile: he proudly gathered up his followers
and led them into the wilderness himself. Unfortunately, they per-
ished there.

The irony is, we can now see that high development theory made
perfectly good sense after all. But in order to see that, we need to adopt
exactly the intellectual attitude Hirschman rejected: a willingness to
do violence to the richness and complexity of the real world in order
to produce controlled, *silly* models that illustrate key concepts.

This discussion, then, is a meditation on economic methodology,
inspired by the history of development economics, in which Albert
Hirschman appears as a major character. I hope that it is clear how
much I admire his work; he is not a villain in this story so much as a
tragic hero.

The Fall and Rise of Development Economics

The glory days of high development theory spanned about fifteen
years, from the seminal paper of Paul N. Rosenstein-Rodan (1943) to
the publication of Hirschman's *Strategy* (1958).[2]

Loosely described, high development theory is the view that development is a virtuous circle driven by external economies—that is, that modernization breeds modernization. Some countries, according to this view, remain underdeveloped because they have failed to get this virtuous circle going and thus remain stuck in a low-level trap. However, government activism is a way of breaking out of this trap.

It is not that easy, of course—just asserting that there are virtuous and vicious circles does not qualify as a theory. (Not everyone would agree with this assertion. Myrdal, for example, emphasizes the importance of "circular and cumulative causation," but, unlike Hirschman, does not provide much in the way of concrete examples of how it might arise.)[3] The distinctive features of high development theory came out of its explanation of the nature of the positive feedback that can lead to self-reinforcing growth or stagnation.

Most versions of high development theory traced the self-reinforcement to an interaction between economies of scale at the level of the individual producer and the size of the market. Crucial to this interaction was some form of economic dualism, in which "traditional" production paid lower wages and/or participated in the market less than the modern sector. The story then went something like this: modern methods of production are potentially more productive than traditional ones, but their productivity edge will be large enough to compensate for the necessity of paying higher wages only if the market is large enough. In turn, the size of the market depends on the extent to which modern techniques are adopted because workers in the modern sector earn higher wages and/or participate in the market economy more than traditional workers. So if modernization can be started on a sufficiently large scale, it will be self-sustaining, but it is possible for an economy to get caught in a trap in which the process never gets going.

The clearest and simplest version of this story was told by Rosenstein-Rodan himself. He illustrated his argument for coordinated investment by imagining a country in which 20,000 (!) "unemployed workers . . . are taken from the land and put into a large shoe factory. They receive wages substantially higher than their previous meager income *in natura*."[4] Rosenstein-Rodan then went on to argue that this investment is likely to be unprofitable in isolation, but profitable if accompanied by similar investments in many other industries. Both key assumptions are clearly present: the assumption of economies of scale, embodied in the assertion that the factory must be established at such a large scale, and the assumption of dualism, embedded in the idea that these workers can be drawn from unemployment or low-paying agricultural employment.

I regard Rosenstein-Rodan's Big Push story as the essential high development model. Admittedly, some of the classics of high development theory differed in their emphasis. On one side, Arthur Lewis, in his famous analysis of "economic development with unlimited supplies of labor," focused on dualism while ignoring the role of economies of scale and circular causation. On the other side, J. M. Fleming, for one, argued that owing to the role of intermediate goods in production—later memorably dubbed forward and backward linkages by Hirschman—self-reinforcing development could conceivably occur even without dualism.[5]

There were also disputes over the nature of the policies that might be required to break a country out of a low-level trap. Rosenstein-Rodan and others appeared to imply that a coordinated, broadly based investment program—the Big Push—would be required. Hirschman disagreed, arguing that promoting a few key sectors with strong linkages, then moving on to other sectors to correct the disequilibrium generated by these investments, and so on, was actually the right approach. Indeed, Hirschman structured his book as an argument with what he called the "balanced-growth" school. He did not acknowledge that he had far more in common with Rosenstein-Rodan and other balanced-growth advocates like Nurkse than any of them had with the way that mainstream economics was going.[6]

For mainstream economics was, by the late 1950s, becoming hostile to the kinds of ideas involved in high development theory. Above all, economics was going through an extended period in which increasing returns to scale, so central to that theory, disappeared from discourse for some time.

It may not be obvious just how crucial economies of scale were to high development theory. One of the characteristics of the writing of many of its expositors was a certain vagueness that makes it hard to know exactly what their arguments were—a vagueness that, as we will soon see, was no accident. Still, if one reads their works carefully, one finds that increasing returns are invariably crucial to the argument.

Consider, for example, what may have been Hirschman's most cited concept, that of "linkages." Some crude followers of Hirschman have identified these directly with having a lot of entries in the input-output table.[7] But Hirschman's own discussion makes it clear that the idea involved the interaction between market size and economies of scale.

In Hirschman's definition of backward linkages, the role of market-size externalities linked to economies of scale is quite explicit: an industry creates a backward linkage when its demand enables an upstream industry to be established at at least minimum economic scale. The strength of an industry's backward linkages is to be measured by the probability that it will in fact push other industries over the threshold.

Forward linkages involve an interaction between scale and market size as well; in this case the definition is vaguer but seems to involve the ability of an industry to reduce the costs of potential downstream users of its products and thus, again, push them over the threshhold of profitability.

So economies of scale were crucial to high development theory. Why did that present a problem? Because economies of scale were very difficult to introduce into the increasingly formal models of mainstream economic theory.

The Evolution of Ignorance

A friend of mine who combines a professional interest in Africa with a hobby of collecting antique maps has written a fascinating essay called "The Evolution of European Ignorance about Africa" in which he describes how European maps of the African continent evolved from the fifteenth to the nineteenth centuries.

One might suppose the process to have been more or less linear, with the maps showing increasing accuracy and greater detail as European knowledge of the continent advanced. But that is not what happened. Fifteenth-century maps of Africa were, of course, quite inaccurate about distances, coastlines, and so on. But they also contained quite a lot of information about the interior—such as the location of Timbuktu, the River Niger, and so forth. Since this information was based mainly on second- or third-hand travelers' reports, some of it was also untrue. For example, the maps showed regions inhabited by men with their mouths in their stomachs. Still, in the early fifteenth century Africa on maps was a filled space.

Over time, the art of mapmaking and the quality of information used to make maps steadily improved. The coastline of Africa was first explored, then plotted with growing accuracy, and by the eighteenth century that coastline was shown in a manner almost indistinguishable from that of modern maps. Cities and peoples along the coast were also shown with great fidelity.

On the other hand, the interior emptied out. The weird mythical creatures were gone, but so were the real cities and rivers. In a way, Europeans had become more ignorant about Africa than they had been before.

It should be obvious what happened: the improvement in the art of mapmaking raised the standard for what was considered valid data. Mapmakers could no longer base their drawings on second-hand reports of the form "six days south of the end of the desert you encounter a vast river flowing from east to west." Only features of the landscape that had been visited by reliable informants equipped with sextants and compasses now qualified. And so the crowded, if confused, continental interior of the old maps became "darkest Africa," an empty space.

Of course, by the end of the nineteenth century darkest Africa had been explored and mapped accurately. In the end, the rigor of modern cartography led to infinitely better maps. But there was an extended period in which improved techniques actually led to some loss in knowledge. Between the 1940s and the 1970s something similar happened to economics. A rise in the standards of rigor and logic led to a much improved level of understanding of some things, but also led for a time to an unwillingness to confront those areas the new technical rigor could not yet reach. Areas of inquiry that had earlier been filled in, however imperfectly, became blanks. Only gradually, over an extended period, were these dark regions reexplored.

Economics has always been unique among the social sciences for its reliance on numerical examples and mathematical models. David Ricardo's theories of comparative advantage and land rent are as tightly specified as any modern economist could want. Nonetheless, in the early twentieth century economic analysis was, by modern standards, marked by a good deal of fuzziness. In the case of Alfred Marshall, whose influence dominated economics until the 1930s, this fuzziness was deliberate. An able mathematician, Marshall actually worked out many of his ideas through formal models in private, then tucked them away in appendixes or even suppressed them when it came to publishing his books. Tjalling C. Koopmans, one of the founders of econometrics, was later to refer caustically to Marshall's style as "diplomatic": analytical difficulties and fine points were smoothed over with parables and metaphors, rather than tackled in full view of the reader. (By the way, I personally regard Marshall as one of the greatest of all economists. His works remain remarkable in their range of insight; one only wishes that they were more widely read.)

High development theorists followed Marshall's example. From the point of view of a modern economist, the most striking feature of the works of high development theory is their adherence to a discursive, nonmathematical style. Economics has, of course, become vastly more mathematical over time. Nonetheless, development economics was archaic in style even for its own time. Of the four most famous high development works, Rosenstein-Rodan's was approximately contemporary with Paul Samuelson's formulation of the Heckscher-Ohlin model, while the works of Lewis, Myrdal, and Hirschman were all roughly contemporary with Robert Solow's initial statement of growth theory.

As in Marshall's case, this style was not due to any particular lack of mathematical skill on the part of development economists. Hirschman made a significant contribution to the formal theory of devaluation in the 1940s, while Fleming helped create the still influential Mundell-Fleming model of floating exchange rates. Moreover, the development field itself was at the same time generating mathematical planning models (first, growth models of the Harrod-Domar type; then, linear programming approaches) that were actually quite technically advanced for their time.

So why did high development theory not find expression in formal models? Almost certainly, the basic reason was that high development theory rested critically on the assumption of economies of scale, but nobody knew how to put these scale economies into formal models.

The problem was, they did know how to deal with market structure. From Ricardo until about 1975, what economists knew how to model formally was a perfectly competitive economy, one in which firms take prices as given rather than actively try to affect them. There is a standard theory of the behavior of an individual monopolist who faces no comparably sized competitors, but there is no general theory of how oligopolists, firms that have substantial market power but also face large rivals, will set prices and output. Still less is there any general approach to modeling the aggregate behavior of a whole economy largely peopled by oligopolistic rather than perfectly competitive industries.

Since the mid-1970s economists have broken through this barrier in a number of fields: international trade, economic growth, and, finally, development. They have done this by making some peculiar assumptions that allow them to exploit the bag of tricks that industrial organization theorists developed for thinking about such issues in the 1970s. (We shall see an example of the power and limitations of this kind of intellectual trickery below, when I present a quick formal version of the Big Push story.) In the 1950s, although the technical level of the leading development economists was actually high enough to have allowed them to do the same thing, the bag of tricks was not there. So development theorists were placed in an awkward bind, with basically sensible ideas that they could not quite express in fully worked-out models. And the drift of the economics profession made the situation worse. In the 1940s and even in the 1950s it was still possible for an economist to publish an article that made persuasive points verbally without tying up all the loose ends. After 1960, however, an attempt to publish an article like Rosenstein-Rodan's would have immediately gotten a grilling: "Why not build a smaller factory (for which the market is adequate)? Oh, you are assuming economies of scale? But that means imperfect competition, and nobody knows how to model that, so this paper does not make any sense." It seems safe to say that such an article would have been unpublishable any time after 1970, if not earlier.

Some development theorists responded by getting as close to a formal model as they could. This is to some extent true of Rosenstein-Rodan, and certainly the case for Fleming, whose doctrine of balanced growth gets painfully close to being a full model. But others at least professed to see a less formal, less disciplined approach as a virtue rather than an awkward necessity. It is in this light that one needs to see Hirschman and Myrdal. These authors are often cited today (by me, among others) as forerunners of the researchers who have recently been emphasizing strategic complementarity. In fact, however, their books marked the end, not the beginning of high development theory. Myrdal's central thesis was the idea of "circular causation." But the idea of circular causation is already present in Allyn Young in 1928, not to mention Rosenstein-Rodan, and Nurkse in 1953 referred repeatedly to the circular nature of the problem of getting growth going in poor countries.[8] So Myrdal was in effect providing a capsulization of an already extensive and familiar set of ideas rather than a new departure. Similarly, Hirschman's idea of linkages was more distinctive for the effectiveness of the term and the policy advice that he derived loosely from it than for its intellectual novelty—Rosenstein-Rodan was already talking about linkages, while Fleming explicitly put both forward and backward linkages in his discussion.

What marked Myrdal and Hirschman was not so much the novelty of their ideas but their stylistic and methodological stance. Until their books appeared, economists doing high development theory were trying to be good mainstream economists. They could not develop full formal models, but they got as close as they could, trying to keep up with the increasingly model-oriented mainstream. Myrdal and Hirschman abandoned this effort, and eventually took stands on principle against any effort to formalize their ideas.

One imagines that this was initially very liberating for them and their followers. Yet in the end it was a vain stance. Economic theory is basically a collection of models. Broad insights that are not expressed in model form may temporarily attract attention and even win converts, but they do not endure unless codified in a reproducible—and teachable—form. You may not like this tendency; certainly, economists are sometimes too quick to dismiss what has not been formalized (although I believe that the focus on models is basically right). Like it or not, however, the influence of ideas that have not been embalmed in models soon decays. And this was the fate of high development theory. Myrdal's effective presentation of the idea of circular and cumulative causation, or Hirschman's evocation of linkages, were stimulating and immensely influential in the 1950s and early 1960s. By the 1970s (when I myself was a student of economics), they had come to seem not so much wrong as meaningless. What were these guys talking about? Where were the models? High development theory was not so much rejected as simply bypassed.

The exception proves the rule. Lewis's surplus labor concept was the model that launched a thousand papers, even though surplus labor assumptions were already standard among development theorists, the empirical basis for assuming surplus labor was weak, and the idea of external economies/strategic complementarity is surely more interesting. The point was, of course, that precisely because he did not mix economies of scale into his framework, Lewis offered theorists some-thing they could model by using available tools.

Metaphors and Models

I have just acknowledged that the tendency of economists to empha-size what they know how to model formally can create blind spots; yet, I have also claimed that the insistence on modeling is basically right. What I want to do now is call a time-out and discuss more broadly the role of models in social science.

It is said that those who can, do, while those who cannot, discuss methodology. So the very fact that I raise the issue of methodology in this discussion tells you something about the state of economics. Yet in some ways the problems of economics and of social science in gen-eral are part of a broader methodological problem that afflicts many fields: how to deal with complex systems.

It is unfortunate that for many of us the image of a successful field of scientific endeavor is basic physics. The objective of the most basic physics is to give a complete description of what happens. In principle, and apparently in practice, quantum mechanics gives a complete ac-count of what goes on inside, say, a hydrogen atom. But most things we want to analyze, even in physical science, cannot be dealt with at that level of completeness. The only exact model of the global weather system is that system itself. Any model of that system is therefore to some degree a falsification: it leaves out some (many) aspects of reality.

How, then, does the meteorological researcher decide what to put into his model? And how does he decide whether his model is a good one? The answer to the first question is that the choice of model repre-sents a mixture of judgment and compromise. The model must be something you know how to make—that is, you are constrained by your modeling techniques. And the model must be something you can construct given your resources—time, money, and patience are not un-limited. A wide variety of models may be possible given those con-straints; which one or ones you choose actually to build depends on educated guessing.

And how do you know that the model is good? It will never be *right* in the way that quantum electrodynamics is right. At a certain point it may be good enough at predicting for its results to be put to repeated practical use, like the giant weather-forecasting models that run on today's supercomputers; in that case predictive success can be measured in terms of dollars and cents, and the improvement of models becomes a quantifiable matter. In the early stages of a complex science, however, the criterion for a good model is more subjective: it is a good model if it succeeds in explaining or rationalizing some of what you see in the world in a way that you might not have expected.

Notice that I have not specified exactly what I mean by a model. You may think that I must mean a mathematical model, perhaps a computer simulation. And indeed that is mostly what we have to work with in economics. But a model can equally well be a physical one, and I would like to describe briefly an example from the precomputer era of meteorological research: Fultz's dishpan.

Dave Fultz was a meteorological theorist at the University of Chicago who asked the following question: What factors are essential to generating global weather? Is it a process that depends on the full complexity of the world—the interaction of ocean currents and the atmosphere, the locations of mountain ranges, the alternation of the seasons, and so on—or does the basic pattern of weather, for all its complexity, have simple roots?

He was able to show the essential simplicity of the weather's causes with a "model" that consisted of a dishpan filled with water, placed on a slowly rotating turntable, with an electric heating element bent around the outside of the pan. Aluminum flakes were suspended in the water, so that a camera perched overhead and rotating with the pan could take pictures of the pattern of flow.[9]

The setup was designed to reproduce two features of the global weather pattern: the temperature differential between the poles and the equator, and the Coriolis force that results from the Earth's spin. Everything else—all the rich detail of the actual planet—was suppressed. And yet the dishpan's behavior exhibited an unmistakable similarity to real-world weather patterns, in effect showed the basic elements of actual weather.

What did one learn from the dishpan? It was not telling an entirely true story: the Earth is not flat, air is not water, the real world has oceans and mountain ranges (and for that matter, two hemispheres). The unrealism of Fultz's model world was dictated by what Fultz was able to or could be bothered to build—that is, by the limitations of his modeling technique. Nonetheless, the model did convey a powerful insight into why the weather system behaves the way it does.

The important point is that any kind of model of a complex system—a physical model, a computer simulation, or a pencil-and-paper
mathematical representation—amounts to pretty much the same kind
of procedure. You make a set of clearly untrue simplifications to get
the system down to something you can handle; those simplifications
are dictated partly by guesses about what is important, partly by the
modeling techniques available. And the end result, if the model is a
good one, is an improved insight into why the vastly more complex
real system behaves the way it does.

When it comes to physical science, few people have problems with
this idea. When we turn to social science, however, the whole issue of
modeling begins to raise people's hackles. Suddenly the idea of representing the relevant system through a set of simplifications that are
dictated at least in part by the available techniques becomes highly
objectionable. Everyone accepts that it was reasonable for Fultz to represent the Earth, at least for a first pass, with a flat dish, because that
was what was practical. But what do you think about the decision of
most economists between 1820 and 1970 to represent the economy as
a set of perfectly competitive markets, because a model of perfect competition was what they knew how to build? It is much the same thing,
but it raises howls of indignation.

Why is our attitude so different when we come to social science?
There are some discreditable reasons: like Victorians offended by the
suggestion that they were descended from apes, some humanists
imagine that their dignity is threatened when human society is represented as the moral equivalent of a dish on a turntable. Also, the most
vociferous critics of economic models are often politically motivated.
They have strong ideas about what they want to believe; their convictions are driven more by values than analysis, but when an analysis
threatens those beliefs, they prefer to attack its assumptions rather
than examine the basis for their own beliefs.

Still, there are highly intelligent and objective thinkers who are re-
pelled by simplistic models for a much better reason: they are aware
that the act of building a model involves loss as well as gain. Africa is
not empty, but the act of making accurate maps can get you into the
habit of imagining that it is. Model building, especially in its early
stages, involves the evolution of ignorance as well as knowledge; and
someone with powerful intuition, with a deep sense of the complexi-

ties of reality, may well feel that from his point of view more is lost than is gained. It is in this honorable camp that I would put Albert Hirschman and his rejection of mainstream economics.

The cycle of knowledge lost before it can be regained seems to be an inevitable part of formal model building. Here is another story from meteorology. Folk wisdom has always said that you can predict future weather from the aspect of the sky, and had claimed that certain kinds of clouds presage storms. In the nineteenth and early twentieth centuries, however, as meteorology made such fundamental discoveries, completely unknown to folk wisdom, as the fact that the winds in a storm blow in a circular path, it stopped paying much attention to how the sky looked. Serious students of the weather studied wind direction and barometric pressure, not the pretty patterns made by condensing water vapor. It was not until 1919 that a group of Norwegian scientists realized that the folk wisdom had been right all along—that one could identify the onset and development of a cyclonic storm quite accurately by looking at the shapes and altitude of the cloud cover.

The point is not that a century of research into the weather had only reaffirmed what everyone knew from the beginning. The meteorology of 1919 had learned many things of which folklore was unaware and dispelled many myths. Nor is the point that meteorologists somehow sinned by not looking at clouds for so long. What happened was simply inevitable: during the process of model building, there is a narrowing of vision imposed by the limitations of one's framework and tools, a narrowing that can only be ended definitively by making those tools good enough to transcend those limitations.

But that initial narrowing is very hard for broad minds to accept. And so they look for an alternative.

The problem is that there is no alternative to models. We all think in simplified models, all the time. The sophisticated thing to do is not to pretend to stop, but to be self-conscious—to be aware that your models are maps rather than reality.

There are many intelligent writers on economics who are able to convince themselves—and sometimes large numbers of other people as well—that they have found a way to transcend the narrowing effect of model building. Invariably, they are fooling themselves. If you look at the writing of any people who claim to be able to write about social issues without stooping to restrictive modeling, you will invariably find that their insights are based on the use of metaphor. And metaphor is, of course, a kind of heuristic modeling technique.

In fact, we are all builders and purveyors of unrealistic simplifications. Some of us are self-aware: we use our models as metaphors. Others, including people who are indisputably brilliant and seemingly sophisticated, are sleepwalkers: they unconsciously use metaphors as models.

The Big Push

We can now return to the story of development economics. By the late 1950s, as I have argued, high development theory was in a difficult position. Mainstream economics was moving in the direction of increasingly formal and careful modeling. While this trend was clearly overdone in many instances, it was an unstoppable and ultimately an appropriate change. But high development theory proved difficult to model more formally because the theory's proponents were unable to deal with market structure.

The response of some of the most brilliant high development theorists, above all Albert Hirschman, was simply to opt out of the mainstream. They would build a new development school on suggestive metaphors, institutional realism, interdisciplinary reasoning, and a relaxed attitude toward internal consistency. The result was some wonderful writing, some inspiring insights, and (in my view) an intellectual dead end. High development theory simply faded out. A constant-returns, perfect-competition view of reality took over the development literature, and eventually—via the World Bank and other institutions—much of real-world development policy as well.

And yet in the end it turned out that mainstream economics eventually *did* find a place for high development theory. Like the Norwegians who discovered that the shapes of clouds do mean something, mainstream economics discovered that as its modeling techniques became more sophisticated, some neglected insights could be brought back in.

Since this sounds rather abstract, it will be best if I explicitly present an example of how the classic model of high development theory—Rosenstein-Rodan's Big Push—can be treated formally.[10]

Our paper-and-pencil dishpan—our model economy—consists of a set of assumptions about the supply of resources, technology, demand, and market structure.

RESOURCES.   The only resource in the economy is labor—that is, we neglect the role of capital, physical or human. Labor is in fixed total supply L. It can, however, be employed in either of two sectors: a "traditional" sector, characterized by constant returns, or a "modern" sector, characterized by increasing returns. Although the same quality of labor is used in the traditional and modern sectors, it is not paid the same wage. Workers must be paid a premium to move from traditional to modern employment. We let $w > 1$ be the ratio of the wage rate that must be paid in the modern sector to that in the traditional sector.

TECHNOLOGY.   It is assumed that the economy produces N goods, where N is a large number. We choose units so that the productivity of labor in the traditional sector is unity in each of the goods. In the modern sector, average labor cost is decreasing in the scale of production. For simplicity, decreasing costs take a linear form. Let Q_i be the production of good i in the modern sector. Then if the modern sector produces the good at all, the labor requirement will be assumed to take the form

$$(2\text{-}1) \qquad\qquad L_i = F + cQ_i,$$

where $c < 1$ is the marginal labor requirement. Note that for this example it is assumed that the relationship between input and output is the same for all N goods.

DEMAND.   Each good receives a constant share $1/N$ of expenditure. The model will be static, with no asset accumulation or decumulation; so expenditure equals income.

MARKET STRUCTURE.   The traditional sector is assumed to be characterized by perfect competition. Thus for each good there is a perfectly elastic supply from the traditional sector at the marginal cost of production; given our choice of units, this supply price is unity in terms of traditional sector labor. By contrast, a single entrepreneur is assumed to have the unique ability to produce each good in the modern sector.

How will such a producer set prices? She cannot raise her price as much as she would like. The reason is that potential competition from the traditional sector puts a limit on the price: she cannot go above a price of 1 (in terms of traditional labor) without being undercut by

FIGURE 2-1. *The Big Push*

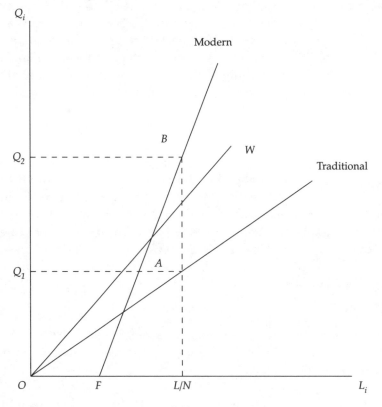

traditional producers. So each producer in the modern sector will set the same price, unity, as would have been charged in the traditional sector.

We can now ask the question, will production actually take place in the traditional or the modern sector?

To answer this, it is useful to draw a simple diagram (figure 2-1). On the horizontal axis is the labor input, L_i, used to produce a typical good. On the vertical axis is that sector's output, Q_i. The two solid lines represent the technologies of production in the two sectors: a 45-degree line for the traditional sector, a line with a slope of $1/c$ for the modern sector.

From this figure it is immediately possible to read off what the economy would produce if all labor were allocated either to the modern or the traditional sector. In either case, L/N workers would be employed in the production of each good. If all goods were produced traditionally, each good would have an output Q^1. If they were all produced using modern techniques, the output would be Q^2. As drawn, $Q^2 > Q^1$; this will be the case provided that

$$(\text{2-2}) \qquad \frac{(L/N) - F}{c} > L/N,$$

that is, as long as the marginal cost advantage of modern production is sufficiently large and/or fixed costs are not too large. Since this is the interesting case, we focus on it.

But even if the economy could produce more by using modern methods, this does not mean that it will. It must be profitable for each individual entrepreneur in the modern sector to produce, taking into account the necessity of paying the premium wage w—and also the decisions of all the other entrepreneurs.

Suppose that an individual firm starts modern production while all other firms continue using traditional techniques. The firm will charge the same price as that on other goods and hence sell the same amount; since there are many goods, we may neglect any income effects and suppose that each good continues to sell Q^1. Thus this firm would have the production and employment illustrated by point A.

Is this a profitable move? The firm uses less labor than would be required for traditional production, but must pay that labor more. Draw a ray from the origin whose slope is the modern relative wage w; OW in the figure is an example. Then modern production is profitable given traditional production elsewhere if and only if OW passes *below* A. As drawn, this test is of course failed: it is not profitable for an individual firm to start modern production.

Suppose, however, that all modern firms start simultaneously. Then each firm will produce Q^2, and production and employment will be at point B. Again, this will be profitable if the wage line OW passes below B. As drawn, this test *is* satisfied.

Obviously, there are three possible outcomes.[11] If the wage premium $w - 1$ is low, the economy always "industrializes"; if it is high, it never industrializes; and if it takes on an intermediate value, there are both low- and high-level equilibria.

One would hardly conclude from this model that the high development idea—namely, that countries can be caught in low-income traps, but that self-reinforcing growth is also possible—is necessarily right. Even within this model, that story is true only for some parameter values. And the specific assumptions are obviously unrealistic. Yet the model illustrates several key points about the relationship between mainstream economics and high development theory.

First, it shows that it is possible to tell high development stories in the form of a rigorous model. The methods of mainstream economics may have created a predisposition to constant-returns, perfect-competition models, but they need not be restricted to such models.

Second, this example, like Fultz's dishpan, shows that the logic of high development stories emerges even in a highly simplified setting. It is common for those who have never tried making a model to assert that underdevelopment traps must necessarily result from some complicated set of factors—irrationality or shortsightedness on the part of investors, cultural barriers to change, inadequate capital markets, problems of information and learning, and so on. Perhaps these factors play a role, perhaps not. What we have just seen is that a low-level trap can arise with rational entrepreneurs, without so much as a whiff of cultural influences, in a model without capital, and with everyone fully informed.

Third, the model, unlike a purely verbal exposition, reveals the sensitivity of the conclusions to the assumptions. In particular, verbal expositions of the Big Push story make it seem like something that *must* be true. In this model we see that it is something that *might* be true. A model like this makes one want to go out and start measuring, to see whether it looks at all likely in practice, whereas a merely rhetorical presentation gives one a false feeling of security in one's understanding.

Finally, the model tells us something about the attitude required to deal with complex issues in economics. This model may seem childishly simple, but I can report from observation that until Murphy and his colleagues published their formalization of Rosenstein-Rodan, its conclusions were not obvious to many people, even those who have specialized in development. Economists tended to regard the Big Push story as nonsensical—if modern technology is better, then rational firms would simply adopt it! (They missed the interaction between economies of scale and market size.) Noneconomists tended to think that Big Push stories necessarily involved some rich interdisciplinary stew of effects and missed the simple core. In other words, economists were locked into their traditional models, while noneconomists were lost in the fog that results when you have no explicit models at all.

How did Murphy and his colleagues break through this wall of confusion? Not by trying to capture the richness of reality, either with a highly complex model or with the kind of lovely metaphors that seem to evade the need for a model. They did it instead by *daring to be silly:* by representing the world in a dishpan, to get at an essential point.

Concluding Thoughts

When I look at the model Murphy and his colleagues used to represent the Big Push idea, I find myself wondering whether the long slump in development theory was really necessary. The model is so simple: three pages, two equations, and one diagram. It could, it seems, have been written as easily in 1955 as in 1989. What would have happened to development economics, even to economics in general, if someone had legitimized the role of increasing returns and circular causation with a neat model thirty-five years ago?

But it did not happen, and perhaps could not. Those economists who were attracted to the idea of powerful simplifications were still absorbed in the possibilities of perfect competition and constant returns; those who were drawn to a richer view, like Hirschman, became impatient with the narrowness and seeming silliness of the economics enterprise.

That the story may have been preordained does not keep it from being a sad one. Good ideas were left to gather dust in the economics attic for more than a generation; great minds retreated to the intellectual periphery. It is hard to know whether economic policy in the real world would have been much better if high development theory had not decayed so badly, since the relationship between good economic analysis and successful policy is far weaker than we like to imagine. Still, one wishes things had played out differently.

One would like to draw some morals from this story. It is easy to give facile advice. For those who are impatient with modeling and prefer to strike out on their own into the richness that an uninhibited use of metaphor seems to open up, the advice is to stop and think. Are you sure that you really have such deep insights that you are better off turning your back on the cumulative discourse among generally intelligent people that is modern economics? But of course you are.

And for those, like me, who try to understand the world through the metaphors provided by models, the advice is not to let important ideas slip by just because they have not been formulated your way. Look for the folk wisdom on clouds—ideas that come from people who do not write formal models but may have rich insights. There may be some very interesting things out there. Strangely, though, I cannot think of any.

The truth, I fear, is that not much can be done about the kind of intellectual waste that took place during the fall and rise of development economics. A temporary evolution of ignorance may be the price of progress, an inevitable part of what happens when we try to make sense of the world's complexity.

Three

Hirschman's *Strategy* at Thirty-Five

Lance Taylor

SINCE it was published in 1958, *The Strategy of Economic Development* has aged gracefully, but increasingly obscurely.[1] It remains on reading lists and has remarkable lessons to teach students who bother to look, but as of 1993 its influence on the mainstream economics profession was not great. Only a dozen index references to Albert O. Hirschman grace the 1,800 pages of the recently published *Handbook of Development Economics,* and few journal articles pay heed to his thoughts.[2]

This lack of interest in what was once considered a prophetic book is puzzling: it remains a good read and addresses issues of current interest in developing economies as well as those in the postsocialist transition. Why Hirschman along with a host of contemporaries faded from the economics profession's sight is an intriguing question. The best answer is that *Strategy* was written near the end of an intellectual pendulum's swing; as the bob moved away, Hirschman and the people with whom he debated became irrelevant to newer concerns.

Before considering his thought, it makes sense to set out the themes from *Strategy* that still carry professional weight. There are three.

—Backward and forward linkages are featured in all the textbooks and show up frequently in applied benefit-cost and regional economic assessments. For the most part, these academic and bureaucratic exercises boil down to big computations with interindustry or input-output matrixes (the more super the computer, the better). Apart from empirical surprises such as the fact that forward linkages from the

59

Russian energy sector are so strong that a cost increase may destabilize the whole price system, they lack intellectual bite.[3]

Paul Krugman rightly emphasizes that linkage connections become interesting only when they are combined with increasing returns to scale in supplying or using industries (see chapter 2 of this volume). Hirschman's careful discussion in *Strategy*'s chapter 6 of the importance of passing thresholds of "minimum economic size" in linked firms is missing in the matrix manipulations. Notable also by its absence from the current discussion is the idea that development is a chain of disequilibria involving linkage effects (more on this below).

—The "Hirschman hypotheses" about how machine-paced factory processes stimulate labor productivity and how the need to maintain modern equipment can enforce its proper handling, since it will otherwise fall apart, have received econometric support.[4] These hypotheses influence the ways in which institutionally minded scholars discuss efficiency questions in such locales as American-owned automobile engine plants in Mexico.[5] As Donald Schön points out in chapter 4, Hirschman-style stimuli serve as incentives for learning, but few economists are likely to be moved by such a "philosophical" observation.

—The material in the *Strategy*'s chapter 9 on inflation as a disequilibrium process provoked by structural imbalances and on "external strangulation" from the balance of payments underlies the macroeconomics of the neostructuralist school.[6] Hirschman himself made subsequent contributions to these lines of thought, for example, in his "Exercises in Retrospection" about recent Latin travails, including "heterodox shock" anti-inflation programs aimed precisely at breaking down structural price rigidities.[7] But it is also fair to say that neostructuralists are a distinct minority among the economists of the 1990s.

Although they are equally striking, other messages from *Strategy* have simply vanished from sight. As already observed, the book's central theme—that development should be seen as a sequence of transitions from one sort of disequilibrium to another—does not enter current thought. This chain-of-disequilibria metaphor could not transcend the intellectual environment in which *Strategy* flourished. It was written for scholars who automatically thought of Josef A. Schumpeter's description of development as a passage between *equilibrium* positions of "circular flow" (an idea that Hirschman neatly and characteristically stood on its head), Ragnar Nurkse's distinction between "vicious" and "virtuous" causal circles, and *Strategy*'s bête noire of balanced growth.[8] Such world-encompassing institutional descriptions are alien to modern academic minds.

Likewise forgotten are the *Strategy*'s discussions of complementarity versus substitution among different types of investment; of possibilities for development via shortage or via excess capacity; of the role of imports in inducing industrialization, with exports as a key complementary source of demand (a point considerably elaborated later by Hirschman himself); and of methods of integrating market- and nonmarket-mediated adjustment mechanisms.[9] Planners in Japan (see chapter 11) and later in the Republic of Korea paid profound attention to such ideas; however, it is likely that they learned them less from Hirschman than from Alexander Hamilton and Friedrich List. Regardless of their sources of inspiration, East Asian economic bureaucrats were certainly well aware of the distinctions between the "balancing" and "unbalancing" roles of the state that Hirschman emphasized in *Strategy*'s conclusion.

The fact that Hirschman and his contemporaries focused on the planning process and the role of the state is one big reason why their ideas ultimately fell on deaf ears. Post–World War II development economists were neither naively pro-state nor diabolically antimarket; they just saw room for public intervention. How could they think otherwise, after experiencing the depression and the war, and after being under the intellectual spell of Keynes?

Strategy acknowledged limitations on a government's ability to handle certain tasks, but its author also thought that enterprising states might want to take a whirl at investing in productive industry as opposed to boring, pork barrel public works.[10] How to make planning effective and bring the pros and cons of both public and private economic activity into one train of thought were concerns of early development economics that later theorists rejected or ignored. Hirschman and friends talked vigorously to one another but had little to say to the following "market-friendly" generations.

Did these messages fade just because they were stated in the wrong idiom? Krugman's view is that the dearth of formalized arguments in *Strategy* doomed it to obscurity (see chapter 2). One cannot dismiss this point out of hand, since economists obviously *are* influenced by neat little models. The other side of the coin is that they tend to reject ideas presented in the conditional mode, drawing on personal observations and practical lore—forms of argument that Hirschman never disdained. However, it may be that Krugman gives the profession's attachment to its intellectual playthings too much weight. The simple truth is that by the 1970s *Strategy* no longer fit the spirit of the times. A neoclassical reaction against the worldview of Schumpeter, Paul Rosenstein-Rodan, Nurkse, Hirschman, and company was well under way by then.

The counterattack was launched on three fronts: agricultural price and technological reform, as set out by Theodore W. Schultz; trade liberalization and the abandonment of industrial policy (especially of the import-substituting industrialization, or ISI variety), as advocated by Ian Little, Tibor Scitovsky, and Maurice Scott; and the elimination of financial repression, as preached by Ronald McKinnon and Edward Shaw.[11] The doctrine that distorted markets were holding back real income growth in poor countries took the profession by storm soon after these authors sounded the call. As underlined by such proclamations as the World Bank's 1991 *World Development Report,* which put great emphasis on market-friendly development strategies, its hold is powerful still.[12]

When he published *Strategy* in 1958, Hirschman argued at least as formally as the economists who supplanted him: Schultz used hardly any algebraic and graphical apparatus, and Little and his colleagues supplied not much more (although the country studies underlying their book made extensive use of the then new-fangled notion of effective rates of protection). To date, there is no generally accepted formalization of what "financial repression" really means.

In fact, formal models of his ideas designed to fit contemporary tastes were available when Hirschman wrote. In one influential example, Hollis Chenery cast input-output linkages and increasing returns to scale into integer programming form: his insistence on the need for nonmarket intervention arguably influenced policy in South Korea and elsewhere.[13] Planning models of the 1950s used more sophisticated mathematics and are not isomorphic to the market-based scale-economy machines that Krugman artfully constructs (see chapter 2). Chenery's solutions could not be realized in unregulated markets, while Krugman's in principle could (under strong enough assumptions about stylized oligopoly behavior).

Even so, the central messages of both sorts of models are the same:

economists have known for generations that increasing returns can give rise to multiple equilibria in the sense that the economy can maintain relevant demand-supply balances with diverse patterns of resource allocation. (Of course, some of these positions could contain "disequilibrium" phenomena, in Hirschman's sense of the word, such as inflation, balance of payments pressure, or unemployment.) Extra-market policy intervention may be necessary to shift the economy between rest points, and economic evaluations based on the price system associated with one equilibrium can be completely misleading for another.

Such results can be read from both Chenery-style planning models and contemporary oligopoly stories featuring firms with decreasing average production costs. Hirschman's conditional policy view in *Strategy*—that "some interference . . . may be justified if it can be demonstrated that a certain growth pattern of consumption would exert far more powerful backward linkage effects than the pattern that is likely to develop in the absence of interference"—is in accord with the formal analyses of both Chenery and Krugman.[14]

This message was lost in the 1970s, as modeling adjusted to neoclassically market-friendly ideological ends. In the 1960s, University of Chicago economists would have nothing to do with input-output calculations in general and backward linkages in particular. Such techniques smelled too strongly of state intervention and planning altogether. They rejected the idea that establishing an industry might stimulate a supplier upstream, given that it received enough demand to realize increasing returns and permit its new buyer to attain low production costs.

A few years later, in the wake of Little, Scitovsky, and Scott and their numerous followers, the Chicago Boys inverted linkages in orthodox calculations of effective protection: a potentially exporting industry could be severely handicapped by high cost suppliers set up upstream under wrong-headed ISI programs. There was no mention in the effective protection literature of the *Strategy*-style notion that expensive suppliers are not likely to stimulate strong forward linkages in the production chain. (Russia's inflation problems with energy cost-push perhaps illustrate that subsidized suppliers can propel forward linkages too far.)

Much more important than Hirschman and his colleagues' alleged aversion to formulas with Greek letters and graphs for the orthodox conquest of development economics was their apparent lack of concreteness: they did not give strong, simple policy advice. This "weakness" can be summarized under three counts:

—The post–World War II cohort of development economists thought in metaphors—vicious and virtuous circles, big pushes, growth poles and trickle-down, balanced and unbalanced growth—which did not seem to be terribly helpful in actual policy practice: "The knowledge of the approximate ranking of an industry from the point of view of forward and backward linkage effects . . . is . . . useful to the economist-planner in underdeveloped areas. It is something to be added to his criteria-box."[15] Fine, but this information does not look immediately useful to someone who has to make a decision about tariff T, quota Q, or subsidy S for industry X today. Orthodox advice to devalue, "tariffize" the quota, and reduce both tariff and subsidy rates posthaste sounds much more crisp. Whether it is helpful or not is another question; I argue below that it may well not be.

—One reason why simple policy recipes usually fail is implicit in Hirschman's complex worldview. What is possible in a given country's circumstances depends largely on its previous history and existing technology and institutions. How the latter factors change drives unbalanced growth but is impossible to foretell ex ante. One has to deal with possibilities and contingencies in a situation filled with uncertainty: As Bishwapriya Sanyal points out in chapter 7, Hirschman was personally well acquainted with Keynes's "dark forces of time and ignorance." Aware of his own (and the profession's) dim foresight, he was not willing to come up with the one-liners that the politicians pay policy advisers to recite. "Get the prices right" may or may not be useful advice, but it *is* succinct—music to the ears of a political chief executive overwhelmed by endless complications.

—As already noted, the first generation of development economists thought that public intervention made sense in the appropriate circumstances. They may have been naive about the limitations that developing country governments confront, but they were not unalloyed devotees of the invisible hand, as exemplified in Hirschman's evenhanded treatment of market and nonmarket adjustments.

The neoclassical position that took over the mainstream is in opposition on all three points:

—Market reformers had a "concrete" suggestion: get rid of distortions and make all efforts to get (set? let be?) the prices right. Such advice purports to be directly relevant to policy decisions.

—A market-centered worldview can be complex and nuanced à la Krugman, but it does not have to be, which is a useful escape valve for propagandists and practitioners. The 1991 *World Development Report*, for example, begins with the cautious opinion that "consensus is gradually forming in favor of a 'market-friendly' approach to development policy" but concludes confidently that "what remains is to put these ideas into practice everywhere."[16] No room for unforeseeable contingencies, politics, and institutional surprises in a market-friendly environment, according to the World Bank.

—In vulgar neoclassical economics, intervention is counterproductive after steps have been taken to set the market system right.

As the World Bank's rhetoric makes clear, simple, strong, market-friendly recommendations carried the day after 1970 in development economics. Will they continue to do so? There are reasons to think not. Changes in economic thought are lagging indicators of current events; much will depend on what happens in the greater world. Robert Wade talks about a "cusp of neoliberalism," which we may cross as the realization sinks in that mainstream policies in the United States and United Kingdom throughout the 1980s were thoroughly wrong-headed.[17]

Along similar lines, the failure of highly orthodox economic packages in postsocialist economies (just think of the former German Democratic Republic, Yugoslavia, Poland, and Soviet Union) and the success of evolutionary, unbalanced policies in places like Hirschman's old stomping ground Colombia, Hungary in Eastern Europe, and China suggest that reassessment may be in order. Indeed, the lesson of recent experience seems to be that mainstream ideas embody misplaced concreteness. Setting prices to "right" values (or letting them move there) is not easy: the target prices are impossible to define and the economic effects of the transition toward them can be fatally destabilizing.

If mainstream economics has to reinvent itself in the light of recent events, both forgotten and still quoted lessons from *Strategy* may come into view again; the book is at least a partial exception to Schumpeter's lament that "economists don't read!"[18] But however remarkable they may be, Hirschman-like ideas will not take over the academic economists' world. The profession, especially its American branch, does not cope easily with admittedly exploratory, conditional approaches that learn from their own mistakes: historically based lore is not nearly so compelling as theorems, and unbalanced growth looks suspiciously like unbalanced thinking to the mainstream mind.

Four

Hirschman's Elusive Theory of Social Learning

Donald A. Schön

IN *The Strategy of Economic Development*, first published in 1958, Hirschman contends that mainstream economists, bemused by illusions of "the big push," "balanced growth," and uniform "prerequisites for development," fail to grasp the processes of social learning entrained by *imbalanced* growth through which developing countries actually follow their various paths to modernization.[1] However, the view of social learning behind Hirschman's idea of imbalanced growth and his guidelines for policymaking never fully surfaces: one does not know just what this view is, whether it is one or many, or how it relates to Hirschman's other main ideas.

What adds to the sense of elusiveness is that Hirschman tends to refer to the role of learning in development by way of analogy—it is as though he were using familiar examples of learning to highlight a process fundamentally understandable in another way. In *Strategy*, for example, Hirschman compares a country that sets out on the road to development to a person who "decides in a fit of enthusiasm to learn a foreign language," in blissful ignorance of the difficulties that lie ahead.[2] As these difficulties appear, "'practice' may be reduced, contradictory and harmful economic policies are being adopted, and development will be slowed down and perhaps halted. On the other hand, if income growth reaches a point where the benefits of development are felt to outweigh the dislocations it brings with it, 'practice' becomes pleasant and is gradually increased, and the country will reach its development goals" (p. 48).

67

From this analogy, Hirschman argues "in favor of some forcing of the pace in the early stages of development, to overcome the resistances that then are strongest." And when in a later chapter he considers whether by exporting production machinery to developing countries industrial countries may be "committing economic suicide," he again draws a learning analogy: "It would be more correct to compare the exporting of certain manufactures to the imparting of a lesson which is finally learnt as home production is started in the heretofore importing country: when a tutor has successfully accomplished his job and has as a result made it possible for the pupil to dispense with him in a particular subject, we do not consider that he has committed suicide" (p. 123). Here, too, a learning analogy seems to allude to a process understandable in other ways. But if these other ways *also* rest on a view of learning, then Hirschman's analogies may be acting as camouflage for the true wellspring of his thought.

The task in this chapter is to begin the search for this wellspring, for if it could be uncovered, the fruitfulness and originality of Hirschman's thought would come into clearer view, as would perhaps even a glimpse of the connections between the kinds of learning he attributes to developing countries and the ways in which he himself learns about development. What we are looking for here may not be a "theory" or "model" that subsumes development under the broader category of learning, but a generative metaphor.[3] Hirschman *sees* development *as* learning in the same way that someone who sees the mind as a computer, or an organization as an organism, thereby comes to think of such things in new ways. We may even regard his metaphor of development as learning with the same "constructive skepticism" and "serious playfulness" that Michael McPherson attributes to his work as a whole.[4] In our search, we might also gain a clearer picture of Hirschman's intellectual relationships to other thinkers with whom his name is not usually associated (Jean Piaget and Lev Vygotsky, for example), and a better grasp of the implications of his work for other fields of study where his work is not as well known as it should be (cognitive and organizational development, for example). A critical elaboration of Hirschman's view of development as social learning might also reveal its implications for mainstream economics. Before setting off on our search, however, we would have to establish what we think a theory of social learning must do.

What a Theory of Social Learning Must Do

A theory about learning must deal with performance that improves over time. Performance that deteriorates, regresses, or merely swings from one mode of action to another does not qualify as learning. In addition, learning activity must be new to the actor, begin and end with more than one event, and be transferable from one kind of situation to another. These additional restrictions add layers of complexity to any such theory, however, and therefore it may not be able to do much more than to identify or clarify them.

Above all, the theory must identify *what* is learned, including the possibility that this may consist of more than one kind or level of content. The theory must explain how changes in performance relate to changes in beliefs, understandings, attitudes, or values; also the means and the *how* of learning; why performance tends to improve under some *circumstances* and not others; and, if the theory claims practical *utility*, how improvement in performance can be enhanced.

Not least, the theory must answer the question, *"Who learns?"* Social learning implies an agent whose performance may improve—for example, an organization that tackles a recurrent problem, or a project in which individuals negotiate a chain of related difficulties. One might even attribute social learning to a whole country or society, but such a view would mask the individuals, groups, and institutions whose complex interactions may result in improved societal performance.

Hirschman addresses all of these topics in his treatment of development as social learning addresses, but with varying degrees of clarity and explicitness.

Learning's Place in the Argument of *Strategy*

For Hirschman, underdevelopment is not a matter of "villainous obstacles" or a lack of "prerequisites," such as capital or education. He thinks "countries fail to take advantage of their development potential because, *for reasons largely related to their images of change,* they find it difficult to take the decisions needed for development in the required number and at the required speed" (p. 25, emphasis added).[5] These countries, he says, must learn to adopt a "group-and-ego-focused im-

age of change" that "takes cognizance of the possibility of mutual benefits and all-round growth" (p. 19). This would free them (a) from the
idea that change comes about for the whole group or not at all (which
leads to stasis or to a reliance on luck or magic); and (b) from the
equally pernicious idea that change can come about only through the
heroic manipulations of an individual entrepreneur. Rather, such a
change of ideas can be effected only through "practical, direct experience with development as it proceeds," taking time, "like any correction of a deeply implanted idea about the nature of the world in which
we live" (p. 19).

In short, Hirschman traces the difficulties of development back to
"where all difficulties of human action begin and belong: in the mind"
(p. 11). They are to be overcome by a process of imbalanced growth in
which shortages, tensions, conflicts, and difficulties continually arise,
stimulating agents of development to make development decisions,
through which they learn to make such decisions, which provoke further disequilibria: "development draws new strength from the tensions
it creates. *By running up against difficulties, development makes it possible
to tackle them*" (p. 209, emphasis added).

Hirschman's *Strategy* is mainly an elaboration of this idea: people
learn to become development decisionmakers by participating in creating and coping with the disequilibria that are inherent in development. Development is "bred in some fashion in the developed sector
of an economy" (p. 40), because that is where people are "effectively
transformed into modern decision-makers." The trickle-down growth
of the modern sector can be "painfully slow," Hirschman admits, but
it also gives rise to "complementarity effects." When an investment is
made in commodity A, in period 1, it functions as a "pace-setter for
additional investment" in period 2 by requiring more production of
commodity B and lowering the marginal cost of producing commodity
C, "virtually compelling" certain additional investment decisions with
a "will and logic of their own," thereby propagating the growth of "the
ability to invest" (p. 42).

Complementarity effects are particularly strong, Hirschman notes,
in industries such as iron and steel, which have strong "backward and
forward linkages."[6] But when the natural course of development does
not yield such effects at a rate sufficient to make development self-
sustaining, policymakers must *induce* the change by aiming to "*keep*

alive rather than to eliminate the disequilibria of which profits and losses are symptoms in a competitive economy" (p. 66).

This idea of using naturally occurring or artificially induced disequilibria to trigger social learning is economic jujitsu: the very difficulties ordinarily seen as obstacles to development now become its energizers. Nowhere is this notion, which pervades *Strategy*, clearer than in Hirschman's ironic questioning of the frustrating effects of population growth (p. 176): *"the learning a community does when it reacts to population pressures* increases the total stock of its resources much as investment adds to total productive capacity. . . . The basic determinant of development which we have called 'the ability to invest' is decisively enhanced in the course of the struggle to accommodate more people" (p. 177, emphasis added).

Hirschman's Underlying Model of Social Learning

Hirschman also believes that certain kinds of doing—making investment decisions, producing things, maintaining capital equipment, allocating public resources, setting development policies—are inherently instructive for development. Whatever the unit of "instructive doing" (my term) may be, its improvement over time is a function of repeated performance. As Hirschman puts it, in full awareness of the apparent tautology, people learn to engage in development by engaging in development.

But such learning by doing depends on the learner's willingness to plunge into instructive doing. This *will to learn* may be confused by contradictory drives. People "invent all kinds of difficulties and obstacles" (p. 25). As in Simon's Berlitz model of learning, the will to learn may be frustrated by the pain of practice, or it may be resisted through the operation of mechanisms such as "defensive ignorance," which reflect an absence of the feeling that "change and progress is possible" (p. 11). And "if this feeling is due primarily to outside demonstration rather than to one's own experience, it may lead to a variety of misconceptions about the process of change that inhibit the achievement of the new goal *until a modicum of learning has been achieved*" (p. 11, emphasis added).

Learning here depends on a willingness to do something for the first time, a disposition learners may resist in the absence of feelings and understandings that impel them to do it, feelings that can be acquired only through the experience of doing it.[7] But how are people to be drawn into the right sort of doing when they are not ready to undertake it of their own free will? Through a variety of attractions, pressures, equivalent forces, Hirschman responds. If, for example, naturally occurring forcing mechanisms may not break the vicious cycle (p. 43) or advance the process with sufficient speed, public policies might create the necessary *"pacing devices or inducement mechanisms"* (p. 26). Governments may locate new enterprises in cities, where complementarity effects are greatest; and projects or firms (terms Hirschman uses interchangeably) can become "self-induced" along their own development paths so as to escape "the all-too-common fate of stagnation and deterioration." Those projects that are "best at calling forth other ventures are most likely to do well themselves," because they will be disciplined by the external demands they bring to bear on themselves: "Paradoxically, a road that is not traveled is likely to deteriorate sooner than one that has to support heavy traffic: the former will surely be neglected whereas there is some hope that the latter will be maintained" (p. 134).

Anticipating the argument of *Exit, Voice, and Loyalty*,[8] Hirschman also considers how pressures, generated from within, remedy "the typical shortcomings that undermine the efficient functioning of many firms in developing countries" (p. 136). This is one of the moments when Hirschman's underlying learning metaphor comes most visibly to the surface. In examining the "pervasive and paradoxical trait: the inadequate care for existing capital in capital-poor countries" (p. 141), he observes that maintenance is predominantly an administrative process, a preventive activity that "must be performed at fairly long intervals that are neither known with precision nor signalled by the capital itself." The difficulty might be solved by introducing technology that is virtually maintenance-free, like Roman roads (and certain high-technology forms of development assistance); but, aside from its limited applicability, this approach "perpetuates the problem by considering the difficulty of *learning* maintenance insuperable" (p. 142). Hirschman proposes, therefore, the paradoxical hypothesis that the "maintenance habit" will be best learned in just those enterprises

where lack of maintenance carries stiff penalties in the form of serious breakdowns and accidents instead of simply leading to a slow deterioration in the quality and quantity of output. . . . It is this *compulsion to maintain* that is characteristic of . . . airlines—nonmaintenance here means certain disaster—while highways can be left to deteriorate for a long time until they become actually impassable. . . . Our hypothesis . . . is in this instance nicely borne out by observation: the performance of airlines in these countries is usually quite creditable, that of the railroads mediocre, and the highway system is frequently in a parlous state of disrepair (p. 142).

Hirschman then takes the logic of this example a step further, arguing that developing countries may actually have a "comparative advantage in 'narrow-latitude' jobs that must be done well if they are to be done at all" (p. 144).

Beyond the ideas of learning by doing, the will to learn, forcing mechanisms, pacing devices, and tasks of narrow latitude, Hirschman's core model of learning contains an additional element: the tendency of instructive doing, once set in motion, to beget its own forcing mechanisms, which promote further learning. Thus, once a large and complex development project is under way, difficulties of control and maintenance inevitably arise that managers have to cope with or else they will fall flat on their faces. At the microscale of development projects, such effects mirror the disequilibrating effects of the development process as a whole.

The peripheral elements of Hirschman's view of learning have to do with features of tasks or settings that foster better performance. Their primary function is not to draw people *into* instructive activities (which is the job of forcing and pacing mechanisms) but to enhance people's ability to learn *through* them. Hirschman refers to a number of "learning factors."

—*Publicly visible feedback.* Task situations are especially conducive to learning when the difficulty to be resolved, the shortage to be filled, or the error to be corrected is publicly and dramatically visible both to the performer and to others who have a stake in the enterprise. Hirschman quotes with approval, for example, the report of a World Bank engineer who favored coating road surfaces in Colombia with bituminous pavement because "neglect of a bituminous surface is more obvious than neglect of a gravel and stone surface" (p. 143). Less tangibly, Hirschman finds an argument in favor of establishing basic industries in developing countries because "their presence brings into view some of the supply limitations that would otherwise remain hidden by the 'foreign exchange illusion'"—an illusion of unlimited supply of (foreign) materials that can be secured only at the expense of a nation's balance of payments (p. 167). The public visibility of negative outcomes is thought to be functional both because it reveals problems, "bringing them into view," *and* because it tends to stimulate demand for remedial action.

—*Rapidity of feedback.* Learning is enhanced when feedback is not only visible and dramatic but also rapid, as in the case of breakdowns in chemical processing plants or airlines, as opposed to the "slow deterioration of quality and quantity of output" (p. 144) that is characteristic of highways and many batch-processing industries.

—*Clear objectives, measurable and consequential indices of performance.* In contrast to services, especially in the public sector, manufacturing plants tend to experience continual improvements in performance because factory managers have relatively clear, consequential, objectively measurable performance goals (p. 148). Similarly, a production department is more likely to be disciplined by performance measurement than an administrative department (p. 154).[9]

—*Work templates inherent in technology.* Technology-intensive manufacturing, such as smelting or cement making, enhances efficiency because of the three factors just mentioned; it also provides a template for work, "a basic structure and rhythm which in effect deal out functions and determine sequences" (p. 147). Furthermore, efficiency is enhanced more by machine- than worker-paced production. Like the production rituals practiced by primitive peoples, advanced technologies both prompt and reward the behavioral patterns of efficient production. Exposure to such powerful industrial teaching aids might well be used in the training of public administrators (p. 155).

—*The pull of the image.* A vivid image of the product enhances learning by providing a model for imitation.[10] In product-based industries, "the image of the final product still acts both as a spur to everybody's efforts and as an objective test of achievement or failure" (p. 154). And products imported from industrial countries can play a tutelary role for domestic producers by demonstrating the existence of a market and the features important to product quality (p. 120).

Although he does not propose an explicit theory of imitation, Hirschman clearly regards it as a reconstructive rather than a reproductive process. Latecomers to an industry, he notes, discover that "the task of adaptation always remains, but is often underestimated just because everything *appears* to be so cut and dried" (p. 138).

—*The implicit principle of productive differences.* In Hirschman's heuristic account of learning, the process is enhanced by observable differences in the quality of performance. By way of example, he cites the learning-enhancing effects of productive differences between industrial and developing countries; imported and domestic products; "northern" and "southern" regions; and better- and worse-performing firms, industries, and sectors. Virtual productive differences may have similar effects; for example, the rated capacity of a manufacturing plant (p. 148) may stand in for a plant that actually achieves such a rating. Much of the strategic thinking in *Strategy* goes to explain how such differences arise in the natural development of an economy; how, when they do not already exist, they may be artificially created by governmental action; and how they may be more efficiently exploited.

At various points, Hirschman mentions the effects of complementarity, demonstration, competition, and migration and seems particularly interested in their combined operation. For example, the difference between better- and worse-performing industries may lead to disequilibria that generate complementarity effects; but it may also stimulate learning by reducing uncertainties (about markets, for example), demonstrating the feasibility of improved performance, presenting models of improved products or processes for imitation, and functioning as schools for training agents of diffusion.

Although Hirschman gives no general account of the variety of ways in which productive differences may enhance social learning, his many observations and analyses suggest the directions in which such an account might be developed.

Gaps, Ambiguities, and Apparent Contradictions in Hirschman's View of Social Learning

Hirschman makes no claim to a systematic theory of learning. Given his diffident, playful, and thoroughly skeptical approach to theory of any kind, he would probably recoil from so Germanic a prospect! He is much more at home either with limited special-purpose models, such as his formal analysis of labor productivity in capital-intensive industries, or with rich narrative accounts of development phenomena. Nevertheless, gaps, ambiguities, and apparent contradictions arise when Hirschman's views of learning are treated *as if* they made up a systematic theory. Such a theory of social learning might cover at least four aspects of performance: learning and doing, instructive doing and changes in beliefs and attitudes, salutary difficulties, and who learns and what they learn.

Learning and Doing

Agents learn the skills required for development, Hirschman argues, when they are attracted or compelled to engage in instructive doing. But how does the very first performance of the new action occur? No matter what the incentives for performance, how are prospective learners able to do the thing for which they lack the requisite ability?

There are three possible answers. Depending on the one we select, we will have a different view of what is learned by doing and, perhaps, a different attitude toward whether learning has occurred at all.

First, the agent may already know how to perform the activity in question (for example, make an investment decision) and may not do it because he fails to see the point of it or wishes to avoid the pain involved. In this case, he acquires certain understandings, attitudes, or views (for example, a belief in the possibility of change) as a result of carrying out the activity, which he knew how to perform all along.

Second, the agent may know how to perform the activity, but his know-how is rough, approximate, incomplete. He may get better at doing the thing in question as a result of practice, which may be seen as a process of repetition that "stamps in" new behavior, or a cumulative detection and correction of small errors, or a more radical improvement in performance through on-the-spot experimentation. Whichever view we take, such practice may lead to new understandings, beliefs, or attitudes.

Third, the learner may be unable to perform the activity in question. Perhaps she may never be able to do it, because there is no way of breaking her vicious circle of nonlearning; or perhaps she may be *taught* to do it. Such teaching might proceed by coercion, as is the case when a determined parent walks a toddler across the floor and the first, mechanical performance of the activity might be said to give the learner a "feeling for the activity"; by demonstration or instruction, so that the agent learns by imitation or following directions; or by the learner's somehow setting and solving the problem of doing it on her own.[11]

Hirschman at one time or another suggests each of these views but frequently leaves unspecified which of them he has in mind. When he speaks of learning to invest by practicing investment, for example, he seems to attribute to the learner some initial but limited capability for investing, which is presumed to improve through practice. When he speaks of the roles of imported products, or of the work templates inherent in advanced technology, he seems to emphasize the importance of tutorial functions external to the learner. When he speaks of backward and forward linkages that induce attempts to supply needed inputs or utilize available outputs, he seems to emphasize the learner's experimentation. When he speaks of more disciplined performance called forth by tasks of narrow latitude, he sometimes hints that the agents already know what to do and how to do it, although they may be insufficiently motivated or disciplined to act on what they know.

A theory of development as social learning would distinguish among these accounts of instructive doing. It would make explicit the kinds of activity agents of development know how to perform *ab initio*; what they need to learn to do, mainly (or exclusively) on their own; and in what cases they require externally available models or tutorial assistance. Such distinctions would determine to what degree a strategy of development can safely confine itself to the design and deployment of appropriate forcing and pacing mechanisms; or how much such a strategy must be concerned, in the design of mechanisms, with conditions and processes conducive *in the first instance* to the acquisition of appropriate know-how, belief, or understanding.

Instructive Doing and Changes in Beliefs and Attitudes

Hirschman says developing countries lack an ego-and-group image of change and the ideas and habits associated with Weberian rationality, discipline, and achievement motivation. In his view, these factors are essential to modernization. Yet he stresses instructive *doing* and the mechanisms for eliciting it. What, then, are the relationships between learning by doing and the images, beliefs, and attitudes that he takes as hallmarks of modernity?

Hirschman's answer is that instructive doing *entrains* the requisite changes in belief and attitude. For example, investors and managers are said to learn to think, feel, and believe in the manner of their counterparts in industrialized countries by virtue of their participation in modern industrial life (p. 41).

Such secondary effects are examples of what Gregory Bateson calls second-order learning, or "deutero-learning."[12] They arise, Hirschman suggests, because as individuals experience particular learning episodes they form habits of anticipation that shape their images of future transactions. So, when private operators learn to compel governments to remedy shortages of services triggered by new development ventures, they also learn that "bottlenecks and shortages will be efficiently taken care of" (p. 204). And when entrepreneurs manage to satisfy their urgent needs for capital by calling on foreign sources, the "spirit of enterprise" is strengthened "through the assurance that the pressures and tensions which may arise will not be allowed to boomerang, but will be temporarily relieved pending a more fundamental solution of the supply difficulties that have been revealed" (p. 207). In cases such as these, "practical, direct experience with development as it proceeds" (p. 19) yields the *general* lesson that shortages, setbacks, and difficulties can be effectively dealt with if and when they arise. This is very close to the "sense of the possibility and desirability of change and progress" that Hirschman places at the center of the modernizing ethos.

There are honorable precedents (most notably in the writings of William James) for the idea that a change in belief or attitude may *follow* behavior rather than set it in motion. But if inducement effects and forcing mechanisms must be designed in order to get more people to do the things that will cause them to acquire the appropriate beliefs, experience the appropriate feelings, and think in the appropriate ways, then there must be "designers" who already possess these development-oriented virtues and are able to convert them to action. Hirschman offers no evidence for this unstated premise of his argument.

Nor does Hirschman offer more than hints of how new experiences of doing may stimulate new connections between means and ends or demonstrate the possibility of achievements and enjoyments hitherto judged unlikely, thereby engendering new beliefs. One is left to wonder why an experience of learning by doing should always, or mostly, influence feelings, thoughts, and beliefs to change in the same promising direction.

Salutary Difficulties

Hirschman's theory of imbalanced growth depends, as we have noted, on the mental jujitsu by which he recasts the difficulties that arise in the course of piecemeal development; they then become spurs, rather than obstacles, to further development. Yet at some points Hirschman designs ways to *reduce* the difficulties experienced by agents of development, as, for example, when he considers, with the aid of an analogy to jigsaw puzzles, how best to order a sequence of development investments so as to promote efficient learning. He suggests that if the time needed to fit in a piece of the puzzle (or carry out a discrete development step) varied inversely with the number of neighboring pieces (or investments) already in place, then we should surround by "neighbors" those pieces that are "intrinsically most difficult to fit in" (p. 82), thereby putting off the most difficult development investments until they can be more *easily* executed.

The policy advice Hirschman derives from this analogy seems to contradict his injunction to keep productive disequilibria alive by maximizing—or, at any rate, embracing—the difficulties that stimulate social learning. Are all kinds and degrees of difficulty salutary for development? Or only some of them, under certain circumstances? In *Strategy*, Hirschman leaves this point moot, though he returns to it in his later writings.

Who Learns, What Do They Learn?

Hirschman adopts certain umbrella slogans for what needs to be learned in and through development—for example, "the ability to invest," or a "group-and-ego-focused image of change." But his global picture of the development curriculum quickly ramifies when he turns to the experience of different learning agents who operate in different sectors, levels, regions, and roles in a developing society. In Hirschman's thought, the "who" and the "what" of learning are intimately connected: each type of learner needs to master a different set of lessons.

Private investors need to learn the art of selecting wisely among investment opportunities, nicely balancing a prudent awareness of risk against an overestimate of risk based on an unwarranted skepticism about the capabilities of domestic producers. Owners of firms need to learn to change "their preference for a stagnating enterprise that stays 'within the family' over expansion that is bought at the cost of partial surrender of control" (p. 136); managers, to practice advance planning, cost accounting, and capital maintenance; entrepreneurs, to coordinate resources and "engineer agreement among all interested parties" (p. 17); and public investors, to prefer a strategy of "development *via* shortage," which sets up incentives and pressures for induced investment, over a strategy of "development *via* excess capacity," which is "merely permissive" of new investment.

The kinds of learning appropriate to different agents of development are conceived as complementary: this is essential to the efficacy of chains of development. Larger social actors, such as development projects, firms, industries, and economic sectors, make their appearance from time to time in Hirschman's drama of imbalanced growth; they play the part of learners of lessons and generators of curricula for other actors; and their curricula, too, are complementary.

Hirschman gives a remarkably full account of the lessons that should be learned by the various types of agents. But he cannot describe them all. His model, he says, is neither closed nor rigid, but open-ended, continually subject to real uncertainties, contingent on the vicissitudes of shifting contexts. He is highly selective in his attempts to give a fine-grained account of his strategy of development; and his principle of selection is largely determined by the "negative template" of conventional development economics against which he fashions his larger argument. So he focuses on backward and forward linkages, internalization effects, investment choice, capital formation, and the like. Around these topics, by way of disconfirming conventional economic wisdom, he spins his tales of disequilibria and learning.

These contributions do not add up to a coherent theory of development as social learning—a theory tantalizingly implicit in the structure of Hirschman's argument. It would need, were it attempted, a language other than that of traditional economics. In *Strategy*, Hirschman is in transition, spinning out a radically new approach, which is organized, nonetheless, around familiar economic categories.

Hirschman's View of Social Learning after *Strategy*

In his next two books about economic development, Hirschman focused more explicitly on issues of social learning just below the surface of *Strategy*. Consider, for example, *Journeys toward Progress*, published in 1963. Hirschman designed this study as though he wished to approximate a schema much used by the cognitive psychologists of the 1950s: a series of trials in which a learner repeatedly engages a persistent or recurrent problem. In this case, the learners are governments or collections of policymakers, and the units of performance are broad policy initiatives. *Journeys* reports on three such learning sequences, centering on drought in Northeast Brazil, land reform in Colombia, and inflation in Chile. Each "is particularly favorable to *the unfolding of a learning process:* the policy makers are presented time and again with essentially the same difficulty and they accumulate a large stock of experiences in grappling with it, and in seeking to avoid or cushion its impact" (p. 14, emphasis added). Hirschman's view of these learning processes remains essentially as presented in *Strategy*: difficulties provoke learning by doing. But shifts of emphasis occur in the treatment of mechanisms that provoke instructive doing and of the learning to which it gives rise.

The discourse shifts by and large from private or public investment to public problem solving, highlighting the ways constituents' dissatisfaction can trigger social pressures that force governments to take new approaches to old problems. Social or political pressures play the main forcing role that Hirschman reserved in the earlier book for pacing mechanisms and complementarity effects. For example, the Inspetoria, Brazil's first federal agency for works against the droughts, was created in 1909 "not so much as a *direct* response to the droughts as *because of dissatisfaction with the way in which the fight against them had been conducted since 1877*" (p. 23, emphasis added).

Through this more frankly political perspective, Hirschman explores the likely contents and limitations of social learning. Thus, problems such as inflation or natural calamities—since they "victimize certain groups in such an abrupt manner as to make them protest and press for help or redress" (p. 161)—generate political pressures that capture the attention of policymakers and lead them to learn to correct their errors, "since the original pressure that led them to act in the first place will not abate and may even increase" (p. 235). But the kinds of problems policymakers decide to tackle seriously will vary from society to society, depending on "the mechanisms that citizen and interest groups have at their disposal for *commanding the attention of policy makers*" (p. 229). Where violent protest is the principal method open to citizens, "only a limited range of problems is likely to be attacked at all forcefully" (p. 230); and when countries lack a "complex web of linkages between the public and the government," it may not be very helpful to advise them to "get to work and develop one, for such a web is the result of a lengthy process which is not easily hurried" (p. 231). Nevertheless, it may be feasible to ride "the coattails of the problem which the policy-makers were anxious to tackle" by appealing to ideologies that link privileged and neglected problems.

The second shift of emphasis evident in *Journeys* bears directly on what is involved in learning by doing. Hirschman continues to stress the importance of the doing itself, but he gives far more weight in these long-term historical narratives to conditions that foster or impede *"genuine learning about the problem"* (p. 139).[13] He faults local policymakers whose "eagerness to jump to a ready-made solution" cuts short that "'long confrontation between man and a situation' so fruitful for the achievement of genuine progress in problem-solving" (p. 240); also "pseudo insights" that block genuine learning, and the "almost morbid insistence [of governments and societies] on declaring past policy-making to have been a series of half-hearted, piecemeal efforts, doomed to failure" (p. 243). Such "writing down of the past," he suggests, may energize a new round of problem solving by blotting out the relative failure of earlier trials, but it becomes dangerous when it leads to the repression of "useful information and elements of incipient and partial success" (p. 245). In fact, "the principal task of technical assistance may then be not so much to bring in *new* knowledge but to acquaint the policy-makers with their own successes" (p. 246).

These shifts of emphasis—toward political pressures that force governments to take problems seriously and conditions that foster genuine learning—come together in two main ideas. First, for some problems "the crisis induced by the very aggravation of the problem may make it possible to understand it better" (p. 262). Writing of inflation in Chile, for example, Hirschman suggests "a rate of almost 100 per cent a year is qualitatively different from an inflation of 20 percent," because a threshold for forceful action is crossed somewhere between the two rates, and because "certain insights into the inflationary process are gained more easily at the faster rate" (p. 201). He also observes that the periodic drought crises in Northeast Brazil led to the convergence of the motivation to solve the problem, the support of powerful allies, and the production of genuine insight.[14]

The twin themes of motivation and insight also come together in a distinction between "two 'ideal type' problem-solving paths or styles: one where advances in understanding tend to induce motivation, and the other where, on the contrary, motivation races ahead of understanding" (p. 236). Motivation tends to race ahead of understanding especially in developing societies, with their revolutions in expectations and their calls for radical, comprehensive solutions of difficulties and for the creation of new institutions (p. 238). But Hirschman does note the possibility of "an ideal or 'balanced' path where both understanding and motivation, or to put the matter into somewhat different terms, both the possibility of effecting change and the aspiration to carry it out, expand in step" (p. 238).

In *Development Projects Observed*, published in 1967, Hirschman returns to one of the main focuses of *Strategy*, the development project. As he examines the histories of eight such projects, ranging from the Karnaphuli pulp and paper mill in Pakistan to a countrywide pasture improvement project in Uruguay, he pursues his idea that development depends not on prerequisites but on "what a country *does* and . . . what it *becomes* as a result of what it *does*" (pp. 4–5).

Hirschman persists in describing behavior as the prime generator of learning; and the capabilities he considers essential to development (risk-readiness, investing capability, maintenance capability, achievement motivation) he treats in the main as *consequences* of behavior. "Assume a virtue if you have it not!" (Hamlet's advice to his mother) captures a central feature of Hirschman's strategy of development; and the strategic problem he frames remains that of inducing the behavior that will engender the desired capabilities.

Because Hirschman is primarily concerned here with project selection and design, he focuses on a version of the idea of tasks of narrow latitude that he had advanced ten years before. It can be shown, he writes, "that some projects and technologies have a special vocation for inducing certain types of learning, attitude change, and institutional reform (and not others), that different projects—because of their different structural characteristics—are, as it were, *specialized* with respect to the kind of changes they will work" (p. 5).

In this book, Hirschman deliberately explores several of the gaps, ambiguities, and contradictions noted above. He follows his characteristic inclination to seek out countervailing truths, relishing the discovery of lessons that seem to contradict those he has expounded earlier—"in blissful ignorance," as he might say. The result is often a recognition of disturbing complexity, in response to which Hirschman calls for the exercise of an art of judgment.

For example, his famous principle of the hiding hand, foreshadowed in *Strategies*, reinterprets two thorny questions: namely, what kinds and degrees of difficulty are salutary (or noxious) for development, and how useful (or hurtful) is it for development agents to be aware of them in advance? The principle's insight hinges on the fact that while projects are vulnerable to the threat of unpleasant surprises, the creativity by which such threats may be remedied also comes as a surprise: "therefore we can never count on it and we dare not believe in it until it has happened. . . . Hence, the only way in which we can bring our creative resources fully into play is by misjudging the nature of the task" (p. 13).[15]

Hirschman's key illustration is the story of the Karnaphuli pulp and paper mill. The premise underlying its construction was that bamboo could be used as raw material for paper pulp. The planners had badly overestimated the permanent availability of bamboo. Had they been aware of the difficulties, they would not have undertaken the project, because they also underestimated their remedial learning capability— and the availability of alternative raw materials (p. 10).

Hirschman underlines the hiding hand's function as a "transition mechanism through which decision makers *learn to take risks*" (p. 26, emphasis added). He adds, however, that "the shorter the transition and the faster the learning the better" (p. 28); also, that it was fortunate that the difficulties showed up later in the project, when the sunk costs were higher, and retreat was therefore less likely (p. 19). Finally, he remarks on the revisionist tendency of development agents to smooth over difficulties that have already occurred, and the corollary tendency of project promoters to mask difficulties they may actually foresee by deceptively portraying a new project as a replica of an existing model.

The principle of the hiding hand points to the central role of *uncertainty*, and ways of dealing with it, in projects of economic development. Hirschman notes that uncertainty is equally central in projects of industrial research and development.[16] He describes a strategy of decisionmaking that is "correct" for research and development projects: flexible goal-setting and coordination, reliance on multiple and parallel approaches, frequent review and modification of means and ends in the light of newly acquired information (pp. 77–78). And he observes that an analogous strategy applies in the design of settle-ments: "when there is considerable uncertainty about the direction in which road traffic and new settlements will develop, it may be possible to build several cheap roads in lieu of a single expensive one and to wait for cues from the ensuing traffic to decide which one should be improved and perhaps paved" (p. 83).

Hirschman advocates flexible project design and the parallel devel-opment of cheap alternatives designed to reduce the costs of mistakes by making it easier to change course. He also shows how projects may be structured so as to increase the likelihood that unanticipated diffi-culties will be effectively dealt with—as, for example, by delegating substantial authority to local project managers who have better chances of learning on the spot how to invent new methods or re-formulate old objectives.

Uncertainty, manifesting itself in surprise, is essential to Hirsch-man's view of social learning, since if there were no surprises there would be very little to learn *about:* no unanticipated difficulties to serve as inducements to creative problem solving, and no desirable second-order learning such as developing a taste for a more exciting life or reducing risk aversion. Nevertheless, some conditions of uncertainty are so dangerous as to be inimical to development. Seeing both the positive and negative effects of uncertainty, which may induce learning or undermine performance, Hirschman advises project designers to embrace *"optimal* rather than minimal uncertainty . . . [as] the appro-priate as well as the only feasible goal" (p. 85, emphasis added).

Hirschman explicitly addresses the question of "salutary difficult-ies," which in *Strategy* he left for the most part ambiguous. Distinguish-ing between the strategies of "trait-making" and "trait-taking," he con-trasts such negative traits as sloppy maintenance or risk aversion and such attributes of modernity as rigorous maintenance and vigorous, planful entrepreneurship. Taking the negative traits as given and un-changeable "may miss important opportunities for effective positive changes in these attributes—on the contrary, it may even strengthen them" (p. 130). But when the project's success hinges on a change in "some of the attributes of backwardness," "then the project's fate be-comes a wager; if the wager is lost, so that the needed change does not occur and the project's success is thereby jeopardized, the project planners will be accused of ignoring local circumstances, traditions, and sociopolitical structure and of incorrigible naivete and lack of realism in general" (p. 131). This dilemma is central, in Hirschman's view, to the art of project design; and the "wager" implicit in a trait-making approach to such design is a bet on learning. For, as Hirschman now points out, "one can at times not be wholly certain that the alien attitudes, types of behavior, and skills will ever be learned." Some positive traits—such as the readiness to appoint people to jobs on the basis of objective qualifications rather than family, tribal, or religious affinity— involve abrupt changes in values rather than gradual on- or off-the-job learning, and their acquisition "is more a matter of one-time choice, commitment and turnaround than of gradual learning" (p. 137).

To say, then, that particular difficulties, and related uncertainties, are salutary for development is to judge that people will learn to acquire the traits necessary for coping with them, which is more likely to be true when trait acquisition is a matter of gradual learning than when it involves an abrupt shift in values. This is an explicit confrontation with issues that *Strategy* had left ambiguous—not only the question of "salutary difficulties" but of learning-by-doing's relationship to changes in beliefs and values. These ambiguities are not entirely resolved, however. Change in values is excluded here from the universe of "learning," presumably because such a change is conceived as "abrupt" rather than "gradual." But what would Hirschman say about the possibility of gradual changes in values? Or, for that matter, about learning that may occur abruptly when people are faced with tasks of narrow latitude?

When Hirschman returns to the theme of latitude, which he had introduced in *Strategy* with the example of aircraft maintenance, he corrects the attractive simplicity of his earlier formulation. Now he recognizes that, while the great disciplinary advantage of narrow latitude remains, the presence of wide latitude has also been shown in some situations to "foster training in rational decision making or the adaptation of imported models of economic behavior to local conditions and requirements" (p. 127). Tasks of narrow *and* wide latitude may be desirable, depending on the circumstances. Hirschman frames the choice in terms of the kinds of learning to which each type of task is appropriate, linking this analysis to the trait-making wager.

Trait-making is less risky, and a more practical possibility, he argues, when the traits in question, from "simple skills to administrative ability," lend themselves to gradual learning on the job or alongside it. In this case, latitude for poor performance has its proper place: "The idea is that one starts at the poor end of the scale and slowly improves his performance. This expectation has long been a principal argument for infant-industry protection" (p. 135). But when traits are so compellingly required that "in their absence high penalties would be incurred or the task simply could not be undertaken at all," and when the traits in question are ones whose acquisition involves an abrupt change of values, then the structural condition of narrow latitude is appropriate: "the radical demands of a task with no latitude for poor performance not only facilitate such turnarounds in values and behavior, but provide a strong barrier against any backsliding" (p. 138).

Yet again Hirschman sounds a cautionary note: the capabilities developed gradually through the performance of tasks of wide latitude may be more "lasting *and also more transferrable* [my emphasis] to areas other than the one in and for which the behavior was actually learned" (p. 136, emphasis added) and hence more deserving of being called learning.[17]

At this point, Hirschman introduces a telling footnote:

I must relate here a personal observation. While living in Bogota in the fifties, I observed with some surprise that the Bogotanos would show the utmost discipline in queuing up for city buses—even as few as two people would often stand in a rigid line. Upon inquiring about the reasons for this "modern" behavior, I was told that the habit had been literally beaten into the citizenry by the army which after the famous 1948 riots, when almost all the streetcars were burned, provided urban transportation in army trucks. Significantly, the discipline that was thus learned under duress had no visible spillover effects on behavior in general, not even under favorable circumstances: even though it is well known that the number of tickets sold for an airplane flight cannot exceed the number of seats available, the opening of the gate at the Bogota airport frequently gave rise to real stampedes (p. 136).

"Standing in line" is as clear an example as Hirschman affords of an action that people already know how to perform, where the significant question is whether, by virtue of a "turnaround in value and behavior," they choose to perform it.[18] If such cases are exemplars of learning, then one might think of learning as a matter of exerting the pressures likely to induce such "turnarounds" and judge the effectiveness of learning, or whether it had occurred at all, on the basis of the learner's transfer to new settings of behavior acquired in one setting under duress.

Hirschman concludes his discussion of salutary or dangerous difficulties and uncertainties with the reminder that "latitude and lack of latitude can both be valuable in facilitating that learning or acquisition of needed skills and traits which we have here called trait-making" (p. 139), depending on whether gradual or abrupt learning is in question. The ability to judge which type of task is appropriate, in any given situation, Hirschman relates to an "art of project design." This reference recalls a passage in the early pages of *Projects* where Hirschman characterizes his principles of design as "meant for selective use rather than for mechanical application all the way through to any and every project" (p. 6). Hirschman's principles may happily coexist with their contraries, their application depending, among other things, on which version of learning by doing one adopts. And this judgment varies, implicitly or explicitly, with the type of learning exemplar one has in mind. Hirschman's art of project design is one that would enable project designers and policymakers to judge just how, in each unique case, contrary design principles, derived from different exemplars and based on different views of the relationships between task structure and performance, should be variously applied or combined.

Learning and Teaching

For whom does Hirschman write? Certainly for his fellow economists and theorists of development. He draws on his practical experience to disconfirm and propose alternatives for certain elements of received economic wisdom. But he also writes for practitioners: for policymakers in developing countries and for those who seek to provide them with aid, assistance, or advice. In the preface to the 1961 edition of *Strategy* he says, "My hope was and is that [this book] will contribute to making planning and programming activities more effective" (p. vii).

If Hirschman's theory of the strategy of development is based on an underlying view of social learning, then its practical application will be a paradoxical kind of *pedagogy*. This is because Hirschman believes that the critical learning occurs through doing, rather than through the kind of teaching that communicates explicit, systematically organized knowledge. His exemplar must be more like a coach than a classroom teacher. In *Strategy*, however, as in *Journeys* and *Projects*, Hirschman seeks to teach the coach—a rather paradoxical enterprise in its own right.

His primary message to development policymakers, inside and outside the developing country, is that they must learn to set up the incentive effects and pacing mechanisms that will attract or compel the dialectical sequences of imbalanced growth through which the relevant actors are most likely to engage in instructive doing; or that they must craft their development projects to call forth appropriate types of learning, attitude change, or institutional reform. The interest of his proposed pedagogy lies in his manner of advising policymakers, and their advisers, just how to go about these tasks. In his view, "it is more fruitful to investigate directly how development activity is determined and grows in underdeveloped countries than to start with some preconceived idea of what it should be" (*Strategy*, p. 38).

The direction, timing, and magnitude of the moves should be keyed to an awareness of how, at a specific time and place, development activity is naturally unfolding—an awareness that can only be acquired through direct, on-site observation. As he recalls in his "Confession," my "instinct was to try to understand better *their* patterns of action, rather than assume from the outset that they could only be 'developed' by importing a set of techniques they knew nothing about."[19]

Hirschman displays an untiring interest in exploring how people who are engaged in a process of development think about what they are doing. He refuses to treat his subjects as empty vessels ready to be filled with externally supplied wisdom, or as passive targets of development strategies (though he *is* willing to treat people as subjects manipulable by incentive effects and pacing mechanisms). He wants to understand the images of stasis and change held by societies, traditional or in the early stages of development, in order to make allowance for how, and with what "strange, unintended, and unexpected results" (*Strategy*, p. 23) they are likely to evolve.[20]

Although Hirschman clearly wishes to accelerate the progress of underdeveloped societies toward modernization, he is ever ready to learn how local knowledge outperforms the expert knowledge of outsiders and always relishes the "hidden rationalities" of apparently irrational local practice. Hirschman's books on development are studded with such examples. In his discussion of backward and forward linkages, he emphasizes that, since "the industry with the highest combined linkage score is iron and steel, perhaps the underdeveloped countries are not so foolish and so exclusively prestige-motivated in attributing prime importance to this industry!" (*Strategy*, p. 108). Similarly, "what looks like a puzzling preference for capital intensity on the part of capital-poor countries in effect turns out to be the incidental result of a perfectly commonsense way of husbanding capital" (*Strategy*, p. 131). He even concludes that

> under certain circumstances it may be rational for governments in underdeveloped countries to concentrate on "show-pieces" because ... when a government undertakes the construction of a large hydroelectric station or of a steel mill, it simply cannot afford to let such ventures go wrong—it places itself under a far stronger compulsion to "deliver" than if it were to spend the same funds on a large number of small projects (*Strategy*, p. 144).

If development policymakers, advisers, and assistants must learn to discover ongoing paths of development from the inside and, as far as possible, without preconceptions; if they are to pay close attention to the thinking of their constituents and clients and remain continually on the alert for the hidden wisdom of existing practice, even when it appears irrational—then it is clear that the pedagogy of development, like the practice of a development policymaker or project designer, is inherently an art. This art may draw on the models of economic development theory, but it is just as likely to serve as a stimulus to the modification of that theory. Hirschman's books on development are themselves cases in point.

Implications of Hirschman's View of Social Learning for the Theory of Economic Development

In the past ten or fifteen years, the notions of public, governmental, and organizational learning have rapidly become ideas in good currency throughout the world. With Japan's exceptional economic growth, and the even more startling growth of the East Asian Tigers, "learning" now epitomizes the capabilities firms and governments require to respond effectively to the challenges of global competition.

"The learning organization" has become a slogan of reform dutifully espoused by managers as well as consultants, and in schools of business a cottage industry devoted to the study of "organizational learning" has sprung up.[21] In this climate of opinion, it would seem natural that the social learning perspective, which Hirschman did so much to advance, would have become central to thinking about development.

And so it has for some people—for example, those who apply to countries the learning and experience curves favored by business strategists—but not for mainstream economists, many of whom still avoid explicit reference to learning. How do the economists manage it? By ellipsis. Economic processes are explicitly modeled in terms of the Newtonian metaphor of economic forces or the (cybernetic?) language of price signals, while the learning inherent in such processes is left implicit.

Even when economists treat their models as heuristic metaphors, they still manage to avoid an explicit account of learning. In this volume, for example, Paul Krugman's essay in chapter 2 introduces a model of "increasing returns to scale," for which, he argues, the development economists of Hirschman's era had no formal representation. According to this model, an individual entrepreneur's decision to shift to modern production is rational when the wage premium required to induce workers to make the shift is consistent with its being profitable for each individual in the modern sector to produce, that is, when the marginal cost advantage of modern production is sufficiently large and/or fixed costs are not too large. The likelihood of meeting these conditions is shown to be greater when all modern firms start simultaneously than when an individual entrepreneur is the *only* one to modernize. This formalization, which reveals strong increasing returns to scale, also shows, in Krugman's words, how "a low-level trap can arise with rational entrepreneurs, full information—and not a whiff of reference to cultural influences, or problems of information and learning."

Nevertheless, such a model makes elliptical reference to learning in at least three ways: the slope assigned to the modernization curve, the setting of the level of total production at which economies of scale are said to set in, and the decision to modernize, which is treated in the model as though actual modernization followed instantaneously from the decision to undertake it. In each of these respects, the model represents processes that actually depend on learning—the learning essential to modernizing, increasing productivity, and exploiting the potential advantages of large-scale production—but it represents them in such a way as to wipe learning out.

If Krugman and like-minded economists rely on models that sidestep learning, it is because they believe the requisite learning will occur automatically once the appropriate economic conditions are put in place. They must believe, in other words, that there is no need to model learning per se because its occurrence can be safely subsumed under other variables (such as wage and productivity rates, or the marginal cost advantage of modern production) without the loss of explanatory power or policy significance. But development theorists pay a significant price for their failure to take explicit account of the learning involved in a shift from traditional to modern production. They are, as Krugman freely admits, unable to explain differences in economic development performance from one country to another, or to say much of anything about particular development projects—both of which are, of course, central to Hirschman's treatment of economic development.

What would it mean to base development theory, explicitly and systematically, on a view of social learning like Hirschman's? At first blush, this might seem to be a wildly improbable surmise. As Krugman points out, formal models are the coin of the realm in economics; and he attributes both the decline of development economics, in general, and Hirschman's declining influence on the economic mainstream, in particular, to the fact that Hirschman and others like him failed to formalize their insights into development. Hirschman's argument points inexorably to a situational, open-ended approach to development, the application of which would only take the form of an art of judgment—the very opposite of the high generality of formal models in economics.

Nonetheless, some economists have recently addressed, from various points of view, questions of learning; and some aspects of Hirschman's view of development as learning may be modelable, even if others are not. It may be worth exploring some of the issues that would arise if "modeling learning," in a Hirschmanesque sense, were to become a respectable enterprise among economists.

At least two ways of interpreting the phrase "modeling learning" are represented in current economic thought. As might be expected, these attempts are oriented primarily, though not exclusively, toward explanation and prediction; and they deal with economic phenomena at different levels of social aggregation.

First of all, some economists construct models that capture the *effects* of learning, usually by means of learning curves that show how the value of a performance variable changes over time, in order to relate such effects to economic conditions of various kinds. Dalia Marin, for example, has tried to explain the comparative economic performances of Austria and Germany in recent decades, in order to draw lessons for economic development in Eastern Europe. Marin bases her work on Alwyn Young's model of "bounded learning," according to which, when a new technology is introduced, learning by doing yields productivity gains until a point is reached at which additional increments to experience yield no further gains; at this point, in Young's model, learning by doing cannot be sustained without a continuous flow of new inventions. Bounded learning, Marin points out, will lead to a trade structure that exhibits some persistence over time and in which learning generates a movement up the technological ladder.[22]

Some economists also model the processes by which the decisions of economic agents change over time as a consequence of learning. Their schema of learning consists in a sequence of decisions made by economic agents in response to successive appearances of a constant or recurring problem. In such cases, modeling may take the form of creating artificial learning agents programmed with decision algorithms "calibrated to reproduce human learning" in the context of strategic choice.[23] A main interest in such research is the degree to which successive decisions converge on norms of economic rationality.

Neither of these ways of modeling learning captures the kinds of relationships, and the insights, afforded by Hirschman's studies of development. However, different reasons for this shortfall suggest themselves, and different kinds of difficulties in modeling learning come to light, depending on which aspect of Hirschman's view of development one emphasizes.

To begin with, Hirschman shares the interest of a researcher such as Young or Marin in representing relationships between learning *effects,* as indicated by learning curves, and conditions that affect their slopes. Hirschman remains an economist, moreover, insofar as he thinks in terms of the structures of *incentives* that affect the performance of an individual, an organization, an economic sector, or a society as a whole. However, the scope of incentives he considers relevant to learning extends beyond those directly related to economic gain. He gives at least as much attention to *political* incentives, such as the pressures for government action triggered by national crises, and to *institutional* incentives, such as those created by tasks of wide or narrow latitude. Taking these variables into account would require a political-economic-institutional model of learning effects and the conditions on which they depend.

Hirschman is interested in explaining development in ways that contribute to the construction of principles for its stimulation and guidance. And because he does not believe in the feasibility of a macroeconomic framework from which uniform policy prescriptions (along the lines of "Get the prices right!") can be derived at the country level, he tries to provide leads for stimulating the kinds of learning essential to development at the level of the region, sector, organization, and project.

Also, in the light of Hirschman's later revisions of his principles of development, a model of learning would have to capture features of *context* critical to the relationships it describes. As we have seen, Hirschman regards his principles of development policy or project design as having limited scope and thus as being applicable in one kind of situation but not in another. Either a model of learning faithful to Hirschman's views would have to be limited in its application to particular kinds of development situations or else it would have to embody general hypotheses about the factors that determine a principle's relevance to one situation rather than another—as when Hirschman himself suggests a general relationship between task latitude and gradual or abrupt learning. Even if such factors could be discovered and built into a model (no small task!), could they be reliably recognized at the point of application? One might still need to appeal to an art of judgment.

A distinction also has to be made between the task of modeling learning *effects* (and their relationships to economic, political, or institutional conditions) and the very different task of modeling learning *processes*. Here we meet again the ambiguity inherent in Hirschman's treatment of learning by doing. Should we assume for the purpose of modeling learning that we can safely ignore learning processes—those essential to the first instructive doing as well as those presumed to follow from it—because such processes can be assumed to occur auto-matically once appropriate incentives are put in place?

One senses that Hirschman may favor an affirmative answer, albeit with some ambivalence, as though he wished to retain at least this much of the economist's point of view. On the one hand, he suggests such an inclination when he considers defining "learning" as behavior acquired under duress that then takes on a life of its own, a possibility he floats in close conjunction with his story of Colombianos who ac-quired under duress the habit of standing in line for the bus. On the other hand, Hirschman's discussion in *Journeys* of genuine versus pseudo problem solving, and his discussion in *Projects* of creative re-sponse to unwelcome surprise, suggest a very different view, according to which modeling learning would have to include modeling the pro-cesses as well as the effects and conditions of learning. We know scarcely enough about such processes to consider modeling them. And if we were to attempt to do so, we would clearly be swept well beyond the bounds of prevailing conceptions of economic rationality.

Part II
Some Development Assumptions in Retrospect

Five

Psychological Modernity in Historical Perspective

Emma Rothschild

"I SAW many ants, travelling for pleasure: they were all black, very clean, and almost varnished, but without any individuality. They all looked like one another. If one has seen one Ant, one knows them all." This is the beginning of George Sand's satire of the British Empire in 1840, or of the "Empire Formique," with its motto "Rule, Formicalia!" The ants are marvelously busy, Sand's narrator says, coming and going and packing and unpacking commodities. They are particularly keen on exchange, and they are indeed prepared to resort to the use of force to defend "formic honour and commercial freedom." "You have a lot of grain and we have none, but you are lacking wood, and we have a lot: shall we exchange?" the ants say at one point to some underdeveloped neighbors; when the neighbors balk—when they behave, in fact, in a way that for Formic citizens is "contrary to the laws of good sense"—then the ants simply send their warships to enforce the principles of international trade.[1]

Albert Hirschman has been profoundly opposed, in all his economic writings, to the conception of individuals as uniform, self-interested, "purely economic" subjects: to the economic theory of Sand's Formic Empire. He has been concerned, instead, with the depiction of economic diversity, and it is this concern that I would like to consider here. Developing countries, Hirschman argues, should not be expected to follow a simple, uniform sequence of industrialization. There are instead important differences in the experience of economic development, both across countries and over time. There are differences, too, in the economic experience of individuals within countries.

99

There are also differences, or dissonances, within the experience of particular individuals, or across the different "sides" of their lives. If one has seen one economic subject, one does not thereby know them all.

Hirschman has been skeptical, since his earliest economic writings, about the effort to identify an economic side of life, within which the diversity of experience is of minimal importance. It is quite difficult, he wrote in 1945 in *National Power and the Structure of Foreign Trade*, to conceive of "normal economic activities" or of "true economic purposes": "True it is that ever since Max Weber economists have had some doubts about the meaningfulness of the term economic when applied to ends and not to means." It makes no sense, for example, to think of a country's having "purely economic relations with the totalitarian states." The exegesis of "purely 'economic man,'" he says, is not helpful in understanding foreign trade; people should instead be seen as buying "imports which create consumption and production habits," and as having "needs" in an "enlarged sense." There is, moreover, no "uniform structure" of foreign trade determined by "the 'industrial' or 'agricultural' character of a country," and no "definite 'law' according to which the commodity structure of foreign trade changes in the course of an economic development such as industrialization"; "any future reconstruction of world trade should take into account the complexity of its structure which our statistics reveal."[2]

The dissonance of persons—the diversity of experience across the different sides of people's lives—comes into prominence in Hirschman's *Strategy of Economic Development*. "Our approach," Hirschman writes, "views the obstacles [to "economic progress"] as reflections of contradictory drives and of the resulting confusion of the will." Modern industry coexists with "preindustrial, sometimes neolithic techniques"; "while dualism no doubt brings with it many social and psychological stresses, it has some compensating advantages." Hirschman's view of policy is concerned, in part, with the psychology of development. Developing countries are seen as operating "under the grand tension that stems from the universal desire for economic improvement oddly combined with many resistances to change"; this condition, Hirschman suggests, should be broken down into "smaller and more manageable tensions." He is opposed, thereby, to the oversimplifying influence of Freud; "difficulties, conflict, and anxiety" should be seen as something more than uniquely "pathogenic agents."[3]

Hirschman's criticism of the conventional development policies of the 1950s is connected, in turn, to his rejection of simple development psychology. The "contempt" of people in rich countries for people in poor countries—or of development policy experts for their subjects of expertise—is in Hirschman's description founded on an excessively simple psychological theory. Like Alexander Gerschenkron in *Economic Backwardness in Historical Perspective,* Hirschman rejects "the idea of the uniformity of industrial development in the sense that every industrialization necessarily must be based on the same set of preconditions."[4] "The Western economists who looked at [less developed countries] at the end of World War II," Hirschman writes, "were convinced that these countries were not all that complicated: their major problems would be solved if only their national income per capita could be raised adequately." They were expected to "perform like wind-up toys"; "their reactions to change were not to be nearly as traumatic or aberrant as those of the Europeans."[5]

It is interesting that the uncomplicated prescriptions took the form, at the time, of imposing simple models of economic planning. Hirschman himself went to Colombia in 1952 as adviser to the "newly established National Planning Council," recommended by the World Bank, "which had taken an active part in having the Planning Council set up in the first place." But he had a "healthy respect (based on watching the misadventures of the French economy) for the efficiency of the price system," and a corresponding distrust ("based on watching Fascist economic policy") for "grandiloquent plans." The Bank "attempted to condition its lending on countries' establishing some form of overall economic planning," he writes; "I almost lost my advisory job in Colombia because I refused to push hard in this direction."[6]

The recognition of complexity is of central importance, finally, to Hirschman's account of the history of economic thought. His splendid book on seventeenth- and eighteenth-century discussions of commerce, *The Passions and the Interests,* has a melancholy ending. Adam Smith's work is seen as marking the end of a long period of openness and experiment in political economy. Smith was concerned, in Hirschman's description, with the simple interests of ordinary people. He tended to disregard the passions and conflicts of the great: "The ordinary mortal was not thought to be so complicated. His principal concern was with subsistence and material improvement, generally as ends in themselves, and at best as proxies for the achievement of respect and admiration." *The Wealth of Nations* is described as initiating a new and reduced epoch in economic thought. Economists were preoccupied, after Smith, with "his proposition that the general (material) welfare is best served by letting each member of society pursue his own (material) self-interest." Smith's work made possible "intellectual specialization and professionalization"; it "represented a considerable *narrowing* of the field of inquiry over which social thought had ranged freely up to then."[7]

The "simple" or uniform theories of modern economists are for Hirschman a consequence and culmination of the long process of intellectual reduction that began in the 1770s. Economics has been grounded, he writes, in the postulate "of the self-interested, isolated individual who chooses freely and rationally among alternative courses of action after computing their prospective costs and benefits." In the so-called economic approach of contemporary theory, economists have applied this model of human existence to "ostensibly non-economic phenomena"; Hirschman's own suggestion is that the model is excessively "simple-minded" in relation to "even such fundamental economic processes as consumption and production." He argues that economics should instead take better account of "the incredible complexity of human nature," including the characteristics of individuals that they are "self-evaluating," beset by "unresolved, and perhaps unresolvable tensions," and subject, in particular, to a tension between "self-interest" and "public morality."[8]

It is this tension, between public and private lives, and between the desires and duties associated with the two sorts of life, that is at the center of Hirschman's work. Countries have interests in power, and also in prosperity; this is the premise of *National Power and the Structure of Foreign Trade*. Individuals seek happiness in public and also in private activities; they oscillate between the two sides of their lives, Hirschman suggests in *Shifting Involvements*, and they are "consumers who are also conscious of being citizens."[9] They are different from one another, that is to say, in part because they have political as well as economic interests. They listen and talk, as well as buy and sell. They have diverse opinions, diverse information, and diverse passions.

I would like to suggest, in what follows, that Hirschman's restless, conflict-ridden economic subjects are in fact very similar to the women and men whom Adam Smith described; that his criticism of simple theories of economic behavior is close to Smith's own and to that of some of Smith's friends in the struggles of the 1770s and 1780s for freedom of commerce, including A. R. J. Turgot and M. J. A. N. Condorcet. I put the onset of "uniform theory" in political economy a little later than Hirschman does in *The Passions and the Interests:* after Smith, and after the first years of the French Revolution. But my concern— like Hirschman's—is also with the modern uses of ideas of psychological uniformity. One use is in economic theory; this is the enterprise, which Paul Krugman describes in chapter 2, of the self-conscious theorist, aware that his or her simplified models are no more than heuristic devices. There is a different use in economic policy. It is the enterprise, in policies for economic development, of psychological modernization. The uniform or ant-like conception—in which everyone is much the same, and similarly self-interested—is in this sense prescriptive, as will be seen; it is a view of how people behave, of how they should behave, and also of how they should be helped to behave, in more modern or more developed societies.

Adam Smith and Human Nature

Adam Smith is, in Gary Becker's view, "the principal founder of the economic approach"; of "the combined assumptions of maximizing behavior, market equilibrium, and stable preferences, used relentlessly and unflinchingly," and thereby of the "unified framework for understanding behavior that has long been sought by and eluded Bentham, Comte, Marx and others." [10] But Smith's own description of his "framework" was strikingly different. He presents it, indeed, as a criticism of what were understood, at the time, as slightly comical theories of self-interest. The first words of Smith's *Theory of Moral Sentiments* are thus as follows: "However selfish soever man may be supposed, there are evidently some principles in his nature, which interest him in the fortune of others, and render their happiness necessary to him." By the end of the book, he is thoroughly skeptical: "That whole account of human nature, however, which deduces all sentiments and affections from self-love, which has made so much noise in the world, but which, so far as I know, has never yet been fully and distinctly explained, seems to me to have arisen from some confused misapprehension of the system of sympathy." [11]

Smith's own account of human nature, both in the *Theory of Moral Sentiments* and in the *Wealth of Nations,* is considerably more complicated. He is quite skeptical, in general, of "the propensity to account for all appearances from as few principles as possible." The desire or principle of pleasure was "most obvious and familiar"; it was not thereby the foundation of all other principles. Smith's famous account of self-interest—"the desire of bettering our condition . . . comes with us from the womb, and never leaves us till we go into the grave"— should thus be understood as much less than a theory of human behavior. His view seems to have been that people are often (but not always) motivated by self-love; and that their self-love is gratified sometimes (but not always) by commodities and leisure.

The principle of self-improvement is "universal, continual and uninterrupted" (or "uniform, constant and uninterrupted"). But it is not the only principle of human behavior, and it is not fulfilled in any unique way. "An augmentation of fortune," Smith writes, "is the means by which the greater part of men propose and wish to better their condition"; it is simply "the means the most vulgar and the most obvious," whether for the poor or the rich. And indeed some of his harshest polemical language is directed against the futility of the desire for what he called "trinkets," "baubles" or "gewgaws," as when he describes the preference of proprietors for commodities (such as "diamond buckles") over authority in relation to their tenants and retainers: "and thus, for the gratification of the most childish, the meanest, and the most sordid of all vanities, they gradually bartered their whole power and authority." [12]

R. H. Coase's summary conveys the skeptical, unrelentless tone of Smith's descriptions. "It is wrong to believe," he writes, "that Adam Smith had as his view of man an abstraction, an 'economic man,' rationally pursuing his self-interest in a single-minded way": "Adam Smith would not have thought it sensible to treat man as a rational utility-maximizer. He thinks of man as he actually is—dominated, it is true, by self-love but not without some concern for others, able to reason but not necessarily in such a way as to reach the right conclusion, seeing the outcomes of his actions but through a veil of self-delusion." [13] Men and women are sometimes single-mindedly self-interested, that is to say, and sometimes not; they differ from each other, and also from their own earlier and later selves.

It is interesting that Smith makes very little distinction between the rich and the poor as diverse and dissonant subjects. It is often the rich, in fact, who are particularly likely to pursue the "most vulgar and the most obvious" means of gratification. Smith was criticized by Malthus for being excessively concerned with "the happiness and comfort of the lowest orders of society." He also paid a great deal of attention to their conflicting sentiments. The view of individuals as self-interested, and interested mostly in commodities, was already widespread in the 1760s; it was seen as a description, above all, of the sentiments of the "common people." Kant, for example, distinguished in 1763 between the soulful few and the self-interested multitude:

> Most men are among those who have their best-loved selves fixed before their eyes as the only point of reference for their exertions, and who seek to turn everything around *self-interest* as around the great axis. Nothing can be more advantageous than this, for these are the most diligent, orderly and prudent; they give support and solidity to the whole, while without intending to do so they serve the common good, provide the necessary requirements, and supply the foundation over which finer souls can spread beauty and harmony.[14]

For Smith, by contrast, the rich and the "fine" are at least as likely as the poor to be self-interested. Smith's view of natural equality—"a philosopher and a common street porter" are born "very much alike," he says, and remain so for six or eight years—extends, in this respect, to the natural propensity to self-doubt. The most vulgarly self-interested individuals in the *Wealth of Nations* are university teachers, for whom the existing structure of emoluments (or "incentives") is said to lead ineluctably to "careless and slovenly" work. Workmen are often finer souls; "it seems not very probable," Smith says, that they should work better "when they are disheartened than when they are in good spirits." They are also tormented by self-doubt: the woman of the lowest order in England who would be thought to have fallen "into extreme bad conduct" if she appeared in public without shoes, or the laborer who comes from a small village to work in the great city, and finds himself "observed and attended to by nobody."[15]

Smith made little distinction, too, between the "economic" and the "non-economic" sides of people's lives. There is a heuristic interpretation of the economists' postulate of self-interested behavior, in which the conception of man as a relentless maximizer of his own utility is said to be not substantive but in some sense methodological. It is no more than a reasonable abstraction on which to found economic theories; it corresponds to the "economic side of life," or to the territory of economic investigation. Yet the division of life into its constituent sides is quite remote from Smith's own conceptions. He does suggest that merchants have "a superior knowledge of their own interest," and are "exercised rather about the interest of their own particular branch of business, than about that of the society." But they are also friendly during their working lives; "colleagues in office, partners in trade, call one another brothers; and frequently feel towards one another as if they really were so."[16] In this, at least, Smith is at one with the economic approach of modern theory: "human behaviour is not compartmentalized," and maximizing (like friendliness) is not restricted to some elusive territory of purely economic (or noneconomic) life.[17]

It is interesting, finally, that the characteristic form of inner conflict, in the *Wealth of Nations,* is very much like the form Hirschman describes. It is the conflict, that is to say, between one's public and one's private life, or between the pursuit of one's interests through honor and through profit, or between the pursuit of profit through influence and through competition. Smith's late feudal proprietors are torn, as we have seen, between using their resources to buy power and to buy trinkets. Innkeepers receive high remuneration to compensate them for the "dishonour" of their profession; corn merchants have the reputation of "wretched hucksters." The different estates of society are distinguished, in part, by their varying propensities to reflect on the public interest.

Even in his famous evocation of the invisible hand, in the *Wealth of Nations,* Smith refers to merchants who profess that they are seeking through their investments to further the public good. People who make this claim are often disingenuous, Smith says, and even when they are well intentioned their efforts tend to be unsuccessful. But their dilemma, all the same, is between the pursuit of their private interests and their public renown. The eighteenth-century merchant, in Smith's depiction, is beset by conflicting objectives, and also by uncertainty about the conditions in which he is likely to trade. He can further the interests of society by his private investments; he can further his private investments by influencing public policy, for example, by bullying or bribing a "timourous legislature" to protect his own enterprises. Freedom of trade will never be "entirely restored" in Britain, Smith says; "not only the prejudices of the public, but what is much more unconquerable, the private interests of many individuals, irresistibly oppose it."[18]

Theories of Public and Private Interest

"The French have been particularly forward to favor their own manufactures," Smith wrote, and theories of public and private interest are prominent in the work of Smith's great reforming contemporaries in France. Both Turgot and Condorcet, with whom Smith had close intellectual connections, were deeply engaged in efforts to reform the commercial policy of France; Smith described Turgot as "a person whom I remember with so much veneration," and wrote of his Reform Edicts of 1774–76 that they "did so much honour to their Author ... and would have proved so beneficial to his country."[19] Both recognized that individuals have diverse, changing opinions, and that political and commercial opinions are thoroughly intertwined.

Turgot and Condorcet were explicitly opposed to the hypothesis of uniquely self-interested behavior, in both the substantive and the heuristic versions. The "laissez-faire" political economy of the 1770s was presented as quite independent of early proto-Utilitarian theories: the theories of Helvétius, for example, of whom Hume wrote to Smith that his work was "worth your Reading, not for its Philosophy, which I do not highly value, but for its agreeable Composition."[20] "Men are not machines who calculate and who always decide on the outcome where there is most to be won," Condorcet wrote in his *Reflections on Corn*, published a few weeks before the *Wealth of Nations*.

"The effect of the forces which act upon the mind of the narrowest merchant is far more difficult to calculate," Condorcet said, than the most recalcitrant problem in celestial mechanics; it depends "on this moral quantity, which itself depends on opinions and on passions."[21] Their opinions and passions, moreover, are expressed in discussion. They listen and try to predict, even in the course of buying and selling. It is interesting that Turgot, a hundred years before Walras, used the metaphor of price formation as a process of *tâtonnement*. But it is a process of discussion or what Turgot calls "debate": "The debate between every buyer and every seller is a sort of *tâtonnement* which makes known to everyone, with certainty, the true price of everything."[22] As in Charles Sabel's description of monitoring institutions, in chapter 11, transactions are in fact discussions; they are part of "the process by which parties come to reinterpret themselves and their relation to each other by elaborating a common understanding of the world."

Turgot, who has been subject, even more than Smith himself, to the charge of "ruthless atomism" in economic policy, was entirely disdainful of early Utilitarian ideas. He seems to have seen no role at all, in political economy, for the expository device of maximizing or "rational" man. He indeed criticizes Helvétius for his superficial understanding of human feelings. The proposition that "interest is the only principle which leads men to act" is for Turgot either trivial or false:

> In the sense that this proposition is true, it is childish, and a metaphysical abstraction from which there is no practical result to be drawn, because it is then equivalent to saying that "man only desires that which he desires." If he [Helvétius] is talking about a reflective, calculated interest by which man compares himself to others and prefers himself, then it is false that even the most corrupt men behave according to this principle. It is false that moral sentiments do not influence their judgements, their actions, their affections. The proof is that they need to make an effort to overcome their feeling when it is opposition to their interest. The proof is that they feel remorse. . . . The proof is that they are touched by novels and tragedies, and that a novel whose hero acted according to the principles of Helvétius . . . would be most displeasing to them.[23]

Turgot and Condorcet were quite skeptical, more generally, of the notion of a purely economic or commercial side of people's lives. Self-interest is not limited to commerce, and moral sentiments are not limited to religious, military, or domestic life. One of the most intriguing preoccupations of the late Enlightenment political economists is indeed with the evolution of moral rules in relation to commerce. The territory of moral prescription changes over time, and it can be expected to change particularly fast in a period—such as the time of Turgot's reforms in France—when the regulation of commerce is itself in a process of transformation.

Manufacturers, Smith says, have a tendency to "intimidate the legislature"; successful traders, in Condorcet's description, use their money and influence to avoid the "competition of merchants who are not rich enough to have protectors"; Turgot shows how wealthy individuals together prevent all reforms, by blocking only those changes that would affect their own interests.[24] But the process of reform is itself difficult to predict. A merchant does not know "if the laws under which he has bought will be those under which he will sell," Condorcet says; this uncertainty inhibits "real" merchants, and favors "men who know how to profit [from] prohibitive laws."[25]

The territory of moral custom is itself changing, that is to say, in the course of commercial reform. Merchants pursue their own self-interest, and one way to promote one's interests is by influencing legislation. But the forms of regulation are changing, together with the norms of political influence. Each merchant, in choosing how to pursue his interests, must thus decide on which forms of influence he thinks are right, which are likely to hurt his reputation, which will help his trade, and which, even, will hurt his trade because they hurt the commercial system of the country. The conflict is of determining importance, meanwhile, for the idyll of perfect competition. Each individual is supposed to know and to pursue his own interest, and the pursuits are supposed to sum to collective success. But the idyll presumes an unchanging (and therefore unimportant) moral environment: the rules of licit competition are known, observed, and uninfluenced by even the most prodigiously successful individual competitors.

Complexity and Simplicity in Economic Thought

The "complicated" or "rich" psychological intuitions of eighteenth-century political economy have an odd relationship to modern economic thought. On the one hand, Smith and Turgot are evidently preoccupied by the conflicts and diversities of individual lives, by the "incredible complexity" that is disregarded in conventional economic theory.[26] On the other hand, they are themselves the founders of much of this theory. Their insights are thereby subversive, apparently, of their own theories. Turgot, even more than Smith, is the great precursor of the late nineteenth-century theory of general economic equilibrium, with its conceptions of *tâtonnement*, of true prices, and of economies that, in Turgot's words, "approach a point of equilibrium."[27] But in the presence of agents who are remorseful, prone to reading novels, and under the continuous influence of their moral sentiments, general equilibrium theory is often unresilient. The theory of the invisible hand is seen, perhaps wrongly, as Adam Smith's most significant contribution to economic thought; it is a theory that makes very little sense if agents pursue their own interests by influencing the political rules that govern investment.

The recourse of nineteenth-century historians of economic thought, faced with this apparent subversion, was to partition the principles of the earlier theorists. In accounts of the "Adam Smith Problem," for example, the *Theory of Moral Sentiments* is contrasted to the supposedly more simple view of self-interested economic life in the *Wealth of Nations*; the two works, it is suggested, are concerned with the different sides of people's lives. Smith's philosophical principles can thus be ignored for the purposes of economic understanding. If they were taken seriously, they would indeed pose problems for the consistency of economic theory; as it is, they can be renounced in the interests of rigor and of the deeper insight that is the consequence of the construction of theories. "If it were generally realised that Economic Man is only an expository device," in Lionel Robbins's words, "it is improbable that he would be such a universal bogey."[28]

Economists are as full of intuitions as anyone else, in this view, but they put their moral and psychological observations to one side for the purposes of being theorists. Like Gunnar Myrdal's ideal investigator, who distinguishes the "intellectual" from the "emotional sphere" (and thus from his "personal political opinion"), the theorist distinguishes his personal intuitions about other people from his enterprise as a scientist.[29] As in Paul Krugman's engaging picture (see chapter 2), the self-conscious theorist is aware that his or her simplified models are no more than devices, but dares, nonetheless, to be "silly." He is prepared to renounce his "deep sense of the complexities of reality," to come to terms with the "narrowing of vision imposed by the limitations of one's framework and tools."

This choice, or the dichotomy of asceticism and complexity, is in fact a distinctively eighteenth-century one. Burke said that the "gross and complicated mass of human passions and concerns" could never be depicted in a simple theory; Herder said of the political economy of the 1770s that "it has offered us a bird's eye view in place of an arduously acquired knowledge of the real needs and conditions of the country."[30] Kant, in his polemic with Herder of 1784–86, answers in the pure voice of the theorist. The notion of knowledge without theory, he says, is impossibly confused. Herder wanted a sort of unphilosophical chart, "on which nothing must be indicated except what makes for human diversity, but this considered in all of its aspects and manifestations." This leads, Kant says, to "a chaos of causes and effects," and of "circumstances" that are "impossible to order." Even in "a general natural history of humanity," there must be a "historically critical mind which would select from the enormous mass of ethnic descriptions or tales of travels."[31]

The Kantian or ascetic choice—of the simplicity of thought over the "enormous mass" of complexity—is not now especially controversial. There is no understanding without selection, and no selection without simplification. This certainly seems to be Hirschman's own position, for example. He is in some respects one of the most susceptible of modern economists to the orderly seduction of simple ideas. His work can be seen as a succession of expository devices, or theories; some subsequently to be "self-subverted," he says, but Kantian nonetheless (see chapter 12).

The interesting question—in the eighteenth century and in modern theory—is whether the simplifications chosen are good ones, whether they do increase understanding. Smith's and Turgot's and Condorcet's individuals, torn between public and private goods, suggest troublesome problems, here, for economic theory. The problems are troublesome, at least, for those generalizations that rely—like the hypothesis of the invisible hand—on the simplifying assumption of self-interested behavior under fixed rules (including rules for the transformation of income into utility).

Some individuals, in Smith's account, will sometimes act out of ingenuous public spirit; some individuals will pursue their self-interest by influencing public officials to introduce restrictions on the trade of their competitors. They are well informed, as Smith says, about their "local conditions"; these local conditions include the likelihood of local changes in the rules and the norms of licit competition. The universal pursuit of self-interest, under these circumstances, is not uniquely conducive to social well-being. The invisible hand, in a world of unstable preferences and endogenously determined rules, is not a particularly good simplification, nor is it particularly conducive to economic understanding.[32]

The choice of simplifications has very little to do, in these circumstances, with disputes over economic technique, with being for or against the commitment to what Krugman calls "tightly specified models." There are very serious arguments among economic theorists about the extent to which economics is now influenced more by its tools than by the world it seeks to explain, that its technology has become an "end" more than a "tool" (for Maurice Allais), and a "guide" more than a "servant" (for Tjalling Koopmans).[33] But the point here is different. If it is an important characteristic of the world that people behave in complicated and disparate ways, then this characteristic can itself be depicted in "nice" models (or nice words).

The complex eighteenth-century view of public and private interests—or Hirschman's view—is itself something to be modeled. Some of the newest exercises in high economic theory are thus concerned with precisely the problem of the heterogeneity of preferences. J.-M. Grandmont, for example, is concerned in recent work to find "a fruitful formal language (that is not exclusive, of course, of others) to talk about and quantify such things as the dispersion, the variance, the shape, of the distribution of behavioural characteristics in a socioeconomic system," and thereby to reduce rationality assumptions on individual agents.[34]

Within noncooperative game theory, too, the object of much recent work is to relax conventional assumptions with respect to "payoffs" and "rules." If people have conflicting "tastes," in David Kreps's description—a "taste for the dollar," for example, and also a "taste not to be a dupe"—then "to model this situation with a game that supposes that such a simple model is correct will lead to bad predictions." The prospect is thereby one of "reconsidering how we model the actions of individuals in a complex and dynamic world," and in particular of "dealing with situations in which the rules are somewhat ambiguous"; it is to get around the tendency "to take the rules of the game too much for granted, without asking where the rules come from . . . [and] whether the rules that prevail are influenced by outcomes."[35] In several respects, this is a Smithian agenda; it is a search for useful simplifications.

Prescriptive Policies in the Modern Period

George Sand's utility-maximizing Formics sent their warships to enforce the principles of rational self-interest, and the "economic postulate" has been understood, since well before Adam Smith, in a prescriptive as well as a descriptive (or heuristic) sense. To act "eco-

nomically" is considered to be good, or at least to be good for development—a precondition, of sorts, for economic modernity. "It has been
for centuries the object of united Europe, to erect herself into a despot,
compelling all the nations of the Earth to be happy in her way," Herder
wrote in 1784. Nations that saw themselves as "philanthropic, disinter-
ested, noble and virtuous"—Herder mentioned the Spanish, the Jesu-
its, the Dutch—were trying everywhere to introduce the "opulence"
and "civilisation" of Europe: they will soon become "good, strong, and
happy men, just like us!"[36]

It is this prescriptiveness of economic thought—a relationship to
policy, or to the world—with which Hirschman has been concerned
since his first ventures with the World Bank. Good theories explain
things about the world. It is a necessary (although not sufficient) condition for good economic theory, under these circumstances, that the
theorist should have some interest in looking at the world.[37] Léon Walras and Carl Menger were interested in general economic interdependence, and also in the prodigious increase in the intermediate consumption of commodities in the 1850s and 1860s; Turgot, Smith, and
Condorcet were interested—like economists now—in the turbulence
in the rules of economic competition that is characteristic of economies
in transition. But economic theories influence the world, as well as
being influenced by it. The "uniform theory" is seen as a description
of how people behave in their economic lives and of how they should
behave if they are to be successful in these lives; it is also—as it was
in the high development policy of the 1950s—a blueprint for economic
development.

The development prescriptions of the early 1950s have an overween-
ing self-confidence that seems to have been founded, to a considerable
extent, on psychological theory. "The government of an underdeveloped country," in the words of a United Nations "Group of Experts"
in 1951, should provide eight "preconditions" of economic development. The group included both W. Arthur Lewis and Theodore W.
Schultz, and its policy conditions are peremptory: the government
should, for example, "establish a central economic unit" and "an-
nounce its programmes for expanding employment." Its historical theories are similarly grand: "progress occurs only where people believe
that man can, by conscious effort, master nature." It incorporates the
political conditions for growth: "there cannot be rapid economic progress . . . [without] the creation of a society from which economic, politi-

cal, and social privileges have been eliminated." The group in effect demands a revolution, in moral and social life: "ancient philosophies have to be scrapped; old social institutions have to disintegrate; bonds of caste, creed and race have to be burst; and large numbers of people who cannot keep up with progress have to have their expectations of a comfortable life frustrated."[38]

Maximizing or "economizing" was itself a precondition, under these circumstances, for economic success. Its extent determined the differing destinies of countries: the "will to economize," for Lewis, and the degree of "manoevring," are the principal explanations for "the essential difference between societies."[39] "New types of enterprising men come forward," Walt W. Rostow wrote later in his account of the stages of economic growth: "men devoted to commerce: men concerned with fine calculations of profit and loss, men of wide horizons." The "period of preconditions," for Rostow, is one of psychological transformation: "just before and during the take-off, the new modern elements, values, and objectives achieve a definitive break-through; and they come to control the society's institutions."[40]

The objective of governments—of one's own government, and also of the other, tutelary governments that constitute the international community—must in this view be to make economizing possible: to provide the preconditions, as it were, for the psychological preconditions of progress. The suggestion does not seem to have been that the United Nations should itself establish schools of enterprise; that young boys in backward countries, like the eighth-year students in Louis Philipon's plan of education for France in 1784, should be instructed "in such subjects as foreign exchanges, book-keeping, and stocks and shares."[41] It was rather that government should promote the diverse changes that determine what Rostow called "non-economic aspects of the drive to maturity" (and that for Rostow included the "reactive nationalism" that had been a "powerful motive force" in psychological modernization—"at least as important as the profit motive"—and that could also "be turned in any one of several directions").[42]

Education itself was indeed seen as mildly suspect, at least in its more aimless forms. One effect of the policies for modernization may thus have been to induce a mildly skeptical attitude to ordinary or "old-fashioned" education. Even Lewis and Schultz and their colleagues seem at that time to have found in education relatively minor or instrumental value. They observe that "up to a few years ago, the first goal of educational authorities in under-developed countries was to get as many children into schools as possible, and to make the whole population literate as soon as possible." "This is still an important goal," they say, "but it has receded somewhat in importance as the needs of economic development have revealed more urgent educational problems." "Top priority," now, is to be assigned to agricultural extension services, to providing university education for "men capable of framing and executing development programmes" (including "administrative officers for government and business"), and to training the other "personnel" required in such programs.[43]

Ideas of Development in the 1990s

The postwar history of policies for psychological modernity—of the programs in which bilateral and multilateral donors tried to foster the "will to economize"—is oddly familiar in the 1990s. There is only one route to progress, for much of modern development policy, and it is a route of social and psychological revolution. Even Rostow's stages of growth have found a sort of echo in recent development prescriptions, especially for Eastern Europe and the former Soviet Union: to hurtle (and not to "lumber") through successive changes, from the overthrow of old (state) institutions to the invention of new (market) institutions, and to the eternity of new (economic) psychology. Desired policies, including "shock therapies," are justified, in part, on the grounds that they will promote institutional or entrepreneurial change of the required sort ("bonds have to be burst"). Undesired policies, such as expenditure on social security, are opposed on the grounds that they are suited to a later, richer stage of development ("expectations of a comfortable life have to be frustrated"). The "will to economize" is once again the cynosure of economic policies for development. People have to learn to be modern: they have to learn to economize, and they also to have to learn both the rules and the norms of economizing.

The history with which we have been concerned suggests several reasons to be timid in the new enterprise of "development hurtling," to see it as full of perils and also of internal tensions. Smith, like Turgot and Condorcet, considered the emergence of "enlightened self-interest"—of economizing within the norms of a civilized society—to be a process that was both slow and uncertain. The transformation of public opinion about commerce is for Condorcet "the only difficult question" in policies for freedom of commerce.[44] It was certainly not a question to be resolved by some sort of benevolent despotism. The reforming sovereign might be concerned, perhaps, to ensure that his subjects are no longer indolent or lighthearted, or that they pursue their own interests within an orderly system of norms and rules. He might indeed direct them to become busily self-interested. They, being obedient, would do their best to be busy. But the norms of licit self-interest are themselves changing. So is the propensity to obedience. So, too, is the prospect of good government: in Smith's words, of a legislature "always directed, not by the clamourous importunity of partial interests, but by an extensive view of the general good."[45]

Smith was frequently criticized by nineteenth-century economists, especially in the German-speaking world, for his lack of respect for "'organic' social structures": in Menger's words, for "the one-sided rationalistic liberalism, the not infrequently impetuous effort to do away with what exists," which was characteristic of Smith, the "Smithian School," and "the Anglo-French Age of Enlightenment."[46] Yet the transformation of the "confirmed habits and prejudices of the people" was for Smith a modest procedure, subject to frequent revisions, and in which the most powerful instruments of reform are "reason and persuasion." "Of all political speculators, sovereign princes are by far the most dangerous," Smith wrote in a comment that seems to have been directed at Frederick the Great's policies for Prussian modernization: the speculative statesman, he says, "seems to imagine that he can arrange the different members of a great society with as much ease as the hand arranges the different pieces upon a chess-board. He does not consider that . . . in the great chess-board of human society, every single piece has a principle of motion of its own."[47]

The tension between economic reform and respect for individual opinions is of central importance to development policies in Eastern Europe, in the former Soviet Union, and in much of the rest of world. It is of central political importance as well. The conflict between liberal and conservative policies is more intense, in some respects, than it has been at any time since the economic reforms of the 1780s: between the "one-sided rationalistic liberalism" of reform and the "organic" respectfulness of conservatism. Economic reformers are not conservatives—"a barrier is a barrier whether you call it a cultural difference or a tradition or anything else," as Margaret Thatcher once said—and market forces, like self-interested individuals, are not obedient to national sovereign powers.[48] To respect individual opinions is not the same as to respect social institutions. These were the problems with which the greatest founders of modern economics were preoccupied before the French Revolution, which are at the heart of Hirschman's work, and which are also the problems of the 1990s.

Six

Society as Output
Exit and Voice among the Passions and Interests

Lisa R. Peattie

I N CONTRAST TO the technocratic discourse at the heart of development economics, Albert Hirschman has steadfastly insisted that development can be achieved through a variety of economic strategies and institutional structures. One work that conveys these views is *Exit, Voice, and Loyalty.*[1] Because Hirschman considers "loyalty" an important aspect of the contrast between exit (market) and voice (politics), the work ends up focusing on the complex social consequences of the choice of means. In *The Passions and the Interests,* Hirschman turns his attention to social thought at the outset of the industrial era, because he believes the issues addressed by the thinkers of that period are relevant to our own times and are those of the implications of the economic process for society.[2]

In light of these works, I have decided to consider Hirschman's ideas not as a contribution to the theory of economics or the practice of economic development, but as a recent descendant of a long line of attempts to trace the consequences of economic development for social life and human behavior. This approach may help us to better understand not only the analytical tools available to development economists, but also the way in which the development process has drastically altered the social landscape since Hirschman's predecessors worked and thus created a new game for those who seek to define the relationship between social life and economic institutions and to shape that relationship.

I begin by placing Hirschman's work in what I consider its context of intellectual history, that is, by reviewing nineteenth-century at-

118

tempts to conceptualize the relationship between economics and social life. I then turn to some hybrid forms of exit and voice and explain how they are applied in current political practice. The essay concludes with some theoretical and practical suggestions arising from current conditions.

By the nineteenth century, economic development had come to be widely understood as both an inevitable and desirable objective of society: the notion became equated with "progress." Yet economic development was also understood to bring pain and social loss. The "deserted village," the dissolution of community and tradition, were thought to be inevitable consequences of the transition to a market economy. Indeed, the "satanic mills" became a symbol of industrialism. As Englishmen were pushed from their villages to the towns and their children forced to twist threads at factory looms, economic thought seemed to take Malthus's reasoning as irrefutable; economic expansion would increase population and lower wages. From the Luddite framebreaker to the Romantic poet, the population of the industrializing countries saw human loss as an unmistakable consequence of material progress.

The nineteenth-century social philosophers who were Hirschman's ancestors worked in their several ways to accommodate progress and loss within the same framework. The conceptual issue was how to assess the implications for society and human behavior of the growth of economic institutions that seemed to be outside the control of society and to have their own dynamic of development.

One of the strategies devised to deal with this question can be seen in the Marxist theories of this time, which proposed that economic institutions not only produce and distribute goods but, because of the way they produce and distribute these goods, also distribute power, define roles, and shape belief and meaning. In this view, the social consequences of economic development are driven by economic interests and shaped by the powers of coercion and conviction inherent in economic relationships—as is evident in the Marxist ideas of class formation, relations of production, and superstructure.

An alternative conceptual strategy has been to separate "the economic" from "the social" components of human activities, to contrast the two, and to treat economic and social relationships as different and contrasting modes of organizing society. This was the approach of several prominent thinkers of the period. In *Gemeinschaft und Gesell-*

schaft (1887), Ferdinand Tönnies pointed out the differences between a society integrated by the sense of community and a society unified by relationships of mutual utility.[3] Similarly, Sir Henry Maine—in *Ancient Law* (1861)—compared relationships organized around (largely ascribed) status to those based on contract.[4] And Emile Durkheim, in *The Division of Labor in Society* (1893), found in "organic" and "mechanical" solidarity categories similar to the antithesis described by Tönnies.[5] These ideas remain central to Western social thought, having been carried forward in this century by Max Weber, Karl Polanyi, Robert Redfield, and such current writers as Christopher Lasch.

In *The Passions and the Interests* and subsequent works, Albert Hirschman is drawn to the idea of reason, which for Hirschman, along with passion and interest, constitutes a kind of "early triumvirate" in the history of philosophical concepts. Since Plato, Hirschman says, the analysis of human motivation has been dominated by the contrast between passion and reason.

> But it is precisely against the background of this traditional dichotomy that the emergence of a third category in the late sixteenth and early seventeenth century can be understood. Once passion is deemed destructive and reason ineffectual, the view that human action could be exhaustively described by attribution to either one or the other meant an exceedingly somber outlook for humanity. A message of hope was . . . conveyed. . . . Interest was seen to partake in effect of the better nature of each, as the passion of self-love upgraded and contained by reason, and as reason given direction and force by that passion.[6]

The currents and eddies of nineteenth- and early twentieth-century thinking that formed the foundation of theories about economic development clearly indicate that reason played a large role in the views that were emerging at this time. It was not just a third member of a triumvirate, much less simply a mediating force between passion and interest. It was the rational linking of means to ends that lay behind the pursuit of self-interest and gave interest its civilizing power. Interest and rationality are the joint antithesis of passion and unreason. These ideas were accompanied by the idea of science as decontextualized, factual, cumulative, and integrated, with new ideas (thought of as discoveries) incorporating the old at a higher level of generalization.

Before exploring how this way of thinking about things helped provide a setting for economic practice as well as for the discipline of economics, I should point out that historically, reason did not enter in this company, or, indeed, was not associated with individual motives of any sort. Reason was, on the one hand, the project and banner of a category of intellectuals—*les philosophes*—and on the other, a developing ideology for the national state in formation.

I am guided here by the analysis of Zygmunt Bauman:

> The coincidence between the rule of ideas (ostensibly the mainstay of the Enlightenment project) and ... surveillance-based discipline may seem contradictory and paradoxical only if the social roots of the Age of Reason are forgotten. Let us recall that, in the beginning, there was "the crisis of the seventeenth century." That the crisis was, in essence, the bankruptcy, or at least the increasingly apparent inadequacy, of the extant ... means of social control. That this feeling of ... social order under threat arose among the powerful and the wealthy of the time out of the new experience of the presence of "masterless people"—a shifting, homeless, vagabond population.... That the effort to neutralize the perceived threat and to dispel the fears it emanated took the form of political practices ... [involving] the new responsibility of the centralized power of the state for the maintenance and reproduction of social order. And that the qualitatively novel location of controlling and order-reproducing powers created demand for a novel kind of expertise, and a novel function of paramount, systemic importance: ... a professional specializing in modifying human behaviour, in "bringing conduct into line" and staving off, or containing the consequences of, disorderly or erratic action.[7]

As Bauman tells the story, the demand for reason to rule appeared as an ideological aspect of the transition from a preindustrial feudal organization of society to one dominated by central governments—first in the form of the Sun King, later of the Jacobins who made the point by rechristening Notre Dame the Temple of Reason, and in due course in the form of socialism advertised as "scientific" and denigrating "utopianism." The opponent of reason was not so much individual passion as popular culture. "Total and unqualified resentment for popular habits, contempt for the irrational and grotesque, now identified with the peasant and generally 'uneducated' culture was perhaps the only point of agreement between the spokesmen of established churches, Puritans, Jansenists, libertines, learned *philosophes* and practitioners of revolution."[8] From these historical predecessors modern planning has inherited both the ideology of rationality and the emphasis on formal order that privileges elite thought and central control.

But, on a parallel track, the idea of rationality somehow became closely associated with economic behavior. The "countinghouse," not the entrepreneur, symbolized the world of business. With the development of marginalist analysis, the profession of economics came to be dominated by theories built on the basic unit of the (economically) rational decision. Indeed, if we look at the antitheses *gemeinschaft-gesellschaft*, status-contract, organic-mechanical, they all seem to imply a contrast between social relations based on a rational pursuit of interest and relations based on cultural tradition. The loss these contrasts seem to express pertains to the replacement of cultural tradition by economic rationality. The replacement is seen as the inevitable price of progress, but as one on which sentiment may dwell with regret.

Once development planning came into existence as an organized professional activity, it was able to benefit from double-dipping into the ideological well. It could impose reason over the disorderly popular world because it inherited the task, and it could do so because the spread of economic institutions was in itself conceived of as a sphere of rational choice. As Albert Hirschman points out in his article "Industrialization and its Manifold Discontents," the eighteenth- and nineteenth-century critiques of industrialization in *general* have given way to critiques of particular industrializations, which are described as being "lopsided" either in overemphasizing heavy industry or in not favoring heavy industry enough; in these critiques, the desirability of industrialization itself is unquestioned.[9] Thus it became possible for development planning to be shaped as a body of professional practice dominated by technocratic discourse concerning the means to a generally defined and generally accepted end.

Development planning is still very much with us, but a cursory inspection of both the intellectual and the institutional landscape at once reveals that the elements that once served as its ideological context are in general disarray.

As we have seen, the national state, the first vehicle of the rule of reason, is rapidly losing its effectiveness as a social form, and along with this, its claim to rationality. No national state is now able to control the economic processes within its borders; this is evident in the case of the once-dominating United States of America, where pre-election political rhetoric makes it painfully clear that the government is unable to deliver the economic management to which its citizens have come to feel entitled. How do national governments deal with economic entities that operate on an international scale?

If, however, we look at the national state, as the historian Charles Tilly does, as a form that has evolved as the most effective set of institutions for waging war, there is trouble in this direction, too.[10] According to Tilly, the national state brings together two originally distinct ways of exercising power: capital (as in the early city-states) and coercion (as in the early empires). As wars became more and more expensive, it was necessary to get capital to pay for coercion, and the national state represented the institutionalization of the ensuing stabilized bargain. But as a result of the way the technology of warfare has developed, it is now possible to be quite dangerous without having a big army, and the political utility of warfare has become more and more problematic.

One might suppose that under such conditions the state's problems in exerting power directly might lead to heightened claims for rationality and rationalizing, and indeed, I suspect that we may see some such phenomena in the schools of planning, with demands for the planner as orchestrator, interpreter, data provider, and indicator. But in the absence of a validating institutional structure, will the public go along?

The means-focused approach to legitimacy by rationality will not be aided by postmodernist intellectual trends within the world of ideas. The view that knowledge is necessarily contextual and relative, that we must always ask "whose rationality?" certainly still leaves a place for data and grounded argument, but intellectual authority seems much reduced under these conditions.[11]

Meanwhile, the literature on "postmodernism" has been greatly expanded by studies of the irrationality of states, as in the works on the First World War by Paul Fussell and Modris Ekstein, or the literature on the Holocaust that treats it, as Bauman does, as the modernist project of a preeminently modern state.[12]

If the state is capable not only of irrationality, but also of exercising its irrationality on the grand scale, why not turn to the rationality of the market? There are some difficulties here as well.

Even if particular economic decisions by consumers, producers, and other economic actors are in themselves rational (and there is a literature to the contrary), individual decisions do not, in a world of institutions, necessarily add up to rational institutions and rational systems. Michel Crozier's work on bureaucracy is an essay to the contrary.[13] Crozier proposes that if every bureaucrat acts in the way most rational for him or her, the result will be a cumulative pushing of decisionmaking upward and a retention of information downward such that, in short order, the institutional system will have a vast separation between power and relevant information. In economic institutions, prices are supposed to transmit information without the sorts of distortions hypothesized by Crozier's model, but again, institutional process may well intervene. In *The Idea of Economic Complexity*, David Warsh diagrams price setting in three institutional subsystems—medicine, military procurement, and professional basketball—to show how institutional cost-shifting can lead to a system of determining prices that has little bearing on the simple supply-demand models appropriate to freely competitive markets and that certainly transmits information in a very distorted way.[14] As Michael Piore has been pointing out to the formerly communist states, the market is not a system of transactions but a system of institutions. Thus, at the same time that scholars under the flag of the theory of public choice have been trying to develop a theory of politics using the tools of analysis previously developed in the sphere of economics, they have entered the fray via a set of concepts that have already adapted to a world of institutions that assumes that rationality can only be partial at best.

So far, I have been talking about institutional trends in "the world of ideas," meaning by that, I suppose, the world of intellectuals. But there is a realm of ideas outside that, ideas that we can see when they are tossed up by the processes of social movement politics. Here there seem to be some rather interesting developments.

As already mentioned, economic development has always been accompanied by movements of an opposing view. In some cases, as in Romanticism, the participants in these movements saw human passion and experience as the all-important ingredients; some, like the utopian socialists, tried to recreate community on a new economic base; some, like the Luddites, tried to slow down the technical change or, like the proponents of an eight-hour day, to alter the conditions it imposed on people. But I think that these movements tended to take the position that economic development is rational and, being rational in its broad outlines, is inevitable: the wave of the future. The Indian dialogue between Gandhism and the modernizers following Nehru has been conducted along these lines.

But the modern ecology movement seems to be sounding a new theme. This is a view that treats economic development as a kind of collective madness.

When I was looking at controversies surrounding airport construction—there are quite a few of these—I found that what often began as opposition to the taking of homes or farms and resistance to the noise of landings and takeoffs almost inevitably escalated into opposition to the ideas of progress that had legitimized the airport project. Once into this terrain, these movements soon find a position from which there is little possibility of returning to the language of normal planning negotiations; the controversy has become part of a social movement with quasi-religious overtones. This social movement is not simply a movement against progress—development—as perceived: Romanticism was that. These movements assert that progress is itself irrational.

When those who were opposed to enlarging the Frankfurt airport built a little "village of resistance" in the woods, dramatizing a search for "meaningful relationships in a communal context," they were doing exactly what the utopian socialists had done in England and America in another century. But in our century, the anti-airport struggles seem tinged with a rejection even more radical than Fourier's.

Opponents often use the most extraordinary language. In Boston, Massport was called an "octopus," a "sand sucker," a "monster with cancerous tentacles"; the opponents of airport expansion spoke of "moral annihilation."[15] A French account of six airport fights in France describes how, from grievances related to noise and land taking, the issues become "globalized" into the struggle against "a society which stakes all on the production of merchandise, on profitability, on 'economic overbidding,' on 'progress,' even if it is at the 'risk of death.' . . . This would be the project finally of a system of flight into the future (*fuite en avant*), which drives to go ever faster, so as to privilege means of transportation like aviation, even if this speed contributes nothing in fact to that society."

"Thus," says the French author, "opposition movements cannot be other than movements which campaign for another direction of society, for a society decentralized, deconcentrated, in which power can be exercised locally, in which rational solutions can be found to meet the needs of all: collective transport, de-urbanization, creation of activities in rural zones . . . a society in which new practices can be created, with other links between individuals, links of solidarity, mutual aid."[16]

In the little book that introduces Hirschman's concepts of "exit" and "voice," he makes it perfectly clear that the distinction arises out of the time-honored one, which he calls a "fundamental schism," between economics and politics.[17] "Exit belongs to the former realm, voice to the latter." He begins here, and goes on to show how exit and voice may be employed to improve the performance of institutions both economic and political, the circumstances under which they may fail to do so, and something of the relationship between voice and exit. In the course of the analysis, the boundary between the economic and the political comes to be crossed, if not blurred, by these alternations and interrelations of the two corrective mechanisms. This property of the analytic scheme is especially appropriate for the world I have just sketched, in which economic institutions are seen as thoroughly intertwined with political ones, and in which each is understood to have functions of the other.

But this world also presents some other novel conditions for exit and voice. A serious change is the decline in the status of the idea of rationality. The idea of reason has fallen into disrepute and is not thought to be found embodied in the institutions of either government or business. The use of voice will not assume a reasonable hearer and a reasonable response. The use of exit may not simply express product dissatisfaction, but rather a general disgust with the purposes of the enterprise.

The most straightforward version of the exit response as political statement is the decision by individual customers not to purchase the output of some politically obnoxious producer. "After the Soviet invasion of Afghanistan, Americans hunting for a way to protest it seized upon dumping bottles of [Stolichnaya vodka]. Sales dropped 40 percent. They climbed back up, only to plunge again after Korean Air Lines Flight 007 was shot down by a Russian fighter in 1983."[18]

As a political tool, however, exit almost inevitably has to be combined with voice—a combination known as boycott. A simple reduction in consumer demand is likely to be ineffective from the point of view of incentive, and, even more basically, is not likely to convey the information. I do not know how successful the farmworkers were in reducing the sales of grapes, but I suspect the publicity campaign that drove the boycott also served to magnify the effect of sales differences on the growers. To the degree that the target of the boycott is seen as being not only in error but also irrational, voice will take the form of both complaint and of distaste and opposition.

Sometimes the exit part of a boycott seems to function less as a direct incentive to the producers than as a symbolic device through which persons, representing themselves as outraged consumers, can play a political role for which we have as yet found no institutional channel. The INFACT organization, in its boycott of General Electric, apparently used the consumer role to enter into the peace movement.[19] INFACT had first become organized to check the marketing techniques of the Nestle company for infant formula in the Third World. The device used was a highly publicized boycott. Having led Nestle to capitulate, the INFACT group, looking about for another life-threatening product on which to use their organization and experience, identified nuclear weapons. They then spent some time selecting GE as a corporation with a substantial history of weapons manufacture, which also had a large enough civilian line to provide a consumer target. INFACT then set up ironing boards (an emblem of domestic life) in parking lots and other public places to solicit signatures and postcards vowing to boycott GE lightbulbs, toasters, and other products.

The GE boycott campaign seems to have been fairly successful, although, I would guess, more from the ironing boards and the prize-winning documentary produced as part of the campaign than from the exit device per se. And some have raised questions about that. Is it appropriate to boycott *civilian* products in the context of a campaign to cut weapons production and move to a civilian economy? Would it not make better sense to cut demand for the military products? (Meanwhile, as an officer of a small organization dedicated to building a political constituency for exactly that, I am all too aware of the difficulties of implementing this strategy.)

A recent analytic history of the Neighbor-to-Neighbor campaign to boycott Folger coffee presents a fascinating account of the interaction between exit and voice, politics and economics, which ambitiously intended to affect not only the policies of the U.S. government but the policies of the government of El Salvador. Neighbor-to-Neighbor, a national grass roots organization that had grown out of the United Farm Workers and Food First decided—not without debate—to move from congressional lobbying to boycott as a way of changing U.S. policy in Central America. The boycott, which was conspicuous enough to attract repeated negative attention from the State Department and to lead the four major U.S. coffee-selling corporations to place ads in favor of peace negotiations in the Salvadoran newspapers, involved not only the U.S. State Department but unions, bishops, and political leaders in both countries and is now moving into an effort to arrange marketing services for Salvadoran cooperative coffee producers.

The Neighbor-to-Neighbor evaluation concludes that the boycott's first goal, to "involve a dramatically larger and more diverse segment of the U.S. population in efforts to end the war in El Salvador," was met in part only. "While the boycott didn't build an enormous army of activists, it did give citizens a bullhorn to magnify their voices to Congress, and contributed to a belief that a small number of people can make a difference." A second goal—to make the war "a subject of national debate"—was clearly met. "The boycott became a part of the political environment." The third goal, to "squeeze off the flow of U.S. consumer dollars," was more problematic, for "the campaign had little economic effect on the growers." However, the psychological threat of a huge economic attack and the actual attack on their image created much concern among the far right and applied key and timely strategic pressure to a deadlocked negotiations process.[20] Again, there is in the boycott the use of exit as a way of creating a forum for voice.

The ecology movement, by focusing on the destructive effects of industry, has generated a whole constellation of small movements to exit from certain products, so as to "make a statement." There are now consumer guides to identify products that are more ecologically sound. There is a boycott against the state of Colorado for its antigay ordinance, against American Express for underwriting a ski resort in a wilderness area, and against makers of war toys, cigarettes, and products tested on animals. The Institute for Consumer Responsibility publishes *National Boycott News*.[21] The discussions that arise in this political world are often complex and difficult to resolve. There has been, for example, a vigorous movement opposing the use of paper diapers because they are contributing to a crisis in landfills. Although this position appears to be the predominant one among the ecologically enlightened, research into the diaper issue challenges this position with some other questions: How about the use of energy in washing? How about the bleach in cotton diapers? How about the heavy use of pesticides and—yes—the relations of production and encompassing politics typical of the cotton industry? Surely this situation is no different from the coffee one.

The truth is that for those who see economic development as a mad *fuite en avant*—as do the anti-airport extremists—neither exit nor voice offers clear channels of action. Those who, like the German Greens, have tried to build a political movement around the restriction of growth, run immediately into the issue of jobs; that is to say, the issue of consumption and of style of life. This means that the voice of politics must combine with a movement for consumer exit. And all this must take place in a world in which economic institutions are becoming more and more transnational, and in which the national state seems less and less able to inspire respect. The current state of exit and voice is therefore one in which people are struggling to work out how to manage their lives under conditions that are unprecedented. The only thing that can give one confidence in these circumstances is the thought that all the conditions human beings have confronted in the past have were, at the time, equally unprecedented.

It is important, therefore, to consider Hirschman's work not from the point of view of his contribution to economics, but of his effort to turn the attention of economics to the study of society. I suspect that his clear, civilized voice, with its elegant antiphony of exit and voice, may not do for our visibly unreasonable times. But then, the situation, as I have already said, is unprecedented and wants invention on all levels.

One of the areas crying out for invention is, of course, development economics. Here, Hirschman's interest in the role of exit and voice in correcting institutions may help point the way to what has to be done.

It appears that the solutions of the nineteenth century offer some guidelines for dealing with today's theoretical and practical problems. There were, as mentioned, two solutions. One, the Marxist, integrated economy and society as base and superstructure; social institutions and human beliefs were developed out of and shaped by the economic base. The view endowed the state with privileged power as the shaper of the "productive forces" and put the needs of daily life at the end of the queue. We know what happened to that solution.

Development economics took the other fork in nineteenth-century theory in the Western world. That version separated *gemeinschaft* from *gesellschaft*, community from association; status, as institutional tradition, from the ad hoc associations of contract; the institutional linkages of mutual utility from those of commitment and caring. Development economics became the domain of rational planning; society and culture were in another department.

The airport battles and the boycotts can be construed as messages indicating that it is not an acceptable strategy to separate the "economic" from the "social." The ecological movement and the women's movements are heard at the World Bank. Religious and ethnic commitments shape the meaning of "interest."

The concepts and the analytic techniques of development economics have evolved in a way that has made it possible to keep the discipline outside all that passion and shifting meaning. The world of macroeconomics is a world of clean ideas and generalized strategic recommendations. When development economics looks at institutions, it looks at a narrow range of institutions and does so in a specialized way.

What would a postmodernist development economics look like?

Seven

Social Construction of Hope

Bishwapriya Sanyal

W HAT appeals to me most about Albert O. Hirschman's
intellectual approach to developmental issues is his
bias for hope.[1] It is the arguments underlying this bias that I want to
probe in this chapter.

Hirschman is, of course, not the only developmental economist with
an optimistic bias. International donor agencies, whose headquarters
are typically decorated with colorful photographs of poor but smiling
people, are filled with economists who are hopeful that if the poor
countries listen to their advice, they will soon become prosperous. But
Hirschman is different from these economists. He is no cheerleader.
He does not root for any "system," any "theory," or any "paradigm."
In fact, his hopeful worldview derives from demonstrating the opposite—that there is no one way to move toward progress.

One could, of course, argue that although Hirschman's development
strategies differ from those of international donor agencies, his bias
for hope is grounded in the same belief held by those agencies—
namely, that the drive for modernization and progress that started with
the Enlightenment in Europe is a universal objective; and that to attain
this objective developing countries must transform the current structure of their socioeconomic relationships through the rational use of
their resources. A logical extension of this argument might be that
there is nothing unique about Hirschman's bias for hope that could
justify an analysis of the kind presented in this chapter, since his hopeful approach to developmental issues goes back to the underlying assumptions of the great "modernization project" of the last two centu-

ries. And, since we are already familiar with those assumptions, why spend valuable time in reinventing them?

It would be foolish to ignore Hirschman's hopefulness on that ground. Why so? First, there is much more to Hirschman's intellectual approach than the utopian visions embedded in most writings on the Enlightenment, modernization, and progress. It is not that Hirschman is more sophisticated in articulating *his* vision of development; he has never been eager to engage in such an exercise. Instead, he has been primarily interested in understanding the intricacies of the institutional processes necessary for development. That is why Hirschman's hopefulness is not expressed in the form of a grandiose development theory. Instead, it expresses itself in his rich and often counterintuitive analysis of the developmental process—a process whose complexity has been misunderstood by many, from both the right and the left of the ideological spectrum, who have seen in such complexity the negation of their simple expectations.

A second characteristic of Hirschman's hopefulness is its political, as opposed to moral, underpinnings. Hirschman does not perceive the development process as a morally necessary struggle between "good" and "evil," at the end of which the former is bound to win. That black-and-white portrayal of social reality has never been a part of Hirschman's intellectual approach. Rather, he has been more concerned about the gray areas of life, where good and evil are difficult to delineate, where changing circumstances make one look like the other, and where the outcomes are open-ended—meaning they can be influenced by human action. It is these intricacies of human action—as expressed by interaction between human beings and the institutions they have created—that interest Hirschman. How such interactions move us forward, incrementally, toward a better quality of life is the centerpiece of the story he has been narrating for nearly six decades.

There is a political undertone to Hirschman's story, although it is not political in the sense of struggles between opposing social forces. Hirschman's story is about the politics of everyday life, best captured in his analysis of the so-called tunnel effect, which explains why and how we react to income inequality in the developmental process. In addressing this intense political issue, Hirschman does not rely on any classical model of political behavior. He interweaves strands of popular psychology, economic principles, and—most important, institutional elements—to convey the message that the problem is neither as grave a situation as others portray nor an inevitable by-product of the developmental process. What is more, it may inadvertently produce some socially positive outcome.

What kinds of argument does Hirschman rely on in providing this complex and hopeful view of development? Which intellectual thread binds the paradoxes, surprises, and ironies into a convincing argument that, indeed, the development glass is half full? These are the questions I want to probe in the following pages. I realize that an adequate analysis of these questions would require much more space and time than can be devoted to this brief discussion. These are questions more appropriate for a full-length intellectual biography of Hirschman. So, what follows is a somewhat sketchy and tentative portrayal based on my limited reading of Hirschman's published work. It should be read more for the questions it raises than for the answers it suggests.

Pessimistic Views of Social Change

To fully appreciate Hirschman's positive view of the development process, one must remind oneself of the pessimistic rhetoric—from the right as well as the left of the ideological spectrum—that is common in development discourse. Let me take the arguments from the left first. Left-leaning developmentalists have always been deeply suspicious of small, uncoordinated reforms, arguing that such changes are really intended for cooptation of the poor and are too feeble to significantly alter basic structural relationships.[2] These critics, in general, advocate not only comprehensive and revolutionary changes but changes that are carefully planned to take into account all key variables and are consistently executed without any deviation from their well-defined, original goals. In this mode of thinking, unexpected and unintended effects of change are usually viewed as having a negative effect, which causes the process of planned change to deviate from its original goal.

The emphasis on planning in the leftist tradition is fairly strong. According to this tradition, good planning requires "a theory" implying full knowledge of the causal relationships among the key variables, an efficient administrative system for the consistent application of this knowledge to goal-directed action, and citizens who appreciate the value of collective production as well as consumption and are motivated to cooperate with one another toward that end. Lacking these prerequisites, social effort in pursuit of change may not achieve the desired results, according to this school of thought.

The arguments against reform from the right of the ideological spectrum are described by Hirschman in detail in his most recent book, *The Rhetoric of Reaction*.[3] I will not reiterate Hirschman's arguments here, except to note that conservative critics typically rely on three arguments to discourage reform efforts: namely, that the effect of reform would be the opposite of what it intends to accomplish; that the reform efforts would jeopardize social progress on other fronts; and that the reform efforts, though well intentioned, could not be implemented well. Although Hirschman attributes these arguments to conservatives, they are not unlike critiques from the left that dismiss incremental reformist policies on similar grounds—pointing out that such policies would not resolve the problem at which they are directed but, rather, would create "new contradictions within the system."

The right and the left also share the belief that certain prerequisites must be fulfilled before deliberate social change can be initiated. For example, many leftists argue that unless "the productive forces" of the country are liberated from the control of "private capital," the benefits of accumulation will never reach the masses. And the liberation of productive forces—particularly labor—cannot be achieved unless workers are liberated from the bondage of "false consciousness." On the right, the emphasis has also been on workers, but not on their "false consciousness." Rather, the complaint here is that unless the workers are imbued with the right kind of work habits and act rationally in exploring the labor market for the highest return to their labor, neither can the speed of accumulation be increased, nor is labor likely to enjoy the benefits of its full productivity.[4] Although Hirschman never addressed these issues about labor directly, he categorically opposed the logical premises on which these sorts of arguments rest— one of which is that unless the prerequisites are fulfilled, poor countries will not develop. Hirschman referred to this fetishization of prerequisites as a hindrance to change, arguing that if indeed all the prerequisites were fulfilled, the country in question would not need any developmental assistance.[5]

Yet another similarity between the two politically opposite camps is their use of "moral absolutes" in assessing the effects of social change. Numerous arguments have been made from the right about the socially destablilizing effects of industrialization and urbanization. There is a body of literature, started in England during the process of industrialization, that criticizes the impact of urbanization and industrialization on social order.[6] In the United States, as Richard Hofstadter has noted, there was an equally shrill outcry against social change as a result of industrialization, because it coincided with large-scale migration from Europe.[7] What is particularly noteworthy about these arguments is their strong emphasis on a moral code of conduct, which the critics feared was being eroded by the rapid social change associated with industrialization and urbanization. This anxiety about social change and its impact on the existing moral fabric of society is still very much with us. The language and rhetoric of anxiety might have changed somewhat, thanks to social policies that discourage racism, sexism, and other prejudices, but, as Alan Bloom's book demonstrated, intense anxiety about social change can provide a great rallying point for many conservative causes.[8]

As for the leftists, the attack on "consumerism" and "commodification" as a result of economic modernization has been a central element of their criticism of capitalist development since the early 1960s. And many on the left have heavily criticized the morally degrading and corrupting effects of urbanization, such as the densely crowded slums and shantytowns in developing countries.[9]

True, some see in these aesthetically ugly changes the positive seeds of revolution; but at times even they have complained that these changes undermine the development of a working-class identity and political consciousness. To put it simply: both the left and the right have evaluated the effects of changes in social values against a set of fixed moral norms that guided their theorizing about development. The relationship between moral norms and theorizing, however, was not one-way. Insofar as certain types of moral norms led to certain types of theories, the relationship worked the other way also: the need to construct neat and conceptually tight "theories" could only be met by adhering to fixed and well-defined moral norms against which the effects of social changes could be evaluated. It did not occur to many individuals in either camp that this form of theorizing can miss much of the complexity of social change.

The Joyful Explanation of Social Change

Hirschman's intellectual approach to developmental issues differs from the dominant views in several respects. For one thing, he has rarely, if ever, written about development and change with apprehension about its outcome. On the contrary, his writing is marked by an almost insatiable curiosity about the development process, which he views as having no fixed destination and no set path. Hirschman has also been more appreciative than others of the effects of development, often pointing out positive, unintended side effects that were neither planned nor foreseen. What is more, these good effects were often the result of a breakdown in the planning and implementation process.

These types of counterintuitive findings have allowed Hirschman to argue against the notion of planned change. This is not to say that he believes planning has no constructive role to play in nudging the economy strategically, through small pushes. Rather, what he argues against is all-encompassing planning of the Soviet variety, which drew its inspiration from German war planning during World War I. Unlike many who perceive developmental tasks to be similar to a war—on poverty, illiteracy, child mortality, or whatever—Hirschman believes they are very different in nature. He has argued that there is no prerequisite to development; and what others have specified as prerequisites, he considers to be the outcome of development.[10] He has also suggested that, unlike war, which requires much planning and coordination between the different components of the defense forces, development efforts can rarely be coordinated, primarily for institutional reasons. In fact, an attempt at all-encompassing coordination and planning in pursuit of so-called integrated development would be bound to falter and create more problems than it solved.

Hirschman has therefore focused on the benefits of small, incremental changes, which, as I pointed out earlier, were considered inconsequential by many developmental experts of the postwar period. In Hirschman's view, small changes appear to be small only because planners envision development as a process of immense changes; however, this perception is not grounded in the history of small changes through which Europe and North America have gradually evolved over many, many years. Development planners were simply astounded by looking at the huge differences in living standards between the developed and developing countries after World War II, and that led them to define the developmental task as one requiring "major transformation." This way of defining the developmental task, Hirschman says, may be well intentioned but counterproductive, as it could make the task appear so great that the planners would never attain the confidence to engage in it in a strategic way.

A third way in which Hirschman differs from most of his peers, both to his left and right, is in his position that progress can be achieved without premeditated goals and without prior knowledge of how to achieve those goals. Implicit in many of Hirschman's writings is the notion that institutions come to define their goals in a more precise way as a result of engaging in action, often with very limited knowledge about the possible consequences of their action. He has even argued, explicitly, that this lack of knowledge on the part of institutions might be a blessing in disguise, because if the institutions engaged in developmental efforts were fully aware of the various difficulties of the task ahead, they would have probably decided not to engage in those efforts.[11]

Underlying this approach to development—without well-defined goals, without "a theory" of action, and without the information necessary to proceed—is Hirschman's deep trust in the ability of both people and institutions to learn from their action. In fact, one could go a step further and suggest that to Hirschman, action is probably the key to knowledge. It is in the act of doing that people and institutions come to define and modify their goals and learn, through fumbling, about how to proceed.[12] Most interestingly, they do all this not by mobilizing new resources, but by discovering and utilizing existing resources, which, until the need arises, are hidden from their own eyes.

Which term should be used to characterize this approach to action and learning? Marxists, when they discuss action as a basis for verifying and building theory, use the term "praxis" to capture the dialectical nature of the relationship between practice (action) and theory. Although Hirschman's approach to knowing is somewhat similar to what this term denotes, it also differs in the sense that he does not subscribe to any specific theory of development and change that could be perfected through cumulative knowledge. To Hirschman, this absence of theory is the basis for creativity and innovation.[13] It is a source of intellectual curiosity and provides the joy of discovery—two key factors that are somewhat similar to what John Dewey, William James, and other so-called pragmatists at the turn of the century identified as

essential elements of learning.[14] Like them, Hirschman, in his approach
to the issues of development and change, is not guided either by strong
normative principles based on some kind of definite philosophy of
individuals and society or by any "laws of motion," or even by any
dictums such as "history repeats itself." As Louis Menand has remarked, the pragmatism of John Dewey, William James, Randolph
Bourne—and I would include Hirschman—follows from the view
"that there is nothing external to experience—no world of Forms, City
of God, independent cognito, a priori category, transcendental mind,
or far off divine event to which the whole creation moves, but only the
mundane business of making our way as best we can in a universe
shot through with contingency."[15]

This intellectual approach to social processes is what underlies
Hirschman's open-ended view of development and change. His deep
awareness of contingencies of the moment made him reject moral absolutes, led him to downscale planners' grand expectations of the
"great transformation" of poor countries, and is behind the wisdom
embodied in several of his insights: namely, that all good things do not
go together; that what many consider critical prerequisites for development are, in fact, the outcome of development; and that because most
developmental problems result from an interconnected set of causes,
the response to these problems does not necessarily need to be a set
of integrated policies.[16] Such integration is neither feasible nor desirable in a context fraught with contingencies. These insights account
for Hirschman's hopeful view of development—which, for want of a
better term, might be described as "pragmatism." And the culture
whose ethos seems most marked by this essence is that found in North
America, on whose shores Hirschman arrived in 1941.

The European Hirschman?

Hirschman is not entirely like the North American pragmatist, however. His writings on the industrialization process in Latin America
and even on various economic issues in the United States reveal a
strong penchant for the use of history in critical thinking. This is not
to say that the pragmatists did not use any form of historical analysis;
but, as Hofstadter has pointed out, there was an ahistorical component
to pragmatist thinking because of its preoccupation with the here and
now.[17] Hirschman, in contrast, frequently relies on historical evidence

and historicism as a methodology in arguing for an intellectually open-ended approach to issues of social change.

I want to emphasize the term "open-ended approach" because historical analysis has been used by many others—including Karl Marx—to demonstrate a fixed and predetermined pattern of social evolution. Hirschman's use of history conveys the opposite: it is meant to demonstrate how institutions and ideas evolve and change with time, how what was once considered a good trend may become a target of intense criticism over the years; how people's passions for social causes and interest in their own well-being swing, like a pendulum, creating new opportunities for progressive reforms. In all these cases history is used to provide hope, not in the Marxian sense of an eventual victory of the proletariat, but of a transformation of social reality, which is by and large the result of small, invisible, and often unplanned changes. This description of social evolution does not make one unabashedly hopeful about the future. Rather, it heightens one's appreciation for what is often rejected as mundane, inconsequential, or unnecessary. In other words, it imparts wisdom—wisdom that provides intellectual patience, a sense of irony, and a resilience against small as well as big surprises.

Hirschman also differs from the pragmatists in their position on the role of the state in social change. Unlike the pragmatists—who strongly believed that individuals are capable of improving their well-being if undeterred by a regulatory state and were generally skeptical of the state's ability to foster social progress—Hirschman, as a development economist, approved of a necessary role for the state in the development of late industrializing countries.[18] But Hirschman was also "a dissenter" among the development economists of the early 1950s, many of whom subscribed to the notion that without a strong and comprehensive push by the government, late industrializing countries in Asia, Africa, and Latin America would not be able to improve the living standards of their citizens. Hirschman's argument against the big-push theory, however, was not a moral one; it was not the type of argument Hayek, Popper, and others had used after World War II to discourage continuing state involvement in the economy.[19] Hirschman's argument was primarily institutional in nature. Unlike the pragmatists, he did not distrust the intention of the government but did question its institutional capability to mount an integrated "big push" for achieving a "great transformation" of the European kind.

Hirschman is not libertarian, either: he never wrote about government as if it were a barrier to the free expression of individual will. On the contrary, having lived through the Great Depression of the 1920s, and having been trained as an economist in Italy and England at the height of the Keynesian revolution, Hirschman's view of the state and the role it can play in strengthening "the hiding hand" has been, generally, quite positive. There is a European texture to Hirschman's view of the state that is distinctly different from the one that marks popular and, in many instances, academic discourse in North America about the inherently negative role of the government in social progress.[20] Kenneth Dyson and others have traced this difference—not between Hirschman and his North American contemporaries, but between Western Europeans in general and North Americans—to the different intellectual traditions about the state on the two continents.[21] Likewise, Bernard Bailyn has suggested that whereas North Americans had envisioned a "no-state state" as the ideal form of institution, needed primarily to protect private property, the Europeans had experienced, firsthand, the transformation of the royalty to "the imperial state."[22] Although Hirschman can hardly be characterized as one whose intellectual approach to the relationship between state and society is guided by the notion of "the imperial state," it is true that he never subscribed to the idea of "the no-state state," which, since the 1980s, has gained a new popularity under the guise of public choice theory.

On the issue of the relationship between state and society, Hirschman is somewhat in the middle: he is skeptical of the ability of the state to orchestrate the process of "great transformation," yet appreciative of the strategic role it can play at critical moments in the process. To what extent is this intellectual middle ground the product of Hirschman's upbringing, until well beyond his formative years, in Germany—the country of Max Weber, the first to theorize about the productive role of the bureaucracy in capitalist development, as well as of Adolph Hitler, the first to use a modern bureaucracy for the annihilation of millions of innocent people? Or, is Hirschman's balanced position on the state's role a product of some other factor, such as his intellectual associations with Gerschenkron at Harvard? And what about his brief stint in Europe as an economist employed by the U.S. State Department to supervise the implementation of the Marshall Plan? How did that return journey to war-ravaged Europe shape his thinking about the state's role in the reconstruction of market and civil society?

Anthropological Economist?

So far, I have argued that a uniquely North American pragmatism, enriched by an appreciation of history and a European *statism*—if I may use that word without its pejorative connotation–are the two hallmarks of Hirschman's approach to developmental issues. Yet a third intellectual strand differentiates Hirschman from most of his contemporary economists—that is the way he incorporates anthropological analysis of institutions in his explanations of macrolevel, economic trends. But my primary interest here is not the hybrid quality of his methodology, which results from the unique blending of two distinctly different epistemological traditions—one relying on a detailed understanding of individual and collective human behavior without the dictates of any "theory," and the other virtually the opposite, an inclination to aggregate human behavior so as to explain broad, macrotrends that either validate or modify preconceived theories.[23] What is intriguing is how this blending influences Hirschman's view of why individuals and collectives act the way they do, and whether that, in any way, leads to his bias for hope.

That Hirschman is, first and foremost, an economist is evident. He has written extensively on the behavior of firms and the functioning of national economies; and the conceptual categories he has chosen to explain these fall squarely within the disciplinary boundary of economics. He even relied on economistic categories—as can be seen in his use of the term "consumers"—to explain social phenomena that at first glance do not appear to be driven by economic logic. For example, his account of why social preferences swing between preoccupation with private interests and passion for public causes relies heavily on the notion of consumer preferences, as if political choices could be reduced to the same level as buying and selling goods and services. To a large extent, this use of conceptual categories familiar to economists can be explained by Hirschman's desire to communicate with other economists. But Hirschman is also an economist at heart, in that his "natural" inclination is to explain any social phenomenon by drawing an analogy with the functioning of the market.

At the same time, in explaining individual and collective behavior Hirschman has never been restricted by the traditional economist's view of social reality. He is not obsessed, as many economists are, by the need to change the status quo so it may move closer to the ideal state of a perfectly competitive market, whether in the case of capital, labor, or commodities. Hirschman rarely writes about either "market imperfections" or "market distortions" and how such problems can be rectified. On the contrary, if one were to adopt his approach, one would probably search for the unexpected benefits such problems may yield. Like most anthropologists who search for hidden rationalities in individual and group behavior that, on the surface, may appear to be odd, Hirschman also searches for unexposed social logic not anticipated by orthodox economists.[24] This curiosity about why individuals and institutions may not act in expected ways demonstrates Hirschman's misgivings about the explanatory power of orthodox economics, which reduces all human behavior to market-based calculations. This is not to say that Hirschman does not believe in the notion of "market"; rather, he skillfully moves beyond the traditional definition, modifying it to incorporate the influence of institutions in the way market actors operate.

This ability to transcend orthodox economic logic in explaining social phenomena is in part due to Hirschman's affinity for microlevel interactions between individuals and institutions, which he observes with an anthropological eye. It is an eye guided not by normative principles of what the world should look like—as is common among economists and planners who prescribe the modernization theories—but by an understanding and appreciation of the way the world is. As Hirschman recognizes, embedded in that world are numerous surprises, paradoxes, and ironies that usually escape the ordinary eye. In articulating these surprises and paradoxes, however, Hirschman does not urge development planners to abandon their normative vision; instead, he suggests that planners ground their normative vision in the existing world and learn from its hidden rationalities. In this way, Hirschman believes, planners may gain the confidence to act in a strategic and selective way and not be disillusioned by the enormity of developmental problems.

Epilogue

The ability to strike a middle ground between apparently opposing worldviews—between that of an economist and that of an anthropologist, between that of a here-and-now pragmatist and that of a historicist, between that of a protagonist of change and that of one curious about the status quo, and between that of a statist of the European variety and that of a libertarian North American—is what provides the intellectual sophistication to Hirschman's bias of hope. It would be a pity if this unique hopefulness about the developmental process was appreciated by only a few scholars. As Hirschman noted himself, many planners and economists in Latin America are afflicted with a deep sense of pessimism, a sense that they can never succeed in any of their efforts to foster social change.[25] Hirschman's writings are not unfamiliar to this group.[26] Many of them are grateful for Hirschman's nuggets of hopeful evidence in the face of their largely pessimistic assessment of their own actions. They are also aware that unlike most U.S. advisers to Latin America in the 1950s, Hirschman did not impose his "theory" of development on them; instead, he constantly searched for the rationale implicit in their action, however disorganized it appeared on the surface.

Still, one can now barely see the imprint of Hirschman's advice on the Latin America countries. This has been particularly true since the middle of the 1970s, when developing countries in general, and Latin American countries in particular, began to move away from "import-substitution" to "export-promotion" policies. Much of the complexity of Hirschman's approach to developmental issues was lost in this shift. As one country after another joined the bandwagon of export promotion in shaping their economic policy, Hirschman, along with other development economists, was not simply ignored, but was loudly blamed for all the economic problems facing these countries.

It seems, however, that the times are changing again. With the general slowing down of the global economy and the corresponding decline of the ideology dominant during much of the economic boom of the 1980s, the complexity of Hirschman's approach may again appeal to policymakers who do not see the world in black-and-white terms. Fortunately, the collapse of the former Soviet Union and the Eastern bloc countries has created a political climate in which policymakers in the developing world can pick and choose a mix of economic strategies without being branded communist sympathizers. In other words, both the political and economic conditions in the world now seem right for a Hirschmanesque approach to developmental issues. In fact, I can go one step further and argue that the complexity of Hirschman's intellectual approach is appropriate not only for the developing countries but also for the developed countries. The latter can benefit as much as the former from Hirschman's creative synthesis of apparently opposing worldviews. And if that fosters a hopeful view of social change in developed countries currently struggling for a new wave of development in the face of deindustrialization, it will benefit the developing countries as well.

Part III
Restructuring Institutions, Policies, and Programs

Eight

Intraocular Lenses, Blindness Control, and the Hiding Hand

Elliot Marseille

"WANT to play some Ping-Pong?" Larry asked.
"Sure," I said.

We walked into the game room. Table, net, two paddles, but no Ping-Pong ball. We looked around, opened a cabinet or two, still no ball.

Larry said, "Nicole wants you to be her operations officer, right? Let me know when you've found a Ping-Pong ball. I'm ready to play any time tonight."

Was he serious? It was nine o'clock and we were a three-hour drive from Vancouver. If there were stores with Ping-Pong balls any closer than that, they were surely closed.

It was the 1982 board meeting of the Seva Foundation. We were at a small retreat center in the lush woods of the British Colombian coast. Seva had invited me to the three-day meeting because it appeared that I was going to be working with board member and key program manager Nicole Grasset on Seva's major project, the Nepal blindness program. They wanted to get to know me better, and they wanted me to get a better sense of what Seva was, and what Seva valued. At the moment it appeared that what Seva valued was Ping-Pong balls.

I walked through the halls of the center, opening closets, looking through shelves of drawers. This was obviously futile. Well, no problem. I could simply pretend to have taken Larry's request as the joke any reasonable person would have assumed it to be. Besides, who was he to subject me to such a humiliating test? As these thoughts drifted by, I stopped everyone I met and explained that I badly needed a Ping-Pong ball and that if anyone knew where one was to be found, they should please tell me. Meanwhile, I kept looking. Finally, someone said, "Here you go," handed me a ball, then turned and walked away. Reflecting on this incident later, I could not recall who my benefactor had been, much less where he had found the Ping-Pong ball. Nonchalant as could be, I walked over to Larry and said, "Ready to play if you are."

He dropped one stitch, but only one. "Rally for serve."

Eye Camp in Pondicherry

If you were to meet someone at an unspecified location in Pisa, you would naturally choose the Leaning Tower. It was midnight when we finally reached Pondicherry. I directed our taxi to the Samadhi at the Sri Aurobindo Ashram not because I had much hope of meeting Dr. Govind Venkataswamy there, but because it was the center of town and because we could think of nowhere else to go. But we were in luck. No sooner had the driver shut off his engine than we spotted a Land Rover on the other side of the street bearing the logo of the Aravind Eye Hospital. A white-haired old man climbed out and started across the dimly lit street in our direction. We got out of our taxi to meet him. "Dr. Venkataswamy?" I asked tentatively.

"Yes, yes. How was your trip, Mr. Elliot?" No surprise. It was perfectly natural to him that we had come to this spot.

We made plans in short order. My traveling companions and friends Dick Litwin, an ophthalmologist in private practice in Berkeley, his wife Judith, and I were to stay at the Hotel Europa ($7 a room) that night. We were to meet Dr. Venkataswamy and the rest of the surgical team for the eye camp's opening ceremony the next morning at 7:00.

India had few plans to bring hospital-based eye care to its million villages. The social and geographic distances are too great and the costs too high. The Indians have instead pioneered simple, low-cost cataract surgery at massive eye camps held throughout the subcontinent. At these two-week camps, charitable groups sponsor hundreds of operations and thousands of outpatient examinations. Most of the roughly 1.2 million cataract operations performed each year in India are carried out at such eye camps.[1] Care is provided free or at nominal cost.

Cataract is a gradual opacification of the eye's crystalline lens. Over the course of years, it causes a loss of vision and eventual blindness. Its etiology is not well understood, though old age is by far the greatest single risk factor. Cataract is the major cause of blindness worldwide. The backlog of operable cataract blindness is estimated at 14 million to 17 million cases in the developing world alone.[2] Perhaps one-third of these people live in the Indian subcontinent, where the annual incidence is about 3.8 million cases.[3] At the current level of surgery (1.2 million cases a year), this means that the backlog of unoperated cases in India is actually increasing. Global demographic trends make for an Alice in Wonderland phenomenon. You have to run faster and faster just to stay in the same place: the aging of the population means that without major new commitments to blindness control, cataract rates will rise in the foreseeable future.

Dick Litwin had come to India bearing gifts for Dr. Venkataswamy. Chief among them was a small supply of intraocular lenses (IOLs). IOLs are plastic lenses that are inserted into the eye to replace the natural lens that is removed during cataract surgery. Many IOL designs had been tried in the United States since the mid-1970s, with significant differences in complication rates and final quality of vision. By 1981, when we departed for India and Nepal in search of adventure and a chance to do some good, IOLs had been approved by the U.S. Food and Drug Administration as an "experimental device." They were routinely implanted in cataract operations in the United States. The great advantage of lens implantation over ordinary cataract surgery is that the patient gains nearly perfect vision without glasses (except, perhaps, ordinary reading glasses). In most of the world, cataract patients receive no IOLs and must wear thick glasses to compensate for the lost focusing power of the natural lens.

Dr. Venkataswamy had had one previous experience with IOLs brought by another American ophthalmologist. These had been of a different design—anterior chamber lenses that sit in an area of the eye forward from the site of the natural lens. The results had been poor, and the Aravind staff had not been moved to experiment further. Dick's lenses were designed for posterior chamber implantation. These are attached to the same anatomical structures that supported the natural lens, and the staff was curious to see if these worked any better. Dr. Venkataswamy began cautiously. He scheduled just one operation on that first morning of the eye camp, for Dick to demonstrate his IOL.

The patient was a completely blind former carpenter named Krishna.

The camp at Pondicherry had been arranged by Guru Sai Baba's social action group. (Sai Baba is famous in the West for his Afro hair and his ability to materialize objects in his hand, though the latter is subject to dispute. Some say that instead of actually manifesting things from nothing, he merely teletransports them from a nearby warehouse.) Sai Baba's devotees had carried out the extensive publicity and outreach for the camp, arranged for an auditorium to be used as a temporary hospital, and tended to the feeding and postoperative care of the patients. They also furnished a generator to supply electricity to the camp. This was important, since India's regular power grid is unreliable. You could be sure that the power would go out at least once in the middle of surgery, plunging the operating theater into total darkness.

The auditorium stage had been cordoned into a surgical area with six operating stations. Each station had two tables. On one, a surgeon from the Aravind Eye Hospital was conducting an operation. On the other, paramedical ophthalmic assistants were preparing the next patient for surgery—placing a sterile green sheet over the face (leaving only the eye uncovered), administering the xylocaine local anesthetic, retracting the eyelids, and inserting the first suture through the upper portion of the sclera (the white of the eye), to hold it still during the procedure. When the surgeon had extracted the cataract and sutured the wound, the patient was bandaged by assistants and removed to the recovery, while the surgeon moved to the second table and began operating on the patient just prepared by the ophthalmic assistants. They, in turn, helped the next patient onto the first table and began the preparation routine.

The rest of the hall was devoted to open ward space—scores of low cots in straight rows on the floor (women on the left side, men on the right), with a wide aisle down the middle. After surgery, each patient was helped to a cot by a female volunteer resplendent in pink sari. Viewed from the stage, the nurses looked like bright butterflies as they clustered first around one cot, then another. There were hundreds of people in the room, yet the auditorium was silent. Everyone moved with a slow, dignified sense of purpose: the patients, the volunteers, the ophthalmologists. I felt I was witnessing the enactment of an ancient drama, the surgeon and ophthalmic assistants melding into one multiarmed Hindu God of Healing.

As expected, the municipal power did go out. The operating room switched over to the generator. Then the generator failed too. The medical teams said nothing. Flashlights appeared, and the operations continued. I went outside to see what had happened to the generator. The volunteers were hard at work trying to get it started but seemed at a loss. I asked what had caused the breakdown.

"It was the consciousness of guru Baba-ji passing near the generator."

I watched Dr. Venkataswamy do a case. It was not until I saw his hands at work that I realized how profoundly arthritic they were. It was as if each finger had a mind of its own, determined to point in a different direction, bent and stiff. So crippled were those hands that Dr. Venkataswamy had to have surgical instruments specially designed for them, yet he has done over 100,000 cataract operations personally. He began his career in public health ophthalmology after his retirement from the government health service in 1978. Starting by converting a small private house into a six-bed eye hospital, he now heads the largest eye hospital complex in the world. The main hospital in Madurai has 925 beds, 325 for paying patients, 600 for free care. There are an additional 400 beds in the satellite hospital at Tirunevelli and 100 at Theni. In 1992, Aravind performed 61,000 sight-restoring operations. Sixty-one percent of these are carried out free of charge; the remaining 39 percent are paid for by patients who stay in private or semiprivate wards. Their fees subsidize the free care.

When asked what he needs most for the expansion of his organization, Dr. Venkataswamy almost invariably starts talking about McDonald's. "McDonald's is able to provide good, inexpensive food for the ordinary man in any city, isn't it? You see, they are using modern management to do everything very inexpensively, very efficiently, so you get the same quality whether it is a McDonald's in San Francisco or a McDonald's in Singapore or wherever it may be. If the ordinary man, even the poor man, can afford to buy a hamburger, why can't we do this one for clean water, for basic medicine, for eye care?" Dr. Venkataswamy is known to many as "Dr. V" and to his friends as "Dr. McV."

For Dr. V, blindness presents two kinds of problems, spiritual and managerial. His guru, Sri Aurobindo, taught that our highest purpose is the integration of the spiritual, what he called the "supermental," with the unconscious material world. This is the practice of Integral Yoga (Sanskrit for "union"): the intentional work of infusing the material world with supermental essence. Selfless service, another name for this practice, is the core teaching of the *Bhagavad Gita*. Do your work impeccably but with no attachment to its fruit; cultivate the tree and the fruit takes care of itself. It is Dr. Venkataswamy at an eye camp: the frightened mother holds her infant up to be examined, incurably blind from xerophthalmia when a little vitamin A, a few green vegetables, would have saved his sight. Now it is too late. Inhale, let the suffering in. No protection behind the persona of medical expertise. He turns to tell her softly there is nothing to be done for her baby. He has had this exchange so many times. Exhale, let it go. Let it be complete. No attachment means no attachment to the drama of suffering and pain, either. There is work to be done. What is next?

What is next is solving the managerial problem. For Dr. V, Integral Yoga means developing a system to provide affordable eye care and then finding a way to replicate it. He knows that this requires a large organization and cannot depend on his personal magnetism. But he also knows that the job of controlling blindness will take a dedication exceeding that of the average Indian Health Ministry ophthalmologist. Joining replicable organizational structure with the spirit of service: that is arduous yoga.

Unless there is a complication at surgery, the convalescent cataract patient requires little care. In the United States, cataract surgery is usually done on an outpatient basis. In the eye camp, patients are kept for five or ten days. This is to make sure that any infections or other complications can be treated immediately. Once they go home, they are usually lost to follow-up.

On the second day of the Pondicherry eye camp, Dick joined the Aravind surgeons for the first examination of the operated patients. One by one they entered a small examination room equipped with a slit lamp. The eye patches were removed, and the patient could see for the first time in many years. This moment is less dramatic than one might imagine. I expected to see joy and excitement in that room and was disappointed that these patients seemed so unmoved by the miracle of modern eye surgery. I chalked it up to the legendary equanimity of the Indian soul. I learned later that their nonchalance was perhaps not so philosophical: their new vision was nothing to be very excited about.

This is in part because the eye needs about two weeks to recover fully from the trauma of surgery and even longer for the new vision to reach its full acuity. But part of the problem inheres in the particular surgical procedure they had received. In traditional intracapsular cataract extraction, no IOL is implanted, and the natural lens is removed along with the entire capsular sack that ordinarily holds the lens in place. To compensate for the loss of the lens, the patient must wear heavy glasses that look like the bottoms of Coke bottles set in thick plastic frames. These *aphakic* (lensless) patients are far from blind but a long way from having normal vision. Their glasses enlarge images by one third. Patients must look directly through the center of the glasses to avoid disorienting distortion. In practice, they are afflicted by varying degrees of fish-eye effects, astigmatism, and farsightedness. One tell-tale sign of the *aphake* is the way he crosses a threshold. He steps high into empty space before bringing his foot down onto the step. Data from Nepal suggest that more than half of the *aphakes* are functionally blind, primarily because they have lost or broken their cataract spectacles.[4]

In extracapsular surgery, the cataractous lens is removed, but part of the capsular sac is left in place. This is the scaffolding that supports the implanted artificial lens. With this procedure, the patient typically gets a visual acuity approaching 20/20 and with far fewer secondary distortions. Compared with the intracapsular procedure, the functional outcome is therefore even better than the improved visual acuity alone would suggest.

Dick's patient, the carpenter Krishna, came in for his exam. An ophthalmic assistant removed the gauze patch from his eye. Krishna took one look at Dick, fell to his knees, and bowed his head to the ground, his hands held palm to palm high above his forehead in the honorific *Namascar* gesture. "*Bhagwan, Bhagwan*" (God, God), he repeated. Dick, both moved and embarrassed, tried to raise Krishna to his feet, but he was not to be deflected from his devotion. Two ophthalmic assistants, one under each shoulder, finally raised him to the wooden chair facing the slit lamp. Dick directed a plane of light through the pupil. Clear cornea, deep anterior chamber, unobstructed visual axis, and no signs of infection. The plastic lens glinted from the center of his eye. The operation was a success.

Dr. V saw the implications of IOLs immediately. The social and economic value for the blind man's family were enormous, for it meant that Krishna could go back to work as a carpenter. Now here was something worth franchising!

Blindness Control in Nepal

From South India, we flew to Nepal to meet Nicole Grasset, World Health Organization (WHO) program manager for the Nepal Blindness Program and, like Dr. V, a member of the Seva Foundation board. We met in her office overlooking the smoky bus stop at Hanuman Gate. The sun was fading and the 22,000-foot peaks of the Ganesh Himals glowed orange against the sky. As I listened to Nicole speak that first evening, it seemed to me that for the second time this trip I was in the presence of someone truly single-minded in purpose. Nicole spoke at length about her five-year plan for a 90 percent reduction of avoidable blindness in Nepal. She spoke of the insupportable contrast between the resources that are brought to bear to save someone in an emergency in the West and the meager efforts to stop the emergency of impending blindness that so many face in the developing world. She felt that nothing less than a comprehensive, nationwide program was needed both to help the blind of Nepal and to show the world what could be done in a five-year period. For if it could be done in Nepal, it could be done anywhere.

Nepal has a population of about 18 million (according to 1990 estimates) and ranks near the bottom on every important demographic and economic indicator: it has a high rate of population growth, 2.5 percent a year; per capita income is $170; the mortality rate of children under the age of five is 183 per 1,000 for females and 175 for males; the adult literacy rate is about 20 percent; life expectancy at birth is fifty-two years; and 95 percent of the population lives in rural areas.[5]

Lovely, accursed Nepal: one of the ten poorest countries in the world, with an infrastructure to match; a mosaic of cultures, languages, and tribal, religious, and ethnic groups, divided by formidable terrain and ruled by a divine Hindu monarch who presided over an officialdom that could teach the Byzantines a thing or two about bureaucracy. It was not fair. The Nepalese are custodians of an exquisite culture. They are ingenious and hard working and receptive to innovation. Why do so many things go so badly there?

Nicole had helped direct the smallpox eradication for WHO for South Asia. Through the sheer power of her will, she had played an important role in ensuring that sufficient resources were available for the eventual eradication of smallpox from the region. This occurred at a time when it was widely believed to be impossible to immunize India's 1 million villages. Just as it appeared that a victory over smallpox was within reach, malaria incidence began to rise. Certain government officials sought a balanced approach to the control of both diseases and planned to shift key Indian personnel out of the smallpox program and into the malaria program. Nicole opposed this seemingly reasonable policy because she saw that there was a historic opportunity to finally eradicate one of the world's greatest killers. She argued that WHO's limited resources were sufficient to eliminate smallpox if the money was used in the most effective possible manner. She and her staff implemented a surveillance system that allowed them to concentrate immunization activities in the areas of actual smallpox outbreak. This strategy isolated and eliminated the disease wherever it appeared and obviated the need for a universal vaccine program. It worked and helped produce one of the greatest public health successes of all time.

Nicole had been moved by the plight of the many blind people she encountered during her years in India and resolved that after the smallpox effort she would try to do something about it. She seized her opportunity in 1978 when WHO sponsored a conference in Delhi on blindness control in Southeast Asia. Nicole presented some thoughts on what India might do to reduce its backlog of untreated cataract blind, but the Indian ophthalmic leadership did not seem very receptive to her suggestions. During a break, Nicole had coffee with Dr. Ram Prasad Pokhrel, another conference participant and Nepal's premier eye doctor, the royal family's ophthalmologist. Nepal had even less eye care than India, and Dr. Pokhrel explained that the Nepalese government would be very interested in the type of effort Nicole had described at the conference. If she were willing, Dr. Pokhrel would throw his weight behind the establishment of a national eye care program in Nepal.

The Seva Foundation was founded by three overlapping circles of friends: veterans of the smallpox campaign who had worked under Nicole; a group of American devotees of the guru Neem Kairoli Baba (Maharaji), including Ram Dass, also known as Richard Alpert, former colleague of Timothy Leary at Harvard; and members of the Hog Farm commune in Berkeley, of which Wavy Gravy, most famously master of ceremonies at Woodstock, is chief clown. ("A clown," Wavy likes to say, "is a poet who is also an orangutan.") At the juncture of these three circles stood Dr. Larry Brilliant.

Soon after obtaining his medical degree, Larry got on the Hog Farm bus when it left for India and Nepal. He and his wife, Girija (then Elaine), got off at Maharaji's ashram in Nainital, in north India. Maharaji told his devotees to feed people and serve them. When Larry asked what he should do next with his life, Maharaji said that smallpox would be eradicated and that he would be part of the effort. He should take a bus to Delhi and ask to work with WHO. Larry, bearded and beaded and with shoulder-length hair, presented himself to the staid officials at WHO regional headquarters and said that his guru had sent him to work on the smallpox program. Neem Kairoli just laughed when he returned to the ashram empty-handed and said, "Don't worry. Try again next week." And the next week. Eventually he got a meeting with Nicole. When she met Larry, she saw not a hippie, but a new member of the smallpox eradication team.

Shortly after Nicole's conference with Dr. Pokhrel in Delhi, Larry Brilliant convened a group of friends for the founding meeting of the Seva Foundation. They were interested in forming an organization that could be the vehicle for inspired service that had been their shared experience in the smallpox program, with Neem Kairoli Baba and elsewhere. Seva was not conceived as an eye care organization and never saw itself as one, even after eye programs came to constitute 80 percent of its program budget. The founding members were clear about their guiding purpose and would allow program content to reveal itself in time. It was to be a research and development initiative for new modes of conscious service. As a first effort, Seva proposed to support the blindness program in Nepal. Blindness? Nepal? Why? Why not? Nicole was committed to it, and, for the time being, they did not need to know much more.

Seva brought an epidemiological and public health orientation to the planning of the Nepal blindness program. In 1980 a national survey of blindness was carried out under the direction of Larry Brilliant and Seva and with Dutch financial support channeled through WHO.[6] This was the first comprehensive national blindness survey ever carried out in the developing world. It showed that 0.8 percent of the population of Nepal was blind and that 80 percent of this blindness was avoidable. The survey also indicated that certain diseases are endemic to certain areas. Xerophthalmia, a blinding complication of vitamin A deficiency, is concentrated in the eastern *terai* (plains), whereas trachoma, a chronic infection of the eye lid (also potentially blinding), is found primarily in the western *terai*. By far the major cause of blindness, about two-thirds, is cataracts.[7]

Cataract cannot be prevented and can be cured only through relatively expensive surgery requiring highly trained ophthalmologists. It does not lend itself to a program based on health education or the training of community health workers. This reality required a shift in orientation for Seva, which would have preferred to be involved in a public health approach to blindness prevention based on education and village-level empowerment. Such an approach would have been more in keeping with Seva's organizational culture, which has its roots in 1960s radicalism and the psychedelic counterculture. Seva is skeptical about the hierarchies of established medicine and the wealth and power they represent. (From his first day as a medical student, Larry Brilliant began organizing his fellow students to strike against the oppressive internship system with its long hours, low wages, and inhuman power structure.) Seva is also committed to a public health orientation. Fundamental to that point of view is that medicine is usually only a small contributor to health status. The structural conditions of society, environmental factors, and personal health practices make far greater contributions to health than access to medical care per se.

Cataract is an exception to this principle. While progress has been made in understanding its etiology, there is still no consensus regarding effective preventive measures. This was even more the case ten years ago when Seva was shaping its role in the Nepal blindness program. Cataract requires surgery, which implies medical expertise, technology, and relatively high costs per case. Prevention, health education, and other nonmedical interventions were more important for the other major blinding diseases. But for cataract, health education is limited to informing people that the disease is curable and motivating them to come forward for surgery.

Seva was also committed to the idea of replication. Models developed in Nepal could be implemented in India or elsewhere in the future. At the same time, elements of the exemplary program being carried out by Dr. V at the Aravind Eye Hospital might help inform the work being carried out in Nepal.

All three elements of Seva's strategy—epidemiological data, an intensive program designed to drastically reduce the backlog of untreated blind within a few years, and the hope of replication—were very helpful in winning support from the donor community. The epidemiological data meant that donors were in the rare position of knowing the dimensions of the problem at the outset. There were benchmarks for measuring progress and some assurance that resources would be deployed efficiently. Trachoma screening would be concentrated in the far west, xerophthalmia in the east, and cataract everywhere, but particularly in the central *terai*. The idea of an intensive assault on blindness held out the prospect of accountability, success within a limited time, and protection against being drawn into open-ended commitments. And replication meant that program costs need not be justified by the Nepal program alone, because its benefits would not be confined there. Donors could see their contributions as part of a pioneering effort in a global blindness control campaign.

But, as important as it was in winning donor support and mobilizing other resources, belief in an intensive five-year program with direct transferability to other countries suggested an underestimation of the real difficulty of the enterprise. This belief was based in part on the idea that some of the lessons of the smallpox program could be applied directly to blindness control. Some of this thinking was sound. Surveillance and the application of epidemiological data to program design and implementation really *did* make for a more cost-efficient program. To cite one example among many, when caseloads at the eye centers were low, we knew that this could not be due to a low prevalence of eye disease. It had to be the result of ignorance or the inability of patients to reach the centers. This led to an expansion of outreach and field-based services.

As I learned more about the problems of blindness control and what it would take to build an effective eye care program, the idea of a rapid and dramatic reduction in the prevalence of blindness seemed less and less useful as a guiding principle. Strictly speaking of course, everyone understood that, unlike smallpox, blindness cannot be eradicated. Each year brings a crop of new cataract cases to be treated; and a small minority of the blind might be unwilling to submit to surgery. The goal was therefore not eradication per se, but elimination of 90 percent of the avoidable blindness. But there are other, more profound differences between the control of blindness and smallpox eradication. In the smallpox program the goal was, for one moment, to outmaneuver the virus and surround it. It did not matter what it took to achieve this configuration, and it need not persist in time. Transformation of the health sector was not required. But effective blindness control meant the painstaking development of a technical and managerial structure capable of delivering eye services year after year. It is a different type of problem altogether.

Nicole is impatient, and impatience is one of her virtues. During the fighting in Lebanon, she coordinated a program for the International Red Cross to furnish prosthetic limbs to war-maimed children and adults. In Biafra she braved the gunfire of Nigerian national troops to get vaccine to the vulnerable population. She brought the same sense of urgency to blindness control. Seva's original strategy for Nepal had called for major participation by expatriate ophthalmologists so that the backlog of unoperated cataract cases could be eliminated in just five years. Concurrently, new Nepalese ophthalmologists and ophthalmic assistants would be trained and deployed to handle each year's new cases.

The prospect of rapid reduction of the blindness backlog in a developing country in just five years had captured the imagination of Western donors and had helped raise the program's initial funding. It had served a useful purpose even though Seva spoke less and less about eliminating 90 percent of the backlog of blindness as time went on. This was not because things went badly. On the contrary, surgical volume increased substantially every year, new eye centers opened in formerly unserved areas, and new ophthalmic personnel were trained. The eradication metaphor was abandoned as the difficulties of that goal were understood better over time. For example, during the program's early years, a major obstacle to more surgical volume was a lack of ophthalmic personnel. The solution was to train more people, and the program did so. Over time, however, it became clear that the real challenge was to get reasonable levels of productivity from the ophthalmologists that did exist. This turns out to be a far thornier problem that was not fully anticipated at the program's inception and still has not been fully resolved. It arises from perverse incentives faced by doctors within the Ministry of Health, and these in turn stem from a deeply ingrained administrative culture that puts initiative and productivity low on the list of criteria for promotions and other rewards.

This is not a problem that fits naturally within the conceptual framework of a five-year assault on the blindness backlog.

In 1989, the year I left Nepal, the program carried out about 22,000 cataract operations, up from about 300 in 1982. We estimated that this might be roughly equal to the annual incidence.[8] In other words, the program was about at the break-even point but had not begun to reduce the size of the unoperated cataract backlog. Because of the ever-increasing incidence, due to the expansion and aging of the population, the surgical caseload will have to continue growing by thousands per year just to contain the numbers of blind at their current level.

Replication had a similar fate. Originally, it had appeared that WHO would play a major role in the Nepal blindness program. It could bring an administrative coherence to the nationwide effort, so that when people talked about replicating the Nepal program, they could refer to a single identifiable entity. In fact, WHO's role diminished over time. Instead of becoming a coherent national program with uniform policies and practices, it was balkanized into several zonal programs, each run by a foreign nongovernmental organization (NGO), with only the broadest central direction from Dr. Pokhrel's organization in Kathmandu. There were profound differences between these NGOs. Some, like Seva (and to a lesser extent the Swiss Red Cross and Norwegian Church Aid), emphasized field activities and village-level screening for eye disease, whereas the German Christoffel Blinden Mission confined its activities to hospital-based care. Other differences lay in the choice of surgical technique, the level of technology, duties and remuneration of the paramedical ophthalmic assistants, the role of expatriate ophthalmologists with respect to their Nepalese counterparts, and the interpretations and levels of commitment to fostering Nepalese self-reliance in eye care. As a result, there was no *one* Nepal blindness program to replicate. The program demonstrated several models, each with its own strengths and weaknesses, and each perhaps appropriate to a different situation or country.

Or did it? My experience with the Nepal program has made me wary of the model of models.

The Hiding Hand in Nepal

Economist Albert Hirschman's doctrine of the "hiding hand" is pertinent here. The hiding hand has subtle and far-reaching implications for the development enterprise, yet the basic idea is simple: in undertaking new programs, people tend to underestimate the difficulties to be overcome, but also underestimate their ability to overcome them when they appear. The hiding hand obscures both. For the most part, this is a good thing. If the problems were fully appreciated at the outset, people would never begin, since they would be even less capable of visualizing conceivable remedies. (But it does lead to the strange conclusion that the optimal amount of ignorance at the start of a new undertaking is some level greater than zero.)

The hiding hand employs a number of different strategies for veiling difficulties. One is to disguise the risky and innovative aspects of a project in the idea that success merely requires the application of a model previously shown to be effective in a different but parallel situation. Blindness control in Nepal is almost nothing like smallpox eradication in South Asia. Yet, had Seva not believed that many of the lessons of the smallpox program could be applied in Nepal, and had donors not found the comparison plausible, they might well have turned their backs on the Nepal program. In that case the other aspect of the hiding hand would have had no chance to operate—to inspire creative, new solutions to unfamiliar problems.

It simply was not known what type of program would work best in Nepal. Far from being a process of replicating a known formula for success, the Nepal blindness program was actually "a voyage of technological and administrative discovery"—much closer, in fact, to a process of research and development.[9] While Seva decried the declining role of a strong, centralizing WHO presence, the withdrawal of WHO inadvertently allowed the program to develop along lines more appropriate to research and development. Hirschman describes three desirable features of such a process:[10]

—Avoid early, rigid specification of performance characteristics. There may be many routes to success, not all of which can be foreseen at the outset.

—During the early stages of program development there also should be no firm stipulation of the way in which different program elements may be fitted together and accommodated to each other. That can come later, after each team (each NGO in our case), has had sufficient opportunity to innovate.

—It is unwise to determine in advance which program design is likely to be best. Important virtues and important problems of each design cannot be anticipated. It may be cheaper to develop a number of prototypes in order to let these virtues and problems reveal themselves before committing to any one.

The Nepal program came to fit these prescriptions exactly, though not by original design or intention. After the withdrawal of WHO, the NGOs established semiautonomous programs in their respective zones. Officially, they were under the direction of Dr. Pokhrel and the government, but they operated quite independently, in part because of their independent funding bases and their strong and distinctive organizational cultures and philosophies, and equally because of Dr. Pokhrel's management style and instinctive understanding of the workings of the hiding hand. The result was better than what would have come out of a rigidly specified, national program tightly controlled by WHO. IOLs would have had great difficulty getting approval from a WHO regime. Supplies and equipment would have been more standardized across all eye centers, and there would have been less technical innovation in general. Nepalese philanthropists, having less sense of involvement in the affairs of their own community, would have been less likely to donate land for hospital construction. Fewer volunteer ophthalmologists would have participated. There would have been less experimentation with incentive structures, staffing patterns, health education and outreach programs, and the physical design of eye hospitals. The Nepal program was the first comprehensive blindness prevention and control program carried out on a national scale in the developing world. Engaged as we were in research and development, it was appropriate not to be confined to a single model.

Kathmandu. Shangri-La. The most exotic city in the world. The city with more temples than people and more dogs than temples. I arrived in November 1982 as a Seva-sponsored semivolunteer. My job was to provide administrative support to Nicole while we awaited WHO funding for the post of operations officer for which Nicole had nominated me. Seva originally agreed to support me for three months. When the WHO funding was not approved during this period, they extended funding for another three months. When that term expired, it was clear that the WHO money would never materialize, and Seva gave me my first one-year contract.

By mid-1983, the program was in crisis. It had become obvious that

WHO was doing little to find new funding for the program in the field and was even threatening to cut support for headquarters in Kathmandu. With weak support from her own organization, Nicole realized that she could no longer function at the level of effectiveness she demanded of herself. She gave six months' notice and resigned in December of 1983. With the announcement of Nicole's departure, Seva found itself at a crossroads.

During its early years, Seva (Sanskrit for "service") was a foundation in name only, since there was no endowment. Its budget was raised from a mailing list of Ram Dass fans, from Ram Dass's lectures, from a few wealthy donors, and from benefit concerts by Wavy Gravy's rock 'n' roll friends, including Bonnie Raitt and the Grateful Dead. It took pride in maintaining low cash reserves, trusting that if it ran good projects money to finance them would turn up. In the meantime Seva's purpose was to serve people, not to be excessively concerned with organizational survival. It saw itself as a catalytic agent for public health. Its job was to raise seed money, to inspire, and to furnish the critical resources and expertise that larger, more bureaucratic agencies sometimes could not provide, or could not provide in time to make a difference. Seva's board included a large complement of effective people with unusually high ethical and professional standards: Dr. V, Nicole, Ram Dass, Larry, Wavy, and others. They knew what relatively small amounts of money could accomplish in the right hands. Part of Seva's credo, therefore, was that "Seva doesn't support projects, it supports people." That is why it was important for my future with Seva that I passed the Ping-Pong test. I passed, first, because I had understood that it really was a serious test, and then because I found the ball by enlisting the support of strangers. Something had been accomplished that was unreasonable, something that could not have been predicted. For Seva often operated in the realm of what Jung called synchronicity—an element of what Hirschman calls "a passion for the possible."[11] It is the fortuitous convergence of preparation, intention, an open mind, and luck. Call it coincidence, but it happens too often to certain people and in certain undertakings to be entirely without explicable agency. Wavy Gravy occasionally remarks, "As I was saying to the mirror this morning, 'It's all done with people.'"

With Nicole's departure, Seva had lost the original impetus for its involvement in the Nepal blindness program. WHO was not going to fund the program at a high level, and it was not clear that new resources from NGOs would be forthcoming now that the program's only internationally recognized leader was gone. The capabilities of her Nepalese counterpart, Dr. Ram Prasad Pokhrel, were not well known to Seva at this point. Just when Seva's previous modus operandi (support for Nicole plus other small but catalytic contributions) was no longer viable, the nationwide program appeared to me in danger of collapse.

During the following year I was assigned to work with Dr. Pokhrel and the new all-Nepalese staff of the program. As the only native English speaker, my main function was to support the flow of paperwork to and from WHO regional headquarters in Delhi. Receipt of money to the program depended on a continuous stream of progress reports, action plans, revised project documents, budget projections, expense statements, and supply requests. All of this effort was needed to ensure the release of funds designated for eye camps, for equipping Nepal's few permanent eye centers, and for the training of a cadre of one hundred ophthalmic assistants.

During this period Dr. Pokhrel was able not only to hold the faltering program together, but also to attract new NGO support from the Swiss, the Germans, the Dutch, the Norwegians and later from Johns Hopkins University and the University of Michigan. Each of these NGOs was responsible for eye care in one or two of Nepal's fourteen administrative zones. In early 1984, Dr. Pokhrel asked Seva to provide eye services for the 2 million people of Lumbini Zone, the birthplace of Lord Buddha. Seva accepted, but only after much agonized soul searching, for taking on Lumbini Zone meant becoming a new kind of organization. Seva would need to build an eye hospital although money for bricks and mortar ran against the grain of its public health ethos. The zonal program would also require a much higher and steadier level of funding than would ever have been necessary in Seva's "catalytic" incarnation.

Starting in 1984, I became Seva's country representative for the Nepal blindness program. This included the comprehensive eye program in Lumbini Zone and support for various national blindness control activities. I worked closely with Dr. Pokhrel's new national eye care organization, Nepal Netra Jyoti Sangh.

Master of the Hiding Hand: Management by Saying "Yes"

A Nepali attending a convention in Mexico City button-holed one of the Mexican participants and said, "I keep hearing this word *Mañana. Mañana* this, *Mañana* that. What does it mean?" The Mexican replied, "*Mañana* can mean many things. If you look in a dictionary, it says 'tomorrow,' but it can also mean 'in a few days,' or 'in a few weeks.' It can even mean 'never, it won't happen at all.'" "I see," said the Nepali. "We have a similar expression in Nepalese, but without the sense of urgency."

Dr. Pokhrel's face is as round and impassive as those of the bronze images of the Malla kings presiding over every ancient Durbar (palace) Square in Kathmandu Valley. He keeps his own counsel. He never engages in direct conflict. In a planning meeting he might say, "The Landcruiser will leave for Narayanghat on Friday. Dr. Adhikari can begin operating Saturday morning." "But Dr. Pokhrel," someone says, "the vehicle isn't scheduled to be back in Kathmandu before Friday night." Without missing a beat: "We will just send the Landcruiser to Narayanghat on Saturday." As if there had been no discussion of Friday.

Dr. Pokhrel's existential stance is *yes*. Yes, it can be done. Yes, that is a good idea. And, yes, I will increase your per diem and travel allowance. He does not always deliver on his *yes*, nor does he intend to. (Madness awaits any Westerner who fails to acquire at least some skill in deciphering the many meanings of the Nepalese *yes*.) But *yes* is what has allowed Dr. Pokhrel to survive and flourish in the killingly jealous atmosphere of Nepalese politics. No one feels shut out.

People hoping to make a contribution sometimes come to Nepal with unrealistic ideas of what that might be. Dr. Pokhrel lets them try out their ideas even when he knows that they will prove wasteful and inefficient. He trusts that people will somehow learn the lessons they need to learn and eventually will find a way to do something useful.

Dr. Pokhrel is a master of the hiding hand. Though I have never heard him articulate anything like it, he practices Hirschman's doctrine intuitively. People bring to a project more than the calculus of predictable costs and benefits. To understand this fully and to incorporate it into one's administrative style demands a high degree of tolerance for ambiguity and uncertainty.

For example, a group of volunteers flew into Nepal every year for four years with a team of ophthalmologists, an anesthesiologist, nurses, even their own administrators, just to do several eye camps. They were all busy people and in Nepal for only a few weeks. They therefore expected Dr. Pokhrel to furnish them with vehicles, supplies, ophthalmologists, and ophthalmic assistants according to their schedule and with little regard for the demand for these scarce resources elsewhere in the country. It was overkill. Staging these camps meant the disruption of other eye care activities, so it is not even clear that these camps produced a net reduction in blindness. Most western administrators would not have allowed this to continue, but Dr. Pokhrel kept saying yes. I shook my head at the time: Development tourism, I thought. Just send the Nepalese what this team spends on plane fare to Kathmandu alone, and they would be able to do far more than what is being accomplished with the whole budget for these eye camps. If Dr. Pokhrel had such thoughts, he kept them to himself. The volunteers were happy. They filmed their exploits and showed them on television. This raised more money, and they kept coming back. This group recently inaugurated a major eye hospital and is now providing eye care for an entire zone.

The Nepalese dutifully write their project documents and five-year action plans because they know that the flow of foreign aid depends on it. They often seem surprised when Western development workers seem to expect that they will then seriously attempt to carry out the program as described in the documents. It is a common mistake for Westerners to believe that the Nepalese are cynical or insincere about the planning effort. They are not. They just do not believe that there is much correspondence between the thoughts of a planner working in his office and the way the world actually works. It is two different compartments. I found that the most important elements of the plan do eventually come to pass; it is just not in the way the planners described, and definitely not on the same schedule.

I once had a conversation with Chet Raj Pant that forever altered my understanding of Nepalese time. Dr. Pant was working for Seva as ophthalmologist and program manager for the Lumbini project. We were sitting on the construction site of the planned Seva eye hospital, and he was asking me about the difference between Christianity and Judaism. At one point he inquired whether Christians and Jews believed in hell and heaven. I said, yes, both believe in them, but the Christians emphasize them more.

He then asked if hell was eternal. I said yes, you just get one lifetime to prove yourself, and the consequences last forever. Dr. Pant was silent for a while, and then said, "So that's why you are always in such a hurry." The scales fell from my eyes. Exactly right! That is why we are so driven! In Hinduism, we are all manifestations of the Infinite, pretending to be finite beings, the ultimate hiding hand. Work through your karma and you merge again with Brahman. For most of us, this process of burning karma will take thousands, even millions of lifetimes. What is the difference if it takes one or two more or fewer? Everyone makes it in the end, because, from the viewpoint of the eternal, you have *already* made it. Why would God be in a hurry?

Intraocular Lenses: An Appropriate Technology?

Every eye camp season, several American ophthalmologists come to work with the program on short assignments, usually three to eight weeks. At first they were needed to supplement the few fully qualified Nepalese ophthalmologists in completing each year's ambitious eye camp program. Over time, as more Nepalese ophthalmologists were trained, the volunteers were not needed for the extra surgical capacity, and their role shifted to that of informal trainers. But what could they teach about ordinary cataract or glaucoma surgery? At a good eye camp, a Nepalese surgeon might do 200 operations in ten days' time. A successful American ophthalmologist is happy to do that much surgery in a year. "These guys are good!" was the typical reaction from a new volunteer emerging from the operating theater after a first experience working alongside a Nepalese surgeon. I would smile, say nothing, and think, "Sure, but why do you sound so surprised?"

Some of the techniques the Nepalese used, particularly the older ophthalmologists, were a bit out of date, and the Americans were able to suggest some changes. More sutures to form a watertight wound closure at the end of the cataract operation was one such improvement. But it worked both ways: more than one American ophthalmologist returned to her practice in the states with a technique learned on some hilltop in Nepal. But there was at least one truly important area of new knowledge that the Westerners imparted, extracapsular cataract extraction with IOL implantation. The volunteers could not avoid at least demonstrating it because most of them were not even able to perform the traditional intracapsular procedure. The younger ones had done their training after the IOL revolution; the older ones had learned the new extracapsular technique so long ago that they would not have been confident doing a cataract any other way.

The push from the volunteers was exceeded only by the pull from the Nepalese. They knew that extracapsular surgery, with or without IOLs, is the state of the art for cataract surgery. Normal professional pride would lead them to adopt it. Nepal offers few opportunities for in-service training, and like all educational opportunities, they are highly prized by the Nepalese. Perhaps, too, living in a poor country, the Nepalese are even faster to adopt new technology than they would otherwise be. Nobody wants to be perceived as backward. One day, no one in Kathmandu has heard of fax machines. The next day they are on every second desktop. The same with personal computers, television, VCRs, mountain bikes, Japanese cars, and heavy-metal rock. But there is another simple reason they wanted to learn extracapsular surgery and lens implantation: it is good medicine.

Each Seva volunteer ophthalmologist brought in a small supply of IOLs, no more than one hundred or so, that they were able to beg from the manufacturers. This usually was not hard because the 1980s were a time of rapid innovation in IOL design. Companies were happy to donate last year's lenses and take the tax deduction. By 1984 Seva had launched a major effort to ship donated ophthalmic equipment and supplies to Nepal. This made materials available to the program that were otherwise unaffordable. It also did good things for Seva's books. On the accounts, in-kind donations could be treated like cash. They therefore had a powerful positive effect on Seva's overhead-to-program expenditure ratio. At a book value of about $250 per IOL, a few lenses went a long way, and manufacturers were giving us thousands.

Seva made no formal decision to introduce IOLs and the new surgical techniques they required and, at first, did not think systematically about their consequences for the program. For the American volunteers, and soon for many of the Nepalese as well, anything else was second-rate ophthalmology. Supply seemed to be no problem, so what could be bad? *Plenty*, according to most of the official international ophthalmic community. Their criticisms came down to three arguments:

IOLs are unsafe under Nepalese circumstances. The country lacks appropriate instruments for IOL implantation, particularly high-quality microscopes. Follow-up care is spotty at best, and at the more remote eye camps it just does not happen. You could perpetrate a disaster on someone's eye or on the eyes of scores of villagers in an isolated hill area and never know it. It is bad practice to perform the more delicate, complex surgery required by lens implantation when you have so little ability to monitor the results.

IOLs mean Cadillac care for an affluent minority while the poor do not even get Volkswagens. IOLs encourage a fascination with high-technology procedures centered at the Nepal Eye Hospital and the University Teaching Hospital in Kathmandu. Rural Nepalese ophthalmologists will be made to feel that they are doing second-rate surgery if they are not implanting IOLs. The gravitational pull of Kathmandu, already powerful, will become irresistible. It will become more difficult to motivate ophthalmologists to practice in the areas of high need, which are practically anywhere other than the capital. Such geographic maldistribution of resources has been seen over and over both in the developing world and in the West. The last thing a public health ophthalmology program should do is aggravate this tendency.

IOLs are not an "appropriate technology." Nepal does not have the technological capacity to manufacture IOLs itself. The technology is therefore not sustainable and will serve only to keep the country dependent on foreign aid. This dependence is both physical and psychological. It undermines the Nepalis' confidence in their own abilities and denigrates the appropriate effort to bring cheap, sustainable care to the poor, rural majority of the population. When aid is withdrawn, or when the supply of donated lenses dries up, the Nepalese ophthalmologists will have to revert to ordinary cataract operations. Doctors and patients both will be demoralized. It will set back eye care in Nepal for many years.

We heard these arguments first from our Swiss, Norwegian, and German colleagues in the Nepal blindness program. But as the Nepal program became better known in ophthalmic public health circles, one or more of these arguments were leveled against us by prominent European ophthalmologists, WHO, the National Eye Institute of the National Institutes of Health, and other eye care NGOs.

At first, lenses were used primarily at the better-equipped eye hospitals in Kathmandu itself. During this early period, the second criticism (first-rate care for the affluent only) was heard most frequently. Later, as the technique spread to rural eye hospitals, and finally to the eye camps, this criticism lost some of its salience and we heard the first criticism (safety) more often. The third criticism (inappropriate technology) was a lower-volume refrain audible in the background throughout the controversy.

The second criticism really stung Seva, and Larry Brilliant in particular. It was painfully ironic that his organization should be perceived as technology-infatuated and insensitive to technology's negative potential for the rural poor. That is what *other* organizations did. Seva tried to take Gandhi's injunction seriously: "Think of the poorest man you have ever seen. Ask yourself before you take your next action: Will it help him?"

For my part, I was influenced by the perspective of the American ophthalmologists, and they tended to discount the arguments of the Europeans. IOLs were just being introduced in Europe in the early 1980s, and they were still experimenting with some inferior designs that tended to produce complications. Most of the European ophthalmologists in Nepal did not use extracapsular techniques themselves and had an exaggerated estimation of their difficulties and dangers. They also had an ideological commitment to appropriate technology that sometimes struck me as the "It's good enough for them" school of technology transfer.

They pointed out that the Nepalese passion for IOLs, and for high technology generally, had been engendered by Westerners. The aid and development enterprise had set up a system of incentives that rewarded the Nepalese for adopting Western styles of development. The Nepalese elite—those in a position to take advantage of the high-paying jobs in the development industry; those eligible for the training and fellowship opportunities abroad sponsored by the United Nations and the U.S. Agency for International Development; those able to market their Western training among the privileged classes in Kathmandu—had succumbed to cultural imperialism and were being richly rewarded for it. Their privilege was being purchased to the detriment of the rural poor and at the cost of the economic and social well-being of their country. The alternative was to foster a style of development that was appropriate to the Nepalese context. The appropriate-technology proponents felt that they were an important countervailing voice speaking on behalf of the powerless, low-caste rural majority.

Like pornography, "appropriate" is hard to define, but the leaders of the European blindness NGOs in Nepal knew it when they saw it. It seemed to mean cheap, easy to maintain, and possible to build from indigenous materials and expertise. By these criteria, satellite-linked telecommunications, motor vehicles, and aircraft are "inappropriate," though they are essential to the economy of a resource-poor, land-locked country, where tourism and carpet manufacture are major sources of foreign exchange and employment.

Since Nepalese technology choices stemmed from false consciousness inculcated by the West, the correct type of technology had to be demonstrated to them. Certainly no impetus for appropriate technology originated with the Nepalese. It is just as much a Western idea as high technology. In practice, it sometimes simply meant second-rate tools. For example, a European surgeon designed a simple, low-cost microscope that could be built and maintained in Nepal (though the optics had to be imported). It was better than loupes, but it was clumsy, could not easily be transported to eye camps, and the optics and illumination were poor. It never caught on with the Nepalese. For about $1,200, a portable, versatile Japanese scope could be ordered with good optics and coaxial illumination. Was this an appropriate technology? It was not cheap enough for Nepal to buy without foreign aid, but it meant that modern microsurgical techniques could be performed in the thatched-roof and mud-floor operating room of a rural eye camp. Certainly eye camps were an appropriate public health technology. For their part, the Europeans saw us as naive if not downright ugly Americans, throwing money at problems and seduced by technology that could never be sustained in Nepal after the withdrawal of foreign aid.

The issue can also be understood in the terms of another useful Hirschman notion: "trait taking" versus "trait making."[17] A play on the microeconomics concept of price taking, "trait taking" is accepting the current modus operandi in a developing country, flawed though it may be. The advantage of trait taking is that the success of a project is not linked to a risky attempt to change the way things are done (as with nepotism, passing the buck, or extremely bureaucratic styles of decisionmaking) The disadvantage is that one may forgo opportunities to institute changes in organizational or political culture that could have positive effects extending beyond the boundaries of the project itself. The trait-making project bears that risk in the interest of creating a more positive context for development. In the blindness program, some of the NGOs attempted to be trait makers with regard to technology. They sought, with some success, to inculcate new attitudes and practices that would generate a sustainable small-scale industry in ophthalmic equipment. In this instance, Seva opted to accept the program's dependency on foreign aid in its technology choices. The blindness program would require substantial foreign support for the foreseeable future, and fostering an indigenous ophthalmic equipment industry was not an area of Seva expertise. You pick your battles.

Among the ophthalmologists, lines were neatly drawn on the IOL question. Those trained to do extracapsular surgery were for it, those not trained were against it. The American volunteers were largely unconcerned with the first criticism—the safety argument. They *saw* the cases postoperatively and knew the complication rate was low. While it is true that there are some complications peculiar to extracapsular surgery, there are others peculiar to traditional intracapsular techniques. Even when intracapsular surgery is successful, the "complication" of *aphakia* must be weighed against the potential complications of extracapsular surgery. In any case, complication rates are no mystery. The overwhelming majority show up during the ten days that the cataract patient is kept under surveillance at the camp or hospital. As time passed, confidence increased. By 1986 or 1987, the extracapsular surgeons came to feel that if IOLs were causing a *big* problem, they would know about it by now.

My own thinking about the question of how to maintain the IOL supply was that India would probably produce an acceptable cheap lens before our donation sources in the United States dried up. (India had already developed a number of *un*acceptable cheap lenses.) But assume the worst: that donations ceased and that no decent third world lens became available. This just meant that tens of thousands of Nepalese would receive first-rate cataract surgery before the program returned to its previous methods. Who would have been made worse off? Perhaps it would be a demoralizing experience for the ophthalmologists, but could one justify withholding IOLs on those grounds?

During this period of controversy, Seva was also supplying lenses to Dr. V's hospitals in India. At Aravind, they charged paying patients a premium for IOL surgery and used the extra income to finance free, mainly non-IOL surgery for the poor. While this Robin Hood approach to finance was built into Dr. V's idea for Aravind from the beginning, it soon became obvious that IOLs were a potential source of unprecedented new revenue. Dr. V wanted a steady supply of lenses and began speaking of building a lens factory at Madurai. Dr. McV, indeed.

Larry Brilliant was not happy with these developments. He heard world-class ophthalmologists argue vehemently on both sides of the question of the safety of IOLs in rural eye camps. No ophthalmologist himself, he resisted making judgments on this clinical question. But when the director of the National Eye Institute expressed misgivings about IOLs in the third world (Cadillacs for the elite), his own concerns were reaffirmed, and Larry became unhappier still. Even developments at Aravind looked unhealthy. He felt that Seva had unwittingly contributed to Aravind's addiction to IOLs. Aravind's financial health was becoming dependent on demand for a type of surgery that was not in the best interests of the poor of India and was an inappropriate precedent for other third world eye programs. And he was not the only one who was worried. Ram Dass felt that IOLs were so seductive that they could distort the allocation of resources toward eye care and away from other important sectors of the health budget. He put the point very bluntly on more than one occasion, saying that every time we put an IOL in some sixty-year-old's eye, we condemned a Nepalese baby to die of diarrhea. Resources are fixed. All games are zero-sum games. As Wavy Gravy said, "When you lose your sense of humor, it's just not funny anymore."

Beyond the possible substantive merit of the anti-IOL arguments, Larry was displeased that such an important innovation had occurred hiding hand–style, without any formal planning or policy decision by the Seva board. At the same time, he realized that there was no good way to terminate Seva's involvement with IOLs. The Nepalese wanted them, and American volunteers would not want to do any other type of surgery. In any case, IOLs could not simply be suppressed. They were the present and future of cataract surgery in the West and would eventually be used in developing countries, too. By this time (1990), the Swiss Red Cross had also started using them at their eye hospital in Bheri Zone. The Nepal program would have to come to terms with them one way or the other. In the end, it would be better to keep Seva's hand in, so that it could have a positive influence on the direction of IOL adoption.

The solution, in other words, was *aikido:* use the energy in the direction it is going. With impetus from Larry and Dr. V, Seva became the prime mover behind the establishment of an IOL factory at Aravind. Starting in 1992, this facility began producing U.S.–quality lenses at a cost that makes them viable for many eye programs in developing countries. The factory at Aravind now produces enough to meet the needs of their own program and sells additional lenses to Nepal for $8 each. Cheap as this is compared with the $250 American-made lens, at an average cost of about $20 per cataract operation in Nepal, $8 is still costly.[13] At that price, IOLs probably could not be supplied to all patients without foreign support. It appears that the price is about to fall dramatically. The Australians are now in the process of building an IOL factory in Nepal, so that it too can become IOL-independent and possibly export them to other developing countries.

What makes a technology appropriate? IOLs had all the classic hallmarks of "inappropriate": expensive, high-tech, unsustainable, a gift to the affluent elite who soaked up scarce health resources at the expense of the poor. It turns out that at Aravind, IOLs are one of the major vehicles for transferring eye care resources from the affluent to the poor on a sustainable basis. Aravind was able to capitalize on the research, and development investment of the American pharmaceutical industry, combine it with inexpensive but skilled Indian labor, and turn out an export-quality product. It looks as if Nepal will be in a similar position within the next few years. The Lumbini eye hospital is now financially self-reliant, in large measure because of IOL-related revenue.

There is another unexpected virtue of IOLs that may actually help lower the cost of rural cataract programs, although the evidence on this point is equivocal.[14] As IOLs came into increasingly common use in Kathmandu and at the Seva program in Lumbini, patients coming to the eye centers started to ask for *ankhaa bitraa chassma* (glasses in the eye). IOLs make the operation more desirable, so more patients are willing to come for surgery on their own motivation and at their own expense. (After the introduction of IOLs in the United States, surgical volume increased 400 percent.) This means less investment in costly outreach and publicity efforts. There is also anecdotal evidence that IOLs increase the service radius of the permanent eye centers and reduce the need for expensive eye camps. In the context of a public health ophthalmology program, this means more and better services to the rural poor, exactly the group that appropriate technology advocates feared would be damaged by IOLs.

The Nepal experience shows that high technology can support egalitarian, appropriate technology–type values. It thus cautions against any simple-minded categorization of technology. It also tends to support the currently disreputable idea that technology is value-neutral. The benefits of IOLs could have been confined to the affluent elite if their adoption had been allowed to develop that way, but their actual effect was the opposite. How general is this lesson? Is this likely to be true of many other "inappropriate" high technologies? I do not know. At a minimum, the IOL story suggests that one's political culture may bias one's perception of the possible ways that a technology can be applied. Understanding this bias may make one more open-minded and ultimately more effective in selecting technologies for development.

Nine

Bringing Hirschman Back In
A Case of Bad Government Turned Good

Judith Tendler and Sara Freedheim

MORE THAN thirty years ago, Albert Hirschman chided development economists for being too optimistic about the capacities of developing-country governments to manage economic development.[1] This put him at odds with the enthusiasm of those times for central government planning and "balanced growth." Today, Hirschman's early skepticism about the capacity of government would *seem* to place him in good company with the new generation of development economists and political economists: they are singularly negative about the capacity of developing countries to govern and to invest wisely, and of individuals to act in the public interest—even more skeptical than Hirschman was in that earlier period. But this interpretation of Hirschman's early works and their relation to the development thinking of today represents only half the story.

Shortly after issuing his early words of caution about developing-country governments to the industrialized world, Hirschman turned toward the developing countries and chided them for being too *pessimistic*. They were ignoring the accomplishments of their own governments, he told them, and giving undue prominence to their failures. He issued these warnings on three separate occasions over an eighteen-year period, starting only five years after his earlier message of skepticism.[2] Perhaps because of this chronology, his writings about developing countries are viewed as "hopeful" rather than skeptical, an interpretation that he himself encouraged by entitling his first book of collected essays *A Bias for Hope*. That the skepticism seemed to give way to hope, however, does not represent a change of heart. Today, he would be just as critical of development economists for their pessimism, after all, as he was for their optimism thirty years ago.

A more accurate interpretation of the skepticism followed by hope is that they always coexisted, and represent the long-standing and intricate *balance* with which Hirschman chronicled development processes, despite his reputation as the inventor of the concept of "*un*balanced growth." Hirschman's balance did not necessarily yield the simple and elegant theories of today's development economics and political economy, with their corresponding spinoffs in terms of policy advice. At the same time, his work was in many ways more grounded than this recent literature in observing how the economies and the governments of developing countries actually worked.

This chapter represents a small attempt to describe the world with balance or, more simply, to celebrate Hirschman's approach to it. It was provoked, in part, by the current imbalance of the development field in the direction of skepticism about the nature of governments and human beings. This is where the chapter starts, just as Hirschman's treatise thirty years ago was provoked, in part, by the optimism of that earlier period. In what follows, we confess to a bias toward the positive. But that does not worry us because it may help to counterbalance the stronger bias toward the negative in the sea of literature that surrounds us.

Today's negative views on the public sector of developing countries have grown out of keen disappointment over the failures of governments to cope with corruption, persistent poverty, and problems of macroeconomic management. Regardless of how customary poor performance in the public sector actually is, however, it has become customary to expect it. This is partly because it has been so well documented and so elegantly explained by the recent theories of public and rational choice, particularly those of "rent-seeking elites."[3]

Out of the convergence of the disappointment and the new theories has come a familiar litany of the causes of poor performance: public officials and their workers pursue their own private interests, rather than those of the public good; government spending and hiring is overextended; clientelistic practices are rampant, with workers being hired and fired for reasons of kinship and political loyalty rather than merit; workers are poorly trained and receive little on-the-job training; and, tying it all together, badly conceived programs and policies create myriad opportunities for graft and other forms of "rent seeking."

These explanations have generated a corresponding body of policy advice oriented toward reducing the role of the public sector as much as possible. This more cautious view of the role of government, together with the theoretical attempt to explain the problem of poor public sector performance, represents a healthy evolution away from the simpler, more optimistic views criticized by Hirschman in the 1950s and 1960s. Although these new theories have been good at explaining why governments so often do badly, they are remarkably silent about the occasions when governments perform well.

The lopsidedness of development thinking in explaining government performance represents more than the understandable failing of a good theory that throws important new light on a problem but cannot explain everything. It also means that developing countries and the donors that advise them have few models of good government that are grounded in these countries' own experiences. The revolutionary transformations of the last decade in Eastern Europe and the former Soviet Union, moreover, have brought considerable urgency to the task of providing good advice about good government. To continue with the current empirically thin basis for advice represents, in certain ways, as naively optimistic a view about the capacity of "the market" or marketlike approaches to solve problems as was the view of the earlier period about the capacity of government to solve those same problems.

This chapter offers some explanations for why developing-country governments sometimes do well. The idea for the research reported on here started with our reading of an article published in the *Economist* in December 1991. Three pages of a special supplement on Brazil were devoted to the remarkable accomplishments of two successive governments in one of the country's poorest states, Ceará, an area of 150,000 square kilometers with nearly 7 million inhabitants.

The *Economist* article was followed by similar ones over the next two years, in *Newsweek, Time,* the *Christian Science Monitor,* the *Washington Post,* and the *New York Times,* as well as various Brazilian newspapers and magazines. The stories told of how the state increased tax revenues markedly by collecting taxes already on the books, freed the public payroll of thousands of "phantom" workers, and introduced some outstanding programs in the area of preventive health, public procurement from informal sector providers, and an emergency employment-creating public works program in the face of severe drought.

The Ceará stories were striking because this particular state government belongs, with eight other states, to the country's poorest region—Northeast Brazil—where one third of the population of 45 million lives in absolute poverty. The governments of the nine northeast states, which occupy an area the size of France, are legendary for their chronic poor performance and clientelistic practices.[4] How could a poorly performing state "suddenly" do so well that, as the news coverage reported, it became a "model" of public administration sought out by other states in Brazil and other countries of Latin America and was feted by international institutions like the World Bank?

This question became the topic of a research project in Ceará, in which Judith Tendler worked together with seven research assistants looking into six programs that showed varying degrees of good performance.[5] Certain themes ran across the explanations for good performance of each case, even though the cases involved different sectors. The most clear-cut case of success was a rural preventive health program, created by the state in 1987, and the subject of this chapter.[6] After only a few years, the program had contributed to a 36 percent reduction in infant deaths from one of the highest rates in Brazil (from 102 per 1,000 to 65 per 1,000). It also tripled vaccination coverage for measles and polio from the lowest rate in Brazil, 25 percent of the population, to 90 percent.[7] Only 30 percent of the state's counties had a nurse before the program started, let alone a doctor or health clinic, but the program was operating in virtually all the state's 178 counties five years later.[8] For these accomplishments, Ceará won the UNICEF Maurice Paté prize for child support programs in 1993, the only Latin American government to do so since the prize's inception twenty-seven years ago.[9]

We chose the health case to illustrate the more general findings about public performance because, of the six better-performing programs, its achievements were most institutionalized, reached the largest number of people, and involved by far the largest number of public workers: 7,300 health agents and the 235 nurses who supervised them. This kind of public service involves considerable unsupervised contact between workers and clients—the health agents met formally with their supervisors only once a month—similar to other "street-level bureaucracies" like agricultural extension, policing, social work, and teaching.[10] The state hired this veritable army of workers from scratch, moreover, at the same time that it was shedding hundreds of "phantom" workers.

The large contingent of workers, their mass hiring over a short period of time, and the unsupervised nature of their contacts would seem to create numerous opportunities for the patronage hiring practices and rent-seeking behavior explained and predicted by the new theories.[11] That such a large field-based bureaucracy did not become the rent-seeking nightmare of the current literature requires some explanation. In attempting one, we hope to contribute to the understanding of public sector performance in developing countries and to a more grounded basis for advice.

Getting Satisfaction

Given the prevailing low expectations of government in developing countries today—let alone the mediocre history of Ceará's public service—anyone who accompanied this research could not fail to be surprised by the high performance and commitment to their work of such a large number of public servants. In numerous interviews, the health agents and their nurse-supervisors revealed a distinct sense of satisfaction and personal fulfillment from their work. Issues of "job commitment" and "worker productivity," however, hardly appear in the current literature on reform of the public sector in developing countries. Much of the focus is on how to "shed labor," on which functions would be better performed outside government, and on arrangements that simulate market competition between agencies or introduce marketlike pressures on public agencies to perform. As one Brazilian state secretary of planning said, in a typical lament, "We've succeeded in shedding some of our excess labor, but the poor quality of what remains stands out as even more of a problem. Nobody seems to be dealing with that."

The relative unimportance of worker-commitment issues in the public sector literature on developing countries stands in stark contrast to the *centrality* of these issues—and the rich treatment of them—in the current literature on industrial performance, competitiveness, and workplace transformation in the industrialized countries.[12] This body of research and thought concerns "reform" in the *private* sector—including a variety of now widely known subjects such as decentralization, flexible specialization, total quality management, worker teams, trusting customer-supplier relationships, and reengineering. Although some of the concepts of this literature have started to spill into the thinking on the public sector, this has happened mainly with respect to the public sectors of already industrialized countries.[13]

It was only against the background of these literatures that we were able to discern the threads of worker satisfaction and increased performance that ran through the health case and the others. This does not mean that we found total quality management or worker-management teams flourishing in the backlands of Ceará, where the health program unfolded. Rather, the explanations people gave for why they liked their jobs better, and of how their work was different from normal, had much in common with the explanations of the industrial performance literature for why these practices have been associated with better performance in the industrialized world. The way citizens talked about the public workers who served them in the health and other programs, in turn, was reminiscent of the way this literature describes the relations of "trust" between customers and the firms they buy from, or between customer firms and their subcontractors.[14] As in the development field, moreover, those concerned with industrial performance are paying considerable attention to "labor shedding" and how to do it. In these debates, however, labor shedding stands out as only one of a *variety* of approaches being discussed to improve productivity in the private sector, including also worker teams, decentralized management, job "enlargement," quality circles, total quality management, and just-in-time inventory systems.

These comparisons between the fields of development and industrial performance are not meant to suggest that the public sector of developing countries should adopt the best practices of firms in industrialized countries—although many are proposing just that for the U.S. public sector.[15] Rather, and more simply, the contrasts serve to reveal the narrowness of the development field's approach to improving performance in the public sector, dominated, as it is, by issues of labor shedding, reduction of the spectrum of government functions, and introduction of marketlike pressures to perform. Now that poor performance is so much better understood and considerable labor shedding, privatization, and other reforms have already taken place, there may be more room in the development field for concern about the conditions under which workers providing public services show high commitment to their work and perform well.

The Workings of the Ceará Health Program

Ceará's rural health program started in 1987 as part of a temporary response to the unemployment caused by one of the periodic droughts that afflict this semiarid state every four to seven years. For its first twelve months, the program was financed by temporary disaster-relief funds from the federal government. Unlike the typical public works jobs offered to the unemployed during these droughts, the jobs for community health agents were available mainly to women. Although the health-agent jobs never amounted to more than 5 percent of the temporary jobs offered by the state during the drought, the program was so successful that the state decided to fund it permanently in 1989, after the drought and the emergency funding for it had ended. By 1993, the program's 7,300 paraprofessional health agents visited 850,000 families in their homes every month—about six per day per agent—providing assistance and advice and collecting information about oral rehydration therapy, vaccination, prenatal care, breast feeding, and growth monitoring.

Program costs averaged US$2 per capita served—totaling approximately $7 to $8 million a year—compared with the $80 estimated per capita costs of Brazil's existing health care system.[16] About 80 percent of the costs represented payments to the health agents, mostly women who lived in the communities where they worked and earned the minimum wage (US$60 a month with no fringe benefits); nurse-supervisors earned an average of five times the minimum wage, $300 a month, often higher than they would have earned in urban clinics and hospitals.

The health program represented a first move toward the decentralization of health services, with municipalities required to hire a nurse-supervisor, pay her salary (about 15 percent of program costs), and support the program in other ways.[17] The state paid the lion's share of program costs (85 percent), covering the wages of the health agents and their uniforms and supplies. A nine-member coordinating team ran the program out of the state Department of Health and traveled extensively in the interior. It recruited and hired the agents and supervised the program with a strong hand; at the same time, it gave considerable discretion to the supervising nurses. After a rigorous selection process by the state, as discussed below, the newly hired agents received three months of training and substantial on-the-job training; nurse-supervisors had three days of orientation and numerous subsequent meetings with the coordinating team.

The health agents of the new program constituted the most visible public sector presence in the communities where they worked, and often in the towns where the program was headquartered. They wore "uniforms" of white T-shirts emblazoned with the name of the program, blue jeans, and blue backpacks with supplies.[18] Mindful of the critical appraisals of earlier preventive health programs run by non-government organizations, the program insisted on ministering to community members in their households rather than out of a health center. Although this was done in order to achieve better health coverage, it had another significant effect on program performance. The health agents were constantly seen by the community moving from house to house and, for their more rural visits, traveling by bicycle, donkey, and even canoe.

The health program's achievements were clearly striking, most notably its rapid growth throughout the state and the dramatic changes in the indicators reported above. Furthermore, the program represented an unusual success in "paraprofessionalization." It overcame the typical resistance of physicians and nurses to the introduction of less skilled workers and, in so doing, brought down the costs of service drastically.[19] The explanation for why the program worked so well is complex, but we focus here on the following themes, which, in one way or another, reveal a work environment that differed substantially from the way the work of public sector agencies is often organized, or how experts think it should be organized.

—Both health agents and nurses saw their jobs as giving them more prestige and status than usual, particularly in the communities where they worked.

—The state government played an unusual role, sometimes inadvertently, in contributing to this prestige by creating a sense of "calling" around these particular jobs—through publicity, the hiring process, the training of workers, and prizes for good performance.

—Although the health program *seemed* to represent a case of successful decentralization from state to municipal government, the actions of the more centralized state government seemed more important to an explanation of the program's success.

—The approach to decentralization, together with the state's public relations efforts around the program, succeeded in heading off the opposition to such programs that frequently occurs, from professionals resisting the use of paraprofessionals in health care and from mayors resentful of the state's usurpation of their powers to hire municipal health workers.

—Workers voluntarily took on a larger variety of tasks than was normal, often in response to their perception of what clients needed. These included tasks that are usually viewed as not what an agency or worker is "supposed" to do and as representing bad practice.

—Although these "self-enlarged" jobs and their vaguer limits would seem to make supervision more difficult and to provide more opportunities for misbehavior, certain mechanisms came into play that hemmed public employees in with pressures to be accountable from *outside* their agencies.

The Unskilled Meritocracy

Existing accounts of civil servants working in health programs similar to Ceará's often convey the same sense of hopelessness as the broader literature on public sector performance in developing countries.[20] Because of that, along with the generally stressed environment of Ceará's public administration, it surprised us to encounter such profound satisfaction among the program's health agents and supervising nurses. As one agent reminisced, in a typical comment, "This town was nothing before the health program started. I was ready to leave and look for a job in São Paulo, but now I love my job and I would never leave—I would never abandon my community." This kind of satisfaction went along with the intense dedication, unpaid after-hours work, and voracious learning observed among a large number of the agents and nurses working in the program. It is worth noting, in this context, that the health agents (as distinct from the nurses) received only the minimum wage and were hired without the job security that public sector employment usually offers. What accounted for this commitment and the high performance associated with it?

Interestingly, the origins of the commitment can be traced back to what happened *before* the health agents started working—namely, the hiring process. The program carried out a remarkable process of merit hiring, which, when it occurs at all or is respected, usually involves jobs in the more professionalized echelons of government agencies rather than those of unskilled workers like the health agents. Merit hiring, moreover, is difficult to find in rural areas, where mayors customarily hire the few municipal employees under their control according to considerations of patronage.

In the Ceará setting, the hiring of the health agents represented much more than a routine civil service procedure. Given the chronic unemployment in the northeast interior, with its low-productivity agriculture and its periodic droughts, the hiring of 7,300 workers became an event of major significance in the lives of the job seekers and the dozens of towns where they were to work. The state-level coordinating team for the new health program went through three stages to hire each worker. It first required written applications from all applicants (family members and friends helped the less literate applicants fill out their forms), from which it culled out a list of people to be interviewed. Two members of the team (usually a nurse and a social worker) then traveled to each town for an interview with each applicant on the list, which was followed by a meeting with all applicants as a group. A subsequent round of individual interviews was often held with those likely to be selected.

For most applicants, regardless of their age, this was the first time they had applied for a job or, at least, been interviewed for one. Many were perspiring and trembled with fear during their interview. In the small interior towns where the interviews took place, townspeople saw the hiring "event" as boding well for the town's future: important professionals from the state capital would stay for more than a few hours—indeed, overnight—to run a competition that seemed to herald a new public service for the community. The coming of the state team thus inspired widespread curiosity and comment, not to mention eavesdropping from outside the open windows and doors where the meetings with applicants were held.

Why would the state have lavished so much attention on the hiring of a large force of unskilled, minimum-wage workers without civil service status—and for a program that was perhaps only temporary and, in essence, local? Clearly, this kind of hiring process must have helped the hiring committee select the best applicants and, hence, partly explains the program's success. But this is not the main reason we bring it up: the hiring process, as "staged" by the state government, had a major impact on the way the program was subsequently perceived by the communities where it operated and on the way its workers viewed their jobs.

The state government advertised the program and the jobs widely in the regions where hiring was taking place through health centers, hospitals and, particularly important, on the radio, the most broadly used medium of communication in the interior. Even though the hiring of the new agents was often phased over a year or more, the number of jobs offered at any particular hiring was frequently the largest one-time public sector hiring in these rural towns, perhaps twenty, thirty, or forty jobs at a time. Later, as already mentioned, the "uniformed" health agents became the most conspicuous and numerous public sector presence in the area.

The health program was also unusual for the interior towns in that it hired mainly women (95 percent), because of the focus of its health messages on mothers and children. Many of these women had seldom had paid employment, not even the temporary employment of the periodic drought-relief programs; others had worked as primary school teachers for the municipality, typically earning less than the minimum wage. This situation is quite common in rural Brazil, where teachers themselves frequently have no more than an elementary school education. In earning the minimum wage, the new women agents were receiving up to twice the wage paid to male agricultural labor, the principal occupation of the poor population of these areas.[21]

In retrospect, the state seemed to be using the hiring process quite cleverly as an opportunity to educate the community—the program's "customers"—about the new service. In interviewing the job applicants, the state committee took just as much care to inspire and inform those whom it would *not* hire—the overwhelming majority, of course—as those whom it did hire. It provided strongly inspirational messages about what the program could do to improve people's lives and how the community could—in taking the program seriously—gain control over its destiny. "This program is yours," the state team told the assembled applicants, "and it is you who will determine its success, whether you get the job or not." The community "does not have to" lose so many of its infants, they continued, and sickness did not have to be so common; it was not "right" to have high infant mortality, a community "could do better," it had a "right" to demand support for such a program from its municipal leaders.

The program's coordinating team also told the applicants that it would be an immense "honor" to be hired. Just as significant for the program's future performance, job applicants were also told that it had been an "honor" for them simply to have applied and been interviewed; participating in the process had proven their "commitment to the community" and their status as "leaders." This was so, the team told them, even if they were *not* hired.

Because the hiring took place in stages, the "image creation" around the process was even more effective. In a *municipio* slated for 150 health agents, for example, the first competition might call for only 30. Three or four subsequent competitions would hire the rest over as much as a three-year period, each time in the same way. In addition to introducing a large new program at a manageable pace, the phased hiring sustained the image creation around the program and its agents well into the implementation period.

FROM REJECTS TO MONITORS.   The state's approach to the hiring process also helped, ultimately, to subject the program to strong pressures to perform, as well as to legitimate its workers. "Those of you who are *not* selected," the traveling committee advised, "must make sure that those who are chosen abide by the rules." This turned a group of 200 or 300 unsuccessful applicants into informed public monitors of a new program in which the potential for abuse was high. Among other requirements, the applicants were told, health agents had to live in the area where they worked, work eight hours a day, visit each household at least once a month, attend all training and review sessions, and not canvass for a political candidate or wear or distribute political propaganda. Although all these requirements certainly do not seem out of the ordinary for such a job, they are not often observed in Brazil or in many other countries. "If these rules are breached," the committee warned the assembled applicants and eavesdroppers, "we want to hear about it." The warning was clinched with the admonition that "we are keeping all the applications, just in case any of those we hire do not perform well."

For those who were hired as agents, the specter of reprisal for malfeasance and of the waiting line of eager replacements formed by the rejected applicants translated itself into pressure to perform well. The drama of the hiring process, in turn, had created an informal and powerful monitoring presence in the community at large. Community members, indeed, subsequently reported to nurse-supervisors when agents were violating the rules and not, for example, living in the community where they worked (these agents were fired). Less drastically, a family that had not seen its health agent in more than a month would often let the nurse-supervisor know.

The image of disgruntled job seekers watching the job winners like hawks for one false step is certainly not one usually associated with increased worker commitment and productivity. Indeed, it smacks more of the "scab-labor" tactics reviled by labor unions. But the dynamic created by these instructions and admonitions was more complex and more positive. Rather than merely create opportunities and incentives for individuals to "whistle-blow" behind people's backs, the hiring process and advertising around the program fostered a sense of *collective* responsibility for it among the community and its workers.

The educational process had endowed prestige on those who won the job competition, and on the program itself, not only in the eyes of those who lost but among the users of the program and the community at large. In addition, the selection committee's instructions to job applicants who were not chosen made them feel involved with the program, so that they also reported to the nurse-supervisors when they were *satisfied* with what a particular agent was doing. Finally, the hiring process and its warnings—far from intimidating the new workers—made them feel they had the *support* of the state government should they have to deal with local politicians who might want to divert the program to their political ends. They now had an excuse to say no, and someone more powerful to whom they could report an abuse; they also knew they could not be fired by the mayor, as was common, for refusing to go along with political or personal abuse of the program.

The importance of "protection" for dedicated public servants crops up frequently in case studies of successful programs like this one— protection from local politicians, as in this case, or from another arm of government or the public.[22] In these studies protection is usually conveyed as making it possible for a group of "apolitical" and highly educated technocrats to carry out programs in the public interest, shielded from political meddling. In this case, however, it was *unskilled* workers who were being protected, and among the protectors were the politicians themselves, namely, the state's governors.[23] Regardless of these differences, one of the conclusions to be drawn from these studies, together with the health story, is that a public agency's performance at any one moment is partly dependent on the balance of power between "protectors" and "spoilers," as well as between dedicated and self-serving public workers.

Although the portrayal of public workers as being "liberated" by their protectors to serve the public good is common in case studies, it is inconsistent with the theoretical view of civil servants as inherently self-seeking; or, at least, it complicates that view. It also points toward a different explanation for some of the *poor* performance in the public sector, as well as the good.

PUBLICITY AND ITS BY-PRODUCTS. The esteem and support heaped on the preventive health program and its workers by the hiring process extended well into the implementation period because of the staged expansion of the program. Other actions by the state had this same effect without, interestingly, necessarily intending to. Seeking additional financial and other support for the program, the state Department of Health successfully approached large private firms to raise funding for radio and television campaigns advertising the program and its preventive health messages and for the training of existing curative care personnel in vaccination and oral rehydration therapy. The state also successfully lobbied the medical schools operating there to require that medical students take courses in preventive health care as a requirement for board certification. The resulting blitz of publicity about the program and, later, its eventual successes—on radio and television and in the newspapers and newsmagazines—placed the health agents and their nurse supervisors in an unusual spotlight of recognition and praise.

The state also awarded prizes—again, with much fanfare—to the municipalities achieving the best immunization coverage. By 1992, 43 of the state's 178 municipalities had received prizes for the best DPT-III coverage (diphtheria, pertussis, and tetanus).[24] The prizes were set up partly with the goal of getting program personnel to take seriously the collection of health data, which is always a problem in such programs. At the same time, the fanfare and the recognition surrounding the prizes were immensely satisfying to the workers in these programs, enhancing their prestige in the communities where they worked and lived.

By 1993 the state's constant publicizing of the health program and its other achievements had attracted highly laudatory press coverage.

It is not clear, however, if the state understood the positive impact of this publicity on the program's workers and their performance, because it had other reasons for making the program well known. First, as mentioned earlier, the publicity was meant to get people to adopt preventive health measures. Second, and assuming greater importance as the program wore on, the publicity simply reflected the effort by a state government to capitalize politically on its own successes. The two governors who reigned over the program in succession had political ambitions nationally; by the early 1990s, the first had become president of an important recently formed Social-Democratic party, and the second was highly conspicuous on the national political scene. Their administrations had been clever and aggressive at publicizing all their accomplishments, not just health, throughout Brazil and abroad.

More skeptical observers of these two state administrations questioned the reality of their claims, suggesting that the publicity exaggerated their accomplishments. Whether or not this was the case is not relevant to our argument: regardless of the intentions, the publicity would have had the same powerful effect of bestowing public recognition on the health program and its workers. Indeed, attention to the other ends served by the publicity may well have helped to cause this particular result to go unnoticed, preventing the state *and* its critics from seeing the value of publicity for these other purposes.

Perhaps it would not have taken much to get good performance from a newly hired contingent of rural women workers, most of whom had no more than a sixth-grade education and had never before had paid employment. But the nurse-supervisors talked about their feelings of "being respected by the community" just as much as the health agents they supervised did. Not only were these nurses trained professionals, but many had left previous jobs in hospitals in larger cities to work for the program.

The Good Professional

The quality of supervision in preventive health and other programs deploying large paraprofessional field staffs is key to their success. Evaluations of poorly functioning preventive health programs routinely cite the absence of good supervision.[25] Any study of the achievements of Ceará's program, then, must ask why supervision was better than in most such programs. In addition, physicians and nurses often object to preventive health programs like Ceará's, or simply have no interest in promoting them. This resistance or lack of interest—sometimes even from previously trained groups of paraprofessionals themselves—contributes to the difficulty of getting the public sector to pay adequate attention and funding to preventive health, as compared with curative health programs. Part of the resistance is due to a genuine concern about compromising professional standards and jeopardizing the health and safety of the patient. Another part, of course, bespeaks worries about losing power, professional distinction, remuneration, and access to jobs. From the glowing reports of the supervising nurses of Ceará's health program, it is clear that a large number of a key group of potential resisters to the program became its ardent advocates. This also requires explanation.

In the urban clinics and hospitals where many of the nurse-supervisors had worked previously, they had been inferior in status to the doctors they assisted, who treated them as subordinates rather than coprofessionals. Now, each nurse was supervising and training an average of thirty paraprofessional agents, who referred to their supervisor as "doctor" and hung on her every word. She suddenly felt herself an important local personage in the community and local people addressed her as "doctor" when they passed her on the street.

In addition, the nurse-supervisors felt that in their previous jobs they had really not been able to "practice nursing." Many hospitals had given them more and more administrative work and met nursing needs by hiring less-trained and lower-paid paraprofessional workers. Not only were the trained nurses less able to practice nursing, then, but they were angered by the lack of "professionalism" in the way nursing was run in their hospitals—using less-skilled workers, for example, to assist physicians at surgery. This led to various protest meetings, which were of little avail and left the nurses feeling powerless, alienated from their work, and ignored as professionals. Similarly, evaluation studies of preventive health programs in various countries have found that the poor quality of supervision, usually by nurses, is a result of their not being called upon to participate in the planning of the programs they administer or of their being allowed little discretion in managing the programs.[26]

In Ceará's preventive health program, the situation was quite different. Although the nurse-supervisors may not have been practicing nursing directly, they had virtual control over the way the program ran in their municipality. As a result, they were able to put into practice their ideas about how public health programs should work. One important sign of the nurse-supervisors' newly gained discretion was the variation in the details of each program from municipality to municipality. Some nurse-supervisors, for example, believed their agents should know how to give shots and take out stitches; others were adamantly against teaching these "curative" tasks; others believed family-planning messages should be central to the agents' advice giving. (Indeed, one nurse-supervisor initiated family planning into her municipality when she found, in conversations with her own agents, that many of them had sexually transmittable diseases and did not know how to prevent or treat them.) The state deliberately allowed this variation from one municipality to the next, not pressing standardization too strictly, in order to give the supervising nurses the autonomy that would cause them to "own" the program they were responsible for.

All this was a far cry from the nurses' subordinate relation to the physicians of their previous jobs and their exclusion from decisions that were central to their identity as professionals. Although they may not have been practicing nursing in their new jobs any more than in their old jobs, they felt more "like a professional" because they were making decisions about how to run a program of public health and saw direct health effects of their work. That their salaries in the preventive health program were higher than in their previous urban jobs must have clearly been important in attracting some of the better nursing professionals and ensuring their dedication. But the dramatic increase in status from being near the bottom of a professional hierarchy, and their new place as health "professionals" at the center of decisionmaking about a program, must certainly have made a difference as well.

It is ironic that the nurse-supervisors, who had criticized the use of paraprofessionals in their previous jobs in urban hospitals, were now feeling more professionally fulfilled in a job that involved the supervision of a large group of just such workers. In addition, the nurse-supervisors adamantly defended the use of paraprofessionals in the preventive health program against the predictable criticisms that eventually came from their urban colleagues in nursing. The new power of the health program's nurses to decide what the unskilled workers could or could not do was key to the change in their view about paraprofessionals.[27] More generally, the nurses supported the program and provided quality supervision because they were given a more central role in planning and operating a health program than they had been in their previous jobs.

Civil Service as a Calling

Through a conspicuous civil service hiring "event," the state created a sense of public "calling" or "ministry" around a particular set of public jobs and the program of which they were a part. Merit-hiring processes are valued, however, for other reasons: they ensure better-quality candidates and public servants and protect the public sector from patronage hiring. In the United States and other industrialized countries, moreover, merit or civil service hiring is so accepted that it is taken for granted; indeed, it is often criticized for being too rigid and for stifling creativity. But in developing countries, where patronage influences public sector hiring to a much greater degree, the hiring process described above represents an outstanding accomplishment.

Good public managers in Brazil often fight major battles to have meritocratic hiring procedures followed in their agencies. In a previous research project, for example, Tendler interviewed successful public managers of infrastructure and agriculture agencies in the Northeast on what they considered to be their most significant achievements. Rather than referring to program accomplishments like getting roads built or wells dug, several reminisced about victories in getting merit-hiring procedures for a particular set of new workers, usually after a battle against political pressure to do otherwise.[28]

The health story shows, in addition, that such conspicuously merit-based hiring can cause newly hired workers to start out viewing their jobs and themselves *differently*—and hence lead them to behave differently—because of the prestige accorded to them by the selection process. Getting the job is, in a sense, like being awarded a public prize. That the selection process itself could bestow prestige and influence performance is not, of course, new or unique to Ceará's health program. Professionals who work in public agencies known for serious merit-hiring procedures often cite this fact, like an item on their curriculum vitae, even when the competition took place many years ago; they proudly and disdainfully set themselves off from others in the public sector who were not hired in this way. In Brazil, Bank of Brazil managers talk this way, as do professionals in the National Development Bank. Outside of Brazil, the Indian Administrative Service provides another excellent example of civil servants who feel themselves an elite simply for having won their jobs.

The health program's hiring process differed from these typical cases of meritocratic public agencies in three interesting ways. First, by publicizing the hiring so intensely in the interior communities, the program conferred status on the job in the very communities where the agents worked. Second, the hiring process and the accompanying publicity around the program linked the prestige not just to the particular individuals who passed the rigorous competition, but also to the program's "noble" mission—bringing the community "into the twentieth century" by reducing infant mortality and disease. In other words, in contrast to the meritocratic cachet among other public servants, the prestige and the glory lay not so much with the public agency into which one was drafted, but with the impact one's work would have on the future of a community.

Part of this difference had to do with the fact that the responsibility for the program was split between the state Department of Health and the municipalities. Although the state clearly maintained the upper hand in the hiring process and supervision of the program, the municipalities hired the nurses; and the agents worked under the nurses' supervision, even though the agents were hired and paid by the state. This meant that neither the agents nor their supervisors "belonged" to the health agency that conferred so much prestige on them. Their prestige, rather than being grounded in the reputation of an agency that hired them, derived from the "mission" of their program in the community, as defined and declared repeatedly by the state government in advertising the program and in hiring and training its workers.

Third, the status the health agents enjoyed was not, as distinct from the more typical case of meritocratic public service, the result of their being an educated elite. The reward for their having passed the competition, in turn, did not come in the form of job tenure. As had become the practice of other fiscally strapped state governments in the 1980s, Ceará had gone out of its way to "contract" these new workers rather than hire them, so as to make it clear that they were not winning a permanent home in the state's public sector.[29] Indeed, the governor customarily stressed this as one of the keys to the program's success, proudly noting that he had always resisted pressures to turn the agents into "state employees." "If you [do so]," he liked to say, "this programme will die".[30]

Unlike the other cases, then, the winning of these jobs was not a result of "being educated." Rather, education was something that the job would *confer* on these workers as a reward for their having been "chosen." It took the form of the program's three-month training period (unusually long, particularly for unskilled, minimum-wage workers), subsequent training, and substantial feedback from supervisors. For most people living in Ceará's interior, access to this kind of training was beyond the realm of possibility.

Workers in low-paid jobs requiring no initial skills often perceive no opportunity for upward mobility in their work. This is a recurrent theme in the attempts to explain poor productivity and worker performance in the industrialized countries.[31] Ceará's program seemed to avoid the productivity problems resulting from paying low wages and providing no job security by giving its health agents substantial ongoing training and conferring status on them from the start. Together, these two attributes of the program were enough to make these workers highly dedicated to their jobs.

Distrust and Respect

It is ironic that selling the idea of the "good public servant" would have been possible at a time when the public sector was so discredited in Brazil and elsewhere. In the 1960s and 1970s, the image of public service had become heavily tarnished because of its association with the military government that took over in the mid-1960s and gave up power to a civilian and democratically elected government only twenty years later. The repressive tactics of the military government, whose targets included peasant organizations in the interior of states like Ceará, created a profound distrust and fear of government agents, which persisted even after the civilian government took over in 1984.

Partly because of the distrust, the health agents found it quite difficult to gain access to people's homes when they started working. Mothers would not answer the agent's knocks on the door, or would hide their children when the agent crossed the threshold. Needless to say, this is a frequent problem for health programs in areas like rural Ceará, where people rely more on traditional medicine and local faith healers.[32] But in Ceará's case, as in many others, this reaction was also a legacy of the mistrust of anything coming from the "government."

Although the public associated the "bad" public servant with the military government, the democratic opening that everyone yearned for unleashed a new wave of contempt for the public servant. Starting in the late 1970s with the first gubernatorial elections and culminating in the first presidential elections of the mid-1980s, the return of democratic politics was said to have brought with it a "recommencement" of patronage politics and its ways of hiring for public sector jobs. An analysis of employment trends in the 1980s, for example, noted a marked increase in public sector employment in the Northeast in the early 1980s, in relation to the rest of the country, and linked it to the gubernatorial elections there for the first time in eighteen years.[33]

During the years when Ceará was hiring its new army of health agents, the next president of Brazil was successfully campaigning on a promise to "get rid of the 'maharajas' (*marajás*)"—public sector workers who lived off the income and perquisites of their jobs without doing much work. He portrayed himself as being particularly qualified for this task, because of his alleged success in reducing public sector employment in the small state of Alagôas, where he had been governor. His failure as president of Brazil to make substantial inroads on the turf of the "maharajas" and, more important, his involvement in major corruption scandals himself led, in 1992, to a successful public outcry for his impeachment by a disappointed electorate now more cynical than ever about public service.

In the late 1980s and early 1990s this environment of public skepticism about government, together with fiscal stringency, generated widespread popular support for reformist politicians to carry out, like Ceará's two governors, "lean-and-mean" policies in running the state's public sector. Like the presidential candidate just described, the two governors claimed they were going to reduce the state's public employment substantially by getting rid of "phantom workers" (*fantasmas*)—those who received paychecks but did not appear at work. After succeeding in eliminating several thousand such phantoms from the state's payroll, the state made good political capital out of publicly advertising that feat. It was in this same environment, however, that the state *hired* a large contingent of new workers for the health program and was able to create an image of "the good public servant" around them. Remarkably, the state succeeded in convincing the public, as well as the new workers, that a dedicated army of new public servants was, in those sorry times, perfectly imaginable.

The Central in the Decentralized

Standard diagnoses of poor performance of developing-country governments point, among other things, to the overcentralization of government functions.[34] Over the last decade, therefore, decentralization from central to local governments has become an important item on the agenda of development research and advice. This literature and its accompanying prescriptions have focused considerable attention on the responsibilities, capacities, weaknesses, and virtues of municipal government as well as other local institutions.

Given the current enthusiasm for decentralization and its strong association in Brazil and a number of other countries with "democratization" and "grass roots control," it would be easy to interpret the new health program as a fine story about decentralization. But this would be a mistake. While giving considerable discretion to the supervising nurses hired by the municipalities, the state has still maintained iron control over certain aspects of the program, as illustrated by the story of the hiring process, among others. (The programs in some of the municipalities, nevertheless, were weaker than the rest because they lacked the support of the mayor or were poorly supervised.)

The agreement dividing labor between state and local government called on the state to finance 85 percent of the program (health-agent wages mainly, and supplies), and the municipality 15 percent (from one to four nurse-supervisors, usually half-time and working the remaining time in curative care for the municipality).[35] The state was responsible for hiring the workers and supervising the nurse coordinators, and the municipality for hiring the nurse-supervisor and paying her salary. These were the only formal commitments required of the municipality.

Before the health program was launched in 1987, most municipalities had no such services. At best, the mayor had an ambulance at his disposal and kept a small dispensary of prescription medicines at his home. Mayors typically doled out these medicines, as well as ambulance rides, to relatives and friends, and to needy constituents in return for political loyalty. The new Brazilian Constitution of 1988 augmented the mayor's access to revenues for health expenditures by increasing the share of federal transfers going to local governments and mandating that 10 percent of these new revenues be spent on health (plus 25 percent on education).[36] Many mayors, however, continued spending less than the mandated amount on health, because enforcement mechanisms were not strong enough; or, if they did increase health expenditures, they continued dispensing services in the traditional clientelistic way. Given this history, the new health program did not enter a municipality without first explaining to the mayor that he would have no control over hiring the health agents and without first obtaining a formal commitment from the mayor to hire and pay a nurse-supervisor half-time.

In a certain way, then, the new program reduced the power of the mayors. They had no control over the hiring of a large number of new public employees in a program under their jurisdiction, and they had to finance part of the program out of funds that they could have used to their political benefit in other areas without such constraints on their power. It was not surprising, then, that some of the mayors were not very enthusiastic about the program when it began. One actually hired his own health agents out of municipal funds to accompany the state-hired agents on their rounds to households so that his agents could also distribute campaign leaflets on these visits—a frequent practice in field-based public services in Northeast Brazil—which the state's health agents were strictly prohibited from doing. Thus the mayors became as strong a potential source of trouble for the new decentralized program as the health professionals who were against the "paraprofessionalization" of health care. In response, the state found an ingenious solution to the problem, which eventually elicited municipal participation and capacity building.

Ironically, the program's division of labor between state and municipality was somewhat of an accident, and "second-best" from the state's point of view. Moreover, this division was nearly the opposite of what might have been expected. That is to say, the Department of Health would have preferred to have had complete control, particularly over the hiring of nurse-supervisors; it understood how crucial good supervision was to such a program, and it was worried about the patronage practices endemic in municipal hiring. But given the cutbacks in the transfers received by the state from the federal government, and the rechanneling of some of them directly to the municipalities, it could not afford to finance the program completely on its own. It also could not go against the political popularity of decentralization, as mandated in the new constitution. Any program so grounded in the municipality would need some form of at least tacit support from local authorities in order to function smoothly.

Instead of maintaining control over the more technical, supervisory jobs, the state chose to control the hiring and training of the much more numerous *unskilled* jobs of the health agents. Under this arrangement, the hiring (and firing) of the nurses could have been just as subject to patronage and cronyism as the state feared the hiring of the agents would be; or, the mayors could have simply decided not to come up with their 15 percent of the funds. But because the position of supervising nurse played a key role in the program, and because there were only one or two such positions available, it was quite conspicuous in each municipality's program.

In addition, although the mayors may have preferred not to commit municipal funds to a health program so much outside of their control, they were subject to strong pressures from the community to enter the program. These pressures—to initiate the program, to hire qualified nurses, and to run it cleanly—were in themselves a result of the state's flurry of publicity around the program: communities without the program pressured and educated their mayors into getting it and making sure it worked. Once a program was in place, additional pressures and information from the army of health agents, as well as the community, elicited further contributions from mayors for items to which they had not been formally committed, such as bicycles, canoes, and mules for the agents so they could reach more remote households, or chlorine for campaigns against cholera.

As a result of the state's publicity about the program, then, both the state government *and* the community exerted a kind of "scissors" pressure on the mayors that forced them to support the program and to not misbehave. Once the team of thirty or more agents and their nurse-supervisor were ensconced in a municipality, they became a formidable force in educating, as well as pressuring, the local government to live up to its responsibilities for providing health services. Ultimately, the mayors found that when the program operated well, it was quite popular and they could take much of the credit. In creating an informed and demanding community, the state had initiated a dynamic in which the mayors were rewarded politically for supporting the program. This helped it replace the old patronage dynamic with a more service-oriented one.

The state actually saw a certain advantage to having the nurse-supervisors hired by the municipality rather than by the state, which counterbalanced their concern about patronage in hiring. If the nurse-supervisors were to be hired by the state Department of Health, agency managers reasoned, their professional futures might well lie in the capital city and not the communities where they worked. As it turned out, the nurses *did* value their jobs, although for more positive reasons than not having a ticket to higher-level state jobs.

Most decentralized programs are, like Ceará's, a mix of local *and* central elements. But the literature on decentralization, with its agenda for reducing the disadvantages of centralized government, has focused mainly on the new possibilities and responsibilities of *local* governments and other local institutions and on the new capacities and revenue sources they must acquire. This lack of emphasis on the tasks of the *central* government in the new order is understandable, of course, since local governments are weak and need attention. In addition, asking central governments to do *less* of what they normally do would not seem that demanding or complex, albeit sometimes politically difficult. As the health story shows, however, the state government was not simply doing "less" of what it had been doing before. Indeed, its actions in the health program represented more than it had been doing in the health sector before and consisted of quite different tasks.

The health program also represented a more incremental and indirect path to decentralization than that usually taken or, at least planned. The state surrounded the mayors with community pressure to "voluntarily" take on more responsibility and be more accountable. As a result of the initial lack of enthusiasm of some of the mayors and the voluntary nature of their participation, the program spread through the state at a gradual pace over a period of a few years, in accordance with the rate of requests backed by commitments from municipalities. Rather than being the result of a full-blown decentralization, then, the program's achievements represented some first steps in that direction. By proceeding in this way, and by luring mayors into the program one by one, the program was given increased financing, responsibility, and, ultimately capacity for local control.

The literature concerning decentralization and the proper division of labor between local and more centralized levels of government tends to see central governments as specializing in inputs and services in which they have a comparative advantage—technical expertise (including supervision and monitoring) and activities with economies of scale (such as financing and capital-intensive facilities). These are usually the more sophisticated, more costly, and "harder" parts of the package. Elinor Ostrom's study of the decentralization of police services in U.S. cities, for example, shows that police headquarters does best at providing evidence labs or vehicle maintenance, while the decentralized local precinct stations do best at managing police patrol and other activities requiring constant contact with the community or "outreach."[37]

The health program did, indeed, follow this division of labor, with the state providing financing, supervision, and medicines and other supplies. But it was very active in a crucial aspect of the outreach. It created an image around the job and the program and, through this image, gained community support in monitoring the "outreachers." One would not have thought that the management of outreach or something as "soft" as image creation would be such a key function of the central government in a program of decentralized management.

The Self-Enlarging Job

Many of the workers in the municipalities where the health program performed best did things that did not fall strictly within the definition of their jobs. (This finding was repeated in the three other sectors reviewed in the larger research study—agricultural extension, business extension, and drought relief.) These extra tasks fell into three categories: briefly, the carrying out of some simple curative, as opposed to preventive, practices; the initiation of communitywide campaigns to reduce public health hazards; and the assistance to mothers with mundane tasks not directly related to health. In all these areas, the agents took on this larger variety of tasks voluntarily, without being asked by their supervisors, and they liked their jobs better for having done so.

Extra activities of this nature often creep into preventive health programs, as well as other programs in sectors with considerable contact between workers and clients.[38] Some health planners would argue that this approach undermines enlightened conceptions of how good health programs should function, just as agricultural planners might argue that such extra activities in agricultural extension merely contribute to the poor performance of extension services. How is it that

such "nonessential" activities could be associated with worker satisfaction and good performance in the eyes of workers and with bad
performance in the eyes of experts? The answer may have something
to do with recent findings in the literature of industrial performance
and workplace transformation: namely, that higher performance and
worker satisfaction tend to be *consistent* with enlarged and more varied jobs.

CREEPING CURATIVISM.   The curative procedures performed by the
agents in the Ceará program were quite simple ones: removing
stitches, treating wounds, giving shots, providing advice on treating
colds and flus, taking a sick child to the hospital. The agents contrasted
the immediate results of their curative procedures with the "tedious
and frustrating process" of getting people to change their health and
hygiene practices: teaching mothers how to take care of themselves
during pregnancy and how to take care of the babies after they were
born, and convincing people to take their medicines regularly, wash
their hands before preparing food, filter their water, and add nutri-
tious foods to their diet. It took considerable patience and perseverance
to convince new mothers, who usually preferred bottle feeding,
that breast milk was not "sour" and distasteful to their babies or that
they should take time out of their day to attend prenatal appoint-
ments.

In contrast, the agents viewed their simple curative activities as an
"entryway" into preventive care. "I first earned the respect and trust
of families by treating wounds or giving a shot," an agent reported,
"so that now families listen to me when I talk to them about breast-
feeding, or better hygiene or nutrition—things that don't show immediate results." In the same vein, the agents liked administering oral
rehydration solutions because they seemed like cures, to the agent as
well as the desperate mother: a severely dehydrated baby, seemingly
near death, would be happily playing in high spirits only hours after
taking the rehydration solution recommended by the health agent.
Agents also liked preventive work that, like much of curative care,
involved the provision or handling of physical objects, precisely like
the mixing together of water, sugar, and salt for oral rehydration.

Finally, with respect to curative tasks, health agents often ended up
treating men for minor wounds and other ailments. This went beyond
their obligations, given that the program was targeted on pregnant

women and mothers with children under the age of five. The treatment of men for minor wounds won their attention and respect for the program; one man, for example, stopped a health agent on the street to show her, proudly and thankfully, how well his leg, which she had treated after it had been injured in a bicycle accident, was healing. The respect won from the men of the community turned out to be important in helping the agents to gain access to resisting and fearful households, to get their preventive messages taken seriously in the community—to impress upon its inhabitants that the program was not "just for women and children"—and to garner community support for the communitywide actions designed to prevent health problems from developing.

Using curative tasks to get one's foot in the door for the less dramatic, longer haul of changing people's health thinking and practices would seem to represent a quite sensible admixture to a preventive health program, especially if that is what made health agents do better on the preventive side. But curative care can also be "dangerous" because it tends to crowd out preventive care in practice and in funding, even though well-funded programs of this kind cost only a small fraction of a curative care program.[39] Moreover, although preventive health programs are meant to complement curative care, the users of health services value curative care more because it shows quick results—as the agents in Ceará themselves said—in contrast to the advice giving that is the bread and butter of preventive care. The "infiltration" of preventive programs by curative care is therefore one of the major concerns of the preventive health field, and with good reason.[40]

Public health reformers throughout the world have criticized the "overemphasis" on curative care as one of the main causes of the neglect of preventive care and its disastrous consequences in the form of disease and death.[41] Critics point to physicians as the culprits. Physicians find curative care more interesting and challenging than preventive care, understandably, and they want to practice medicine with the best diagnostic and treatment facilities they can get, which translates into high-cost, large, urban hospitals. The much less capital-intensive and less high-tech work of preventive care is low status for most physicians and hence of less interest to them, just as road maintenance is less challenging and prestigious to civil engineers than road construction. Because physicians play a prominent role in health planning and in professional pressure groups, the taste for curative care gets translated into underallocation of resources to preventive care. The Ceará story shows, however, that doctors are not the only villains in the story. Low-tech preventive care workers *themselves* prefer curative care just as much as the doctors do or, at least, some rustic admixture of it with their preventive routines.

Preventive health programs in developing countries are particularly vulnerable to "creeping curativism." Even if they start with only a few curative tasks, the taste for immediate results causes the curative share to get larger and larger through time, squeezing out the preventive work. Clearly, then, one cannot throw caution to the winds and simply allow preventive health agents to do as much curative care as they want, just to keep them and their clients happy. Nevertheless, it is still important to understand the positive impact of curative tasks on the *preventive* agenda in increasing worker and client satisfaction and hence in improving performance.

The creeping curative care in Ceará's preventive program has not gone unnoticed. Nursing professionals in the state's capital have complained that agents should not be dispensing curative care, no matter how minimal, without at least receiving training as nurse assistants. The program's management, in response, has shown some willingness to consider providing formal nurse assistant training to at least some of its health agents. This constructive response raises the specter of another possible problem, which illustrates just how difficult it is for a preventive program to obtain the salutary effects of a "little" curative care without being overtaken by it. The more narrowly defined technical training in curative care now being recommended for Ceará's preventive health program may simply enable the health workers to go too far in the curative direction, which is exactly what preventive health planners worry about.

FROM HOUSEHOLD TO COMMUNITY.   Many health agents took on, of their own accord, communitywide activities meant to reduce public health hazards—in addition to their job of visiting households. In one case, for example, agents obtained free air time on the radio in order to name families leaving garbage in front of their homes; in another, agents pressured workers and management in a bakery to wear hair nets and wash their hands; in yet another, agents worked with their supervisor to introduce meetings on family planning and female sexuality, which were not a part of the program. Interestingly, this taking on of larger causes was in part the result of the program's initial social-ization of these workers into public service with images of "doing good" and the dedicated public servant.

Some health managers have worried about the tension that such broader activities often create between the program and local authori-ties. Or they complain that such activities distract health workers from the more basic tasks of preventive health. But many public health re-formers, reflecting a strong current of thinking in the fields of preven-tive health and medical anthropology, *encourage* preventive health workers to see themselves as "agents of change" and of "empow-erment." There is a large literature on this subject, but it does not bear directly on the points being made here.[42]

Health agents in Ceará also liked their work when they were pulled away from their routine preventive tasks to participate in community-wide campaigns against epidemics of disease, the most recent example being the state's campaign against cholera. Although not always seeing immediate results, the workers who participated in these campaigns felt themselves swept up in a serious and dramatic public mission, in which the topmost officials of the state were intimately involved. This was more exciting than giving mothers the same message over and over again about breast feeding or prenatal care. The same sense of the heroic also explains the sudden bursts of good performance by workers in agricultural extension services during epidemics of crop disease or pest infestation.[43]

TRUST AND THE MUNDANE.   The third area in which health workers went beyond their mandate voluntarily was related to quite mundane activities. Because agents visited homes during the day when mothers were there alone with young children, they sometimes assisted with the cooking, cleaning, or childcare by giving a baby a bath or cutting its fingernails or hair. The mothers, often lonely and overburdened, found considerable solace in this support and in sharing their prob-lems with the agent. "She is a true friend," a mother said of the health agent working in her community. "She's done more for us than she'll ever realize."

This additional attention might seem to increase the burden of an already heavy work agenda, which required several household visits a day, often to places difficult to reach. Agents reported, however, that the extra help they offered was crucial to gaining the trust of the mothers, as well as the community in general, which they found to be the most difficult task of their work, at least at the beginning.

In addition, and very important to the understanding of these workers' worlds, they saw their clients not only as subjects whose behavior they wanted to change but as people from whom they wanted respect and trust. Indeed, respect from clients and from "my community" dominated their talk about why they liked their jobs—much more than how they felt about their supervisors and other superiors. Although they prized the relationship with a good supervisor, they had much less contact with that person than they did with their clients. In sum, as workers they seemed to need trusting relationships with their clients as much as they needed to see signs of changed health practices. And the "extra tasks" helped to create those relationships. The satisfaction that these workers felt in being trusted by their clients and the community enabled them to convey preventive health messages most effectively to bring change to the communities where they worked.

Although up to now the development literature has concentrated on the reasons for *mis*trusting public sector workers, as noted earlier, the theme of trust between workers and clients or customers is gaining considerable attention in studies of industrial performance. These studies have found a strong relationship between certain high-performing sectors and firms in the industrialized world and the degree of "trust" between the individual worker and customer, or between the subcontractor and supplier firm. With their extra tasks, Ceará's health agents were building this same kind of trust, and that surely explains in part the program's good performance.

Conclusion

—Government workers in Ceará's successful preventive health program felt a strong commitment to their jobs, which endowed them with new status and prestige. This came from a good relationship not only with their supervisors, but also from the communities where they worked. This latter is rather surprising in view of the general public's growing contempt for the government and its civil servants. The new public recognition, in turn, had a significant influence on the workers' performance.

—The state government's widespread advertising of its programs and their achievements—partly informational and, later, partly sheer boasting about its achievements—contributed to the new prestige. Through a remarkable merit-hiring process for 7,300 health agents, a raising of expectations about progress, and an appeal to the collective sense of the program's workers and the community, the state created an aura of dignity and hope around the program and its workers.

—Workers often did things that fell outside their job definitions, things that were not considered to be "best practice." For example, preventive health workers provided a little curative care or helped mothers with household chores. Rather than being viewed as deviations from standard practice, this broader set of tasks cohered together as a more "customized" way of providing service to clients, which in turn further boosted the public's respect for these workers and formed the basis for relations of trust between workers and citizens.

—Certain new mechanisms from outside the health agencies came into play that hemmed public employees in with pressures to be accountable. This offset the greater ambiguity of their job definitions and the greater difficulties of supervision that it might create. Some of these outside pressures were the flip side of the growing public recognition that health agents were experiencing. The state's collective consciousness-raising about the program and the merit-hiring procedure also served to inform the public about what the programs and their workers should or should not be doing and hence drew the public in as informal outside monitors.

—The key to the success of this partial decentralization to local governments was not to be found only in local governments' new powers, funds, or capacities. Rather, the quality of the program was a direct result of the state's iron control over the hiring process for health agents, its constant messages to the constituents of the municipalities about the mayors' responsibilities to support the program and run it cleanly, and its suggestions that citizens vote against mayors who did not do so. What the *central*, rather than local, government was doing, in sum, proved to be the key to the success of this decentralization.

The findings reported in this chapter might at first blush seem to be relevant only to the health sector, particularly to preventive health programs. They might also seem to be a function of the particulars of the Ceará case—namely, the hiring of so many rural women. Clearly, this kind of work force would be extremely grateful for its "scarce" public sector employment. Also, these workers experienced that special excitement of participating in a bold new public venture. And in places like the interior of Ceará, where infant mortality is so high, it is not that difficult to make rapid improvements on this front—in comparison with many of the other areas in which preventive health programs struggle to preserve the community's well-being. Most public programs do not operate in this kind of "honeymoon" environment. *Not* getting good performance in this kind of situation, in other words, would be unusual.

Loosely similar findings, however, emerged in some of the other sectors studied as part of this research.[44] In contrast to the health program, these other programs hired no new workers; on the contrary, the study period was one of personnel cutbacks and fiscal privation for them. With certain sectoral variations, these other workers also reported liking their jobs better for reasons similar to those reported above.

In the new theories of public sector behavior, as mentioned earlier, the main hope for improving performance lies in hemming in civil servants with policies and work environments that restrict their opportunities to misbehave or, failing that, in simply reducing their numbers. In boiling down the study of poor public sector performance to the self-interested individual, surrounded by opportunities to subvert the public good, the current theories ascribe too much determinacy to this outcome. The health story and others like it suggest that things do not work this way. Even when civil servants are surrounded by opportunities to act in their own interest and against the public's, they often do not do so. The story of the health program helps illuminate the circumstances under which public servants will or will not act in the public interest and what governments can do to influence those circumstances.

The way in which Ceará hired and advertised its health program enabled it to *shape* the person who was to become a public worker. This exercise in image creation and its positive effect on worker performance suggests that the self-seeking interest of the public employee is not always as powerful or incorrigible as it is assumed to be. That is to say, if the self-seeking "rational" actor is the basic unit of analysis for predicting behavior, then the person who went through the socialization of the health program as described above would behave no differently, given the same temptations, than if she had gotten the job through family or political connections.

In arguing along lines that differ from the prevailing view, we are also painting a somewhat different picture of the constraints and opportunities for improvement in public sector performance. In our picture, self-interest can be a variable rather than a constant: a government may be able in some cases to broaden the concept of self-interest to include that of a "public calling." That the image of the public servant could have been so effectively reversed in this particular case suggests that the image itself—whether good *or* bad—may play as important a role in determining workers' behavior as their "innate" self-interests.

To make matters even more indeterminate, some in the public sector actually *enjoy* serving the public good, in addition to the self-serving others. At any moment in time, performance will be partly determined by which group holds power. Governments can, in addition, build pressures and incentives into programs, as in the health case, that can even turn some of those leaning toward self-interested behavior into more public-minded beings. The structure of certain programs and their messages, as the new policy advice suggests, can indeed be designed to hem self-interested public workers in with pressures to be accountable. But certain actions by the government can also be transformative—as they certainly must have been in the health story. Although this interpretation suffers from being less elegantly simple and deterministic than the prevailing theories, it also opens up a wider front of choices for program and policy advice.

Ten

Visibility and Disappointment
The New Role of Development Evaluation

Robert Picciotto

I FIRST MET Albert O. Hirschman in 1964, just before he embarked on the field visits that yielded *Development Projects Observed.*[1] He evinced curiosity about my work as a junior project economist in the World Bank, and I proudly described my contributions to the "rate-of-return" crusade that was being waged by project economists to secure a foothold within an institution still dominated by financial analysts and engineers.

Given the prevailing orthodoxy, I was surprised by Hirschman's lack of enthusiasm for the heroic calculations I was producing and could not fathom his insistent queries about the "hidden assumptions" embedded in a project evaluation methodology that was so obviously full of promise.

Since then, as a development practitioner, I have had occasion to reflect on the unspoken hypotheses that underlie traditional economic evaluation. In the process, I have read—and reread—everything of Hirschman I could find, and in the fog of the daily transactions associated with the development business, I have made frequent use of his ideas to make sense of what I saw.

But it is mostly the memory of Hirschman's irreverent, playful, and insistent questioning that has stayed with me. For behind the detachment of his deceptively cool demeanor, a passion to get to the center of development issues came through and proved, somehow, infectious.

So, almost thirty years after my initial encounter with Hirschman, the time has come to respond to his deceptively naive questions about the evolving practice of development evaluation and, in the process, to reflect on his pioneering contributions to the profession.

An Evaluation Pioneer

Hirschman has been consecrated as a pioneer of development economics.[2] But to posit that he is a pioneer of evaluation is far from uncontroversial. Hirschman himself may not relish the proposition since much of the official evaluation literature is not distinguished by elegance or subtlety. Conversely, evaluation professionals steeped in the auditing tradition may find the proposition preposterous, while, at the other end of the spectrum, the "scientific" exponents of theory-based evaluation and social experimentation will consider it improbable.

"The main function of evaluation," according to Michael Scriven, "is the determination of the merit and worth of programs in terms of how effectively and efficiently they are serving those affected, particularly those receiving, or who should be receiving, the services provided and those who pay for the programs—typically taxpayers or their representatives."[3] In the absence of market tests, the function helps stakeholders assess whether a policy, a program, or a project has been effective. Typically, evaluators begin their work by comparing outcomes with original plans. Next, they assess the relevance of these plans, that is, their contribution to country development objectives. Finally, they judge the balance between costs and benefits. Thus evaluation—broadly defined to include the extraction, interpretation, and use of information and ideas relevant to public policies, programs, and projects—is to the public sector what accounting is to the private sector.

Evaluation differs from macroeconomics in at least three ways. First, evaluation is concerned with "micro" phenomena and specific programs and does not normally aim to explain, let alone model, the evolution of the total economic system. Second, it is multidisciplinary. Public administration, engineering, business management, statistics, sociology, and political science all command substantial influence in evaluation organizations. Third, whereas research economists are prone to search for the selected facts or numbers that will confirm (or invalidate) their models, evaluation practitioners are pragmatic and suspicious of grand theories.

Hirschman's down-to-earth method of inquiry conforms to these characteristics, and according to him, "A fundamental characteristic of humans is that they are self-evaluating beings, perhaps the only ones among living organisms."[4] In order to assess the mechanics of reform in Latin America, Hirschman "set out on a hazardous expedition into the vast no man's land stretching between economics and other social sciences such as political science, sociology and history. . . . [He] conducted interviews with numerous government officials, political, business and labor leaders, intellectuals, and economists who had special knowledge about the events that [he] intended to chronicle, often because they had played important roles in them."[5]

Thus Hirschman resists rigid hypothesis testing within the boundaries of a single discipline. He approaches the world "without theoretical preconceptions of any kind." *The Strategy of Economic Development* reflects the dilemmas he encountered as an official adviser to the government of Colombia in the early 1950s, when he used his firsthand observations of how things work to develop views about planning that were at odds with the conventional wisdom of the times, in general, and the doctrines of his World Bank sponsors, in particular. Similarly, he constructed the exit/voice/loyalty framework, arguably the most seminal metaphor of institutional economics, merely to understand the travails of a troubled Nigerian railways administration that he had observed on a field visit.

The development practitioner is accustomed to dealing with the unexpected. Equally, Hirschman is at his best when faced with "seemingly odd, irrational, or reprehensible social behavior." In searching the "hidden rationalities" that underlie the actions of hard-pressed economic agents, he uncovers illuminating paradigms that challenge the conventional wisdom. Hirschman's acerbic remarks about the grandiloquent homilies to which policy-oriented economists frequently succumb have contributed to the sense of solidarity that many of his readers who are foot soldiers of development feel toward a comrade in arms. Almost alone among development economists, Hirschman has articulated the little-publicized role of development agencies and private voluntary organizations in helping to get things done on the ground.

Furthermore, Hirschman's value-laden, policy-oriented paradigms may be rightfully claimed by the evaluation profession, whose principal vocation is to influence policy. By contrast, many social scientists hold the view that the proper function of their work is limited to describing the way the world is—not the way it ought to be. For them, policy recommendations cannot be established through the legitimate exercise of their occupation. Not for Hirschman. This is fortunate since, in the words of Michael Scriven, the value-free doctrine has "kept the ivory tower insulated from the pains and perils of the real world. . . . Society paid a terrible price for this self-indulgence, a policy that kept the social sciences out of the kitchen because of its heat." From this perspective, evaluation may even be viewed as "the discipline that leads social science to expand its previously narrow self-concept."[6]

In what follows, I consider development evaluation in the light of Hirschman's ideas. Inspired by those ideas, I use two interrelated concepts, visibility and disappointment, to illuminate the interaction among evaluation, participation, and the policy reform process. Next, I examine the relevance of Hirschman's metaphor of the "hiding hand" to the evaluation function. Finally, I note how current thinking about development and evaluation is catching up with Hirschman—an unusual circumstance for a chronic dissenter, accustomed to sailing against the wind.

Understanding Policy Reform

Oscar Wilde once observed that architects differ from doctors in that they "cannot bury their mistakes." Visibility could indeed be one of the reasons why master builders have produced awesome works of art since the dawn of civilization, whereas it took millennia for the medical profession to transcend quackery and superstition: before the advent of autopsies, private medical activity was cloaked in ritual and secrecy while construction of large structures has always been a public event.

Visibility

In the same vein, Hirschman's *Development Projects Observed* advances the proposition that technologically complex schemes are implemented more successfully than projects that make limited demands on scarce technical and management resources, even in countries hindered by weak institutions and scarce skills. Probing this apparent paradox, Hirschman has argued that the risk of spectacular failure that large, prominent, and technically advanced schemes entail restricts "latitude" for inferior performance and brings forth extraordinary exertion from project participants, a proposition at variance with the "appropriate technology" doctrine that was then in vogue.

The shock of a natural disaster generates similar pressures for rigorous, time-bound performance. Exactly two months after the 1987 earthquake that damaged oil production fields and a pipeline carrying a significant share of Ecuador's oil to its export markets, the World Bank approved a reconstruction loan. A demanding schedule was agreed and it was met. Streamlined design and contracting procedures were used and innovative repair techniques were pioneered to deal with the rugged terrain and poor accessibility of significant portions of the damaged trans-Ecuadorian pipeline. The project had a rate of return greater than 100 percent, as estimated at inception. For an investment of about $100 million, Ecuador secured a yearly net income of about $500 million.

The visibility of the high-stakes pipeline project and its use of advanced technology restricted the latitude for inadequate performance and led to unusually speedy and effective results. By contrast, technical assistance to the project, which focused on environmental problems and emergency preparedness, entailed broader latitude characteristics and took three years longer than planned to reach completion.

The larger the project, the more visible it is. While the evidence is mixed, there is substantial empirical grounding for the proposition that small is not always beautiful. For example, a 1992 independent evaluation of 274 completed World Bank projects indicated a distinct correlation between the size of individual operations and their satisfactory outcomes. Whereas only 60–65 percent of projects involving loans smaller than $25 million were judged satisfactory at completion, some 80–90 percent of those involving loans greater than $150 million were so classified.[7] Evidently, the higher success rate reflected the strong commitment that large and visible ventures evince from their sponsors. That is to say, large schemes often embody limited tolerance for error.

There is also evidence to suggest that the latitude-reducing impact of technology can be positive: out of 3,159 projects financed by the World Bank, the share of satisfactory outcomes has been found to be larger for technologically demanding sectors (telecommunications, energy, and transport—with satisfactory outcomes ranging from 82 percent to 90 percent) than for "softer" sectors (agriculture, tourism and technical assistance—with satisfactory outcomes in the 64–67 percent range).

This said, it should also be pointed out that spectacular project failures (from steel mills in Nigeria to cement projects in Pakistan) are often associated with large and technically demanding ventures. Conversely, satisfactory outcomes are not limited to "hard," large, modern ventures. For example, the share of successful outcomes for World Bank projects evaluated since 1970 turns out to be lower in industry-related projects (68 percent) than in those connected with human resource development (79 percent). This suggests that Hirschman's idea that performance is enhanced in tasks of narrow latitude is a powerful and useful metaphor rather than a strictly generalizable theory. Factors other than technology or size are evidently at work—for example, institutional structure and leadership—factors that Hirschman has also explored.[8]

The training and visit (T & V) approach to improved agriculture extension, sponsored by the World Bank, illustrates the importance of organization and leadership in achieving development goals.[9] Throughout South Asia and sub-Saharan Africa, T & V has spawned an impressively successful set of projects directed at enhancing agricultural productivity. Hundreds of thousands of small farmers have been reached, and the resulting transfer of knowledge has accelerated the adoption of profitable farming practices, the use of high-yielding varieties of crops, and the effective use of irrigation facilities.

Neither scale nor sophisticated technology explains the favorable results of the new extension system. Most of these projects are small and rely mainly on local skills. They consist of weekly visits by extension workers to designated contact farmers, weekly training of extension workers by research personnel, and a concentrated focus on proven technologies. World Bank funding has been modest and geared to the provision of shoes, bicycles, and jeeps to ensure staff mobility and modest housing, so as to make extension agents less dependent on the hospitality of large farmers.

The key to T & V's success has been a charismatic individual (Daniel Benor) intent on introducing clear-cut management practices in a service that has traditionally been neglected and plagued by low morale. To use Hirschman's language, "trait making" has been the critical contribution of Daniel Benor and his disciples. Guided by a simple set of management principles and endowed with missionary zeal, they have mobilized and motivated the entire extension chain, from the village-level worker to the minister of agriculture, in a wide range of country situations.

The T & V experience demonstrates that the positive impact of project visibility may arise independently of scale or technological characteristics. Organizational design can make project officials responsive to local communities, and external demands for performance can "pull" improved results out of established agencies (as in the case of the visible and regular demand exerted on research agencies by extension agents). Both of these forces can set bounds on the "free-riding" behavior commonly associated with "soft" programs run by government agencies. Thus, T & V participants have been highly motivated not only because they were pressured to perform by the professional supervising them but also because they were involved in a highly visible and prestigious program. Such selective incentives and pressure mechanisms have proved to be powerful instigators of change even in the absence of improved remuneration.

To be sure, organizations require frequent fine tuning and periodic overhauling. Even a successful innovation such as T & V cannot be sustained forever, given its dependence on a stream of profitable technologies, its vulnerability to fiscal stringency, and the limitations of its top-down leadership style. Judith Tendler's study of rural development in northeast Brazil highlights the limitations of large professional bureaucracies and reaffirms the salutary pressures of "bottom-up" beneficiary involvement coupled with the bracing impact of demands and guidance from enlightened political leaders (see chapter 9).[10]

The role that institutions play in shaping project performance can also be seen in Bangladesh. That country's flood protection policy has been shaped by an inadequate appreciation of the alternatives available to expand food production and protect human settlement, as a result of weak executing agencies, inadequate evaluation skills, and a lack of community involvement in project design and execution.[11] Despite decades of development assistance to Bangladesh, the technical and institutional complexities involved in constructing, maintaining, and protecting major embankments have not been mastered. In this particular case, the visibility associated with scale and engineering complexity did not induce effective project outcomes. Instead, visibility had perverse results: whenever exceptional floods and the attendant human misery have been visited on Bangladesh, promoters of inappropriate engineering solutions have grasped the opportunity to harness local and international resources to give new life to their dubious schemes.

Growing evidence of such public sector failures has led to critical reviews of the comparative advantages of public and private provision of infrastructure services and to the design of institutional solutions adapted both to the new technologies and to the specific externalities of particular kinds of infrastructure.[12]

The design of project organizations should make room for competition, participation, and regulation, or, to use Hirschman's terms, for judicious admixtures of exit (the market), voice (politics), and loyalty (trust-inducing mechanisms). For example, the dairy cooperative system pioneered in the Kaira district of Gujarat, India, combines businesslike marketing (exit), strong community participation (voice), and a variety of selective incentives aimed at boosting loyalty. The dissemination of this model to other states of India, financed by the World Bank, was not uniformly successful, partly because it turned out to be difficult to replicate an effective voice mechanism in regions devoid of the strong cooperative tradition of Gujarat.

In short, the visibility that stems from project size and advanced technology may not be sufficient to produce effective results. The organizational engineering of projects is equally important in this regard, and it, in turn, must take into account the larger institutional environment, including the traditions of cooperation, discipline, and participation embedded in the local scene.

Disappointment

As Hirschman has pointed out in *Journeys toward Progress*, the reform-enhancing effects of project visibility are closely linked to the existence and manifestations of public disappointment. Recently, large dams have become a target of public protest because the harmful environmental and social consequences of some projects of this kind have become visible. In response to these pressures, governments have introduced more exacting standards to protect displaced people, minimize environmental damage, and provide recourse to affected communities through independent inspection. Reform is under way to "internalize the externalities" of large public investment projects in India, as a result of public attention on the disruptive consequences of involuntary resettlement associated with the construction of a major multipurpose project on the Narmada River.[13]

But just as project visibility does not by itself guarantee positive outcomes, so public protest also has its costs. With the aid of facsimile machines and other modern means of communication, it has become possible to mobilize small groups and to amplify their "voice" globally through the networks of nongovernmental organizations. Experience shows that countervailing pressure from the mass of domestic beneficiaries of large-scale projects is not so readily organized. The result has been an increase in the transaction costs associated with major infrastructure projects and a policy shift away from such schemes. By contrast, the travails of scattered, unsophisticated, and previously neglected rural works are far less visible, and the potential for effective public protest—and correlated remedial action—is low and uncertain. Such schemes are particularly vulnerable to "takeover" by local vested interests. Paradoxically, large projects may enjoy economies of scale not only in construction but also in terms of the efficacy of public pressure over their perceived defects. Yet small schemes are widely sought after as vehicles of external assistance because public opposition to the large projects schemes tends to linger well after remedial actions have been taken. In time, information about the mixed performance of small schemes will become visible and this may well induce a further swing in opinion, analogous to price movements. This illustrates how the development business is subject to cycles of fashion reflecting the interplay of project performance, the pace of reform, and the stickiness of public perceptions.

All this is consistent with Hirschman's view of policy change. Without public disappointment, there would be no social energy available to challenge authority. Public dissatisfaction resulting from economic shocks, natural disasters, or the visible shortcomings of projects generates pressures for reform. Conversely, where problems do not lead to public disillusionment and protest—either because they are hidden or are perceived to be intractable—the impetus to reform tends to be half-hearted or nonexistent. Hence it is the combination of visibility and disappointment that lights the spark. But whether reform actually materializes depends on the degree to which the institutional environment fosters social learning.

As Hirschman discovered in *Journeys*, social learning cannot take place without institutions that can channel public protest into responsive shifts of public policies. That channeling is done through the generation, dissemination, and interpretation of information that promotes public understanding of policies and programs. Social learning also demands accountability and a credible capacity for independent review. Hence evaluation is vital for improved institutional learning and transparency in decisionmaking. Public protest and participation transform the energy of disappointment into reform when evaluation lends a helping hand. Where evaluation functions are weak, policies tend to ossify and institutional arrangements remain in place well beyond the time when experience shows the need for change. Without adequate evaluation, the visibility of projects and policies may lead planners to prescribe faulty solutions to social, political, and economic problems, and public discontent may hinder reform if it is not channeled through a combination of evaluation and participation capable of triggering constructive engagement.

Figure 10-1 displays some of these relationships. It shows that policy outcomes may vary according to the availability of such factors as project visibility, participation, evaluation competency, and public understanding of policy issues. When project and policy outcomes are unsatisfactory and their workings are visible (a condition commonly described as "transparency"), local involvement in public decisionmaking is activated. This, in turn, yields successful reform if the public also has some understanding of policy issues, which can be enhanced by the evaluation efforts and responsiveness of public decisionmakers, along with public participation. When policy processes and project workings are not transparent, however, the public may become frustrated by poor outcomes and may be prompted to agitate or even engage in subversive activities unless it is smothered in ignorance, in which case it is likely to remain passive and lethargic.

Evaluation and the Hiding Hand

The argument that links evaluation to improved performance, via the visibility of outcomes and transparency of development, runs up against another of Hirschman's ideas, the famous hiding hand. Paradoxically, Hirschman views the hiding hand as providential. A project is more likely to be successful, he says, when there is *less* transparency,

FIGURE 10-1. *Public Response to Policy Shortcomings*

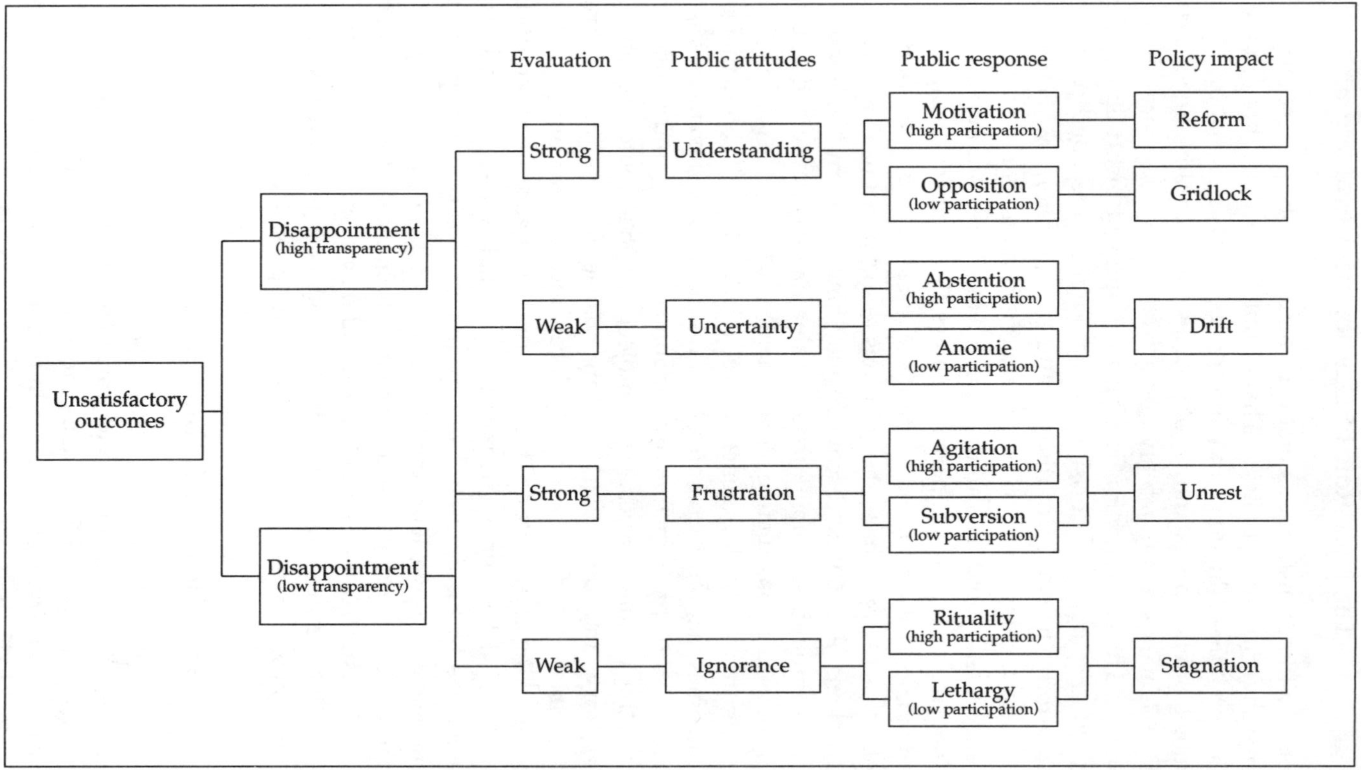

that is, when the true difficulty of a development project is at first hidden from those involved in its workings. In *Development Projects Observed*, agents of development tend to underestimate both the future difficulties they will face *and* the creativity they will summon. By underestimating the risks, they help to ensure that viable projects are undertaken. Thus, the hiding hand postpones the chilling effect of prudence over ambition and adds an aura of excitement and mystery to the development enterprise.

A World Bank–financed urban project in Colombia offers an illustration of the hiding hand phenomenon.[14] At its completion the project had been rated a dismal failure. A few years later, however, it began to show positive outcomes. The project involved the construction of community centers in slum areas in more than twenty-three cities of intermediate size. The buildings were designed on a grand scale, and it took a long time to construct them. The project also included a great many programs, most of which failed to reach the grandiose objectives that had been visualized by project planners. Sophisticated coordination mechanisms and elaborate planning processes proved cumbersome and unworkable in the local environment, which featured a highly centralized system of government.

In the ensuing years, however, the project began to have a substantial impact on development in the cities it served. The infrastructure and the associated training components helped microenterprises and a bustling local economy. Health services were delivered. A variety of social activities sprang up in the wake of community development. Once project funds were exhausted, responsibility for the project fell into local hands, which were able to coordinate activities smoothly and naturally, because of the proximity of services now installed in the vast new community buildings. The very size of the buildings showed that the government cared. Eventually, the project triggered unexpected initiatives and hopes, a rare development in marginalized and neglected slum areas. And the forward and backward linkages of project investments led to highly valuable benefits.

Here, then, is a case where the hiding hand worked. The naive vision of urban development that animated project sponsors induced risk taking and ultimately useful economic and social outcomes. But there are other cases in which side effects have no influence on the final outcome—and where the hiding hand becomes a sleight of hand activated by rent seekers or development con artists. In such circumstances—as in the Danube–Black Sea Canal in Ceaucescu's Romania—forward and backward linkages are weak and the hiding hand does not play a positive role.

More generally, the paths to development are strewn with the carcasses of failed schemes sponsored by leaders who overestimated their capacity to overcome problems and underestimated project risks and costs. In evaluating the pluses and minuses of the hiding hand, it is vital to distinguish—as many of those blinded by the metaphor do not—*what* is being hidden and *who* is doing the hiding and *why*.

Efficient markets thrive on good information: cost-effective transactions assume compliance with contractual conditions so that market exchange requires reliable information as well as credible enforcement mechanisms. Similarly, projects take place through a complex web of contracts and informal obligations. Hence it is essential to handle information in a transparent way if project performance is to be effective. The larger and more technically advanced the project, the more exacting the demand for specialization and coordination and the greater the investment needed to acquire, store, interpret, and disseminate information. Indeed, the narrow latitude for poor performance that Hirschman discovered in technologically advanced projects is, in part, a result of the transparent information flows that technology demands.

This is why the hiding hand can lead to serious dysfunctions if it is allowed to distort vital information about a project. For example, when public officials conceal the true extent of project costs from taxpayers or fail to make reasonable efforts to anticipate such costs, project management may succumb to laxity and even corruption. The lack of transparency about the anticipated benefits of an infrastructure scheme—such as a new highway—may also lead to inequitable windfalls, which benefit individuals with early access to information, for example, concerning strategically located real estate investments.

To reiterate, reliable information and the transparent handling of such information are leading determinants of effective project performance, while the sustainability of project benefits can be ensured in significant measure through rigorous project analyses. Of course, shifts in technologies, products, or practices may stretch the project in directions that are poorly adapted to the investments already sunk into information systems and agency practices. In such cases, project restructuring is needed. One function of evaluation is to provide decisionmakers with timely and reliable information so as to facilitate organizational adjustment and the rechanneling of information flows. In order to shift direction in a timely manner, participants must have a voice in implementation. Conversely, the exiting of project participants must be discouraged since adaptation to changing conditions demands specialized skills, ample experience, and familiarity with internal information channels and systems.

Hirschman defines loyalty as the organizational characteristic that gives scope to voice and discourages valuable participants from exiting. The need for loyalty is especially acute when the recourse to exit by experienced participants in public projects causes organizational performance to deteriorate. Loyalty, in other words, combines the exercise of voice with a voluntary decision not to exit, and its presence in an organization is directly connected to the role that evaluation and participation play in management. It depends directly on the participative content of management practices since participants have an incentive to exercise their voice option only where this may influence the organization. Furthermore, loyalty is enhanced by the availability of relevant information and knowledge: by enhancing stakeholders' chances of influencing decisions, evaluation contributes to improved organizational performance and makes the exit alternative less attractive.

Thus the hiding hand has its advantages as well as disadvantages. When planners underestimate the difficulties of a development venture, the benefits of a timely search for solutions may be lost, but the hiding hand also retards exit and provides a breathing spell for project managers that they may use, in turn, to discover creative ways of handling problems as they arise. Hence, the hiding hand tends to discourage premature exit by participants, that is, it plays a role akin to loyalty. And it is especially beneficial when forward and backward linkages are strong and spawn substantial indirect benefits—even when originally planned outcomes do not materialize. But, as already pointed out, the effect of the hiding hand depends on who hides what from whom.

As an instrument of providence (uncertainty), the hiding hand can be beneficial when it inspires leadership endowed with the right "vision." In particular, unexpected natural challenges can help a leader mobilize the scattered energies of participants. At the same time, when managers deliberately conceal difficulties and obstacles (which are not hidden from them) they may inhibit timely participation and make it more difficult to find the solutions needed to transcend the problems the organization is facing. Such a willful lack of transparency, once discovered, corrodes the very trust on which participation depends.

If overambitious targeting could be shown to be correlated with a favorable development impact, evaluators would not hesitate to commend optimistic forecasts. However, an extensive review of portfolio management practices in World Bank projects has demonstrated that unrealistic projections of benefits and costs are detrimental to project outcomes.[15] Sustainability can be achieved only through a constancy of purpose and the nurturing of consensus among project participants. In the short run, it may be expedient to secure support through over-optimistic goal setting. But to achieve staying power, social frustrations must be kept to a minimum and trust preserved through realistic objectives and transparent exposition of their risks and costs.

A recent study of adjustment lending in Africa concludes that policy reform programs succeed more readily when the objectives and the time frame for implementation are realistic, conditions are clear, and their order of priority is clearly defined. The more successful programs have been based on high-quality analysis, careful assessment of expected outcomes, thorough examination of the potential effects of external shocks such as commodity price declines, and a deliberate effort to build consensus in favor of reform.[16]

Prudent reviews of economic and social aspects as well as systematic involvement of beneficiaries are desirable for broadly based reform programs or large-scale investment projects. For example, a special study of the World Bank's experience with involuntary resettlement associated with major hydropower and irrigation schemes makes clear the need for thorough social impact surveys, accurate planning of resettlement programs, and systematic involvement of affected communities before major civil works are attempted.[17]

It will be particularly difficult to find constructive solutions to problems when the hiding hand conceals collective action dilemmas and project objectives cannot be agreed upon. For example, an excessive preoccupation with physical implementation (such as the construction of schools) may conceal a neglect of the essential development objectives (such as increased enrollment of girls or improved curricula). In such cases, monitoring and evaluation have usually been neglected or misdirected, with the result that remedial measures have not been identified at the time they can do the most good.

Blissful ignorance early in the project cycle is not necessarily followed by timely awareness of obstacles, let alone mobilization of appropriate responses, especially where commitment is weak and consensus is shaky. The hiding hand can be providential if wielded by nature, but its use (or misuse) by project managers or participants can undermine the reform-enhancing effects of visibility, disappointment, participation, and evaluation.

The New Development Agenda and Its Implications for Evaluation

Just as large dams have evoked lofty expectations followed by deep disillusionment, the development enterprise itself can be regarded as a boom-bust cycle in the eye of the public. In recent years, a new development consensus has emerged. Dissatisfaction with past outcomes has given rise to a new agenda that is more appropriate but also more ambitious, and in response to it the World Bank and other development agencies have made far-reaching adjustments in their goals and practices. The new development agenda looks very much like Hirschman's old one, which is not surprising, since Hirschman has had a major impact on it. His main ideas having been vindicated, he must now find himself close to the mainstream—a bittersweet outcome for an intellectual rebel.

Sustainable poverty reduction is once again the overarching theme of the development agenda. For Hirschman, development has always meant striving toward socially progressive ends; as an economist, he has invariably welcomed altruistic values into the profession, thus opposing the advocates of theoretical parsimony and dismal public choice. The new development consensus rejects centralized modes of resource allocation. From the start, Hirschman rejected the early view of development as a centrally planned process, driven by public investment and guided by input-output tables. Instead, he put forward models, as he wrote in *The Strategy of Economic Development*, that depended "not so much on finding optimal combinations for given resources and factors of production as on calling forth and enlisting for development purposes resources and abilities that are hidden, scattered or badly utilized."[18]

The role of institutions is becoming, at long last, a central concern of development economics, which is now focusing on the interplay of market and nonmarket instruments of economic management. As noted already, Hirschman was there first, searching for workable reform through ingenious combinations of politics and markets. Institutionalists are now emulating him as they turn from cynical explanations of failed governance to a search for constructive solutions to the dilemmas of sustainable development through institutional design.

Chastened by its disappointment with the simplistic doctrines of the right and the left, the mainstream development profession is finally catching up with Hirschman's intellectual contributions and shaping a new development agenda that, in turn, carries important implications for the evaluation profession.

A Changing Course for Evaluation

From an overwhelming preoccupation with the evaluation of public investment, through cost-benefit analysis and estimates of economic rates of return, development evaluation has shifted to the analysis of policies and institutions, and the design of flexible enabling environments for private enterprise, local initiative, and social action—all of which is familiar Hirschman territory.

It is instructive that, with the recent increase in the share of policy-based and institutional development operations, only about a third of World Bank project appraisals now include rate-of-return calculations. Development evaluation can no longer rely solely on reestimations of economic rates of return, even though the technique remains useful as a way of ensuring systematic attention to key development factors. There are several reasons for this. First, evaluators are now expected to judge programs and projects on the basis of their contribution to economic growth, poverty reduction, and environmental sustainability; and there is no straightforward method of calculating returns in terms of multiple development objectives.

Therefore, participatory evaluation must consider how consensus can be secured for second-best outcomes instead of merely berating development managers because first-best outcomes could not be achieved. Second, meaningful rate-of-return estimates cannot be produced in situations where indirect benefits and costs lie at the center of the development venture; for all but the simplest of schemes, one cannot possibly capture all relevant project features in a single number, the evaluation equivalent of the philosopher's stone. For these reasons and more, cost-benefit and rate-of-return analyses provide no guarantee of the visibility of outcomes or the transparency of operations. Indeed, the false precision of rate-of-return calculations may lull decisionmakers into a misleading sense of security and exacerbate the negative effects of the hiding hand.

In contrast to such conventional analyses of public investments, evaluation is moving in other directions. It is being increasingly pressed to consider the processes out of which development projects emerge and through which they are executed, the legal and regulatory environments in which projects operate, and especially the growing role that local authorities, nongovernmental organizations, and other elements of the civil society play in development.

Due consideration of the objectives originally set for a development venture remains part and parcel of sound evaluation practice (loyalty has its place), but evaluators also encourage flexible treatment of criteria for project outcomes, in order to accommodate to the shifting plans through which development agents try to adapt to changing circumstances. Recognizing that the economic and social environment is becoming increasingly volatile, development planners have turned away from detailed, long-term, centrally developed blueprints, in favor of a process orientation that emphasizes institutional aspects, rather than physical goals, and takes a flexible, often decentralized approach to the definition of objectives, means, and priorities. For example, the ambitious Chile Public Sector Management project, funded by the World Bank in 1985, was originally designed to address such major issues of public management as public enterprise reform and privatization. Because of procedural bottlenecks, the studies got off to a slow start, and by the time the disbursement of funds began, the government had already made its major decisions regarding privatization. At that point, a flexible approach was introduced that allowed the government to call on local consultants to carry out specific, practical, and timely studies related to the reform program. These changes, together with the appointment of a seasoned local coordinator who was granted considerable autonomy, permitted government commitment to emerge and the project to achieve a substantial measure of success.[19]

Given the new framework and priorities for development evalua-

tion, Hirschman's counterintuitive ideas serve as metaphors for evaluation practice. Knowingly or unknowingly, evaluators draw on Hirschman's metaphors as they explain awkward ways of moving forward as
coping strategies, for example, or treat sharp policy swings as attempts
to reconcile multiple development objectives. More fundamentally,
Hirschman's distrust of pieties paraded under the banner of development planning or efficient allocation of resources and his resistance
to prescription fit the temperament of evaluators who prefer targeted
findings and custom-made explanations to general theories and rou-
tinized calculations.

One of the principal ways in which the new development agenda
has influenced the evaluation profession is that it has focused attention
on participation, both as something to be evaluated and as a desirable
feature of the evaluation process itself. Participatory development is
often fingered as the culprit behind the declining success rate of development projects.[20] According to this diagnostic, participatory development leads to a more complex development agenda, which leads in
turn to projects of greater complexity and thus makes for poor performance. But the premises underlying this chain of reasoning are dubious. Is simplicity at the project level incompatible with a complex and
relevant program? Does participation hinder or help the management
of complexity? Would a simpler agenda secure public consensus in
support of development? There are alternative explanations for the declining project success rate: a more demanding agenda, derived in part
from the more visible shortcomings of past practices, brought to light
by improved evaluation; deterioration in the resource flows, commodity prices, and civil order that contribute to the development environment; heightened expectations for development, triggered by the
harsher environment.

Evaluators are coming to see participation less as a scapegoat for
failure and more as a contributor to success. As mentioned earlier,
popular participation in development policy and projects can help to
improve accountability, transparency, public trust, and "ownership"—
all of which are associated with positive development outcomes. In
hindsight, it is not surprising that unsatisfactory outcomes should be
highly correlated with a lack of ownership, and that this lack should
be attributed to a lack of participation. The time has come to address
explicitly and up front, the conditions that make for local ownership

of development projects, including participatory mechanisms that may keep loyalty to economic and social reforms alive in the face of adversity and disappointment.[21]

In particular, the role of *decentralized*, local participation in achieving development outcomes needs to be better understood. In rural areas, for example, integrated development, which relies heavily on autonomous administrative structures and expatriate technical assistance, has proved to be costly and unsustainable, and its wholesale importation of outside institutional models has not fostered local commitment and learning. On the other hand, decentralized control of development, with its submission to entrenched local power structures, has sometimes had counterproductive results. Because of the lessons of these failed experiments, area development projects have fallen into disfavor. Yet renewed emphasis on poverty reduction and more supportive economic policies have created a resurgent demand for well-designed area development projects focusing on sustainable and productive models of land utilization. A new generation of area development projects, many of them heavily invested in participation, has arisen on the basis of the lessons of evaluation experience.[22]

Participatory development has created a larger and more demanding market for evaluation services and has broadened and diversified the targets of evaluation. Increasingly, evaluation is called upon to reveal the "hidden irrationalities" of excessive centralization as well as those of premature decentralization. Here, as elsewhere, Hirschman has blazed trails of understanding that have influenced the directions of recent evaluation research.

Faced with the task of evaluating participatory development, evaluation itself is under pressure to become more participatory. Self-evaluation, practiced under the oversight of an independent evaluation authority, is a form of participatory evaluation that has considerable merit. However, participatory development means that the locus of self-evaluation tends to be fragmented, which poses further challenges to rigorous evaluation.

Concluding Comments

The new development agenda has shifted the focus of evaluation in directions previously explored by Hirschman. His evaluative methods are calculated to irritate, surprise, and sow seeds of doubt; and in the ensuing puzzlement, he has often brought people together by undermining the certainties and dogmas that divide them. In short, he has sought to contribute to the reform cycle through contrarian means. The evaluation profession is catching up. Within the framework of visibility and disappointment, evaluation contributes to the channeling of information and the encouragement of participation to convert the energy of public protest into constructive learning and reform. Now that the social dimension of development is receiving more attention, cost-benefit analysis is being enriched by multidisciplinary impact assessments, and participatory evaluation techniques are yielding their own contrarian findings. In time, Hirschman's surprising ideas will be included in the basic tool kit of evaluators not only because of their conceptual appeal but because they will be found to be helpful in facing up to reality.

Further, as fresh talent is brought into the field and the current disappointment with development economics finally calls forth a new focus on the institutional dimension of sustainable and equitable growth, we may yet enter the era visualized by Keynes, in which a new generation of social scientists, turning away from methodological rivalries, will join forces in evaluation and be perceived to be as useful as dentists.[23]

Eleven

Learning by Monitoring
The Institutions of Economic Development

Charles F. Sabel

THE CENTRAL DILEMMA of growth is reconciling the demands of learning with the demands of monitoring. By economic learning I mean acquiring the knowledge to make and do the things valued in markets. This, of course, supposes unlearning knowledge that is not so valued. Thus developing economies must forsake subsistence survival strategies and master current know-how while adapting it to local conditions and changing world markets. Advanced economies must escape the routine mastery of the technical and organizational know-how of earlier epochs to master the principles of the current one. Put another way, learning at all levels of economic development is about waking up and catching up. By monitoring I mean simply the determination by the transacting parties that the gains from learning are distributed as agreed. The ability to monitor is thus the capacity of each party to assess whether it is getting enough of a fair deal to continue dealing.

The Conflict between Learning and Monitoring

The dilemma of economic development is that learning undermines the stability of relations normally required for monitoring. Take first the relations among firms. The more settled the definition of products and production processes, the easier it is for firms to write contracts covering the contingencies associated with their transactions. Similarly, when economies of scale and other considerations lead to the concentration of production in vertically integrated firms, stability allows operations to be steered through the formulation of bureaucratic rules that are intelligible to subordinates and enforceable by superiors. But learning is not learning unless it disrupts this regularity and thus gives rise to a potentially paralyzing fear of the breakdown of monitorability. Consider two firms contemplating a project. Each worries that if it dedicates resources to the common project first, the other will delay performing on its promise until the agreement between them is renegotiated in its favor; so neither acts for fear of being held up by its partner. The problem is not generally solved if one firm purchases the other and replaces contractual coordination with hierarchical order. For within a bureaucratic corporation, innovations threaten the principals' control of their subordinate agents. Instructions for the execution of novel projects are by definition so complex and ambiguous—tell me if we are trying to solve the right problem— that agents can interpret them as authority to pursue their own ends, not those of their supervisors; and the redirection of effort may be undetectable to the higher-ups.[1]

A second, analogous conflict between the possibility of learning and the possibility of monitoring arises with regard to the relation between the economy as a whole and the state as the entity that sets the rules of economic transactions. The preponderance of historical evidence is that, regardless of their level of development, economies seldom pull themselves out of long-term, low-equilibrium traps by the bootstraps that market prices theoretically provide individual firms. Rather, unless the state reduces the risk of breaking with subsistence strategies or outdated practices by, say, sheltering domestic markets from foreign competition, facilitating the acquisition of new technology, or subsidizing exports, the routines are the routine. But if the state seeks to advance the common good by sheltering markets in any of these ways, it may put the public interest at the mercy of private ones. Firms may use state protection of their markets as an occasion to acquire competitive know-how and share the fruits of their knowledge fairly with workers, suppliers, and others with whom they collaborate in production. But they may also enrich themselves without regard to their collaborators, or, worse still, use state protection to secure increased revenues without learning at all. Addressing these problems through the application of broad, evenhanded rules—equal treatment for all—increases the risk of wasting scarce resources to no effect; addressing them through programs tailored to particular situations opens the way to the pursuit of self-interest through the multiplication of exceptions and analogies. Nor does successful learning mean that firms will want to continue to succeed by learning. Success produces an inertia of its own; and as those in the advanced countries know as well as anyone, inert firms, regardless of their putative level of advancement, may find it more expedient to seek state protection than to (re)learn to compete.

Current debate offers two contrary but equally unsatisfactory solutions to these twin problems of economic coordination. Thus one solution to the problem of paralyzing fear of deceit among and within firms is often said to be simply a tradition or culture of trust. In such cultures, it is claimed, the fate of each is seen as so entwined with the others that no one would think of exploiting the opportunities created by innovation to hold up a partner or hoodwink a principal. This view reconciles learning and monitoring by asserting that learning is possible whenever monitoring is unnecessary. Because cultures are taken to be historical creations, and groups do not deliberately make their history, it is hard to see how persons who do not spontaneously trust one another can come to do so.[2]

The alternative, game-theoretic solution is more promising about the possibility of instigating cooperation, but only marginally so. The core claim of the game-theoretic view is that if the parties expect to gain from continuing exchange, put a high value on those future gains as against current takings, and know that their partners do the same, then trade will continue. Game theorists are ingenious in demonstrating the precise conditions that can lead to this outcome.[3] But the same ingenuity reveals the fragility of such contingent cooperation: The shadow of a doubt about a partner's intentions is often enough to move the parties in these accounts to forgo the gains of trade rather than make themselves vulnerable to deceit. The game-theoretic view differs importantly from the cultural explanation in taking seriously the possibility that partners with no previous knowledge of each other can discover a propensity for long-term mutual reliance through initially limited trades. But in explaining cooperative behavior as the result of the coincidence of dispositions to cooperate, by a different route game theory, too, arrives at the conclusion that learning is possible only in the rare instances when the parties have clear motives for believing that monitoring takes care of itself.

Explanations of the state's successes and failures in encouraging learning without thwarting monitoring bring the subjacent fatalism of these views to light. Thus the public institution corresponding to the culture of trust is the "strong" state dominated by a bureaucratic elite so dedicated to the public good and so autonomous that it can shelter the economy without becoming the captive of the interests it helps create.[4] But nations are bequeathed strong states just as they are bequeathed cultures of trust; and there is, presumably, no more chance of creating such institutions than choosing one's ancestors. I take it as a sign of the current skepticism about the possibilities of purposeful public action that there is, to my knowledge, no analog in the discussion of public intervention in the economy to the game-theoretic idea of the (fragile) stabilization of trade relations through trade (although it would, in principle, be possible to fashion one from the intellectual building blocks provided by pluralist theories of the state).

In this chapter, in contrast, I argue that the economic actors can often resolve the problem of reconciling learning and monitoring by making the two indistinguishable: by creating institutions that make discussion of what to do inextricable from discussion of what is being done and the discussion of standards for apportioning gains and losses inextricable from apportionment. Through these institutions, discrete transactions among independent actors become continual, joint formulations of common ends in which the participants' identities are reciprocally defining. Put yet another way, these institutions transform transactions into discussions, for discussion is precisely the process by which parties come to reinterpret themselves and their relation to each other by elaborating a common understanding of the world.

I claim further that discursive institutions of this kind can connect the state to the economy as well as actors to one another within the economy, and that by allowing the parties to know what they are getting into from the first, they can be built experimentally and incrementally. As the same principles undergird limited and extensive collaboration, wary partners can gauge their respective reliability and capacity without making themselves imprudently vulnerable or jeopardizing fuller cooperation through initial caution. But even as the partners define common goals and wariness gives way to a recognition of mutual dependence, their institutional obligations require them to continue scrutinizing one another's behavior. Thus by narrowing the gap between an agreement and its execution so much that game-theoretic concerns of defection and deceit cannot enter debate, these restrictions also blur the distinction between mistrust and trust on which the cultural argument rests.

The empirical epicenter of the chapter is a discussion of the Japanese production system as defined by just-in-time inventory management, extensive use of subcontracting, statistical process controls, and value-added engineering. Japan has grown so fast in the last century while maintaining the continuity of certain of its key economic institutions that it counts as the leading example of both a developing and an advanced economy. It is certainly the point of reference in current discussions of trust or goodwill as a precondition of cooperation. Japanese success has also inspired a game-theoretic discussion of the coordination of decentralized industrial organizations in which all those collaborating in production are in effect joint owners of the assets under their control. Thus the Japanese system not only exemplifies the logic and developmental principles of the institutional reconciliation of learning and monitoring, but also provides a convenient vantage point from which to make a first appraisal of the theoretical implications of that accomplishment.

But Japanese experience is also a *locus classicus* for the discussion of the strong state as a necessary framework for growth at all levels of development and hence provides an equally convenient starting point for a reinterpretation of the conditions for successful state guidance of the economy. The argument is that success here has much more to do with joint formulation of goals between suppliers and customers in collaborative subcontracting systems than the common picture of prescient bureaucratic direction of economic actors suggests. I argue that such a concertation of goals occurs in the relations between associations of many kinds and various state entities. We typically understand the purpose of such relations to be the harmonization of interests rooted in the division of labor. But in "developmental" states they serve rather to redefine the participants' interests in ways that reshape the division of labor within the economy and between it and the public authorities—and thus moot the kind of distinctions between state and civil society that the strong-state, weak-state debate takes as fundamental.

By way of conclusion I make explicit the assumptions about the relation between individual and society on which the notion of the discursive formation of interests rests and show them to be a variant of what is often called social experimentalism or pragmatism. This view supposes that individuals are sociable in the sense that they must co-operate to some extent to produce anything from meaning to goods. The claim is that the more deliberately the parties apply the general principles of cooperation to their particular activities, the more effective those activities will be. I argue that learning by monitoring lends credence to this view with regard to just the sphere of activities commonly supposed to exclude sociability by its very nature: the economy. At the beginning, however, I want to set these considerations in relation to the current reappraisal of the postwar debate about balanced versus unbalanced growth and economic development more generally.

Development Economics, Externalities, and Social Learning

If you believe that good ideas may be eclipsed but never truly pass away, then the conditions for the current revival of interest in development economics could have been intuited from Hirschman's elegant but untimely obituary of the discipline, written at its darkest hour a decade ago.[5] The success of development economics, Hirschman argued, had depended on the coincidence of two foundational convictions. The first was that the mechanisms of growth in (and hence the policy measures appropriate to) a growing, essentially self-equilibrating economy are different from those governing an economy trapped in a low-level equilibrium. The second was that international trade could help an economy free itself from such a low-equilibrium trap. Belief in the first conviction was buttressed by the experience of the Great Depression, especially as understood by Keynes, by Alexander Gerschenkron's analysis of the state's increasing role in pooling savings in successive cohorts of developing countries as economies of scale led to apparently inexorable increases in the efficient size of plant (and hence the lumpiness of capital-goods investments), and by Sir W. Arthur Lewis's analysis of the dilemmas of dual economies with unlimited reserves of costless agricultural labor.[6] The second conviction grew out of the same understanding of free trade as a precondition of peaceful growth that made the Marshall Plan the U.S. strategy for reconstructing postwar Europe.

Development economics went into decline, Hirschman continued, as mainstream economists began to doubt the utility of distinguishing low-equilibrium traps as a fundamental type of economy, and Marxist economists, particularly in the developing countries, attacked the idea that international trade benefited the weaker trading partner. The mainstream doubts sprang from increasing skepticism about the effectiveness of Keynesian demand management in the advanced countries and their analogs (particularly market protection through import substitution strategies) in the developing world.[7] This doubt was reinforced by the striking success of such apparently free-market economies as Taiwan, Hong Kong, and the Republic of Korea. When the Marxists looked at their home economies they saw the multinationals and their domestic allies prospering amidst and from the general misery.[8]

Now the shoes are on different feet or so down at the heel that no one wears them. The Marxists have lost confidence in autarkic strategies of development. Many now embrace free-market alternatives with the zeal of renegades; others are silenced by the prospect of a world of unappealing choices. But many of the most mainstream economists now doubt that markets work to equalize growth rates in all economies. More to the point, they suspect that strength can breed strength and the strong can continue to grow faster than the weak.[9] Other mainstream economists and policymakers are now beginning to think that certain kinds of state sheltering of markets are a precondition, not an obstacle to successful international competition. This is the lesson they learn from Japanese economic strength in relation to U.S. weakness and the unexpected discovery of the role of the state—and the "strong" state at that—in some of the export booms of the East Asian tigers.[10] Suddenly almost every economy is in, or could fall into, a low-growth trap—no long-term logic of world-market equilibrium necessarily leads it out—but state intervention of the right kind just might.

This directs attention back to the classic problems of development economics as these were debated in the 1950s by proponents of balanced as against unbalanced growth. The common ground in the debate was the idea that firms pursuing growth strategies together faced different incentives and were more likely to succeed than firms in isolation. Imagine a closed economy composed of firms producing all the final and intermediate goods that under the most favorable conditions would be demanded in that economy. Then if all invest simultaneously, the investments of each, translated into wages, help create the purchasing power that backs demand for the products of all. These are pecuniary externalities. Similarly, if all the users of an intermediate product invest simultaneously, the producer of that good can invest in a larger-scale, and presumably more efficient plant than otherwise, to the benefit of all customers. These are nonpecuniary externalities.

The debate concerned the forms of coordination needed to produce these externalities. Proponents of balanced growth argued that externalities could be achieved only if the actors actually moved simultaneously, as the imaginary example of the closed economy just invoked suggests; and as a result they saw the principal problem of development policy as assuring that simultaneity.[11] Proponents of unbalanced growth, notably Hirschman, countered that no developing economy could ever muster all the resources required for simultaneous action, and that the problem for policymakers was, therefore, how to stagger investments so that the disequilibria created between the supply and demand for various intermediate and final goods touched off self-reinforcing sequences of upstream and downstream investments.[12]

The differing perspectives underlying the current concern with low-level traps have led to a revival of this debate that seems likely to extend it in new directions. For macroeconomists and specialists in international trade who acknowledge the danger of low-level traps and see the achievement of externalities as a precondition for escaping them, the central problem is how to model such externalities so that they are comprehensible in the light of mainstream ideas of market structure, and then to use these models as the authorization for policymakers to actually intervene to realize them. As the details of these eventual interventions appear of secondary importance, the model makers' sympathies are with the parsimonious arguments of the proponents of balanced growth, whose development strategy, after all, was simply to realize in real life the as-if assumptions of stories demonstrating the relevance of externalities.

On the other side are specialists in industrial organization and organizational sociology. They see in externalities the outcome as much as the motivating cause of many firm-level decisions, and they want to understand this relation from the vantage point of individual firms. They focus on the idea, central to the thesis of unbalanced growth, that the prospect of externalities is as important as the reality. Put another way, the actors can come to act in anticipation of complementary responses to separate decisions, so that in retrospect each in turn acted as though all had been deciding simultaneously. Their point of departure for this line of argument is Hirschman's claim that economic actors can be induced to learn to solve problems by the systematic creation of bottlenecks, and that this learning can become a self-sustaining source of growth as they discover how to recognize opportunities and how to profit from them. But in this form the unbalanced growth view is provocative, not definitive. The claim that disequilibrium can induce "social learning" is hardly self-evident (see chapter 4). Shocks, after all, can also induce self-protective strategies of risk reduction through autarky. We need to know what kind of disruptions produce learning, and how.

It is in this connection that the experience of Japan and the broader debate on the reconciliation of learning and monitoring become relevant. As I want to show next, the Japanese production system has honed one variant of learning through the induction of disequilibria in manufacturing, and in a way that illuminates aspects of the general concept left underexposed in the older debate.

Unbalanced Growth in Production

Japanese production methods are often presented as either a collection of loosely related efficiency-enhancing techniques, or as emanations—uninteresting in themselves—of a national spirit of cooperation, horror of waste, or improving zeal. However, I maintain that the separate methods and the broad features of the industrial organizations they help define follow from the application of a simple idea of decentralized learning that has been institutionalized so that the interests of the parts are consistent with the interests of the whole. For ease of exposition, I pass very lightly over the historical complexities of the system's origins and do no more than indicate its competitive shortcomings.

The constant reduction of in-process and finished goods inventory and the strain it puts on the whole manufacturing organization is the obvious point of contact between the Japanese production system and the idea of unbalanced growth. In the volatile markets of the early postwar years, many Japanese firms, and especially Toyota, came close to bankrupting themselves by accumulating inventory as they continued to produce at normal rates during downturns. When their bankers refused to bear this risk, the firms experimented with inventoryless models of production. In part they were inspired by the restocking practices of U.S. supermarkets, which reordered goods only after the last item of a particular kind had been removed from the shelf. Toyota imagined itself as the shopper in a supermarket of automobile components, picking parts off the shelves in just the sequence needed to assemble a car for which it already had a customer. Removal of the parts would signal to those who made them and the components of which they in turn were made to produce a replacement, barring an order to produce nothing or a variant of the previous piece. The closer the assembler came to realizing this ideal, the closer it would be to eliminating the risk of holding inventory.[13]

Inventory is a reserve against contingencies. Production without inventory, therefore, places enormous demands on each manufacturing operation and the logistics system connecting them. Production must be synchronized so that the order for each piece is filled in time to be incorporated into more comprehensive assemblies. Quality must be impeccable because, by definition, defects cannot be replaced with spares from inventory. Rather, the whole system must wait while an acceptable substitute is produced. Because breakdowns, like defects, delay production, operations must be extraordinarily reliable. They must also be extremely flexible, in the sense of quickly convertible from production of one make or model to another, if the system is to respond to variations in the composition of demand. This successive removal of inventories creates bottlenecks in production that make it possible to identify each work station's weaknesses; and in this way it is analogous to the potentially informative disruptions of production caused by, say, the construction of a new steel plant in stories of unbalanced growth.

The Japanese system ensures that the information thus revealed is put to productive use, first, by assigning responsibility for doing so to those—typically production workers—in the best position to learn what is required. Then assurances are provided that no one will be harmed from what is learned, and that those adept at applying it will benefit from their efforts. Since the unbuffered operation of the machines at each work station creates a continuous flood of information about the station's performance, the machine operator is best situated to discover what does not work and what might: if stressing the system in its moment-to-moment operations produces the richest information about the causes of its limitations, those responsible for moment-to-moment operations have to bear responsibility for removing those causes.

Three other closely related institutions move the shop-floor workers to concert their interests in the use of this knowledge with those of the firm.[14] The first is a guarantee of long-term employment security with pay tied to seniority for full-time workers. Although not established for this purpose, the guarantee of employment security means that even workers who do not expect to make innovative use of what they observe have no motive for hoarding their knowledge from others. Whatever happens, they have a place in the company, and the better its fortunes, the better—thanks to the effects of seniority on wages—their own prospects. The second is a system of merit-based promotions administered through a central office, what Masahiko Aoki calls the ranking hierarchy. This system ensured that workers who make innovative use of the information, or successfully encourage whole groups to do so, are rewarded for their efforts and given the opportunity to extend and test their capacities. The third institution, the company union, ensures that the others are working as agreed, although it, like lifetime employment, was certainly not created expressly for that purpose. Although I have introduced them matter-of-factly, their role in the organization of production raises fundamental questions about the de facto ownership of the firm that I take up below.

Through the mid-1960s Japanese industry applied the general manufacturing disciplines immediately supposed by inventoryless operation.[15] Single-minute-exchange-of-dies and other tooling were widely introduced to reduce the setup time required to switch from one part to another. Preventive maintenance was built more and more systematically into everyday operations to ensure reliability. Insofar as it was easier to observe whether a particular manufacturing process was running within certain parameters, and there was a very high probability that parts produced under those conditions conformed to specifications, statistical process controls replaced direct monitoring of component quality. Cross-training of workers meant that production lines could be configured so that the operator at any one station could use different machines as required by different parts, or that operators could be moved from line to line to accommodate larger variations in demand. Just-in-time inventory systems that caused parts to be produced only as needed allowed firms to reap the benefits of each round of improvements and uncover the next set of bottlenecks to address by running the whole production system just faster than its least robust stations could manage.

The more groups of workers maintained, restocked, cut the setup times, and jointly operated clusters of machines, the more autonomous they became and the more they resembled a small factory within a factory. Japanese firms began to formalize and extend this workshop autonomy through the introduction of quality circles. These circles, or the work teams that often grow out of them, bring together operators exercising joint control of a production area and encourage them to improve its performance as a unit in relation to the others. Quality circles and work teams thus invite production areas to do their own industrial engineering and organize their own logistics. At least, they must determine how much autonomy to assume in these regards, and how to cooperate with outsiders—technical staffs from the home company, or outside suppliers of parts of equipment—in securing whatever services the group does not provide itself. Today it is not uncommon for such groups to negotiate with management about the fees they are charged, through the allocation of corporate overheads, for the use of plant facilities. They also frequently have a say in decisions regarding the allocation of capital for their use and in hiring and disciplining members. Taken together, their prerogatives come to resemble those of independent business units.

The same set of concerns that culminated in the formation of quality circles and work teams also shaped and encouraged the extension of subcontracting by Japanese firms. In the late 1940s and early 1950s, Japanese companies turned to subcontracting to economize on direct investment outlays, undercut the influence of national unions, and create a production buffer that expanded and contracted in rhythm with the business cycle, thus sheltering the guaranteed jobs of the core work force from the effects of demand fluctuations. Remember that beyond these immediate considerations, the Japanese producers saw themselves as customers in component supermarkets whose provisions they organized; and this self-conception may have worked in the background to encourage them to delegate responsibility for making even crucial parts to outside firms. More important, the same techniques of decentralizing responsibility for incremental, coordinated improvement through learning could easily be applied across firms. Indeed, as the evolution of the quality circles and work teams shows, the techniques actually foster the articulation of the whole production system into closely linked but increasingly autonomous units.

The evolution of pricing practices between subcontractors and their customers shows this connection between learning inside and learning outside the firm. Initially, subcontracting was by process: turning, milling, or boring jobs, for example, were simply transferred to outsiders who executed them on equipment similar to that originally used and at a price controlled by the market rate for a process of that type. Prices for more complex jobs were calculated by summing the rates for their component steps.

Because the large Japanese manufacturers were reducing buffer inventories, adopting the corresponding manufacturing disciplines, and thus expecting parts suppliers to meet the new system's moving performance standards, the costs of switching subcontractors—once a workable relation was established—were high. Instead of putting each job out to bid at the end of each contract period, as a U.S. firm might have done, the Japanese companies therefore used the detailed cost information from the current agreement as the reference point for negotiations over target prices in the next one. Subcontractors were typically required to cut prices at the average rate expected of firms in their line of work after adjustments for fluctuations in the costs of raw materials, the subcontracting on which they in turn relied, and tooling. Savings beyond the targets were divided between the customer and the supplier according to fixed and generally accepted rules that rewarded superior performance.

This system of historically based price determination could then be extended to accommodate the subcontractors' growing responsibilities in the interfirm division of labor. For reasons connected to the logic of reorganization traced above but not of interest here, the large firms began to abandon the principles of grouping production machinery according to type—all the lathes in one workshop, all the milling machines in another—and started to line them up in the sequence required to produce particular families of parts—first a lathe, then a milling machine, then a lathe. Accordingly, the firms began to subcontract whole production sequences rather than jobs defined by particular processes, and the subcontractors had to assume both the administrative burden of managing the line as a whole and the responsibility for designing or collaborating in the design of the components to be produced. Expenses for the new tasks were charged to the gross margins category (overhead, including labor, plus a profit margin); firms thus had incentives to broaden their competence as well as increase their efficiency of current operations.

The effect of the elaboration and extension of the price rules and related practices was to create a relation between subcontractor and large-firm customer strictly analogous to the one between the large firm and the machine operator or work group of operators. The presumption that agreements with subcontractors will be extended through renegotiation, assuming acceptable performance, is equivalent to the operators' employment security. The pricing rules, in combination with the presumption that the most capable firms will increase their responsibilities and autonomy most rapidly, create an equivalent to the ranking hierarchy that encourages superior performance by rewarding it.

To illuminate the Japanese system from a final perspective, I want to call attention to a characteristic vulnerability. The system works because the participants themselves are induced to better their performance by constantly redefining how that is to be done. The price of this autonomy, however, is agreement at the start that improvements will count as improvements only if they better some historical standard: subcontractors must, for example, cut their production costs by an agreed amount semiannually, where the initial price is simply the prevailing one at the time the rules are first applied. If the target rate of improvement is better than the average rate of improvement in the industry, and the actual rate is close to the target, then the actors better the market while maintaining the freedom to do things by their own lights. Japanese company accounting systems, therefore, characteristically focus on measuring improvement in the output per unit of labor or capital input, rather than on assessing global performance retrospectively by return on capital or other financial measures, as is common in Western firms.

The danger is that changed market conditions, and especially some innovation in process or product, will so alter prevailing performance criteria that the original reference point will become irrelevant. Improving at better than the industry rate is plainly no help when a breakthrough design doubles the competitive performance level or rate of improvement. The precondition of piecemeal improvement is to define the performance of each part by reference to its effect on the performance of the whole, and then to forget about the whole and worry about the parts. The chances of overlooking opportunities for or evidence of global breakthroughs are therefore particularly high for organizations that are especially proficient at piecemeal advance.[16] Even changes intermediate in scope between the local and the global are likely to be suspect because they unsettle so many pieces at once that they potentially jeopardize the system of piecemeal learning by doing.

Just how much the Japanese economy actually suffers from these potential hazards is hard to say. But there is significant evidence from the computer and other industries that at the end of the 1980s Japanese firms were so absorbed by beating their own performance standards that they got better and better at a losing game.[17] Improving faster than IBM on what IBM was doing when it dominated its industry is plainly no longer a world-beating strategy when IBM is no longer dominant. Similarly, Japanese machine-toolmakers got better and better at linking their own products into more and more flexible ensembles with proprietary communications protocols. But their customers increasingly doubt that any one firm can produce the key building blocks of a flexible manufacturing system; hence they increasingly prefer open or nonproprietary protocols that allow combination of equipment from different makers. One result of such missteps is that Japanese firms have become increasingly interested in "Western" measurement standards that force production groups to justify their current projects as the most reasonable use of the resources they immobilize, given plausible alternative investments, rather than by referring to their own historical performance. Alternatively, Japanese firms might extend the system of interfirm cooperation—described below—that is currently used to assess competing technical solutions to the same problem to permit assessment of the performance of whole products or business units using habitual accounting practices. Neither way is adjustment-effortless or assured; and success in recasting the rules discussed so far will depend on the (re)constitutional powers of Japanese society as a whole: whatever else it is, the particular system of firm-based learning by monitoring under discussion here is not an all-purpose machine for adjusting to all possible environments.

This much will suffice, I hope, to demonstrate that the large Japanese firm and its subcontractors are part of a single system of decentralized learning through induced shocks—unbalanced growth—and that the success of that system depends crucially on the way institutions shape the interests of the parties in production. Before extending the argument to the relation between the state and the economy as a whole, I want to stand aside and examine theoretically just what kind of shaping the institutions are doing.

What the Rules Rule Out: Some Implications of the Japanese Example

Schematic as it is, this account of the Japanese system is hard to reconcile with cultural or game-theoretic explanations of Japan's industrial success. On the one hand, the thicket of rules prescribing the kind of activities to be monitored and the use to be made of the resulting information does not square with the idea that a historical propensity to cooperate ensures cooperation. On the other hand, on closer inspection, the rules seem designed more to rule out the kind of considerations of deceit and defection that preoccupies game theory than to regulate them to the end of cooperation.

Take first the anomalous character of the Japanese system as sketched here, from the culturalist perspective. If culturalist explanations of cooperation have any bite, then shared norms and, above all, the shared expectation that all parties to an exchange share common interests must prevent any of them from exploiting the vulnerabilities of another. Explicit agreements of the bare-bones, we-agree-to-do-this variety are required even in such a world to ensure that the partners are fully informed of their joint goal and of their respective parts in achieving it. More extensive agreements enjoining the parties to treat each other fairly or share and share alike might also be consistent expressions of the notion of a culture of cooperation insofar as they—like civic festivals—affirm and thereby reinforce standards of behavior already recognized as binding.

Although it has often been noted that contracts between Japanese subcontractors and their customers do contain such declarations of mutual goodwill, the ensemble of Japanese production rules does not look at all like the I-will-be-good-to-you-if-you-are-good-to-me type.[18] They stipulate the kinds of information to be reviewed, set minimum

performance standards with reference to that information, and say precisely how gains greater than the minimum are to be divided.[19] If you
did not know better, you might in fact easily mistake the Japanese rules
for garden-variety contracts and hence take them to be expressions of
Western or U.S. cultures of mistrust.

Nor does it help the culturalist case to argue that, appearances
aside, the Japanese interpret their rules with a trusting forbearance
that transforms their significance and renders them more robust than
their Western counterparts. It is a staple of U.S. contract-law doctrine
that all contracts are incomplete in the sense of leaving important contingencies uncovered; hence they must be interpreted with forbearance and deference to prevailing custom and practice if cooperation is
to proceed. What distinguishes U.S. from Japanese agreements in the
relevant cases is much more the substance of the rules they provide
than the spirit in which those rules are interpreted. Until the cultur-
alists can explain the extensive presence of rules in Japanese
agreements and their content, the claim that the interpretive spirit of
the agreement is decisive and its letter irrelevant strikes me as, well,
spiritualist.

But in arguing that the Japanese rules are enough like contracts to
discomfit the culturalist view, I do not mean to be saying that the rules
really amount to contracts in the game-theoretic sense of promises to
perform contingent on the other parties' performance. On the contrary,
the rules create a regime in which "agreements," "performance," and
"monitoring" in the contractarian sense do not exist. In a contractual
regime the parties are presumed to be independent entities exchanging
promises to perform as agreed if the others keep their promises, too.
Monitoring is the periodic review of performance to ascertain its con-
formity with the agreement. But if, as in the Japanese case, the agreed
rules do not fix the parties' actions, but rather define how they will act
to revise their joint goals (and their standards for evaluating goals),
then there can be no conventional monitoring. Because the behavior of
one party can influence the goals of the others, it is meaningless for
either to define, let alone measure, a partner's performance in reference
to an anterior agreement.

Another way to put the point is to say that the rules of unbalanced
growth transform what contractarians see as a chain of exchanges or
an infinitely repeated game into a continuous discussion of joint possibilities and goals, where the parties' historical relation defines their

mutual expectations. Just as in a discussion, the parties suppose their understanding of their situation is limited. Therefore they jointly specify what they believe they understand so as to expose and begin exploring the limits of that understanding. Just as in a discussion, they must accept the possibility that their views of themselves, of the world, and the interests arising from both—their identities, in short—will be changed unexpectedly by those explorations.

In a contractarian world, by contrast, there is no joint exploration of novelty and still less any redefinition of identities through persuasion. The world is presumed to be well understood. If an agent does not know what is the case in any particular situation, another likely will. Each party, moreover, has settled interests in the form of ranked preferences for particular outcomes and pursues them strategically. Speech in this world is just the strategy by which the speaker plays on the limits of the listener's knowledge to advance his or her own interests. In speaking, I try to characterize the world so that you will believe it is in your best interest to act in a way that serves my purposes. Since it is common knowledge that everyone uses talk strategically, listeners only credit what they hear if they believe speakers' preferences resemble their own, or unless claims are easily verified or lying effectively punished. The central problem in this world is therefore to determine when speech informatively discloses some known fact about the world, not how discussion might be used to extend the range of knowledge. No wonder, then, that the convention here is indeed to talk of talk rather than discussion or persuasion, as if to rule out the possibility that communication can influence fundamental beliefs and interests.[20]

Or consider, finally, the contrasting views of failure. In a discussion, the participants must accept the possibility that one party may simply be unable to keep up its end of the conversation, and that those who can will seek new interlocutors. One of the many possible reasons for such failure is insufficient understanding of the problem at hand or even of how to pose it in the first place. The core idea of contingent-claims contracting and game theory, in contrast, is that agreements fail because of earthly, self-regarding motives, not haplessness in the face of higher powers. In these views, the very firmness of the parties' identities and interests and the clarity of their understanding of the world allow them to reliably advance their interests by undertaking certain actions in return for like undertakings by their partners. On this view, failure to perform is not the sign of inability, but rather of unwilling-ness rooted in an interest adverse to the original agreement.

Reinterpreting Japanese production against this backdrop makes it possible to address two problems that vex culturalist and game-theoretic interpretations. The first concerns evidence—surprising, given foreigners' expectations of steadfast dealings—of the wariness of Japanese business relations in general. Japanese subcontractors of-ten take pains to avoid dependence on any single customer by diversi-fying sales across industries and among different *keiretsu* industrial groups.[21] Japanese firms also diversify their sources of credit to avoid dependence on any single bank insofar as possible. There is evidence, furthermore, that banks do let client firms fail at rates approximating those in the United States for businesses of comparable size.[22]

These findings do not fit the standard explanations. If the Japanese trust each other for cultural reasons, there should be no fear that de-pendence will be abused and hence no motive for reducing depen-dence through diversification. Indeed, in a trusting world, diversifica-tion would be a sign of disloyalty born of doubt in the partners' sense of responsibility. Every such self-protective gesture would create con-fusion where there had been none. In such a world, bankers with a tutelary relation to firms would be failing to do their duty if they al-lowed those firms to fail.

Game theory points to a similarly refractory result. Firms in this view aim to make themselves vulnerable to one another in order to acquire, by cooperative forbearance, a reputation for trustworthiness. Such a reputation is competitively valuable, the argument goes, be-cause potential partners will prefer dealing with a company or bank that cannot afford to lose its good name by deceit than with a firm that has no name to lose.[23] Alternatively, think of the banks and large firms as insuring their borrowers and suppliers against the risk of failure. They collect premiums in the form of, respectively, above-market inter-est rates on loans and below-market prices for components. Firms would not want to diversify their customers for fear of diluting their insuring partners' sense of responsibility for their fate. Banks that let customers fail would be seen as insurers that collected premiums but refused to pay damages, with the result that payment of all premiums would stop.[24] Hence banks would not let firms fail. Thus in game theory, as in the cultural view, small misdeeds can undo the whole world. Whereas in the cultural understanding these misdeeds are unthinkable, thinking about them in game theory makes them undoable.

The notion of rule-governed learning by monitoring can, in contrast, accommodate evidence of diversification and disruption of relations by shifting attention from the extent to the character of collaboration. As relations become discursive in the sense just described, firms can assess continuously through direct experience whether particular partners are able to advance a joint program, and if they are, whether the result could be a fusion of identities that creates enduring mutual interests. Given the availability of this kind of knowledge about current and potential partners, strategies such as diversification and individual decisions such as the willingness to allow a particular firm to fail need not have the generic and catastrophically disruptive significance attributed to them by the standard views. Diversification, for instance, might in the light of direct experience signify the intention to learn new things rather than fear of dependence mingled with a penchant for deceit. A bank might allow a customer to fail because that customer is indeed a failure. Other clients in different, more promising situations could correctly assume that the bank could tell the difference.

The second recalcitrant theme for the standard view concerns the question of property. The parties to production in the Japanese system take such obvious and extensive account of one another's concerns that it is awkward and misleading to consider them fully independent entities. If ownership means precisely the power to determine how assets will be used when those with a de facto say in their use disagree, who, given this reciprocal influence, owns a Japanese firm? Does the question have a meaning at all in a system of the Japanese kind?

The culturalist view tacitly evades the question by its assumption of general goodwill and forbearance. Where this assumption holds, ownership amounts to stewardship of particular goods that are ultimately regarded as common property. The identity of particular owners is irrelevant because ownership is automatically exercised in accordance with the public good. For game theory, on the other hand, the property question is a real one. If the actors' motives are insufficiently distinct, it is pointless to theorize about the response of each to the autonomous strategic choices of the others. The precise distribution of rights and the evaluation of self-regarding intent is therefore of central interest; and the ambiguities of the Japanese system are perplexing.

An exemplary treatment of the problem from this perspective is Masahiko Aoki's view of the Japanese firm as jointly owned by its employees and an equity-owning bank, with management responsible for reconciling conflicts between them. Because ownership is joint and the owners share a common fate, each has reason to accommodate the interests of the other: hence the reciprocal influence. Yet the owners' interests are distinct enough to provoke strategic maneuvering of the kind familiar in game theory. Hence the need for managerial mediation.[25]

But this analysis does more to cast the explanatory difficulties of game theory into sharper relief than to resolve them. To begin with, it is clear from the preceding analysis that if direct employees are to be counted as owners, then subcontractors must be as well. Including them does more than lengthen the list of proprietors from two to three. It calls into question the very idea of treating the firm and its constituents as distinct entities, as opposed to mutually determining parts of a larger and indistinctly bounded pool of coproducers whose scope exceeds the mediating jurisdiction of any single group of managers.[26] A closely related consideration applies to the equation of managers with arbitrators. In learning by monitoring, employees perform such "managerial" tasks as reorganizing their own work in accordance with the generally recognized interests of the firm. Certainly their interests as a group can, at times, be distinguished from those of creditors or stockholders. But the notion of managers as arbiters confusingly reasserts a distinctness of purpose that the notion of joint ownership rightly, if imprecisely, blurs while correspondingly and implausibly narrowing the responsibilities of management. It seems no more reasonable to think of Japanese managers as mediators than to imagine the director of a Broadway show as simply arbitrating the demands of the cast, orchestra, stage crew, angels, composer, and librettist.

These equivocations I take to be the result of the view's underlying assumptions, not the deficiencies of a particular formulation. The same discursive rules that make it senseless to speak of conventional exchange also make it misleading, I take it, to speak of property in the conventional sense of residual control of assets as well. But what else would one expect of a production system in which the use of assets is determined incrementally by all those who use them?

I now want to extend the discussion to the state's relation to the economy, and show that the same principles that guide the operation of systems of discursive production within and among firms also apply to building them deliberately within whole economies.

The State and Disequilibrium Learning

Debate about the state's role in promoting economic growth is, we saw, deadlocked. On the one hand, it is clear that economies at all levels of development can fall into low-equilibrium traps from which they can be released only by external help, typically from the state. On the other hand, it is unclear how the state could acquire knowledge of the economy superior to that of the firms, and more obscure still how the state could avoid becoming the captive protector of the very economic groups whose transformation it aims to encourage. Indeed, these two concerns are connected in a particularly daunting way: in redirecting the economy, the state must rely on information not directly available to the market participants. Otherwise those participants could redirect themselves. But such extra-market information is politically tainted: its generation and transmission depend on the participation of private groups that are likely to use their influence on public authority to shelter themselves from competition as to improve their response to it. Under these circumstances nothing less than the deus ex machina of the strong state—a prescient bureaucracy independently moving the levers of government—is required to make public action a motor for rather than an obstacle to growth.[27]

These fears, to repeat, are not groundless. Yet the notion of disequilibrium learning as central to economic development suggests that they overstate the obstacles to effective state intervention in the economy by mischaracterizing the kind of knowledge required for intervention to be effective and, relatedly, restricting unduly the kinds of relations that can exist between the state and private groups.

Another Kind of Knowledge

Consider first the character of the knowledge relevant to state intervention. If the state can intervene successfully at all in the standard view, then it is only because its perch above or bestride the economy affords it a breadth of knowledge unavailable to market actors. The claim that this is possible today draws whatever plausibility it has from the related view—familiar from debates about finance capitalism, late development, and corporate governance—that banks with long-term equity holdings in firms to which they also extend credit are better corporate monitors than other stakeholders in part because of their broader experience of business activity in particular sectors and the economy as a whole.[28]

But if the central problem of economic growth is inducing disequilibrium learning, why should the state not do or learn to do *that*, rather than worrying about how to increase the breadth of its knowledge of the economy in general? There are two broad ways public authorities might attempt this; and despite their differences, and their differential efficacy, neither requires the state to pretend to knowledge of markets superior to that of market participants.

The first potential way to induce disequilibrium learning is simply to perturb the existing equilibrium. This was the idea behind the program of staggered investments as advanced by the proponents of unbalanced growth. Knowledge of upstream and downstream connections of various economic activities could guide authorities to the projects most likely to induce complementary investments (as in Hirschman's theory of linkages). But the state's aim was to trigger a self-reinforcing process that could proceed without further public intervention. As any of many possible projects could have this triggering effect, the evident limits to the state's knowledge of these connections were not considered an objection to the practicality of the strategy.

The difficulties with staggering large investments, anticipated above, are clear enough in the rearview mirror of neoclassical criticism of development economics.[29] Projects big enough to create self-reinforcing disequilibria also afford sufficient opportunities for patronage quickly to breed lobbies of state employees as well as suppliers and customers of the public sector. These lobbies subordinate the development program to their own self-interest. The result of economic disequilibrium is therefore not continuing, ever more productive disequilibrium, but rather a new balance of political forces that lives well by perpetuating the new status quo.

The second way to foster disequilibrium learning is to induce firms to agree to learn by monitoring. Instead of perturbing the marketplace in the expectation that firms will react by adopting rules encouraging disequilibrium learning, the state encourages firms to subject themselves to rules that create informative disequilibria in their operations.

Thus the state aims at a relation with the firms that is like the firms' relation with their employees or subcontractors, but with this difference: the goal of learning by monitoring within and among firms is primarily substantive—cheaper, more reliable, more innovative products; between the state and the firms, however, the goal is primarily formal—better rules for encouraging learning by monitoring.

The state need no more pretend to superior market knowledge in this variant of the strategy than if it were itself acting directly in the marketplace. Rather, the state instigates the firms to set goals with reference to some prevailing standard so that shortfalls in performance are apparent to those with the incentives and capacity to remedy them—the firms themselves—and new targets are set accordingly. For its part, the state might undertake to stabilize certain markets by imposing import duties, offering export subsidies, or authorizing firms in those markets to set prices and production quotas. In return, those firms undertake to produce goods of export quality as defined in international commerce. Deviations from these standards orient the firms' broad efforts at improvement just as detection of defects in any one firm's production directs more localized improvements there. Analogously, the state might subsidize collaborative research efforts that grouped producers and users of a process or product with the pertinent research institutions. But the consortium would only get the subsidy provided it demonstrate the ability to evaluate and disseminate the results effectively. In these and other cases, discussion of which rules to apply can establish rules of participation—who is part of the group of potential cooperators and on what conditions—and create precedents that shape the procedures for rule revision.

Sometimes the state's interlocutor in such deliberations will be one or a few large companies, some or all of which may indeed be publicly owned. But much more often the public's interlocutors will be groups or associations of firms. In many developing countries the firms in the traditional industries from which exports first come, such as leather products, ceramics, textiles, and garments, tend to be small and numerous. If the many firms in each industry agree to meet common standards, then each can learn from the shortcomings and accomplishments of the others (an incalculably valuable nonpecuniary externality), and the public authorities can economize on administrative resources that are likely in short supply. In the advanced economies the development and production of complex goods increasingly involves the coordination of many specialists from diverse branches of industry and the service sector with the consequence that here, too, the state is likely to treat groups of firms rather than individual concerns.

I will call such groupings developmental associations to distinguish them from more familiar types of affiliation.[30] In standard accounts associations are cast in two roles. In the neoliberal view, they act as predatory lobbies using political pressure to extract returns they cannot achieve directly in the market. In the neocorporatist or private interest government view, they act more benignly to structure negotiations between interest groups and the state to reach mutually advantageous outcomes otherwise unattainable. Centralization of collective bargaining in deals between peak associations of labor and industry, for instance, reduces the inflationary danger of sequential, leapfrogging agreements when labor markets are tight, but also the threat of competitive deregulation resulting from a sequence of whipsawing give-backs when they are slack. Similarly, the state can authorize employers' associations and unions to shape and interpret regulatory rules provided the latter help police the regulations. The outcome can be rules that are enforceable because they are workable for all parties and effective because they are enforceable. Benign or malign, these two types of association take the members' interests as essentially fixed. The bargaining regime changes the expression of those interests, not their fundamental character. Hence the characteristic tasks of officials of these kinds of associations is reconciling or harmonizing the interests of the group's members with the interests of its external partners.[31]

A central role of the developmental associations that emerge in strategies of disequilibrium learning, in contrast, is to help create the interests and identity of their members.[32] Discussions about the firms' goals and the procedures for revising them in the light of experience necessarily reach into the very constitution of each company, shaping what it wants by shaping what it supposes it can and will eventually be able to do. At the limit, in fact, the formative characteristics of association can dissuade this type of grouping from acting like a conventional interest group at all: if firms in association realize that they can thrive in market competition, they are unlikely to use their association to lobby for protection against the market. Thus, just as the state can learn how to set goals in collaboration with associated firms, the firms in association can learn how to organize and define themselves in collaboration with the state. This mutual vulnerability is the discursive counterpart in the relation between the state and the economy to the interpenetration of identities that follows from learning by monitoring within and among firms, and between them and their representative associations. I will speak, therefore, of developmental business associations when referring to the central institutional actor in this web of relations and of discursive interest formation when referring to the relations themselves.

I note, finally, that the partners' mutual vulnerability in a discursive relation does not imply enduring harmony in their dealings any more than the familiar harmonization of interests in a bargaining regime suggests that the attendant negotiations must inevitably result in mutually beneficial accord. Political groups that believe themselves to share a common end such as the good of the nation or the people, and that do actually put their own identities at risk in its pursuit, can nonetheless disagree so sharply in their interpretation of the common good that they become implacable enemies. Analogous conflicts can arise among firms and between them and the state in the attempt to set the rules of disequilibrium learning.

State and Developmental Associations in Japan

Now I will get down to cases, beginning with the claim that the success of the Japanese economy is due to the strength of the Japanese state. If the state can really discipline the economy as that argument supposes, then investigation should focus on how bureaucracies come or can be made to be so resourceful, independent and public-minded, not how the authorities can instigate firms to set rules that transform their identity. And if any state is strong in this sense, then surely it is the Japanese one.[33]

But in the event the strong-state argument does not bear much weight even in Japan. Two kinds of objections are convincingly raised against it. The first is simply that the state's intentions have been an extremely unreliable guide to the economy's actual performance. In the postwar period, for example, the crucial guiding authority, the Ministry of Trade and Industry (MITI), systematically underestimated the expansive capacity of the domestic steel industry, tried to dissuade automobile firms from undertaking their hugely successful export drive, and urged rigorous consolidation on a machine-tool industry that succeeded brilliantly without it.[34] Public authorities, understandably, are glad to claim credit for every economic success; but only the particularly credulous would accord it to them on this kind of coarse evidence.

The second objection is that wherever the Japanese state has intervened in the economy it has done so in collaboration with private sector interlocutors; and it is this collaboration that explains why these interventions have on balance been beneficial, however inadequate they may appear as efforts to foster economic development by plan. As revealed in studies of the aluminum smelting, petroleum-refining, machine-tool, and aircraft industries, the relation between the state and the economy is characterized by what Richard Samuels calls "reciprocal consent": The state acknowledges industry's right to extensive consultation in the formulation of policy, and industry in return acknowledges its obligation to cooperate in the execution of policies so formulated.[35] Studies of Japanese economic development from the Meiji Restoration to the postwar period, discussed below, confirm the pervasiveness of this pattern.

The notion of reciprocal consent casts too wide a net, however, for present purposes. On the one hand, it includes forms of concertation between the state and business associations typical of neocorporatist interest harmonization. On the other, it captures the collaboration between the state and developmental associations. To establish that the public authorities in Japan encouraged firms to learn by monitoring, it is therefore necessary to look past the debate about the strength of the Japanese state to accounts of the role of business associations in Japan.

What the historical record shows is remarkably consistent with pervasive state support for developmental associations from the beginning of modern Japan in the aftermath of the Meiji Restoration. Between 1884 and 1900 a series of laws and edicts authorized a qualified majority of producers in the same line of business in the same locale to form local trade associations (dogyo kumiai) in such traditionally export-oriented industries as silk fabrics and reeling, cotton textiles and flannel, pottery, porcelain, and intricate matting. The trade associations could regulate prices, market shares, and wages for all firms in their respective industries and locales; they also adjudicated commercial disputes between producers in their jurisdiction. In those respects the *dogyo kumiai* were the successors to traditional guilds. Because the government was well aware, however, that such regulatory authority could be used to protect current practices, these powers were granted on condition that the associations police and improve the quality of the members' products. This was typically accomplished through joint inspection of goods for export. High-quality producers would not want their reputations jeopardized by merchandising their wares with inferior goods; but they could presumably sustain a coalition within the trade association in favor of above-average standards only by show-ing the average performers in the association how to improve their production.[36] There is no doubt that such cooperative inspection played an important role in structuring the relation between the state, the association and its members; and it is sometimes claimed that co-operative inspection was their main function.[37]

Similar principles, moreover, informed the operation of producers' organizations operating in the new, factory-based industries not cov-ered by the regulations regarding local trade association. The powerful All-Japan Cotton Spinners Association (*Boren*) for example, regulated competition in its industry during downturns by allocating its mem-bers' quotas of raw cotton, whose import the association controlled. Members were under substantial public pressure to justify their quotas through superior or at least adequate performance; a ranking of the firms according to efficiency in extracting output from their machines was published monthly in the *Boren* journal. Laggards consulted more technically advanced firms, and members had the right to send their operators for training to associated firms or to request that trainers be sent to them.[38] The organized exchange of production information was also crucial to rationalization of highly concentrated industries such as steel, where the major firms before World War II were either state-owned (Yawata Seitetsujo) or state-founded (Tanaka Kozan, later Ka-maisha Mining Company) and organized by the mid-1920s as a single cartel in which both public and private investments were at risk. Here it was the Iron and Steel Institute of Japan, founded during World War I, that collected and published technical information and discussed its application with engineers from each firm in annual study meetings. The success of rationalization combined with expansion of the domes-tic market and depreciation of the yen to assure the industry high profit rates through the 1930s and thus to moot the question of how allocation of market shares would have been linked to performance in a contracting market.[39]

Public authorities in this period, however, were determined to reaffirm the principle that regulatory authority would be ceded to producers' associations only if the latter could connect its exercise to the generation and dissemination of information that improved performance. Thus in 1930 the Ministry of Commerce and Industry—MITI's forerunner—formed the Temporary Rationalization Bureau to draft and supervise administration of new legislation covering local trade associations and like institutions. The aim of the Important Export Products Manufacturers' Association Law of 1931 was to help small and medium-size manufacturers wrest control of the local trade associations from brokers and wholesalers mainly by ensuring that joint inspection resulted in a reallocation of shares to superior performers.[40] The Rationalization Bureau's model of success was the Striped-Cloth Industry Association, which distributed a fixed quota of the industry's total annual target production among the new or current producers who bettered the current level of productivity.[41]

These principles continue to influence Japanese economic policy down to the present, although trade associations and cartels may not be as central to the diffusion of learning by monitoring as before World War II. In some regional industries, for example, economic development is promoted by the joint efforts of local officials of MITI's Small Business Bureau and established local business people. Together they award subsidized credits to going firms and startups that demonstrate the necessary technical expertise and familiarity with market prospects. The officials know the technology. And the business people know the markets, because they either sell to the same customers as the selected firms or else purchase the latter's products directly themselves. In the first case inadequate performance damages their reputation; in the second it directly threatens their own capacity to produce. Either way, the business people have an immediate stake in the success of the firms they help select for aid; and the process by which credit is awarded and loans monitored becomes part of the larger discussion of how to improve production in the regional industry.[42]

A final case in point concerns the organization of state support for interfirm research. An increasing share of public subsidies for commercially relevant research goes to groups of firms typically organized as Engineering Research Associations (ERAs): nonprofit entities formed to carry out a specific research project, funded in part by member firms and in part by the government, and equivalent in law to private trade associations. The first ERA was founded in 1961 in the automobile industry; like *Boren* and the Iron and Steel Institute, it collected, generated, and publicized information in ways that allowed firms to improve performance while assessing it. In that first association, forty-seven automotive parts firms, none with research capacity of its own, used equipment and personnel provided by a national engineering laboratory and their trade association to collect data and perform tests connected with projects in the improvement of filters, radiators, suspensions and other components. Because the performance was measured centrally, superior designs were available to all; and once any component maker adopted it, the large-firm customers of the others would ensure, via the subcontracting rules, that all the others did so, too.

As more and more firms have built research facilities of their own and ERAs have shifted from mastering and refining foreign best-practice to assessing the strengths and weaknesses of fundamentally different technical approaches to a single problem, the internal structure of the associations has become more complex. Members must, for example, agree on a common standard for evaluating alternative solutions and ensure that assessment even at different locations is by uniform, agreed procedures.[43] Winning results have to be made accessible in industrially applicable forms to those who pursued losing alternatives. Under these conditions, government-supported laboratories—national ones for large projects, regional ones for smaller programs—act as translators and arbiters. They evaluate the research findings of participants and in so doing help articulate a lingua franca for expressing goals, techniques for measuring progress, and protocols for conveying results acceptable, and therefore reassuring, to all.[44]

In reviewing the role of developmental associations in Japanese economic policy, I do not mean to suggest that those are the only kinds of business associations in Japan and still less that the national economic policy has had building them as its sole goal. There are lobbies and private interest governments aplenty in Japan, and economic policy, particularly state support for the exclusion of foreign firms and products, seems to reflect concerns for national prowess that have more to do with geopolitical concerns than the desire to increase the learning capacity of the economy, however difficult it may be to distinguish these ends. Nonetheless, by this cursory review I do, on the contrary, mean to advance the claim that learning by monitoring is as central an organizing principle in the relation between Japanese firms and the state as it is in the relations within and among firms, and that no other principle—the bureaucratic ghost in the machinery of the strong state least of all—does as well at explaining the economic success of these relations.

Further Cases: Germany, Korea, and Taiwan

Nor, of course, is the focus on Japan meant to suggest that developmental associationalism is a peculiarly Japanese phenomenon. Even a glance at economic history reveals significant, strikingly similar cases in diverse cohorts of industrializing countries. For much of this century, trade associations in Germany, for example, have divided their respective industries into highly specialized subunits with firms in effect obligated to compete with others in their area of specialization. To expand their markets in this system, therefore, firms have to increase demand for their type of product by improving its performance. The assurance that potential competitors in adjacent specializations cannot enter the market during downturns reduces the risk of concentrating on the increasing refinement of a single type of product. Boundaries between specializations are policed by a technical-norm committee under the aegis of the trade association; and in the very process of setting norms, these committees, like the Japanese analogs, allow firms to learn crucial aspects of what the others know while monitoring their behavior.[45] German interfirm research, to continue the comparison, has developed in ways that recall the Japanese pattern. In the years immediately after World War II, firms with scant research facilities relied on the help of public institutions such as polytechnics to help in the solution of common technical problems. Today such institutions spend more and more time evaluating competing solutions developed by the various firms' own labs within the setting of programs that look much like ERAs.[46]

The economic successes of Korea and Taiwan can be interpreted as examples of the importance of developmental associations in the late-late cohort of industrializers. Debates about the preconditions of growth in these countries are following the pattern of changing analyses of Japan, with an important difference. During most of the 1980s these two Asian tigers were juxtaposed as examples of dynamic, deregulated market economies against the stalled model of import substitution typical of Latin America. Closer analysis, however, revealed the guiding hand of "strong" states that, in Japanese fashion, allocated credit to favored industries and firms while stabilizing their markets through complex import controls and export subsidies.[47] But here, too, further examination of the origins and operations of this state guidance is bringing to light forms of cooperation between the state and organized business in which the latter adopts a learning regime in return for forms of market stabilization that only the former can ensure.[48]

In both countries this cooperation was the result of bargains struck between the business community and state bureaucrats as both sought an alternative to the rampant clientelism that checked economic development in the 1950s. In Taiwan these bargains reinforced sectoral trade organizations that encouraged, measured, and rewarded learning by member firms, as in the Japanese developmental associations, on which the Taiwanese institutions were partly modeled. In the face of a price war in the small domestic market and increasing international competition, for example, the Taiwan Cotton Spinners Association established an Export Encouragement Fund. Members were assessed for contributions to the fund in proportion to their cotton purchases. Producers that exported more than their assigned quota received their contribution back plus a bonus equivalent to 5 percent of export sales; those who exported less forfeited their contributions. The agreement was policed by an arbitration committee that could, as a last resort, call on the state to sanction violators by cutting off their electricity.[49] In Korea the military governments of the 1960s and 1970s allowed the *chaebol* business groups that had established themselves in consumer-goods industries to diversify into the producer-goods sectors, but on the condition that the conglomerates compel their subsidiaries to test their learning capacity in export markets.[50]

The danger of such comparisons is that they invite a counterinterpretation of the illustrations of an allegedly general phenomenon as the expressions of a particular, historically defined type of economic development. Here, for example, the association of Germany and Japan as examples of learning by monitoring can be used to buttress an alternative argument about the particular characteristics of late nineteenth-century industrializers with strong traditions of guild production. Taiwan and Korea were once Japanese colonies. Hence it can always be argued that insofar as they are like Japan, it is because Japanese institutions continue to influence their development either as a colonial heritage or a model for emulation. The more superficially similar the comparative cases, the more likely it is that they *do* have comparable histories, and the effort to document the general applicability of a general principle becomes an argument for its historical specificity. To put an obstacle in the path of such an interpretation and to bolster the claim to generality in a way that connects it to the core concerns of development economics that inspire the argument as a whole, I present a final example of developmental associationalism that cannot be assimilated to the Japanese historical context or, for that matter, export-oriented development models more generally, but does plainly reveal the connection between learning by monitoring within and among firms and developmental associations.

A Developmental Association in a Contemporary Developing Economy

The case is the growth of furniture making in the Brazilian village of São João do Aruaru from a fragmented, rudimentary handicraft to a technically adaptive, highly organized industry from the mid-1980s to the present.[51] Under fiscal pressure from declining tax revenues and decreasing transfer payments from the federal government, the government of the state of Ceará in the northeast of Brazil has tried to cut expenses and foster local development in this period by buying whatever supplies and equipment it could locally. The State Industry and Commerce Secretariat (SIC), a small bureau of economic development specialists with a smaller agency of technical experts, has the responsibility for finding suppliers and brokering the transactions. But, crucially, the authority to make and accept purchases rests with the other government agencies that would actually use the products. Thus even though there is government preference for their products and no competition from imports, local firms do not have guaranteed markets. Consequently, the bureau has incentives to ensure that the producers it finds can indeed meet the requirements of prospective customers.

This it does in the case of the furniture makers of São João do Aruaru by making all producers engaged to fill an order jointly responsible for filling it, making defects traceable to their source, and providing technical assistance to firms that need it. Thus contracts for the manufacture of, say, school desks or tables are signed between a particular government customer and the SIC acting as the agent for a group of producers. Half the total purchase price is due upon the signing of the contract and the remainder upon certification of its satisfactory completion. Metal tags on each product identify the maker. Under these circumstances, the above-average producers have even stronger incentives to share improving information with other firms in their group than their counterparts in Japanese-style developmental associations: if the laggards lag by too much in São João do Aruaru, the leaders, regardless of their reputation, do not get paid. Conversely, the laggards are under extreme pressure to improve their reputation for reliability. Otherwise their quota in the next round of contracting is sharply reduced, if they are allowed to participate at all. The SIC in turn has every reason to encourage and augment the flow of information about difficulties and remedies by putting its technical staffs at the service of the firms.

As the preceding discussion suggests, much of the coordination of relations among firms and between them and their customers, on the one hand, and with the bureau, on the other, is actually the responsibility of trade associations. Indeed, the SIC makes formation of a trade association the precondition for contracting an order to a group of producers: a group that cannot find agreeable rules of association presumably cannot be expected to pool resources or reallocate responsibilities to meet difficulties as they arise. The association then assigns production quotas and uses the government technicians as consultants in addressing common problems; its composition and leadership change to reflect the growing influence of the more capable firms in successive contracts. Thus, although the system in São João do Aruaru does not expose producers to world-market competition, its upshot is to encourage firms and their developmental trade associations to acquire the skills that can eventually result in exports.

This variant of the developmental association, finally, reveals a connection between learning-by-monitoring within and among firms and learning-by-monitoring between the firms and the state that is less apparent in the Japanese case. From the perspective of firm-level learning by monitoring, the SIC and the trade association to which it gave rise look like the purchasing department in a highly decentralized firm. Like a purchasing department, these entities match customers to suppliers in a way that induces learning: in exchange for the prospect of stable relations with their eventual customers, the producers—subcontractors in the one case, furniture makers in the other—have to demonstrate that they can meet the latter's changing demands. Like a purchasing department, the SIC and the trade association have to help organize the flows of information and assign responsibility for performance to serve this end. Seen this way, learning by monitoring in firms and learning by monitoring between the firms and the state are not only informed by the same principles: they can issue in convergent institutions.

Making and Understanding

The great appeal of Hirschman's idea of unbalanced growth was to suggest how public authorities might be vital in economic development without presuming to know more than the economic agents about how to do business. Only a theory that allows for the possibility of such benign public intervention can account for the frequency of vast pecuniary and nonpecuniary externalities that otherwise seem to require extraordinary good fortune, superhuman powers of coordination, or blind faith in the benevolent guidance of a hiding hand when viewed in retrospect. The idea of learning by monitoring tries to make good on the promise of such a theory by showing, from the smallest to the largest setting within an economy, how in transforming exchanges into continuous discussions the actors can induce learning by perturbing the status quo, yet not make themselves hostage to fortune.

In advancing these claims I have helped myself to assumptions about the capacities of individuals in relation to society that are at odds with the contrary standard views of both economists and sociologists. If the arguments carry weight, then they count as presumptive evidence in favor of these assumptions and reinforce the suspicion, hinted at repeatedly above, that current debates about the nature of the economy presume such essential features in common that for our purposes they amount to a false dichotomy more than fundamental alternatives.

By way of conclusion, then, I make the background assumptions of learning by monitoring explicit. The argument is that this form of economic cooperation is a particular case of a broader type of social experimentalism or pragmatism. In this view cooperation is as necessary to the production of meaning in science or politics as it is to the production of goods in the economy. With this mutual dependence goes mutual vulnerability; and hence in all spheres of life the actors must in some measure define their identities and interests in creating a common framework of understanding that allows them to assess the shortcomings of their joint activities. The power of the theory is to show that the more aware they are of this necessity, the more they can make of their possibilities.

The crucible of modern debates about the character of economic exchange is the dispute between Herbert Spencer and Emile Durkheim regarding the limits of contractual arrangements.[52] Spencer argued that all economic relations could be regulated by contracts. Durkheim objected that contracts cannot cover all contingencies and must therefore be interpreted when applied to unforeseen circumstances. In Durkheim's argument the parties, anticipating this, bind themselves only if they can also anticipate that eventual adjudication by third parties will be consistent with their own understanding of fairness. Hence the contractual regime supposes norms of fairness. Society in its formative stages is understood as the collective actor that articulates these norms and imposes them on individuals in rendering the world intelligible to all and each to the others. As the division of labor progresses, professional groups form with distinct responsibilities for the specialized tasks. A sense of mutual dependence obligates each group to the others and guides their members in the fulfillment of their contractual duties.[53] Thus even as the economy advances it continues to depend on society as its regulatory foundation.

Spencer's views, of course, eventuate in modern contractarian and game-theoretic understandings of the self-regarding basis of cooperation; Durkheim's shape two leading variants of economic sociology. The first, which I have already discussed, makes cooperation depend on the presence of community and trust among the actors. Here Durkheimian norms of fairness have direct motivational force, causing the parties to anticipate reciprocity, not guile, and so making cooperation natural whenever it is potentially advantageous.

The second variant focuses on social networks taken as connections among actors that result from trust in action. General norms are stripped of their motivational force in these networks. Rather, the rhythmic accumulation and discharge of small obligations creates routines that in turn shape expectations of cooperation. Differences in these expectations define social networks of different types; and only certain types of networks encourage innovative exchange. In "under-socialized" networks the participants share so few expectations that they are paralyzed by their inability to foresee how others will react to unforeseen contingencies, as in markets. In "oversocialized" networks the rules of reciprocity are so precise and pervasive that they freeze exchange by defining the distribution of its proceeds.[54] If wealth above a certain minimum is shared with one's kin, for example, accumulation above that limit is discouraged. Economic cooperation therefore results in innovation and growth only when networks are neither under- nor oversocialized.

Hence the false dichotomy between economic and sociological views of cooperation that served as the foil for discussion of learning by monitoring. Despite their differences, the heirs of Spencer and Durkheim both assume that cooperation is the result of anterior conditions: the alignment of the actors' self-interests in the one case and the normative characteristics of a group or habits of reciprocity in the other. Because they view cooperation as an outcome, neither is much concerned with the way cooperation actually works; still less do they contemplate the specific possibility that the inner workings of cooperation might transform the actors' understanding of one another in relation to the commonly defined world in which their interests are rooted.

Yet the thicket of rules in the Japanese production system belies the idea that the parties expect to resolve eventual disputes by relying either on self-evident social norms or self-enforcing penalties and incentives that induce cooperation apart from any understanding of the others. What the rules of learning by monitoring do is oblige the parties to redefine their projects and obligations as their joint experience outpaces their initial understanding. It is this constant reelaboration of intent that can produce the fundamental alignment of interests that the sociological account assumes as the precondition of cooperation and the economic account excludes even as a consequence. To understand the world in which this outcome makes sense, the relation between individual and group in learning by monitoring must be distinguished from the conceptual legacy of Spencer and Durkheim.

In learning by monitoring, individuals are, to begin with, sociable. As in the sociological view, what they want and what they regard as a legitimate means to getting it are powerfully shaped by what the groups into which they are born and raised indicate as desirable and legitimate. But in contrast to the sociological view, in the world of learning by monitoring this moral guidance is neither precise nor persuasive enough to determine action. Individuals must interpret the general rules and expectations to bring them to bear on their actual situation. These reinterpretations proceed through argumentative encounters in which individuals attempt to establish an equilibrium between their views and social standards by recasting both.[55] It is this reflexive capacity to embrace different forms of self-expression that defines persons as individuals and creates new interpretative possibilities for society.[56]

Such notions of reflexive sociability are in turn at the core of current debates about meaning and conviction that grow out of or are influenced by pragmatic or other notions of social experimentalism. Modern analytic philosophy, to take the canonical example, holds language in use to be so irreducibly ambiguous that meaning can only be produced cooperatively, through joint elaboration of a common framework of understanding in discursive conversation. Such are the linguistic ambiguities analytic philosophy reveals that I must interpret what you say to make sense of it at all. To manage that, I must assume as a rule that you are truthfully and conscionably advancing some part of a general understanding of the world, and that I can grasp what you are saying. Put another way, I must assume that you are speaking a language, and one that I can translate sufficiently well into my own so that we can clarify your meaning by further exchanges.

This turns the contractarian view of talk on its head. The contractarians assume that meaning is self-evident, but that the interests of speakers and listeners are so likely to diverge that determining the credibility of utterances is the central problem of understanding. For the analytic philosophers, meaning is so tenuous that discussion partners must provisionally presume convergence of interests to make sense of what they are saying. If I assume guile, incoherence, or untranslatability, I cannot hold the conversation steady enough to venture even a preliminary, clarificatory interpretation of what you might be saying. It makes no difference whether your language with respect to mine is that of another planet, another nation, another party, or another intellectual school, or whether we merely use different dialects of a common tongue. In all cases our very ability to speak at all depends on a background disposition jointly to assume and explore a common framework of agreement potentially encompassing both languages: and this framework, in making meaning possible, also creates the conditions for addressing eventual differences as well.[57]

The idea that corrigible consensus is crucial to the ability to specify disagreements and recompose them in a new, equally corrigible form is also central to debates both about persuasion in scientific controversy and the nature of constitutionalism. Consider the account of science by Karl Popper, Imre Lakatos, and Paul Feyerabend as a continuing exchange among dubious orthodoxies and redoubtable heterodoxies.[58] They argue that orthodoxy and heterodoxy are much more closely related than suggested by Thomas Kuhn's depiction of science as alternating periods of "normal" problem solving and "revolutionary" philosophizing.[59] If there were not always different schools of thought whose adherents picked and solved puzzles mindful of the differences, the scientific puzzle solver would be a drone. Good scientists, then, must learn to depend on ideas while assessing their dependability: Feyerabend, for example, speaks of a "principle of tenacity" by which scientists determine to maintain a belief *despite* indications of its infirmity.[60] But such rules of tenacity can work only if they rest on an understanding, shared by all schools, of what in the end counts as good evidence and good argument in a particular area of inquiry. That understanding is the discipline in the scientific discipline and simultaneously the ground for consensus and dissent.

In deliberative constitutionalism, finally, the actors are not individuals but social groups with persistently different interests and ideas of public order. These groups, it is presumed, recognize the need for long-term cooperation in pursuit of large common ends; but they recognize as well that such enduring, intimate relations both presuppose and contribute to changes in their identities without necessarily erasing their differences. Hence they devise an institution, particular to the particular historical circumstances, that encourages the parties to make themselves mutually vulnerable by limiting the dangers of mutual vulnerability. This institution is the constitution. It is the public, official equivalent of the background understanding of the conditions for elaborating agreement in the cooperative view of meaning; and it is corrigible through amendment, just as the background understanding among particular parties becomes more clearly specified with time.[61]

These views plainly have deep affinities with the account of science as a continuous exchange among dubious orthodoxies and redoubtable heterodoxies. Like this notion of science, the idea of deliberative constitutionalism takes continuing differences of opinion as constitutive of a process of self-(re)definition, not an obstacle to it. Like the former, the latter calls attention to the difficulties of holding the world fixed enough in particular circumstances to assess which parts of it can be fruitfully questioned. Like this view of science, deliberative constitutionalism also assumes that answers regarding the questionable parts will eventually call into question the parts held fixed, but that these "crises" or "revolutions" will (usually) be manageable precisely because they are ultimately recognized as a heightened form of everyday deliberation or debate. Thus deliberative constitutionalism presumes that citizens have and can exercise in public debate the same cognitive faculties as the members of a disputatious scientific community.

But can this general view of the cooperative articulation of understanding be applied to cooperation in economic exchange? Jürgen Habermas clearly objects to this extension in distinguishing communicative from strategic action. For Habermas, too, truthfulness and conscionability are the tacit preconditions of any conversation. In communicative action the interlocutors in effect make respect for these preconditions the goal of their joint effort: they speak to express their best understanding of how the world actually is or morally ought to be and are therefore prepared to revise particular views given grounds to do so. Because they anticipate such challenges, what they say is potentially universalizable in its respect for the most general rules of warrantability. Science, morality, and foundations of law are the preserves of communicative action. In strategic action, on the contrary, the interlocutors try to play on the presumptions required for intelligibility to achieve particular purposes. Talk becomes the cheap talk by which I try to enlist you for my ends. The economy is its precinct.[62] The two realms of action are connected only through the law, which respects the individual's right to self-expression and development as supposed in communicative action while providing the framework for the contractual pursuit of strategic ends.[63]

But this distinction of types of action is doubly suspect. First the notion of strategic action trivializes the problem of economic cooperation. If strategic action were so easily coordinated by contract as supposed, game theory would have a very easy row to hoe; and it would be impossible to understand the commonplace observation that the legal system increasingly relies on the normative consensus of actors in particular settings—labor or securities markets, for example—in place of general rules.[64]

Second, the notion of communicative action suggests that the "universalizable" truths of science, morality, and law produced in discourse are so purified through conversation as to be (almost) beyond criticism. But the modern fascination with the cooperative generation of meaning was a response to the repeated failure to find in any of these realms a categorical language so unambiguous and robust as to remain fixed in the face of interpretation through application.[65] The discovery of the compulsions to truthfulness and conscionability in everyday discussion helps clarify how persons in all circumstances make the meaningful best of a bad situation. It does not by itself warrant the conclusion that the dilemma of ambiguity can be overcome by those who take it especially to heart.[66] In fact, it is a commonplace that the creation of a scientific "consensus" can have more to do with "economic sales strategies" than "any model of a unanimously concluded conversation."[67] Habermas treats science as a counterexample to the view that cooperative truthfulness in collective problem solving refashions previous understandings without purging them of particularity; on such evidence science is better seen as yet another confirmation of it.

Such, in any event, was the view of John Dewey, George Herbert Mead, and other American pragmatists whose work influenced the developments in analytic philosophy, the philosophy of science, and constitutional law indicated here.[68] They saw persons in all spheres of life as shaped in their wants and understandings by their current activities, yet able through reinterpretation of past experience to identify and collectively address in a limited way the limitations arising from those very activities. Science was one example of this capacity, democracy a second, and ingenuity in production a third.[69] Dewey illustrated the position as sparely as possible in defining the state in relation to the citizens. Just as "an alphabet is letters," he argued, "'society' is individuals in their connections with each other."[70] Such sociable individuals can perceive through public debate the burdensome effects of their separate transactions and jointly regulate their affairs accordingly. The group formed in identifying the collective-action problem is the public; its agents are the officials; together the officials are the state. The intended and unintended consequences of state action reshape private transactions, leading in time to a new problem of collective action and a new redress.

Learning by monitoring helps explain how pragmatic "publics" of this sort can function in the economy; pragmatism helps explain how the economic actors can learn to learn by monitoring. Take first learning by monitoring as pragmatism in economic action. From this perspective, the rules I have discussed are designed to oblige the actors to take notice of the unintended burdens created by their transactions and to arrive at a common view of how to reshape their activities so as to avoid them. Learning by monitoring is in this sense an institutional device for turning, amidst the flux of economic life, the pragmatic trick of simultaneously defining a collective-action problem and a collective actor with a natural interest in addressing it. The disequilibria created by learning by monitoring are informatively effective for the same reasons as scientific experiments and democratic rule; and under these conditions the differences between the disciplines of the factory and laboratory dwindle in the face of their similarities.

Consider finally the preconditions of learning by monitoring itself. So far I have emphasized how scanty these need be: because in this system the same rules apply to small cooperative projects as to large, and vigilant attention to the partners' activities is required under all circumstances, the costs of experimenting with learning by monitoring are theoretically so low that it is hard to see why it is not adopted wherever it might be useful. Yet it is clear how difficult it is for American or British firms to learn from the example of their Japanese competitors, although many succeed in the end.[71] Is there anything to say about the conditions that make for success in some cases but not others?

Pragmatism suggests an answer that paradoxically encourages the actors to chance bootstrapping of this sort while casting doubt on the possibility of a predictive analysis of the grounds of success. For this kind of pragmatism, the wellsprings of joint understanding and cooperation are found in the no-man's-land where action is more sociable than the economists' individual preference orderings and yet more personal (in the sense of related to the very nature of personhood) than the sociologists' norms and networks. In this zone it is impossible to predict what persons or groups will do by looking at their interests, values, or institutions because the limits of these can always become the starting point for their redefinition. Whether they do or not depends on the particulars of the situation, including, of course, the actors' changing understandings of their possibilities given different interpretations of their past. Cooperation in this view therefore always has a history. But as long as the contingencies of the actors' reinterpretation of their experience in their self-constitution as a "public" are at the heart of this history, it can only be recounted in retrospect, not foretold.

This view helps make sense of an otherwise puzzling gap in the vast literature on the social bases of cooperation. No one has yet produced a plausible list of the preconditions for cooperative solutions to even the simplest collective-action problems: those concerning common-pool resources. In such cases resources are depleted unless their use is appropriately limited. Otherwise each user assumes the resource is wasting, gets as much as possible while the getting is good, and turns the assumption into a self-fulfilling prophecy. Thus, without regulation, deep-sea fisheries will be destroyed by overfishing, alpine pastures by overgrazing.

But the connection between the formative social context of a common-pool resource problem and the institutionalization of a cooperative solution is quite weak.[72] Settled alpine communities that speak the same language and cannot replace their resources once they are destroyed are more likely to cooperate in managing their affairs than the polyglot fishing fleets from different nations that can move on to new fisheries if they destroy their current one. But the differences are marginal. There are plenty of unregulated meadows and well-regulated fisheries. More fundamentally, investigation reveals important common-pool resource cases where users who once saw their interests as adverse redefine them as compatible in the act of institutionalizing cooperation, and equally important ones where cooperative solutions break down because of shortcomings in the institutions through which they operate. In this sense "community," taken as the historical alignment of interests of a group's members, is neither a necessary nor a sufficient condition for cooperation: cooperation can arise from situations where interests were not aligned, and alignment by itself does not secure continuing cooperation.[73]

This is precisely the result that the preceding discussion suggests. The pragmatist notion of self-reflective sociability lends explanatory plausibility to the finding that cooperation is possible wherever it is advantageous, where "possible" means, as it usually does, not impossible and not necessary. Learning by monitoring helps explain just how institutions of certain kinds can play a role in realizing those possibilities.

The upshot is that the most careful efforts to canvass the preconditions of cooperation put the responsibility for events precisely where
learning by monitoring suggests it should lie: with those who see and
bear the immediate consequences of their decisions. They can never
know the outcome of their efforts at cooperation in advance. But the
successes of learning by monitoring at all levels of economic development show that in speaking of their possibilities they are exercising
the very faculties needed for realizing them.

Postscript

Twelve

A Propensity to Self-Subversion

Albert O. Hirschman

PROBABLY one of the most hackneyed and certainly one of the best Jewish stories is about a Jewish mother who gives her son two ties for his birthday. The next day, to please his mother, he puts one of them on, whereupon she exclaims reproachfully: "And the other, you didn't like?!" The reason this is such a fine story is, of course, that it makes implicitly a general point about human nature. We authors (of more than one book) are, I submit, similarly touchy and insatiable for praise. When a reader sincerely wishes to show admiration and declares, "I liked your book a lot," are we not slightly offended and feel like asking, "Which one?" meaning in effect: "And what about the others?"

Also, and now I may be speaking for myself alone, when a reader praises my critique of the "Search for Paradigms," or of the "Quest for Parsimony" in economic or social science, I tend to be once again ungracious and am liable to rebuff the tribute by exclaiming: "Wait a minute! I am not, you know, all that much set against paradigms or theorizing."[1] For I like to claim that I have come up with quite a few theoretical notions of my own, from the early distinction between the "supply effect" and the "influence effect" of trade in *National Power and the Structure of Foreign Trade* all the way to my last book, *The Rhetoric of Reaction,* where I undertake to array all arguments against change or reform into the three newly created categories of perversity, futility, and jeopardy.[2]

For reasons that will become evident, I shall quickly cite some other instances of theory building on my part. In spite of its title and of its origin in practical advisory work in Colombia, *The Strategy of Economic Development* was widely regarded as a contribution to development theory.[3] A simple principle—"unbalanced growth" or the idea of maximizing induced decisionmaking—was here shown to yield suggestions on a wide range of development problems, from investment priorities to industrialization patterns, from inflation and balance-of-payments policies to new attitudes toward population growth, from the choice of technology to the role of the state in development. Among my subsequent writings on development, I might mention my "tunnel effect" paper, which dealt with the effect on political stability of a growth process that brings with it, as is often the case initially in market economies, increased income inequality. I drew a theoretical distinction between an early phase of political tolerance for this inequality and a subsequent phase of impatience. The resulting model helped to explain a variety of political developments in the third world during the 1950s and 1960s and lent itself to being translated into quite simple mathematics (in addition to its illustration through the two-lane tunnel metaphor).[4] Finally, my theoretical bent is perhaps best illustrated by my book *Exit, Voice, and Loyalty*.[5] In that volume and subsequent elaborations, I tried to show that these simple concepts and their interrelations can be used to throw new light on a vast range of seemingly disparate social, political, and economic situations—surely the hallmark of useful theory building.

So I bristle a bit when I am pigeonholed as "atheoretical" or "antitheoretical" or even as "institutional" and cannot wholly agree when I am portrayed—as Michael McPherson once did in a generally most perceptive paper—as someone who is primarily interested in noticing and underlining what more systematic-minded (theoretical) economists or social scientists have overlooked.[6] I do admit to having frequently a reaction, perhaps something approaching a reflex, to other people's theories, of the "It ain't necessarily so" kind. Skepticism toward *other* people's claims to spectacular theoretical discoveries is, of course, not a particularly noteworthy trait. It is, however, more unusual to develop this sort of reaction to *one's own* generalizations or theoretical constructs. And this has become increasingly the characteristic of my writings that I wish to look at here.

In *National Power and the Structure of Foreign Trade*, I showed how relations of influence, dependence, and domination arise directly from those commercial transactions between sovereign nations that had long been pronounced to be "mutually beneficial" by the theory of international trade. Even if one agreed with the classical theory on the economic gains from trade, it could be shown that the *political* effects of foreign trade were likely to be *asymmetrical* and to favor, at least initially, the larger and richer countries. This basic finding was one reason my book was "rediscovered" in the 1960s when a number of writers—such as Fernando Henrique Cardoso, Osvaldo Sunkel, and André Gunder Frank—developed the so-called *dependencia* thesis. Actually, I never felt comfortable being cast as a "forerunner" of this group, whose economic and political analysis I often found excessively somber. In 1977 an occasion arose to explain my attitude toward the *dependencia* school, and I decided to do so by criticizing my own thesis of a quarter of a century before.[7] I tried to show that the very situation of dependence that a small, poor country may experience initially as a result of trading with a large and rich country can give rise to various countertendencies, both economic and political, that in time would reduce this dependence. For example, while trade between a powerful large country and a small country makes initially for subordination of the latter, this situation will lead to a reaction that has some chance of success on account of what I called the "disparity of attention": the large country is unable and unlikely to focus its attention on its relations to a small trading partner with the single-mindedness that is available to, and characteristic of, the latter ("the [dependent] country is likely to pursue its escape from domination more actively and energetically than the dominant country will work on preventing this escape").[8]

My propensity to self-subversion manifests itself again around my next book, *The Strategy of Economic Development.* One of its principal chapters dealt with the characteristic features of the process of industrialization in less developed countries. I pointed out that industrial development in these countries typically proceeds by means of what I called backward linkages—an industry supplying a good proven to be in demand through prior imports will be established first on the basis of imported inputs, such as semifinished materials and machinery, and domestic manufacture of these inputs will then follow via backward linkage. This sequence is very different from the way in which industry was established in the pioneering industrial countries, where locally made machinery and intermediate materials had to be available from the start. But I celebrated the backward-linkage dynamic just because it followed a different road and could qualify as an original discovery of the late industrializers.

Already in *Strategy* I made some cautionary remarks on the conceivable drawbacks of the backward-linkage dynamic, particularly on the possibility that it may turn out not to be all that dynamic, with the interests of the early industrialists often being opposed (for various reasons) to the domestic production of inputs. In an article that was written ten years later I expanded on this theme and have now come to see this industrialization as liable to "get stuck," or as an example of what I call the "getting-stuck syndrome" that seems to affect a number of intended but potentially abortive sequences.[9]

An example fresh in my mind of arguing against my own propositions concerns my recent attempt to understand the events that led to the downfall of the German Democratic Republic in 1989—with the help of the concepts of my 1970 book *Exit, Voice, and Loyalty*.[10] In that book I had explained at length how exit undermines voice and how the inability to exit can strengthen voice. What happened in the German Democratic Republic in the course of 1989 seemed to contradict this model: here the massive flight toward the West contributed powerfully to the mass demonstrations against the Communist regime, which was brought down by the combined blows inflicted by exit and voice. It was this unexpected and effective collaboration of exit and voice that excited my interest and made me examine closely the sequence of events. In the process, I came upon some complications of the original model that, once being introduced, made it quite easy to understand how exit and voice could work in unison rather than at cross purposes. But, as I wrote, "the inventiveness of history was needed to suggest the complication and to reveal its importance."[11]

Finally I come to my most recent book, *The Rhetoric of Reaction*. This is perhaps the most pronounced instance of my propensity to ferret, undermine, or stand in some tension to propositions I have put forward, most pronounced because I engage in this propensity *within the same book*, rather than some years or decades later in a separate publication. The book was largely written in 1986–89 "as a tract—properly learned and scholarly, but still a tract—against the then aggressive and would-be triumphant neo-conservative positions on social and economic policy making."[12] The major portion of the book is devoted to three arguments that I show to have been marshaled time and again against the principal proposals for change and reform over the past two centuries: the arguments of perversity (the proposed change for the better will actually backfire and make things worse), of futility (the proposed change will be wholly ineffective), and of jeopardy (the proposed change will endanger some earlier advance).

But, as I explain at greater length in a recent paper, it occurred to me, in the course of considering the last of these arguments, that the jeopardy thesis is easily turned around: countering the view that a new reform will endanger an earlier advance, the partisans of that reform will often assert that the proposed reform will complement and strengthen the earlier one.[13] I then looked for other "progressive" arguments that would be similarly, if less obviously, related to the perversity and futility theses. As a result, I wrote a chapter I had not planned to write, "From Reactionary to Progressive Rhetoric," that shows in some detail how "reactionaries have no monopoly on simplistic, peremptory, and intransigent rhetoric."[14]

I do not believe that this chapter blunted the polemical thrust of my book. Still, the demonstration that progressives can be just as given to arguing along doctrinaire and routine-ridden lines as reactionaries modified my overall message and brought me to conclude the book, originally written in a combative mood, on a quite unintended constructive note.

In the follow-up article that I just mentioned, I characterized my "Progressive Rhetoric" chapter as "self-subversive." *Self-subversion* may in fact be apt as a general term for the intellectual wanderings I have been describing here by drawing on various writings of mine. Such self-subversion is probably rather unusual. It may seem odd that anyone should repeatedly *wish* to demonstrate that a tendency or line of causation he or she has suggested earlier needs to be substantially reconsidered and qualified by attention to the opposite line, in the light of subsequent events or findings. A simple reason scientists (social and otherwise) are rarely self critical to the point of engaging in self-subversion is that they invest much self-esteem and even identity in the findings and propositions for which they have become known. In their further work, they are likely to explore, along Kuhnian "normal science" lines, all those domains in which their original findings can be *confirmed*. In this way, much confirmatory evidence will be accumulated and resistance against self-subversion will mount.

Another reason why there is such resistance is the continuing hold on our minds of certain basic conceptions about "the way things are" in the physical world and the analogies to the social world we are apt to draw. Whether the sun turns around the earth or the earth circles around the sun, we are certain that both of these propositions cannot be true at the same time. We tend to forget that, in the social world, things are much more complicated and ambiguous. Here any connection we have established convincingly between events, as though it were a universally valid law, could be found simultaneously to hold and not to hold (or to hold in a very different form) in various subsections of human society—for the simple reason that some underlying assumptions, previously implicit and thought to be general, apply in one subsection but not in another.

Here lies also the reason why my exercises in self-subversion, while often experienced at first as traumatic, are eventually rewarding and enriching. The new dynamics I come upon in matters of dependence, linkages, exit-voice, and so on, do not in the end cancel out or refute the earlier findings: rather, they define domains of the social world where the originally postulated relationships do not hold. Far from having to hang my head in shame on account of some egregious error that needs to be recanted, I can still land on my feet and in fact "come out on top" as I celebrate the new complexities I have uncovered.[15]

In closing, I should therefore like to plead for the overcoming of the normal resistance to self-subversion, even wish to proclaim the virtues and attractions of indulging that activity. In the first place, I believe that what I have here called self-subversion can make a contribution to a more democratic culture in which citizens not only have the right to their individual opinions and convictions but, more important, are ready to question them in the light of new arguments and evidence. Furthermore, just as Gaston Bachelard said of Freudian repression that it is "a normal activity, a useful activity, better still, a joyful activity," so engaging in self-subversion can actually be a positive and enjoyable experience.[16] When I encounter a social situation where exit stimulates voice instead of undermining it, as I had long thought, I may well pass through a moment of perplexity and concern about my exit-voice theory having been "falsified." But past this moment, I feel genuinely more alive as I now have new interrelations and complexities to explore. Wittgenstein is reported to have remarked that "he could feel really active only when he changed his philosophical position and went on to develop something new."[17] At some point of one's life, self-subversion may in fact become the principal means to self-renewal.

Coda

I recall being much moved, many years ago, by Camus and his wartime essay "The Myth of Sisyphus" and particularly by its last sentence: "Il faut imaginer Sisyphe heureux" (One must imagine Sisyphus happy). Perhaps, as a result of my reflections on the uses of self-subversion, I can now go beyond the Camus formulation and propose instead, less elegantly but more radically: One must imagine Sisyphus himself making the rock tumble down.

Appendix A

Seminar Participants: Obiter Dicta

THERE CAN BE QUITE A DIFFERENCE —in voice, sheer candor, and even clarity—between the things scholars say in formal papers and in seminar banter and discussions. Nevertheless, off-the-cuff dicta try to amplify and explain: and even if they do not always succeed, they can be revealing in their nuances, details, and ideas, and in some of the pungent language and unexpected attitudes and values. Since we had notes and tape recordings for most of the sessions, we summarized, closely paraphrased, or quoted a sample of these other angles of vision. Our résumés of the discussions depended in part on whether there were one or two speakers at the seminar, and the length of the presentations, as well as the adequacy of the tapes and our notes. We omitted less relevant items, however, and, on occasion, slightly changed the wording of the quotation—in the main because of grammar, redundancy, or tense. We also shifted the order of some of the remarks to fit the sequence of the chapters and to highlight the more challenging policy implications. The chapter writers did have an opportunity to review and edit the final version. The minutes and the tapes are available at MIT's Rotch Library.

Krugman Discussion: Modeling, Learning, and Policy

Paul Krugman charged that it was the failure of Hirschman and other high development theorists to "formalize" their findings that led to the decline both of development theory and of the influence of its proponents.

Not surprisingly, this thesis raised hackles. "Why did Hirschman have to be the one formalizing his ideas?" asked Lance Taylor. "In any case Hirschman did publish models in *The Strategy of Economic Development*," he added, and "they were more formal than others of the time." There is a difference between some "brilliant insights" in an individual's work and major contributions to a discipline, Krugman replied. Regardless of Hirschman's impact on individuals, Krugman continued, he has not had an impact on the mainstream or entered the formal discourse of economics. "If you don't engage the World Bank, or you are ignored by the World Bank, an important strand has been lost." Krugman dismissed Taylor's downgrading of formalization. It "is not that easy," he said, to construct a convincing model.

Judith Tendler suggested that Hirschman should be judged not by the degree of his international impact through the World Bank but by how well—in comparison with the mainstream—he explains phenomena in specific places. Krugman disagreed. "No one knows exactly why Korea and Japan have done so well; too many factors are at play." Tendler countered that Korea's story is inconsistent with the story "that comes off mainstream economics" and thus called into question the usefulness of the mainstream.

"The Macedonian army performed well when they had an Alexander the Great in charge," Krugman remarked, "but the Roman army was good at management no matter who was in charge." Models are "systems that work," he continued, and "don't require brilliant people to constantly reinvent them." Krugman then underlined the "Kuhnian" view that intellectual succession requires not just negative evidence but also a well-formulated alternative theory. "You overestimate a 200-year tradition," Taylor suggested. "You underestimate consistency of method," Krugman replied.

Hirschman's work must be seen, Michael Piore observed, in the context of the changing relationship between economics and the other social sciences: "a relationship opened up by Keynes and the depression but subsequently closed."

Martin Rein thought an entrepreneur in the midst of a transition from a traditional to a modern sector would have a different model in mind: "You have to look at how the learner is learning, what shapes and governs that process, and what the theory does or does not do to explain it."

Whereupon Krugman quoted Gunnar Myrdal's proposition about

what killed institutional economics: "All the people who wrote about economic history had nothing to say about the Depression. Then other people came along and said 'Increase G.'" Piore demurred: what is seen as resistance to modeling, he said, is an openness to other disciplines that has disappeared today.

Donald Schön called attention to Krugman's "elliptical references to learning. Don't entrepreneurs moving into the modern sector have to learn how to use capital and equipment in order to get the benefit out of it? Isn't there a difference between expressing the results in terms of output, expressing the results in terms of strategy, or conceiving a process by which more output is produced?"

Emma Rothschild distinguished between learning as a cognitive or reflective activity and learning in the sense that a computer is programmed to respond to price signals (the classical economist's model of the market as an exchange of information). By way of illustration, Schön observed, "an improvement in economic performance can be regarded retrospectively as mechanical, but not beforehand, when the choices leading to that improvement are not predetermined, and a good coach can make an enormous difference."

Apropos of Krugman's characterization of Hirschman as a novelist, Tendler said that the ability to depict how the world works is one of Hirschman's special gifts, not a weakness. "Isn't this failing of theory to develop significant development counterexamples the most serious challenge to mainstream economics?"

That may be, conceded Krugman, since there are no convincing models that capture enough factors to explain why some countries do better than others; but the key issue is how over time one can improve the discipline of economics. He agreed with Robert Solow that that is best done by modeling simpler, solvable problems and becoming eventually more proficient, so that it is possible eventually to handle more complex systems. "This is the most critical point to bear in mind, not the inadequacy of economic modeling in particular." What is more, Krugman maintained, it is the justification for the use of theory even as "radically simplified versions" of complex processes (or "useful untruths"). By the "richness of plain English," an author such as Hirschman seduces people "into thinking that they are being offered a more complex understanding of a phenomenon than with formal models; and that is rarely true."

Taylor Discussion: Professional Practice, Modeling, Lore, and Prescription

Like Krugman, Taylor believes that Hirschman is not much read and not too relevant to practice. In vigorous dissent, Karen Polenske pointed to Hirschman's continuing influence in regional economics, both in the United States and in developing countries. Taylor conceded that "some things could be driven out of macroeconomics, but could not be buried in regional economics."

Meenu Tewari said she was startled by Krugman's view, since Hirschman's perspective is "very different from either a Marxist or a neoclassical approach, which would rely on one simple recommendation"; Hirschman focuses on "the way things happen while people are making changes" and she finds his work is a very "useful . . . guide for those observing planning interventions and for those suggesting interventions." Perhaps a distinction should be made, Tendler suggested, between the "macrolevel," which Hirschman does not examine directly, and the sector or projects at the local level, where it seems Hirschman is being read.

Hirschman did not like to make prescriptions, Rothschild noted, and he did seduce "with words," and, no doubt, many economists are "seduced by different means"; but in any case she reminded everyone that Hirschman made an important point for the era he was operating in at the time *Strategy* was written: "his one generalization about development is that there are no generalizations about development, as opposed to the simple models marketed by the World Bank—then central planning and now price prescription."

Taylor added that Hirschman's way of looking at systems—that "you can't talk about a system without looking at the forces impinging on it from the outside"—had influenced other people's work, citing Gillian Hart and her research in Indonesia, in which "what goes on in the village depends very much on what is going on outside the village." Tendler agreed. Hirschman's contribution, she said, went "several steps beyond 'the micro is linked to the macro.'"

Taylor then characterized much of Hirschman's advice as "amplified common sense," which "doesn't formalize very easily": he was more an applied than an academic economist, whose contributions were captured in anecdotes or "lore" rather than formulas or the kind of knowledge economists use. Tendler asked for a definition of "lore."

Martin Rein said it was the "do's and don'ts," without the boundary conditions, or "rules of thumb," while Schön contrasted it with physics and Newton's laws, but Tendler observed that "development planning is not physics, and Hirschman is more than a 'storyteller.'"

The resolution of the problem, Lloyd Rodwin suggested, hinges partly on how one interprets the form of the contributions and the significance of professional as well as disciplinary development. Don Schön agreed. He objected to the pejorative characterizations of Hirschman's observations as "lore" in comparison with macroeconomic representations of the academic economists. The difference between Krugman's little models and Hirschman's little models, Schön observed, is illusory because "little" formal models are hardly more than heuristic, under certain circumstances and specific conditions: "neither one of them has a claim to universality, and both of them are quite situation-specific but rather fuzzy about what the situation is. So in a sense the clear distinction between the formal economists and the lore of practitioners tends to erode. No doubt, too," Schön added, "to apply Krugman's models probably takes quite a bit of skill and attention to nuance, and thus the difference in applying formal economic models and less formal Hirschmanian advice is in fact quite small."[1]

Taylor granted this point: he thought Hirschman was more "humble" than Krugman about any claims to describing "reality" in some global or universal way, although Hirschman made detailed, perceptive observations about how the world works in "a complex social reality." Nonetheless, the hiding hand principle, Taylor felt, could be "misleading and socially dangerous," if used willfully to conceal how hard a given course of action would be.

To Tendler, however, the hiding hand principle pointed to the need to surround policy- and decisionmakers with certain pressures and supports so that when difficulties arise, their ability to deal with them is greater.

Piore Discussion: Practice, Theory, and Interpretive Frameworks

Rodwin asked Piore to clarify his views about Hirschman's relationship to theory. While his own preference is for coherence, Piore said, he did not think Hirschman was ever bothered by whether something fit conventional theory or not, and by "if it didn't fit, why it didn't fit." He stressed that he shares with Hirschman the sense that "practice is very important as a guide to what is reasonable in the realm of ideas," and if the ideas do not fit practice, he "would rather live with ambiguity than resolve it by a set of intellectual constructs that are consistent with each other but do not have much to do with practice."

Rein asked for an example of what Piore meant by practice or experience and by its conflict with theory. Piore turned to Hirschman's idea of voice for that purpose. This concept, Piore argued, "crystallizes a series of ideas" in some areas where conventional economics fails, such as labor economics. But Hirschman "did not look deeply enough into the nature of communication and what is involved in voice or in developing a common framework of analysis"—for all of which "voice" is "a poor term." Piore questioned, too, whether the concept of exit is adequate. "It organizes a realm of experience. . . . It's a little lamp that helps you see how this piece of the world operates." But for Piore that is not good enough, "because it operates in a way that is very different from the way you operate in economic theory."

Schön welcomed Piore's challenge to conventional economic theory and his view that "cognitive structures and interpretive frameworks at the level of persons and institutions are in some sense 'prior.'" There are many benefits, he noted, in the current economics framework. "It's simple, it's uniform, and it lends itself to quantification." And, he speculated, "there are risks if interpretive structures are seen—as they are through Hirschman's lens—to be neither uniform, simple, nor quantifiable—but complicated, different, diverse, and contextually dependent. An economics so based," he suggested, "might not have the power that it currently has."

In response, Piore said he had not "invested" in those simplifying qualities. The Keynesian turn toward empirical evidence, he noted, was precipitated by the traumatic experience of the depression, which "opened a space for a different approach to the world: the Keynsians were willing to tolerate any idea that would explain that event. In the historical evolution of economics since then, practice has been pushed to the periphery, impoverishing economic theory."

But "any theory filters for what it describes as relevant," Lisa Peattie declared, and "conventional economic theory fails to treat coordination as a political as well as an economic activity: power really does not enter in." Piore concurred. "One of the problems with the exit-voice typology," he said, is that "it does not capture that dimension: to call the issue 'voice' is to convert it into an issue of communication."

Schön Discussion: Learning, Expertise, Politics, and Institution Building

Professor Luca Mendolesi—one of the Italian guests attending the seminar—was not surprised that Hirschman's approach is "elusive": the subjects of Hirschman's learning process were not the automatons of neoclassical economics but "people who are learning," consciously and unconsciously. Hirschman's ideas, he observed, "emphasize the qualitative aspect, the art of inducing learning and thus development."

Hirschman may have been a good coach to finance ministers in Latin America, Lance Taylor added, but he had not done much "playing" since his work in Colombia; "so he lies in some vague territory between the academic economists with their strong simple models and the policy economists in the messy world of politics." As for learning by doing, most economists, he said, "especially academic economists, learn and operate not by doing but by relying on nice, neat, simple models." But Hirschman's work, he continued, "is not amenable to strong simple models because of its emphasis on disequilibria and constant adjustment to disequilibria." However, the simple, pragmatic ways Koreans "targeted and prompted exports with clear subsidies and disincentives was in line with Hirschman's thinking, although the Koreans may not have read Hirschman."

Tendler took another tack. Less advanced countries, she noted, often have to handle problems at the same time they are building institutions. "They do not have the luxury of talking about program design without the agency to carry it out. So planners must be parsimonious in their definition of a proper program; they must consider the minimum demands that can be made or burdens that can be placed on a very weak agency." Hirschman, she observed, had been uniquely tuned to these sorts of issues, and his economic advice was always predicated on an assessment of the circumstances impinging on implementation in given places. There is the well-known example of Nigeria where—because of ethnic rivalries—roads were a more practical mode of transportation than railroads. That is to say, because road building can be a decentralized activity, it tends to avoid many of the tribal and related problems that would attend a centralized project. Thus

Hirschman's advice to decisionmakers would be: "do the road rather than the railroad, no matter what the preceding cost-benefit analysis says, and spare this project these problems."

Another example of Hirschman's approach, Tendler cited, had to do with expanding electric power capacity where the public power agency needs the pressure of private producers to keep it on path. "Imbalance will create the help needed for further development, if there is a threshold demand for power." Here, she disagreed with Schön's view that Hirschman had an unfinished and perhaps inconsistent theory of learning. "Maybe he was not interested in it," she said. "At some level, Hirschman is 'a determinist, a micro-Marxist' who believes that technology, along with other forms of resource endowment, determines how actors behave." Perhaps so, Lloyd Rodwin interjected, but Hirschman had told him that Schön's thesis was one of the group's more interesting contributions.

Hirschman was really interested in what people already know— what they knew but could not act on, Tendler continued. He did not tell them how to do things so much as help them to do what they already knew and wanted to do. She described working with him in Brazil and seeing him approach people "not as an expert" but "to learn from them." That was why he was so "revered. Hirschman's style was to stand conventional development advice on its head, which perhaps accounts for the lingering assessment that his ideas were not operational: his rule of thumb for development," she said, "was not to look at the internal capacity of the organization in charge of a particular project, but to look outside it for pressures that would keep it focused." He might say, "Don't do an electric power project unless a lot of firms have bought generators, no matter what the cost-benefit says." His principle of the hiding hand had the implicit premise, "Don't worry about the difficulties—in fact, it is better if you don't know them up front," advice that is "hard to translate into expertise." The closest he got to prescriptive advice, she said, is "make sure you have good people in place and that they are surrounded by 'good' pressures."

Tendler concluded that Hirschman had "unnerved those in the mainstream of development economics by removing boundaries that marked areas of conventional expertise by sector, organization, or analytic mode." In his construction, for example, transportation planners had to know about ethnic rivalry, a demand that "opens up the world too much" and "challenges the whole idea of development planning cast in terms of the transfer of knowledge from the advanced to the backward countries."

Schön shared these views. But he reiterated that Hirschman was not skeptical about giving "subtle, situation-specific, local-level advice," only about making "generic prescriptions" cutting across countries. Hirschman was "happy to be a coach." Rothschild agreed, but Tendler did not: although good at coaching, she said, Hirschman also "tried to understand behavior and practice in specific cases and made powerful generalizations that helped one to understand and support pragmatic institution building and decisionmaking."

Hirschman also explored, Schön observed, the connection between learning (necessary for both economic actors and development economists) and uncertainty. The Big Push model proposes that individual entrepreneurs move from the traditional to the modern sector, and it credits economies of scale, wage differentials, and other factors, "but it does not account for an individual in the process of learning about these differentials. Hirschman was not interested just in economic growth," Schön emphasized, "but in a state of mind, a process of change and institution building in which learning *is* development."

Rothschild Discussion: Economic Rationality Reconsidered

Rothschild drew attention to the arguments among theorists about the extent to which economics is now influenced more by its tools than by the world it seeks to explain; and by simplifications that have little to do with disputes over economic technique, with being for or against the commitment to "tightly specified models." The issue, she argued, "is not that models are oversimplified, but which simplifications are most useful." She suggested, too, that Hirschman's *Strategy of Economic Development* must be seen in the context of the 1950s, when there was the "powerful idea," emphasized by Arthur Lewis, Theodore Schultz, Walter Rostow, and others, that there were prescribed prerequisites— "social and psychological"—for development to occur in less developed countries; and that Hirschman's objection to preconditions was a radical departure from the mainstream position. Indeed, "his skepticism about the impulse within economics to lean on theory and simple messages ... applied similarly in different countries, and his reluctance to provide one-liners for the World Bank may account in part for his alleged limited influence within the field."

Bishwapriya Sanyal observed that development economists such as Lewis thought the proper operation of the market was disrupted in developing countries by the unwillingness of the population to move, a resistance these economists characterized as irrational because people were not going to "the place of highest return." In contrast, he said, "Herbert Marcuse's 'one-dimensional man' was a critique of economics, and of intellectual and cultural life insofar as it was dominated by economic ideas, because it focused on profit and utility maximization as *the* dominant value."

Rothschild's views, Schön found, were not unlike those of Piore, who complained that conventional economists have been inattentive to empirically derived cognitive structures shaping behavior and have accepted a more or less false model. The only difference is that Rothschild takes a historical look at the ways maximization has been stereotyped. "For economists, rationality is significant," Piore added, "as it applies to the behavior of firms; hence profit, rather than utility maximization becomes critical: from the point of view of economic theory, profit is a surrogate for utility."

"What is the appropriate characterization of economic rationality?" Taylor asked. The "spin in Schultz's book on rural development is that people in developing countries *are* utility-maximizers: Doesn't the task then become not psychological shocks but removing the fetters to the economic rationality already there?"

The fetters are still "institutional, external rather than internal," Rothschild replied, and Tendler concurred. Rothschild offered the example of "rationality in the fledgling Russian entrepreneur who bribes the party apparatchik; the entrepreneur's behavior may be rational but will not lead to the establishment of a market unless it is channeled in some way."

The economic theory of rationality, Tendler added, "does not explain why a public official would not accept bribes and ... Hirschman was in search of an adequate theory embracing public-minded behavior as well as narrow self-interest."

Peattie Discussion: Challenging the Rationality of Development

Schön found parts of Peattie's presentation "fascinating," but did not see how her views on the limits of reason and on the breakdown of the exit-voice typology tied in with the story of boycotts. "Hirschman was writing at the end of the phase when rationality was less important in economic theory," Peattie emphasized, mentioning as examples Schumpeter and Keynes, who saw the world in terms of "bounded rationality" and buffeted by the "dark forces of time and ignorance." The exit-voice typology, however, "rests on a conception of the world in which social and economic institutions are discrete and rational: once it does not appear like that, behavior won't fall into categories of exit and voice."

"Does that mean boycotts are not rational?" Schön asked. "Such behavior is a strategy that does not count on rationality in institutions," Peattie responded, and it "assumes no boundary between economics and politics." However, "it does assume a rational response regarding its impact on the bottom line," Rodwin observed.

Martin Rein suggested that a boycott may challenge social norms, rather than interests. Peattie agreed "because activists in a boycott are not trying to change behavior: they want to change reality. You can't argue across frames," she said, "but you have to do something convulsive to change the frame." But "it is a small step from boycotts to sanctions," Taylor observed, and sanctions, "despite their small economic impact, played a role in changing political conditions in South Africa."

Sanyal wondered where Peattie would place violence in a "continuum of gestures" of social protest. In their study of the Narita Airport controversy, *Against the State: Politics and Social Protest in Japan*, David Apter and Nagayo Sawa argued that violence was central to the activists' extra-institutional status and strategy. "The willingness to expose oneself to violence in the form of civil disobedience is one way in which a person grounds the movement in physical experience," Peattie replied. "Look at how antiabortion activists are willing to be dragged off to represent their degree of commitment." Sanyal was skeptical. Peattie seemed to be arguing, he said, that the exit-voice dichotomy has lost its relevance—because new types of social movements now

occur in a context different from "the nineteenth-century world of expectations" on which she said Hirschman still relies; but Hirschman
in his current work on the fall of the Berlin Wall says that "exit still
works." Peattie, however, saw Hirschman's own example as a "mixed
mode," itself part of the stimulus for her own remarks.

Both exit and voice, Schön noted, are "subject to calculation on their
anticipated effects and are both interest-based rational arguments
grounded in some conception of a social order based on reason"; and
if this is so, Schön asked Peattie, "what changed that would make the
exit-voice typology less applicable; and was the problem [one of] getting Hirschman into another story you wanted to tell about social and
political conflicts?"

"I am raising the question," Peattie responded, "of where development economics sits in the world that ... I am describing: where
people go around committing *seppuku* under cherry trees and chaining
themselves to abortion clinics." Development economics, she noted,
"is still outside that world and still manages to operate at places like
the World Bank, but how long can that go on. And I think that leads
to the question of the advantages and limits of professionalism."

Rodwin wondered "whether today's environmental movement
should be seen as a current outside the mainstream comparable to the
Luddites or Romantics of the last century, in no significant way negat-
ing the principal emphasis on development as a form of progress. Or
does it foreshadow a fundamental change in the relationship between
the economy and society?" "The deep ecology movements may go further than the nineteenth-century movements," Peattie replied, "but the
economic institutions may be harder to control or change."

Schön thought the argument depended on distinguishing between
the rationality of means as opposed to the rationality of ends: "If one
is interested in the rationality of means," he argued, "exit and voice
may be a way of parsing all such strategies, and they are inherently
strategies that demand calculation and rationality on the part of people
who are affected by them. If you are interested in the rationality of
ends and what you are interested in is not making institutions work
or perform better but in changing the whole conception of development and progress, then exit and voice are no longer relevant strategies. Nor can you assume that they would work to effect the change
you had in mind because there is no calculation across frames, and
what you require is a convulsive event to change the frame. Hence that

becomes a recipe or a guide for looking at what in our society works to shake up the frames."

Peattie agreed. As examples, she cited her work with a group seeking the demilitarization of American society. From this perspective "the topic of economic conversion is an economistic title for something that turns out to be more complicated." She also cited the diaper controversy. "Cloth was thought to be more ecologically sound because of the landfill requirements of disposables, but then [this] had to be weighed against the energy cost of washing cloth diapers as well as the bleach, pesticides, and horrible social relations of production associated with cotton." David Laws noted that the personal commitment of the researchers to cloth diapers also may have risked their objectivity, but the results of their study came out as "sort of a wash."

Paola Perez-Aleman asked how Hirschman deals with the concept of interest: can it be defined outside of the narrow view of economic interest as pure self-interest? To illustrate propositions about interests, Peattie cited the experience of Jobs with Peace, a group founded by Marxists. Its members believed that because people act on their interests, the constituencies to organize against the military budget were those in the human services, whose budgets naturally compete.

"If both sides view each other as irrational," Laws concluded, "then they are mutually blocked by their perceptions of each other's means and can have no discussion over each other's ends." The airport controversies are good examples of this, Peattie said: "Airports are always couched in the language of progress and so their opponents have to attack the goals of progress and the rationality of planning, treating planners as having phony rationality, like the Wizard of Oz." What is impressive, she added, is that "there is always this antiprogress and antiplanning sentiment floating around."

Asked about her views of the state in the context of social protest, Peattie said "the adversarial relations of state opposition can take different forms: in the sphere of normal politics, there is ordinarily less political space for antiairport activists, as in the Japanese case, but in Germany, the Greens came into electoral politics on the tail of the airport fight, which was a social movement and a piece of parliamentary politics at the same time."

Lynn McCormick was "intrigued" by the idea that planners could be trained to be irrational. "I didn't say it would be easy," Peattie replied. Karen Umemoto asked where to draw the line between rational and irrational: was it helpful to think about that line in terms of what level the appeal is being made? Peattie said the abortion issue provided a good example of that difficulty, a task complicated by the "problem of dialogue across frames."

Robert Einsweiler observed that "in a boycott each side knows the rationality of each other's positions, and only the general public might be confused by the accusations of irrationality directed at each side."

"How about the opposite case?" Tendler asked. Suppose (as in Brazil) "a population is very active in voice because the state has something it wants as opposed to something a constituency sees as irrational and wants to stop." This condition, she said, "does not fit the portrait of the monolithic and oppressively rational state in Peattie's paper: here people see the project as eminently rational and want in." "This is a more traditional complaint," Peattie thought, "in which people want their fair share but not with the same fanaticism as when they are jumping frames and redefining what the nature of the good is. . . . Then they set themselves afire and do all sorts of weird stuff."

"Aren't you stacking the cards," Rodwin asked Peattie, "by "choosing in the main causes with which you are in sympathy, in contrast to other groups [that] you might detest, including the Ku Klux Klan and the current German antirefugee movement, as well as other local communities mobilizing against people moving into certain areas?" Peattie replied that she was in fact examining "such absolutist cases as the abortion controversy, in which she might hold her own convictions but could also see each group preparing their respective acts at their respective church bases the night before."

Rodwin expressed mixed feelings about advocacy for local grassroots control as a way of ensuring more democracy. "This assurance depends in part on the goals being advocated. The means-goals dichotomy also oversimplifies matters: for means are often goals in themselves." Peattie cited a paper she wrote in 1968 against advocacy planning, but hesitated to offer a categorical answer.

Was there a time when she had been more sure about how to resolve these questions, Umemoto asked? Peattie said no. "But this lack of certainty did not prevent you from acting on your convictions," Schön murmured. "I'm sure you don't get on with it by contemplating it alone," Peattie replied.

Schön asked "whether these strategies of protest, when reason fails, serve to reestablish relationships of solidarity over relationships of utility." Peattie thought "they also deny that separation." Summing up, Schön suggested that "what is being protested is separation between economy and society and what begins as a protest against the airport becomes a campaign to re-embed economy in society as a whole and get rid of the hegemony of utilitarian relationships."

In Rodwin's view, Peattie appeared to be criticizing planners for being "overrational and naive," and from her point of view, they were often on the wrong side. Yet, he thought, the work of planners generally "may be regarded as efforts to adjust the economic system to the social system."

Sanyal Discussion: Hirschman's Background and Moral Stance

Sanyal's suggestion that Hirschman has no theory of development drew a protest from Karen Polenske, who wondered whether she or Sanyal were using the same definition of theory. "Hirschman has no set paradigm of causality in his mind," Sanyal replied. "If the theory is x creates y under z conditions, Hirschman is more interested in explaining z than in explaining x creates y, and in arguing that x will not create y unless z exists."

But, Polenske said, *The Strategy of Economic Development* in fact proposes a theory of unbalanced rather than balanced growth. Sanyal disputed that point somewhat: *Strategy* "was essentially a response to theory, to the then mainstream proposition that there was a way—and a single way—to do equal and balanced development." "Maybe the issue was between a theory of development and a theory of a strategy of development," Schön remarked.

Sanyal disagreed and argued again that mainstream theory offered one strategy for all developing countries, whereas Hirschman designed custom strategies after identifying contextual and particularly institutional z variables first.

Taylor observed that the entry-exit debate may not illuminate the course of Hirschman's thinking as much as a more dialectical argument. His world view emerged from a series of circumstances marked by dramatic transitions—synthesized in his Latin American experience. He proposed "defining the Hirschman set by its complements, by what bounds it." In addition, Taylor observed that despite Hirschman's "abhorrence of grand theory," and despite the fact that the *Strategy* was a direct challenge to the mainstream development economists of its day, in it Hirschman shared some of their assumptions: namely, "that planning was working in some corners of the world and the Keynesian revolution said there was a role for government intervention, views that came to sound equally dated, whatever their other contradictions."

Einsweiler suggested that since *Exit, Voice, and Loyalty* was fundamentally concerned with organizational reform, "exit is not just a kind of 'leaving': it is a purposeful action and a more powerful tactic than voice, with some expectation that departing has an effect, thus intended as a hopeful act of reform." Sanyal objected, saying that is the role reserved for voice.

Piore called this a paradox, in that "exit has an effect in a global system but from the point of view of the 'exiter,' the institution or organization has been abandoned—a distinction that may make exit understood differently by economists and political scientists and that revives the question of how it should be understood as an autobiographical idea from Hirschman's own experience."

"Hirschman is a hero within economics," Piore concluded, not because of his individual ideas but "because he comes across as a moral person, . . . he uses ideas to achieve a particular moral stance." What Piore found particularly striking about Hirschman's stance was its tolerance. Global theories, in contrast, "block out so much more than they make you see, . . . and what they block out is going to lead to a mistake sooner or later."

But Piore disagreed with Sanyal's view that the source of Hirschman's stance was the experience of entry. The ability to have ideas that are tolerant of other ideas is less about coming to America and was derived more from the experience of intolerance that drove him from Germany. Piore concluded that "Hirschman must be right when he emphasizes exit. What is more, exit is not just walking out, not a simple act of abandonment."

Rephrasing Piore's question as "Why would exit lead to tolerance?" Sanyal replied that "there are enough examples of people leaving or being pushed out of their country that have not led to tolerant thinking to make it hard to directly associate a capacity for tolerance with the experience of exit." This debate could be addressed adequately only by a biographer, Polenske said.

Marseille Discussion: Learning via the Hiding Hand

Elliot Marseille, reporting on the Nepal blindness program, said he was struck by the incongruity between his organization's emphasis on plans and the problems and opportunities of real life that were not taken into account in those plans. He then summarized the various ways Hirschman's hiding hand hypothesis anticipated these discrepancies.

Rodwin asked what criticism Marseille would make of this hypothesis, given Robert Picciotto's view that optimism does not necessarily, or even often, produce good results. Although setting high goals or standards can lead to demoralization and frustration, Marseille conceded, there are cases, and Nepal is one of them, in which optimism has worked.

Maybe those discrepancies, Schön suggested, are due in part to the fact that "Hirschman's concept of learning was a retrospective idea: in hindsight everything makes sense. My first blindness may turn out to be useful, but only in looking backward. Hirschman himself admits in his later books that some forms of difficulty or blindness do not yield." What is difficult, Schön suggested, "is to operationalize our awareness of the principle." Similarly, David Laws wondered how—given Marseille's retrospective recognition that success was not a byproduct of planning—one can use it as a prospective argument to say "leap."

The prospective lesson for management and organization, Marseille replied, may be that "one needs nimble organizations that can change directions quickly, that are sensitive to error detection. Small organizations are usually able to capitalize on unexpected opportunities and to respond creatively to problems that arise. Planners also must be close to the front-line actions and must talk to people who are not just planners. Small organizations do not have such large constituencies committed to having things a certain way, or to the way suggested in their plans."

Bish Sanyal disagreed. In a very flexible project, the hiding hand suggests that "rigidity, for instance, could sometimes lead to success by providing more time to work on a problem." But he wondered—in relation to nonmarket-type situations—what Marseille had in mind when he referred to the usefulness of the hiding hand. "It takes account of the way the world, as opposed to the mind, is constructed," responded Marseille. "When a project is conceived, it needs to have some boundaries. [Planners] look at the costs and benefits and the effects, but they are all confined in scope because they can't predict the second-, third-, and fourth-order effects over time. Yet [everyone] knows that the world is highly interdependent and in fact third-, fourth-, and fifth-order effects are often the big ones. In other words, the hiding hand is sensitive to the tension between the limitations of our understanding and intelligence, and the thrilling, wonderful, scary messiness of the world."

"Had I been in Marseille's shoes," Picciotto interjected, "I [would have said] the hiding hand is successful or helpful in situations with very good, committed leadership. [But] the hiding hand is often misused for private or vested interest." What is more, he added, when the project is a large economic development effort such as the building of a dam, even if one assumes unique leadership, one cannot "grope" toward a dam. Also, the notion that "small is beautiful" may hold for an organization but not necessarily for economic development. And "trust is broken the moment you lie to get the money." So the hiding hand has its limits. "But at Seva," Marseille noted, "no one was lying: . . . they believed what they were saying."

"Many people do not know that they do not know," Rodwin observed. "Take the housing debates in the 1930s in the United States. The public housing advocates believed firmly they were right. They were not, but those who criticized them knew precious little, too. And, as Senator Patrick Moynihan has suggested, one cannot go to a congressional committee and ask for several hundred million dollars and say they'll grope for a couple of years and then let the committee know if what they are doing makes sense or not, if this is the right way to go."

"There might be two hiding hands," Picciotto concluded, "one applied in the right situation, the other in the wrong one. In the latter case, even though everyone might still be happy, they would still sink." Marseille agreed. The argument "small is beautiful" could apply only when large organizations are not needed, for example, not in the case of a big dam. Many of the problems faced today, however, are big problems and transcend national boundaries, as in the case of pollution.

This is a drawback for small organizations that cannot muster the resources needed to solve these big problems.

Schön wondered if Marseille had drawn the wrong lesson. "The trouble with groping toward a dam is that you often have to make a clear-cut irrevocable decision. Hirschman says don't grope; leap!" Schön thought the lesson from the difficulties is "get yourself started and then grope."

Emma Rothschild emphasized that "groping, or *tatonnement*, was the central metaphor of markets in general equilibrium in modern economics: the margin is what matters, little by little getting closer to the equilibrium price. Standard economic analysis falters when you have big projects . . . and discontinuities."

There is nothing inherently wrong with groping, Picciotto conceded. But in the case of a nonmarket big dam decision one should certainly not leap until having groped enough. "It's too risky when a project involves hundreds of contracts with workers, contractors, suppliers, and others without reliable information: contracts cannot be based on blind faith. For such situations," he added, "there seems to be a big gap in Hirschman's scheme: a scheme where the architecture looks perfect but what is missing is the connection with information theory and with principal-agent problems. This is all cloaked in optimism and romanticism. The architecture of Hirschman," he urged, "needs to be made more precise."

Sanyal returned to one of Marseille's points. "Perhaps his central message—was *not* to have a theory of information because there is so much uncertainty. The lesson he is drawing is that if a plan is based on a theory, sooner or later it will fall apart, and what is needed is an approach by which one can learn from past mistakes."

Rothschild then noted that "one often-discussed virtue of the market is precisely that it consists of people that are in the dark; the individual agent does not have to have a lot of information. [That is] the beauty of the market." "Maybe," Picciotto said, "but not everything can be solved through the market."

"In any case," Schön observed, "the social structure of the market situation is fundamentally different from the social structure of the blindness project. [Whereas] decisionmakers in the blindness program had engaged in some form of intellectual decision process that seemed concerted, deliberate, and rational, in the market situation individual agents are conceived as not [being] concerted."

Even so, Rothschild said, "there is a large and powerful body of economic theory that suggests the market model should also be applied to nonmarket situations such as Marseille's. While this theory would not imply that the unintended consequences are taken into account, it would say, 'There's an optimizing design: that such an optimal outcome could be achieved through these processes.' While no one is intending this outcome, everyone ends up doing what works best." These comments reminded Marseille of the Nepalese project manager, Dr. Ram Prasad Pokhrel, and his intuitive understanding of the way the hiding hand worked and his ability to get nongovernmental organizations (NGOs) to compete with each other for his approval. He was, said Marseille, a "masterful orchestrator of a competitive market of ideas and initiatives that would improve blindness prevention efforts."

The intriguing point here for Picciotto "was that Marseille began with this nonmarket hiding hand and ended up with something that was 'market friendly.' For initiatives at the stage of infancy," Picciotto conjectured, "the hiding hand may be useful to create confusion, to help do things one would not otherwise do, which means that the hiding hand is elusive and does not have a long shelf life. Sustainability requires help from the unseen hand (the market). Proof of this is all the NGO projects that disappear throughout the developing world as development fashions change. Sometimes they will become replicable, at others not."

When asked for an evaluation of the relative importance of Seva's initial planning effort, Marseille conceded that the plan "figured quite heavily in the actual outcomes: although to some extent politics mattered, the initial nationwide comprehensive survey of blindness did provide data that were used to decide where hospitals would be built. The initiative to train ophthalmic assistants to extend the impact of the small number of ophthalmologists was also considered right from the beginning. The plan was more than just a background."

Tendler Discussion: Learning from Pressures

Hirschman's view of the efficacy of unbalanced growth, Tendler observed, was based on an appreciation of the underlying dynamics of an essentially political process. That is to say, a constituent group creates pressure for the state action required to allow development to proceed.

Schön agreed with Tendler that mediocre agencies can become high-performing ones rather quickly "if demand is exerted on them from the outside, if there is a high penalty for not performing, and if [they] can tell measurably and dramatically whether [they] have performed or not, and if there are broadly distributed interests in performance and the exercise of the penalties." The shift occurs under all those circumstances, he said. "But what was the lesson in all this: to find external demand and apply it in some formulaic way?"

On the contrary, Tendler said; she was responding to outstanding problems in a multitude of countries with a set of useful generalizations. She cited "four examples of policies or practices representing changes in the way development planners think ... consistent with, but not attributed to Hirschman: partial privatization, creating competition-like pressures, which are good for service delivery by the public sector; public agencies contracting out services, with a similar rationale that penalties for failure and incentives for doing well improve service delivery, in part because external forces are then impinging on the agency; decentralization, [as in the case of] highway maintenance devolved to localities that depend on good road conditions for commerce because central government agencies are preoccupied with construction (a classic "Hirschmanesque" case of solving a problem by changing the structure of a situation; the key is to put the maintenance where it will be surrounded by pressures to do it from the outside, and keep construction far away because it will consume maintenance funds if you let it be nearby); and rural electrification, where there was already a threshold level of demand."

Tendler maintained that these four practices, now commonplace, could have been "read off of Hirschman thirty years ago," but were not: this led her to reemphasize that Hirschman was far in advance of his time because acceptance of his ideas required a radically different conception of expertise. Citing a study on education reform and Kalyn Culler's work on dissemination of innovation, Tendler noted that where innovations were seen as radically different from current thinking and practice, they were resisted, but this was less the case when the change was perceived as being compatible with, or only marginally different from, the status quo. Recalling Taylor's argument earlier in the seminar that Hirschman's relative acceptance is less a commentary on his work and more a signal of changing paradigms, she said this was consistent with public-sector shifts toward privatization, subcontracting, decentralization, and the general idea that markets work better than the public sector.

Polenske's personal experience, coming from a farm community in the American West and working in rural settings around the world, led her to question Tendler's story, although she could not quite put her finger on the problem. Tendler mused that perhaps Hirschman paid too much attention to forces outside institutions and not enough to continuity within them, a topic she might pursue next in her own research.

Picciotto Discussion: Evaluation and Learning

Picciotto said he found comfort in Hirschman's work because it helped him make sense of what he saw every day. When asked if, in retrospect, he felt the World Bank could do things better at an early stage of resettlement, Picciotto replied that resettlement could indeed be handled successfully if human engineering needs were given as much attention as physical engineering. Both in Thailand and in Maharashtra, India, resettlement was handled quite sensibly. What was needed was grassroots information, and an emphasis, from the start, on compensating people. In the unsuccessful case of Narmada in Madhya Pradesh, he added, "the state administration was retrograde, weak, and reluctant to compensate: it did not want to set a precedent that would later lead squatters and other groups to make similar claims. Now the government of India is paying much more attention to the problems of resettlement." Also, experience with small groups teaches that "it is often much easier to organize the extremes rather than the mainstream that will benefit from the project. The extremes exercise the most clout [whereas] it is difficult to mobilize people or the support of the government and NGOs to *solve* problems rather than to stop projects."

"Can you clarify your definitions of participation and competition?" Polenske asked. "Evaluation in the public sector," Picciotto replied, "parallels auditing in the private sector." Development requires an independent audit of how well things are progressing. "Evaluation is an instrument of loyalty, exit is competition, and voice is participation. Through evaluation one can judge a particular development intervention, that is, locate it properly within this triangle." Development, he added, involves much more than just the private sector or the public sector. One has to look at their interaction. His definition of participation, "admittedly very general, included any transaction between people that led to decisionmaking. In the Narmada case, for example, participation meant talking to people to figure out what their reaction would be to the project, what would get them to resettle, what kind of compensation would have to be paid, and what kind of land they would have to be given."

Rothschild volunteered another example based on the approval process for a public sector project in the United Kingdom. First, detailed plans are drawn, which include an assessment of environmental effects and (more recently) some evaluation of social effects. After all these plans are announced, public inquiries are held, the evidence is presented and discussed (NGO groups participate in that public inquiry process), and a decision is made. If the parties still disagree over the project, an appeal can be made to the secretary of state; there has also been some talk of designing a process that would also allow for participation *after* the construction starts.

The United Kingdom, she noted, "has been a relatively consensual society, without the kind of mismatch seen between the World Bank and the Indian and international NGOs in the Narmada case. In the Narmada project, the costs of leaving their ancestral land were close to infinite [for some individuals in the resettlement group]. Because they happened to be connected to international NGOs they were enormously visible. The 5 million people whose income or well-being could have gone up by 10 percent were invisible; in the English 'model' these issues would have been discussed in some open systematic way through the public inquiry participatory process."

Picciotto hoped the Indian experience would eventually lead the authorities to set up institutions that would allow that kind of a participatory process. The idea, he said, "is to get a workable system that is replicable and affordable, and that provides a decent voice to the voiceless while . . . still ensuring the public good, which is not necessarily the good of only the vocal minority. There cannot simply be participation without hierarchy. The hierarchy itself has to be subject to some other process of control; that is where evaluation comes in: by providing objective evidence to bear on these decisions without having any ax to grind, one may be able to inform the debate, provided it is effectively disseminated."

Sanyal wondered if there was a connection between the two variables—visibility and participation—and whether the hiding hand was likely to produce a better result. Assuming "an appropriate level of participation and excellent evaluation," Picciotto thought a hiding hand was not needed. Others questioned how often those ideal conditions would exist.

When asked to explain his taste for hierarchy, Picciotto said the real job was to construct an institutional setup that would allow the creation of the public good (such as good civil works that benefit many people) to proceed, through the design of the legislation and mechanisms of enforcement, including public hearings, evaluative techniques, and arbitration. "The engineering of this contractual infrastructure is the true job of development," he added, "and that is why Hirschman has become so important. People no longer believe capital investment alone will spur growth. [It is also essential] to create attitudes, rules, and regulations, that is, institutions, and a policy assessment capability—evaluation—which has to be independent, credible, and perceived to be so by all the parties involved. That is all the more reason why evaluation itself has to be participative."

Sanyal suggested Picciotto in effect claims that if the poor—those displaced—are able to participate, then it is likely that the project will be successful. He wondered why the stopping of the Narmada project by NGOs was not considered participation. "What did the term 'participation' mean without this political context?"

"Not all participation is productive," Picciotto replied. "There is an optimal level of participation. Excessive participation leads to excessive transactions costs and few results. You need hierarchy, too. You can't debate forever."

Sanyal argued that one of the goals of participation is not to have a protest: the reason the World Bank is interested in participation, he conjectured, is that "delays in the execution of the project could end up being very costly. In negotiation theory [one would not] even ask someone to negotiate unless they were protesting! In other words, political protest seems to be a *prerequisite* for negotiation, even though we want to believe that by introducing negotiation the need for protest can be eliminated. Why would we ever negotiate with someone unless they are troublemakers?" Sanyal also observed that people cannot protest without information. For both reasons he thought it was difficult to preempt protest.

In South Africa, Judith Tendler observed, it is difficult to determine whom to negotiate with. Each of 110 large urban squatter upgrading and sites and services projects she is looking at there is negotiated with the community or the civic association. "In many cases three, four, or even five groups claim they represent the community. The community almost needs to hold an election before the contractor or the developer can do anything."

In Brazil, she added, peasants organized sit-ins in the offices of the agricultural research stations demanding that the research agendas be tailored to their needs. She reported similar success stories in big squatter upgrading projects. In one instance, "the World Bank and the city administration each had its own ideas of where the projects needed to be done and which squatter settlements would go first. However, [it was] the most vocal community groups that determined whose neighborhoods would be done first."

Tendler felt uneasy, however, about all the attention the seminar had given to the institutional processes of participation in the World Bank. In her view, participation was something that needed to be a little more distant. She agreed with Sanyal's earlier remarks concerning the importance of information and the irrelevance of protest if interested parties do not even know what is going to happen. The key was to let the information out. She had heard NGOs make the same recommendation for years. "If the information is let out, that in itself will elicit tremendous positive pressure on the government. This strategy had actually been followed in the past in getting people on board who otherwise would never have gotten involved. In Latin America, [for example,] priests distributed the news to their parishioners through printed leaflets; people then began to come forward saying that the way it was being done was not the right way. This spontaneous process was at least as important, if not more important, than a formal process of participation."

David Barkin, reflecting on his experience in Latin America, said, "A lot of lip service was being given in Mexico to many of the principles Picciotto talked about, but it was more theater than anything else. Decisions continued to be made by a hierarchy: people were being compensated at market prices, but soon after they became permanently impoverished in a situation of political and economic inequality and inflation." Barkin added that what he heard from Picciotto about resettlement was similar to what many Mexicans thought about the "lonely voices" of Scott Guggenheim or Herman Daly at the World Bank. "My voice is not a lonely one in the organization," Picciotto replied. "The World Bank's policy is quite clear in the case of resettlement: no one should be made worse off in terms of income." However, he conceded, "frequently this policy is not implemented because of a 'principal-agent' problem; that is, the Bank's policies are ignored by the agents that implemented the projects." But he expects the problem will be solved sometime in the future, as participatory techniques become embedded in project design and implementation.

Barkin suggested the problem was actually much more complex, because compensation was being calculated in terms of money income rather than in real income or a standard of living. Economists doing field research often discovered substantial imputed income that accountants had not taken into account. Although there were ways of dealing with this problem, Barkin insisted that implementation is extraordinarily difficult, and the spectacular examples of the application of these methodologies are trivial in comparison with the vast amounts of money that the World Bank and other similar institutions spend.

Picciotto agreed. Barkin then noted the differences of perception between the junior and senior staffers at the Bank. In a recent meeting he had been struck by the views of the younger staff, who were quite convinced that structural adjustment policies were good and that in the long run everyone would benefit from them. "They believed Mexican peasants were inefficient and had to be knocked off the land, that there was no way that maize could be produced effectively by the vast majority of them. Although there were some senior staffers at the World Bank who did contemplate leaving some of the Mexican peasants on the land, the younger people—the operational staff who were actually directing the cadastre, the mapping operations, the credit implementation operations, the allocation of hardware and software— were convinced that peasants were the main obstacles to modernization in rural Mexico; and the conversation between junior and senior Bank staff was like a dialogue between deaf people."

Sabel Discussion: Learning by Monitoring

Sabel focused first on the tension between learning (creating new knowledge and thus change in the current situation) and monitoring (the countervailing need to have instruments to check whether partners are performing as promised) in development, or in fact in innovation at any level. He also examined the role of Japanese industry as the world's leading example of how to introduce *disequilibrium* into the production process and how to align interests and assign responsibilities so people learn from them.

Rodwin wondered whether Sabel's description of Japan was "idealized," since he did not consider what happens to units that fail on the basis of these shared agreements or in the current retrenchment of large Japanese companies. Sabel argued that in Japan people are assured a place in the production community if they meet a minimal standard, and that the subcontractors, once part of a "dual society" within Japan, are improving their position as well. Although there are "deep problems" in Japan, he thought this system in its heyday provides answers to a very obvious question about unbalanced growth and about the more general question, "When do you get learning and monitoring?"

But Tendler felt Japan was not so much an example of unbalanced growth as a pacing device, as defined by Hirschman in *Strategy*. For Hirschman, she observed, "the idea of unbalanced growth is permissive. For instance, overbuilding electrical power capacity might trigger a creative response and not just excess capacity—and pacing devices have to do with increasing penalties. The classic example is airplane maintenance, where the costs of poor maintenance are high, in contrast to the ongoing care of highways, which deteriorate more incrementally and less tragically." She suggested that another class of pacing devices could be inherent in the structure of groups, or the structure of the technology involved or of the social order; in addition, there may be another class of situations in which the state is not in dialogue with a single other party but a more complex discussion the state itself may have elicited may take place with a third party. She also asked how Sabel would incorporate recent work on cooperation by Elinor Ostrom, and how he would explain historically successive periods of success and failure, such as Brazil in the 1960s.

Ostrom's work, Sabel replied, shows that there is not a single list of conditions for cooperation, because there are always crucial local conditions. As for the distinction between pacing mechanisms and unbalanced growth, he agreed it "sounds right exigetically," but he also referred back to Schön's argument that Hirschman had no explicit theory of social learning. In addition, he challenged the familiar Hirschman truism cited by Tendler about airplanes, saying that the current statistics on aviation hazards in the former Soviet Union showed "there is nothing automatic about airline maintenance." He promised to explore the questions raised about third parties, using the case of "management invoking workers to monitor middle management" as an example of the topic's potential fruitfulness.

Sanyal considered Sabel's interpretation of the Japan case "very un-Hirschman-like" because it set prerequisites for the system to function, very much in the tradition of balanced-growth theories; and "while it is fashionable to take economic categories into political science to explain political phenomena, there were other questions about nonproduction activities of the state that cannot be addressed in economic terms, such as deal making, distribution, and enfranchisement of excluded constituencies." Sabel, however, saw no problem in not being "Hirschmanesque." Also, he "had outlined a model for 'bootstrapping institutions' rather than institutional prerequisites for growth. It is now fashionable to apply economic categories to political phenomena," he emphasized, "but it is *not* fashionable to take economic categories and say that they do not work: for the real problem is that there is a political activity, namely, permanent conversation about equity and goal setting, and *that* is what is really going on. The contracts are not really about exchange: they are about establishing this eminently political relation." His paper, he added, "was not about economics invading political science, but about politics sort of running wild over all of economics."

But since the goal setting Sabel laid out is about production, Sanyal felt the objective is production as opposed to distribution, and thus is basically an exercise in economics. "Not so!" Sabel replied. "In contrast to the common view that the most successful economic organization of all time is about economics, it is really . . . a kind of continuous mushy discussion about what it would be good to make and how it would be good to divide it." These distributional issues, he suggested, "shed light on how systems break down and consensus dissolves because of the exclusion of interests."

Schön suggested that the "recursivity of these contracts makes them 'meta-contracts': the parties agree that they are going to keep setting mutual objectives of their transactions within a certain framework and that they are going to keep resetting the strategy by which they are going to reach those objectives, and they are going to keep monitoring how well each of them is doing." *Learning* in these cases applies to both levels, because in monitoring, each party *learns* about the other. In short, "conflict between monitoring and learning that used to arise endemically is structurally resolved by this kind of contract."

Sabel agreed. "The distinction between learning and monitoring in effect disappears, because both sides are using the same information in the same way. . . . The incentives go the right way to make it work because the parties engage in a weird form of joint ownership, which is not a partnership where you can get out your stake, but rather a commitment between the parties to do joint problem solving in perpetuity." Instead of "meta-contract," Sabel preferred the analogy of political constitutions: here "the binding agreement is to build dispute-resolution systems at whatever level is required to take into account the changing mutually determined interests of the constituents, by constitutional amendment if necessary."

Appendix B

Hirschman: Responses and Discussion

PROFESSOR HIRSCHMAN WAS SENT NOT ONLY THE PAPERS of the seminar and the summaries of the discussions, but even the seminar tapes, so the seminar may have played, Lloyd Rodwin confessed, the role of Robert Burns's "giftie" in showing Professor Hirschman a little bit how others see him.

Hirschman told the group he had indeed gone over the materials from all these sources, and he noticed new aspects about his own writings, and even began to make notes about his "cognitive style," which he later downgraded to "broodings."

Hirschman described his cognitive style as the habit of presenting a strong thesis at the outset and then qualifying it, by bringing in complications, which become "more interesting" than the original theoretical assertion. He also mentioned in passing that while he has been encouraged to compose his memoirs, he has refused to do so as long as he still has an idea in his mind, but he expressed his appreciation of an earlier Rodwin quotation from Jorgé Luis Borges and remarked, "with a nod to Borges," that writing essays and books is "an alternative and more interesting way of writing one's autobiography."[1]

Hirschman then made a series of comments "on the nature of change, planned and unplannable." Although he had been long engaged in analyzing "underdevelopment," it became clear over time that many of his observations applied equally to societies in the so-called developed world. When change turned out pretty well, he said, it was often "a one-time unrepeatable feat of social engineering," an outcome that only gives confidence that a similar or similarly unique constellation of circumstances can occur again; but trying to repeat the sequence of events formulaically in another context, he felt, "won't work."

Hirschman also observed he had not been the kind of adviser the World Bank wanted him to be, and eventually lost interest in advice giving because he did not want to boil down his advice to "epigrammatic one-liners," such as "get prices right." To illustrate the uselessly broad homily he sought to avoid, he read a sentence that came from an old World Bank hand: "Successful development depends on getting most policies reasonably right and none of them hopelessly wrong." Rather, his "bias for hope" led him to different recommendations: "Be ready to seize special opportunities as they arise and *learn* to recognize the *gestalt* of when there is such an opportunity." This is hardly the kind of advice for which there is ready demand, he observed.

Donald Schön mentioned Hirschman's earlier "paradoxical" comment about a particular situation being, in the eyes of a Hirschmanian planner, similar to another circumstance in its uniqueness. Returning to an ongoing debate within the group about whether economic development could be considered a science, Schön said that Hirschman's comment seemed in a gracious way to dismiss that possibility and to confirm Lance Taylor's "lore" thesis; also that the relationship between generalization and advice in Hirschman's construction was "not obvious," although it seemed to suggest that while generalizations could be derived from experience, prescriptive advice could not.

Hirschman responded that he would be more reluctant than most advisers to rely on a standard "toolkit," and less than comfortable with the "minimalist" position suggested by the old World Bank hand, a stance that offers no more specific advice than "don't be corrupt, and don't be stupid."

Martin Rein interjected with the first obligation in the Hippocratic oath: "Do no harm." Lisa Peattie suggested there is more than one kind of generalization: not only the case where "*A* follows *B*, as the night the day," but also the more inductive approach of detecting a pattern, or a recurrent factor, "and if you look for it, you might see it." But in order to deal with pattern recognition, Rein replied, one needs to say what it is a case of.

This discussion, Hirschman said, reminded him of Judith Tendler's comments on his advice to Nigerians, in an environment of ethnic strife, on the choice between building highways or railways: although he recommended highways, because they could be built in a highly decentralized system, he "could also imagine a country with ethnic problems but also with the possibility of cooperation, and it would be very good to have a railway precisely because it would be an opportunity for a certain amount of learning. This kind of judgment is what makes a decision fundamentally unique to each case."

Taylor jested that while Hirschman "disparaged" development advisers for one-liners, he had become adept at "one-worders," such as "linkage," "exit," and "voice." Peattie felt these one-worders were "a name for a pattern," and thus were quite different from the imperatives contained in the one-liners. Taylor then suggested that "a taxonomy of one-worders" might be useful. Noting, also, the dialectical way Hirschman's ideas proceed, he asked whether that might be a useful way to think about pattern generation and recognition.

As a footnote, Lloyd Rodwin—citing Hirschman's effort to resolve polarities as well as his obvious familiarity with both socialist and Hegelian thinking—asked how much influence each of those literatures had had on him. Hirschman said that during his education in Berlin, he had been part of a group of high school students who met once or twice a month with a mentor six or eight years older than themselves, and that this constituted "one of his first philosophical experiences"—an influence, he added, that he was still trying "to get rid of." Here he read from the galleys of his article "Exit, Voice, and the Fate of the German Democratic Republic: An Essay in Conceptual History" (published in *World Politics* in January 1993). He noted that "the German language has a peculiar gift for compact terms such as *umschlagen* and the famous Hegelian *aufheben*, which endow such turnabouts with seeming reality. I deliberately avoided these terms, as they evoke the famous dialectic, the negation of the negation, and similar mysterious, if preordained, processes that dissolve all contradictions and reconcile all opposites." He added that while he does not "believe" in the Hegelian system as he once might have, it is helpful for "opening up" arguments (although he also regards "its appearance as a warning signal: Watch out, it's that Hegelianism that's preying on you, somehow").

But, Taylor countered, "the dialectic does not explain the neat categories you found." Hirschman agreed, adding that "the desire for neatness in categories is not just a Hegelian impulse but a desire for shaping things. . . . I don't feel I have anything to write about unless I have achieved a certain amount of neatness." "When people write something contradictory," he observed, "they generally do not flag it, which is why we are still busy trying to sort out the great thinkers." When someone "thinks and puts down a line of thinking, that is the best person in the world to see the opposing argument, for all the time the person is being hit by ideas tending to negate what he or she is just now thinking and has to deal with it." Nietzsche, he said, "is one of the few 'self-overcoming' thinkers, openly and in front of the public. There should be more."

Michael Piore observed that Hirschman made two implicit arguments about his relationship to theory: on the one hand, Hirschman had expressed surprise that people think he is not interested in theory, because he has had strong theoretical ideas in which he takes pride, while on the other hand, an important part of Hirschman's career has clearly been spent being critical of theory, "even his own." Piore said "this represents a paradoxical or (in a good sense) perhaps schizophrenic stance toward abstract ideas"; he asked Hirschman to respond to Peattie's position that Hirschman might be presenting "a different kind of theory, meant to be used in a different way," and that his critique "implied a different notion of theory itself."

Both could be true, Rodwin suggested. Piore replied that there could be still a third interpretation. Hirschman, however, wanted the question made more concrete.

Peattie offered her own work on social movements as an example: she has found it difficult to deal with them in "an ordinary theoretical way," and her daughter suggested that she needed "to borrow from chaos theory," which is premised on nonrecurrent patterns rather than predictable or inevitable sequences. Similarly, she said, social research and advice giving are realms in which nonrecurrent patterns rather than deterministic sequences are appropriate, requiring different styles of thought from more traditional attempts to apply generalizations. Hirschman demurred, saying he was "not the chaos type," and adding that his approach was in part an attempt to be "modest" about ideas and about the extent to which his advice is correct.

Rodwin drew a distinction between a "limited hypothesis" (or pattern recognition) and "systematic theorizing" (or connecting different ideas and making more powerful predictions on the basis of more systematic analysis). Peattie pressed Rodwin on the "loaded" terms in his statement, asking what he meant by "more powerful generalizations."

Rodwin said that one of the ideals of science is to connect different kinds of hypotheses and ideas into a system, a process of cumulative support for a particular observation or hypothesis being tested, extending the range of what one can say.

Robert Einsweiler addressed a different problem in pattern recognition, saying that "language—that is, linear speech—can capture only a static image of an ongoing process and not a dynamic situation with complex sets of relationships changing with time. Patterns may be recognized but remain hard to describe"; and perhaps Hirschman "may have been exploring the *gestalt* of a given situation piece by piece, but then—with inadequate tools to describe it in its entirety and in its dynamism—may have pulled back from theorizing about it." Hirschman responded that he did not see himself "as pulling back but sometimes as challenging my earlier ideas as a result of later perceiving different possibilities: a widening of horizon sometimes to be celebrated (a view spelled out in more detail in my forthcoming book, *A Propensity to Self-Subversion*)."

Hirschman then ventured some reactions to the papers presented during the seminar. He concurred, he said, with Schön's observation that he had stopped short of a full-fledged theory of learning. Using an example from *Development Projects Observed*, Hirschman said that he had seen people in one country queuing up for the bus—a habit formed under a previous occasion of martial law—but not for other forms of transportation. In reading Tendler's paper, he thought of a way to describe this phenomenon: "learning happens when some behavior adopted under duress becomes second nature, or takes on 'a life of its own,' no longer connected to the original impetus." But Tendler wondered why he would not call that "habit" instead of "learning."

Hirschman also qualified his advice on technology, saying that he had hoped, for example, that maintenance of airplanes would extend to maintenance of roads, through a process of diffusion; but he pointed to *fracasomania* (that is, "failure complex," the tendency to interpret policy experiences as a string of failures in situations where Hirschman saw evidence of success) as an instance of denying learning that may have occurred.

Schön reiterated his observation that Hirschman's epistemological position in *Strategy* and other writings "disconfirms" other economic theories. In arguing that development occurs in the course of one-of-a-kind opportunities detected, made sense of, and capitalized on,

Hirschman represented himself as an "economist who learned to distrust economics and trust his own intuitions." Hirschman responded that he had done some reading in learning theory, but did not see "unity" emerging "out of the fragments."

Tendler maintained that in the previous example of the bus queue, Hirschman really had not paid attention to anything resembling a learning process: what is in between the force and the habit is learning, she argued. To Taylor, "it sounded Pavlovian": "Don's interested in learning and you're not."

Hirschman linked his resistance to this kind of thinking as part of his "attempt to defeat prerequisites," preferring to leave it to the mystery of "the cart before the horse."

As for Charles Sabel's paper, Hirschman said that he was all the more interested in it in part because it offered a variant response to the question he himself has often been asked, "'Would you propose unbalanced growth?' Here the Japanese initiate and induce it," he added.

Nor was he "just shadowboxing," as Krugman implied in his paper, "in setting himself against Myrdal, Rosenstein-Rodan, and Rostow"; also, he had operated with the concept of increasing returns to scale (a concept that was tacit knowledge) and that minimum firm size was an important trigger in the linkage model. He then called attention to an important postscript to *Strategy* ten years later, that is, in a 1968 article, "The Political Economy of Import Substitution in Latin America" (reprinted in *A Bias for Hope*), in which he gave an important role in the linkage process to exports. (For further discussion of this point, see Hirschman's new preface in the 1995 edition of *Development Projects Observed*.)

Taylor had noted that he was on the side of state intervention just when social and economic opinion veered in the direction of the free market, but actually Hirschman felt he "really was between the two ends of Taylor's 'eternal pendulum,' and thus remained antithetical to both schools." Hirschman added that while in some cases market and nonmarket forces work together, he had also argued in *Strategy* that "cases of market failure did not ipso facto imply that the task has to be handled by a public authority; there is also the possibility of government failure as well as market failure. There are some tasks that exceed the capacity of society, and these are not necessarily better left to the public rather than the private sector."

To Emma Rothschild, Hirschman admitted he had been "exasperated" with Adam Smith, because in researching the literature of the seventeenth and eighteenth centuries, "I found the 'passions and the interests' everywhere used as opposites, while Smith suddenly treats them as synonyms." In addition, he objected to the facile way Smith separated politics from economics in saying that prosperity rested solely on "peace, easy taxes, and the fair administration of justice," joining "the prerequisite school" in the process.

He agreed, too, with Peattie that the exit-voice dichotomy has something in common with other social dichotomies, including the *gemeinschaft-gesellschaft* split, but he felt that his categories are not so mutually exclusive. Peattie asked whether the *gemeinschaft-gesellschaft* pair had been in his mind when he proposed exit-voice; Hirschman said that he was "so untutored" that he was not aware of his overlap with these prior categories until after he had formulated his own, for which he credited "some kind of Providence at work." But on the question of rationality, he maintained that boycotts, as he had written in *Exit, Voice, and Loyalty,* "are associated with loyalty because they are based on the proposition 'I promise to reenter when certain conditions are met.' In addition, while in normal cost-benefit accounting voice implies costs in time and money, economic 'rationality' can be bestowed on voice when voice-participation is instead counted as a benefit, as becomes plausible when voice is regarded as an investment in oneself." However, he warned "against the idea of considering investing in identity as the highest rationality."

Hirschman credited Bishwapriya Sanyal with "a very fine description" of his "bias for hope." Sanyal, he said, "understood very well that the hopefulness I advocate is not the royal road to progress but a tortuous path to be discovered, and once trod is not necessarily traveled again." But he took exception to Sanyal's linkage of the connections between his work and his itinerant life-history. It was "too simple," particularly the conclusions Sanyal had drawn on the implications of his entry to the United States. On Sanyal's argument that he is antitheoretical, he reminded the group that he has "come up with quite a few theories of his own"; but he agreed that he tends "to have some doubt" about theories built on "stark dichotomies"; in addition, he tends to emphasize the particular inability of many analysts to perceive change already going on, mentioning in passing that one of his own favorite essays was "Obstacles to the Perception of Change," included in *A Bias for Hope*, where his theory of *fracasomania* had been first articulated.

Hirschman also made "another autobiographical declaration": that he had often thought that his work in Colombia and Latin America was an important period of his own development. He recounted how he had become an American "patriot" as a result of World War II and his work on the Marshall Plan, and how in Latin America he began to be more critical, seeing the Alliance for Progress as "too naïve and simpleminded." These views were reinforced by "the events of the 1960s," when he saw other friends (Alexander Gerschenkron in particular) turn conservative; he had often said he was "grateful" to Latin America for having kept up or rekindling the "ardors" of his youth.

Finally, on the question of the difficulties of "ordinary experts" applying his notions, Hirschman said it was even more complex than what Judith Tendler gave him credit for, even more difficult than she is saying. He entered the plea that "at times I was more interested in portraying and celebrating the grandeur of the development enterprise than in giving practical advice. Someone, I thought, had to see this whole extraordinary process as an epic adventure rather than as a commercial transaction. And at the end of my three books on development—*Strategy, Journeys,* and *Development Projects*—I feel that was what I've been after."

Notes

Chapter 1

In citing the views of the contributors to this volume, I drew from their respective chapters and from the Hirschman seminar tapes and minutes (HSM). HSM is based on résumés of the Hirschman seminar presentations, discussions, and tapes prepared by Jean Riesman and Lloyd Rodwin. Appendixes A and B in this volume provide abbreviated, amended, and reorganized versions of these minutes and discussions prepared by Lloyd Rodwin. The tapes and minutes are in the Rotch Library at MIT.

1. Albert O. Hirschman, *Development Projects Observed* (Brookings, 1967).

2. Lance Taylor, *Varieties of Stabilization Experience: Towards Sensible Macroeconomics in the Third World* (Oxford University Press, 1988).

3. Paul Krugman, HSM, September 23, 1992, p. 2.

4. Remark in Donald Schön, HSM, September 17, 1992, p. 1.

5. Hirschman responded to Krugman in a letter dated March 15, 1993. He drew attention to the more formal views he explicitly developed in "The Political Economy of Import-Substituting Industrialization in Latin America," *Quarterly Journal of Economics*, vol. 82 (February 1968), pp. 2–32. In particular, he pointed out the role of scale economies and market size, as well as the ways he modeled the backward linkage process. His position then, and his way of arguing, he added, reflect "as much or more [his argument with] his Latin American 'structuralist' friends (then politically very influential) who were down on ISI [import substituting investment] on exhaustion, income-distribution, etc., grounds and who were not at all given to 'modeling' than with the neo-classicals who were down on ISI on comparative advantage grounds." Hirschman also expressed doubt about whether the eclipse of "high development theory" was due to the lack of formalization rather than the views he spelled out in his "Rise and Decline" article of 1981: that is, the failure to mount an effective reply to the devastating attacks both by the neoclassical right (concerning the misallocation of resources) and by the neo-Marxist left (concerning inequity and exploitation) plus the savage political setbacks experienced during this period. For an interesting sequel to Hirschman's "Rise and Decline" article ("The Rise and Decline of Development Economics," in Albert O. Hirschman, *Essays in Trespassing, Economics to Politics and Beyond* [Cambridge University Press, 1981], chap. 1), see Amartya Sen, "Development: Which Way Now," *Economic Journal*, vol. 93 (December 1983), pp. 745–62.

6. In a striking note of support for Taylor's thesis, David Warsh quotes Robert Samuelson's advice to the Nobel Prize Committee: in view of the sad state of mainstream economic theory, Samuelson (an economics columnist—not Paul Samuelson the economist) suggests that "the committee should give their economic prizes to economic practitioners and activists, or should stop giving them out altogether!" See *Boston Globe*, December 26, 1992, p. 81.

7. The quotations in this section are from Michael Piore's presentation reported in HSM, October 28, 1992.

8. Albert O. Hirschman, *The Strategy of Economic Development* (Yale University Press, 1958), p. 25.

9. Albert O. Hirschman, *Journeys toward Progress: Studies of Economic Policy-Making in Latin America* (New York: Twentieth Century Fund, 1963).

10. Hirschman's quotations in this sections are from *Rival Views of Market Society and Other Recent Essays* (Harvard University Press, 1992), pp. 142, 158–59, 172.

11. Emma Rothschild, HSM, October 28, 1992, p. 4.

12. HSM, October 14, 1992. Subsequent quotations in this section are either from chapter 6 or this résumé of her oral presentation.

13. T. S. Eliot, "London Letter," *The Dial*, vol. 73 (1992), p. 331.

14. HSM, October 21, 1992. Subsequent quotations in this section are either from chapter 7 or this résumé of his oral presentation.

15. This quotation and those cited subsequently are from HSM, November 19, 1993, p. 1, as well as chapter 8.

16. See also Albert O. Hirschman, "Economic Development Research and Development and Policy Making: Some Converging Views," in Hirschman, *A Bias for Hope* (Yale University Press, 1971), chap. 2.

17. This quotation and those cited subsequently are from chapter 9.

18. This citation is from chapter 10. Subsequent citations are from HSM, November 19, 1993, or chapter 10, unless otherwise indicated.

19. Hirschman, *Development Projects Observed*, p. 5.

20. Ibid., pp. 5–7.

21. Ibid., p. 8.

22. This and the other quotations that follow are from HSM, November 18, 1992, or from chapter 11.

Chapter 2

1. Paul Krugman, "Towards a Counter-Counterrevolution in Development Theory," *Proceedings of the World Bank Annual Conference on Development Economics* (1992), pp. 15–38.

2. Paul N. Rosenstein-Rodan, "Problems of Industrialization of Eastern and South-Eastern Europe," *Economic Journal*, vol. 53 (June–September 1943), pp. 202–11; and Albert O. Hirschman, *The Strategy of Economic Development* (Yale University Press, 1958).

3. Gunnar Myrdal, *Economic Theory and Under-developed Regions* (London: G. Duckworth, 1957).

4. Rosenstein-Rodan, "Problems of Industrialization," p. 205.

5. See W. Arthur Lewis, "Economic Development with Unlimited Supplies of Labor," *Manchester School* (1954), pp. 139–91; and J. Marcus Fleming, "External Economies and the Doctrine of Balanced Growth," *Economic Journal*, vol. 65 (June 1955), pp. 241–56.

6. Ragnar Nurkse, *Problems of Capital Formation in Underdeveloped Countries* (Oxford University Press, 1953).

7. One advocate of U.S. industrial policy suggested that we target industries that either "provide inputs to or use inputs from a large number of other industries." I have often wondered what industry does *not* meet this criterion—hand-thrown pottery?

8. Allyn Young, "Increasing Returns and Economic Progress," *Economic Journal*, vol. 38 (December 1928); and Nurkse, *Problems of Capital Formation*.

9. See Edward N. Lorenz, *The Essence of Chaos* (University of Washington Press, 1993), pp. 86–94.

10. See Krugman, "Towards a Counter-Counterrevolution." This treatment is a streamlined version of the exposition in Kevin M. Murphy, Andrei Shleifer, and Robert W. Vishny, "Industrialization and the Big Push," *Journal of Political Economy*, vol. 97 (October 1989), pp. 1003–26.

11. Actually four, if one counts the case where equation 2-2 is not satisfied, so that the economy actually produces less using modern techniques. In this case, it clearly stays with the traditional methods.

Chapter 3

Comments by Albert Hirschman and Lloyd Rodwin on previous versions are gratefully acknowledged.

1. Albert O. Hirschman, *The Strategy of Economic Development* (Yale University Press, 1958).

2. Hollis Chenery and T. N. Srinivasan, eds., *Handbook of Development Economics*, 2 vols. (Amsterdam: North-Holland, 1988).

3. Alexander Vorobyov, "Production Aspects of the Russian Transition" (Helsinki: World Institute for Development Economics Research, 1993).

4. Howard Pack, "Industrialization and Trade," in Chenery and Srinivasan, eds., *Handbook of Development Economics*, vol. 1, pp. 333–73.

5. See, for example, Helen Shapiro, "Automobiles: Trade and Investment Flows in Brazil and Mexico" (Harvard Business School, 1992).

6. Lance Taylor, *Income Distribution, Inflation, and Growth* (MIT Press, 1991).

7. Albert O. Hirschman, "The Political Economy of Latin American Development: Seven Exercises in Retrospection," *Latin American Research Review*, vol. 22 (Fall 1987), pp. 7–36.

8. Josef A. Schumpeter, *The Theory of Economic Development* (Harvard University Press, 1934); Ragnar Nurkse, *Problems of Capital Formation in Underdeveloped Countries* (Oxford University Press, 1953); Paul N. Rosenstein-Rodan, "Problems of Industrialization of Eastern and South-Eastern Europe," *Economic Journal*, vol. 53 (June–September 1943), pp. 202–11.

9. Albert O. Hirschman, "The Political Economy of Import-Substituting Industrialization in Latin America," *Quarterly Journal of Economics*, vol. 82 (February 1968), pp. 1–32.

10. Hirschman, *Strategy of Economic Development*, pp. 65, 165–66.

11. Theodore W. Schultz, *Transforming Traditional Agriculture* (Yale University Press, 1964); Ian M. D. Little, Tibor Scitovsky, and Maurice Scott, *Industry and Trade in Some Developing Countries: A Comparative Study* (Oxford University Press, 1970); Ronald I. McKinnon, *Money and Capital in Economic Development* (Brookings, 1973); and Edward S. Shaw, *Financial Deepening in Economic Development* (Oxford University Press, 1973).

12. World Bank, *World Development Report 1991* (Oxford University Press, 1991).

13. Hollis Chenery, "The Interdependence of Investment Decisions," in Moses Abramovitz and others, *The Allocation of Economic Resources: Essays in Honor of Bernard Francis Haley* (Stanford University Press, 1959), pp. 82–120.

14. Hirschman, *Strategy of Economic Development*, p. 115.

15. Ibid., p. 108.

16. World Bank, *World Development Report 1991*, pp. 1, 157.

17. Robert Wade, "East Asia's Economic Success: Conflicting Perspectives, Partial Insights, Shaky Evidence," *World Politics*, vol. 44 (January 1992), pp. 270–320.

18. Josef A. Schumpeter, *History of Economic Analysis* (Oxford University Press, 1954).

Chapter 4

1. *The Strategy of Economic Development* (Yale University Press, 1958).

2. This is an early appearance of the principle of the hiding hand. Hirschman's reference here is to Herbert Simon's "Berlitz model" of learning, in which Simon supposes, as Hirschman explains on p. 48 of *Strategy*, "that an individual who desires to learn French starts out with a given level of difficulty or ignorance. The more he practices, the more he will reduce the difficulty, but for each level of difficulty there is one rate of practice (hours per day) beyond which practicing is unpleasant so that if this level is reached or exceeded, practice will be reduced the next day."

3. Donald A. Schön, "Generative Metaphor: A Perspective on Problem-Setting in Social Policy," in Andrew Ortony, ed., *Metaphor and Thought* (Cambridge University Press, 1978), pp. 137–63.

4. Michael McPherson, "The Social Scientist as Constructive Skeptic: On

Hirschman's Role," in Alejandro Foxley, Michael McPherson, and Guillermo O'Donnell, eds., *Development, Democracy, and the Art of Trespassing: Essays in Honor of Albert O. Hirschman* (University of Notre Dame Press, 1986), pp. 305–15.

5. It is true that at this very point Hirschman also introduces somewhat different language. He speaks of specific shortages as manifestations of a "basic deficiency in organization" and describes obstacles to development as "reflections of contradictory drives and of the resulting confusion of the will" (p. 25) As we shall see, however, both of these phrases are consistent with his view of learning.

6. By "backward linkage" he means the tendency of every nonprimary economic activity to induce attempts to supply through domestic production the inputs needed in that activity; by "forward linkage," the tendency of every activity that does not by its nature cater exclusively to final demands, to induce attempts to utilize its outputs as inputs in some new activities (p. 100).

7. Cf. Plato's dialogue, *Protagorus and Meno,* trans. W. K. C. Guthrie (London: Penguin Books, 1956), p. 128. Here, Plato shows how Socrates infuriates Meno by exploding his claim to know how virtue is acquired. Meno then exclaims: "But how will you look for something when you don't in the least know what it is? How on earth are you going to set up something you don't know as the object of your search? To put it another way, even if you come right up against it, how will you know that what you have found is the thing you didn't know?"

8. *Exit, Voice, and Loyalty: Responses to Decline in Firms, Organizations, and States* (Harvard University Press, 1970).

9. These three learning factors singled out by Hirschman are central to two other initiatives aimed at promoting organizational learning: the so-called cogwheel experiment developed in the 1950s by the psychologist, John Kennedy, at the Systems Development Corporation in order to train teams of operators for the SAGE air defense system; and the more recently celebrated Total Quality Management Program based largely on the work of Edward Deming. In both instances, task situations stimulate continual improvement in performance by clear and measurable objectives, iterative experimentation, and rapid, public feedback of results.

10. Hirschman draws here on Kenneth Boulding's book, *The Image* (University of Michigan Press, 1956).

11. This last option raises Meno's paradox: since the action is initially strange to the learner, how will she tell that she has done what she set out to do? The possible answers depend on attributing to the learner some initial capacity for *recognizing* what she does not yet know how to *produce.* She may recognize a "mismatch" between the actual and the desired performance (as a novice golfer can recognize a bad swing, though not yet know how to make a good one), or recognize the *end* she wants though not yet know the means of producing it.

12. Gregory Bateson, *Steps to an Ecology of Mind* (Ballantine Books, 1972).

13. He suggests, for example, that reformers have a learning edge over rev-

olutionaries because they *take action* and thereby learn from their mistakes, whereas revolutionaries tend to believe that "the needed changes cannot be effected without a *prior* overthrow of the 'system'" (p. 271).

14. Hirschman also points out, characteristically, that although such crises have a natural tendency to stimulate governmental response, they may induce a level of anxiety that actually inhibits learning. Interestingly, he supports this point with a reference to the literature of learning theory (p. 261).

15. Restated in Jan Elster's theory of "byproducts," which is expounded in his *Ulysses and the Sirens: Studies in Rationality and Irrationality* (Cambridge University Press, 1984), this paradoxical formulation would be: "The creative act that rescues a precarious venture comes always as a byproduct of misjudgment."

16. See Albert Hirschman and Charles E. Lindblom, "Economic Development and R&D and Policy Making: Some Convergent Views," *Behavioral Science,* vol. 7, no. 4 (1962), pp. 211–22.

17. In his appearance at the MIT colloquium on his work in the fall of 1992, Hirschman suggested that his skepticism about the persistence of learning in development may have accounted for his failure to pursue the idea of learning more extensively. He even suggested a definition of "learning" as "the acquisition, under duress, of behavior that then takes on a life of its own."

18. The same can surely *not* be said of the acquisition, through tasks of narrow latitude, of such other patterns of behavior as "rigorous preventive maintenance."

19. Albert O. Hirschman, "A Dissenter's Confession: The Strategy of Economic Development Revisited," in Gerald M. Meier and Dudley Seers, *Pioneers in Development* (Oxford University Press, 1984), p. 91.

20. Among these results, he mentions the oscillation between group- and ego-focused images of change, which he uses to explain the phenomenon of strong-man regimes that begin "with a genuine desire to distribute more equally the fruits of economic progress among all the people, but often end up pitifully in a frantic and unabashed drive for self-enrichment on the part of the dictator and his clique" (*Strategy,* p. 24). His understanding of this phenomenon makes a useful contrast with currently popular "kleptocracy" theory.

21. In the former category see, for example, Peter Senge, *The Fifth Discipline* (Doubleday, 1990); in the latter see, for example, the review article by George P. Huber, "Organizational Learning: An Examination of the Contributing Processes and a Review of the Literature," NSF-Sponsored Conference on Organizational Learning, Carnegie-Mellon University, May 1989.

22. See Dalia Marin, "Learning and Dynamic Comparative Advantage: Lessons from Austria's Postwar Pattern of Growth for Eastern Europe," paper prepared for 17th Economic Policy Panel, Copenhagen, April 22–23, 1993. See also Alwyn Young, "Learning by Doing and the Dynamic Effects of International Trade," *Quarterly Journal of Economics,* vol. 106 (May 1991), pp. 369–405; and "A Tale of Two Cities: Factor Accumulation and Technical Change in Hong Kong and Singapore," Massachusetts Institute of Technology, February 1992.

23. This is the strategy followed by W. Brian Arthur in his "Designing Eco-

nomic Agents That Act like Human Agents: A Behavioral Approach to Bounded Rationality," *American Economic Review*, vol. 81 (May 1991), pp. 353–59.

Chapter 5

1. George Sand, "Voyage d'un moineau de Paris," in Grandville, (P. J. Stahl) *Vie privée et publique des animaux* (1840) (Paris: Hetzel, 1867), pp. 117–23.
2. Albert O. Hirschman, *National Power and the Structure of Foreign Trade* (University of California Press, 1945), pp. 3, 38, 78, 123, 139, 150.
3. Albert O. Hirschman, *The Strategy of Economic Development* (Yale University Press, 1958), pp. 25, 125, 132, 209.
4. Although the Industrial Revolution in England influenced all subsequent industrializations, it should not, for example, be taken as a general pattern (or English paradigm): "the historian, after he has refused to ignore the uncomfortable irregularities . . . can attempt to systematize the deviations from the original pattern by bringing them into a new, although necessarily more complicated, pattern." Alexander Gerschenkron, *Economic Backwardness in Historical Perspective: A Book of Essays* (Harvard University Press, 1966), pp. 31, 41, 360.
5. "The Rise and Decline of Development Economics," in Albert O. Hirschman, *Essays in Trespassing: Economics to Politics and Beyond* (Cambridge University Press, 1981), p. 24.
6. "A Dissenter's Confession: The Strategy of Economic Development Revisited," in Albert O. Hirschman, *Rival Views of Market Society and Other Recent Essays* (Viking, 1986), pp. 6–7; and Hirschman, "The Political Economy of Latin American Development," *Latin American Research Review*, vol. 22, no. 3 (1987), p. 31.
7. Albert O. Hirschman, *The Passions and the Interests: Political Arguments for Capitalism before Its Triumph* (Princeton University Press, 1977), pp. 111–13.
8. "Against Parsimony: Three Easy Ways of Complicating Some Categories of Economic Discourse," in Hirschman, *Rival Views*, pp. 142, 158–59.
9. Albert O. Hirschman, *Shifting Involvements: Private Interest and Public Action* (Princeton University Press, 1982), p. 63.
10. Gary S. Becker, *The Economic Approach to Human Behavior* (University of Chicago Press, 1976), pp. 5–14; and George J. Stigler and Gary S. Becker, "De Gustibus Non Est Disputandum," *American Economic Review*, vol. 67 (March 1977), pp. 76, 89.
11. Adam Smith, *The Theory of Moral Sentiments* (Oxford University Press, 1976), pp. 9, 317.
12. Ibid., p. 299; and Adam Smith, *An Inquiry into the Nature and Causes of the Wealth of Nations* (Oxford University Press, 1976), pp. 341–45, 419. On these passages, see also Hirschman, *Passions and the Interests*, pp. 100–02.
13. R. H. Coase, "Adam Smith's View of Man," *Journal of Law and Economics*, vol. 19 (October 1976), pp. 545–46.

14. Immanuel Kant, *Observations on the Feeling of the Beautiful and Sublime* (1764), trans. John T. Goldthwait (University of California Press, 1960), p. 74. Kant was an admirer of Smith's *Theory of Moral Sentiments,* and it is possible that his evocation of the unintended consequences of the pursuit of self-interest were influenced, directly or indirectly, by the first edition of the *Theory,* published in English in 1759.

15. *Wealth of Nations,* pp. 28–29, 100–01, 760, 795, 870.

16. Ibid., pp. 26–72, 266–67, 361–62; and *Theory of Moral Sentiments,* p. 224.

17. Becker, *The Economic Approach,* p. 14.

18. *Wealth of Nations,* p. 471.

19. Letter of 1785, in Ernest Campbell Mossner and Ian Simpson, eds., *The Correspondence of Adam Smith* (Oxford University Press, 1977), p. 286.

20. Smith, *Correspondence,* p. 34.

21. M. J. A. N. Condorcet, *Oeuvres,* ed. Arago and O'Connor (Paris: Firmin Didot, 1847–49), vol. 1, pp. 281–88, vol. 11, p. 155.

22. A. R. J. Turgot, *Oeuvres,* ed. Schelle (Paris: Alcan, 1913–23), vol. 3, p. 326.

23. Charles Henry, *Correspondance inédite de Condorcet et de Turgot 1770–1779* (Paris: Didier, 1883), pp. 143–44.

24. Smith, *Wealth of Nations,* p. 471; Condorcet, *Oeuvres,* vol. 5, p. 28; and Turgot, *Oeuvres,* vol. 1, p. 620.

25. Condorcet, *Oeuvres,* vol. 11, pp. 148, 200.

26. Hirschman, "Against Parsimony," p. 158.

27. The point of equilibrium, for Turgot, is such as to "procure for the entire society the greatest sum of production, enjoyment, wealth and strength." Turgot, *Oeuvres,* vol. 3, pp. 315, 334. See also Emma Rothschild, "Commerce and the State: Turgot, Condorcet and Smith," *Economic Journal,* vol. 102 (September 1992), pp. 1197–1210.

28. Lionel Robbins, *An Essay on the Nature and Significance of Economic Science* (Macmillan, 1932), p. 87.

29. Gunnar Myrdal, *The Political Element in the Development of Economic Theory* (1929), trans. Paul Streeten (London: Routledge and Paul, 1953), pp. xi–xii.

30. Edmund Burke, *Reflections on the Revolution in France* (1790) (London: Penguin Books, 1982), pp. 152–53; and J. G. Herder, *On Social and Political Culture* (1774), trans. F. M. Barnard (Cambridge University Press, 1969), p. 198.

31. Immanuel Kant, *On History,* trans. Lewis White Beck and others (Indianapolis: Bobbs-Merrill, 1963), pp. 40–47.

32. It is important to emphasize that Smith saw many advantages to the "invisible hand" policy of allowing people to do what they wanted with their investments; they include increasing freedom as well as increasing welfare. See Emma Rothschild, "Adam Smith and the Invisible Hand," *American Economic Review,* vol. 84 (May 1994, *Papers and Proceedings,* 1993), pp. 319–22.

33. "The mathematical tool is indispensable for the analysis and understanding of economic phenomena, but the essential work is not the manipulation of this logical tool, it is the choice and discussion of premises, which

should be founded on the observation of facts." Maurice Allais, "Puissance et dangers de l'utilisation de l'outil mathématique en économique," *Econometrica,* vol. 22 (January 1954), p. 70; and Tjalling C. Koopmans, *Three Essays on the State of Economic Science* (McGraw-Hill, 1957), p. 170.

34. J.-M. Grandmont, "Transformation of the Commodity Space, Behavioral Heterogeneity, and the Aggregation Problem," *Journal of Economic Theory,* vol. 57 (June 1992), pp. 32–33.

35. David Kreps, *Game Theory and Economic Modelling* (Oxford University Press, 1990), pp. 117–18, 129, 184.

36. J. G. Herder, *Outlines of a Philosophy of the History of Man* (1784), trans. T. Churchill (London: Johnson, 1800), p. 224; and Herder, *On Social and Political Culture,* p. 206.

37. "It is a good model if it succeeds in explaining or rationalizing some of what you see in the world in a way that you might not have expected": this is Krugman's account, in chapter 2.

38. *Measures for the Economic Development of Under-Developed Countries,* Report by a Group of Experts appointed by the Secretary-General of the United Nations (United Nations: Department of Economic Affairs, May 1951), pp. 15, 31, 93.

39. "There must be a few people willing to pioneer. . . . Of course, the larger this alert minority, and the more scope it is allowed for maneuvering, the more rapidly the community will grow economically, and it is in the differences of proportions and of scope that the essential difference between societies is to be found." W. Arthur Lewis, *The Theory of Economic Growth* (Homewood, Ill.: Richard D. Irwin, 1955), p. 42. The verb "to economize" is used, here, in the sense of Menger's *wirthschaftender Mensch:* someone engaging in economic activities, which are also activities in the course of which people tend to be self-interested, or of which self-interest is the "mainspring."

40. Walt W. Rostow, *The Stages of Economic Growth: A Non-Communist Manifesto* (Cambridge University Press, 1971), pp. 6, 31, 70.

41. Quoted in Howard C. Barnard, *Education and the French Revolution* (Cambridge University Press, 1969), p. 51.

42. Rostow, *Stages,* pp. 26, 29.

43. *Measures for the Economic Development of Under-Developed Countries,* pp. 52–53.

44. Condorcet, *Oeuvres,* vol. 11, p. 197.

45. Smith, *Wealth of Nations,* p. 472.

46. Carl Menger, *Investigations into the Method of the Social Sciences with Special Reference to Economics* (1883), trans. F. J. Nock (New York University Press, 1985), p. 177.

47. *Theory of Moral Sentiments,* p. 234; see Emma Rothschild, "Adam Smith and Conservative Economics," *Economic History Review,* vol. 45 (February 1992), pp. 89–90.

48. *International Herald Tribune,* September 22, 1989.

Chapter 6

1. Albert O. Hirschman, *Exit, Voice, and Loyalty: Responses to Decline in Firms, Organizations, and States* (Harvard University Press, 1970).

2. Albert O. Hirschman, *The Passions and the Interests: Political Arguments for Capitalism before Its Triumph* (Princeton University Press, 1977).

3. Ferdinand Tönnies, *Gemeinschaft und Gesellschaft: Abhandlung des Communismus und de Socialismus als Empirischer Culturformen* (Leipzig: Fues, 1887).

4. Henry Sumner Maine, *Ancient Law: Its Connection with the Early History of Society, and Its Relation to Modern Ideas* (London: J. Murray, 1861).

5. Emile Durkheim, *The Division of Labor in Society*, trans. George Simpson (Glencoe, Ill.: Free Press, 1933).

6. Hirschman, *Passions and Interests*, p. 43.

7. Zygmunt Bauman, *Legislators and Interpreters: On Modernity, Postmodernity, and Intellectuals* (Cornell University Press, 1987), pp. 74–75.

8. Ibid., p. 62.

9. Albert O. Hirschman, "Industrialization and Its Manifold Discontents: West, East and South," *World Development*, vol. 20 (September 1992), pp. 1225–32.

10. Charles Tilly, "How War Made States and Vice-Versa," New School for Social Research Working Paper Series 42 (1987).

11. Alasdair MacIntyre, *Whose Justice? Which Rationality?* (University of Notre Dame Press, 1988).

12. Paul Fussell, *The Great War and Modern Memory* (Oxford University Press, 1975); Modris Ekstein, *The Rites of Spring: The Great War and the Birth of the Modern Age* (Anchor Books, 1990); and Zygmunt Bauman, *Modernity and the Holocaust* (Cornell University Press, 1989).

13. Michel Crozier, *The Bureaucratic Phenomenon* (University of Chicago Press, 1964).

14. David Warsh, *The Idea of Economic Complexity* (Viking Press, 1984).

15. Dorothy Nelkin, *Jetport: The Boston Airport Controversy* (Transaction Books, 1974), p. 166.

16. Jean-Marie Charon, *Les Movements d'Opposants aux Decisions d'Implantation d'Aeroports et l'Aligne Nouvelle de T.G.V.* (Paris: Association pour la Recherche et la Developpement en Urbanisme [Mars], 1979), p. 102.

17. Hirschman, *Exit, Voice, and Loyalty*, p. 15.

18. Eben Shapiro, "The World Has a Few Too Many Russian Vodkas," *New York Times*, September 6, 1992, p. E2.

19. Matthew L. Wald, "G.E. Boycott Is Working, Group Says," *New York Times*, June 13, 1991, p. D5; and Barbara Presley Noble, "Making a Difference: Going after G.E.," *New York Times*, June 16, 1991, p. C12.

20. Neighbor-to-Neighbor, *The History of the Salvadoran Coffee Boycott* (San Francisco, 1992).

21. Heather Rhoads, "Boycott," *Nukewatch Pathfinder*, The Progressive Foundation (Winter 1992–93), p. 2.

Chapter 7

1. By using the term "a bias for hope," I am not only referring to his book with that title. I think the term aptly captures Hirschman's general approach to developmental issues.

2. See, for example, Peter M. Ward, *Welfare Politics in Mexico: Papering over the Cracks* (Allen and Unwin, 1986); and David Harvey, "Planning the Ideology of Planning," in Robert W. Burchell and George Steinleib, eds., *Planning Theory in the 1980's: A Search for Future Directions* (Rutgers University, Center for Urban Policy Research, 1982), pp. 213–34.

3. Albert O. Hirschman, *The Rhetoric of Reaction: Perversity, Futility, Jeopardy* (Belknap Press, 1991).

4. See Peter D. Anthony, *The Ideology of Work* (London: Tavistock, 1977).

5. Albert O. Hirschman, "Underdevelopment, Obstacles to the Perception of Change and Leadership," in Hirschman, *A Bias for Hope: Essays on Development and Latin America* (Yale University Press, 1971), pp. 328–41.

6. Gertrude Himmelfarb, *The Idea of Poverty: England in The Early Industrial Age* (Vintage Books, 1985).

7. Richard Hofstadter, *The Age of Reform: From Bryan to F.D.R.* (Vintage Books, 1955), pp. 8–9.

8. Allan D. Bloom, *The Closing of the American Mind: How Higher Education Has Failed Democracy and Impoverished the Souls of Today's Students* (Simon and Schuster, 1987).

9. Collin Leys, *Underdevelopment in Kenya: Economy of Neocolonialism* (University of California Press, 1974); and Susan Eckstein, "The Political Economy of Lower Class Areas in Mexico City," in Wayne A. Cornelius and Felicity M. Trueblood, eds., *Latin American Urban Research*, vol. 5 (Beverly Hills: Sage, 1975), pp. 342–60.

10. Hirschman, "Underdevelopment."

11. Albert O. Hirschman, "The Principle of the Hiding Hand," *Public Interest*, vol. 2 (Winter 1967), pp. 1–23.

12. This is similar to James March's position in "Model Bias for Social Action," *Review of Educational Research*, vol. 42 (Fall 1972), pp. 413–29.

13. Albert O. Hirschman, "The Search for Paradigms as Hindrance to Understanding," in Hirschman, *A Bias for Hope*, pp. 342–60.

14. Robert B. Westbrook, *John Dewey and American Democracy* (Cornell University Press, 1991).

15. Louis Menand, "The Real John Dewey," *New York Review of Books*, June 25, 1992, pp. 52.

16. Hirschman cites Robert Packenham's *Liberal America and the Third World: Political Development Ideas in Foreign Aid and Social Science* (Princeton University Press, 1973), as the inspiration for this notion. See Albert O. Hirschman, "The Rise and Decline of Development Economics," in Hirschman, *Essays in Trespassing: Economics to Politics and Beyond* (Cambridge University Press, 1981), p. 20. On Hirschman's view of the prerequisites for development, see Albert O. Hirschman, "A Dissenter's Confession: The Strategy of Economic Development

Revisited," in Gerald M. Meier and Dudley Seers, eds., *Pioneers in Development* (Oxford University Press, 1984), p. 99. On his view of the appropriate response to developmental problems, see Albert O. Hirschman and Charles E. Lindblom, "Economic Development, Research and Development, Policy-Making: Some Converging Views," in Hirschman, *A Bias for Hope*, pp. 63–84.

17. Richard Hofstadter, *Anti-Intellectualism in American Life* (Knopf, 1963).

18. Albert O. Hirschman, *The Strategy of Economic Development* (Yale University Press, 1958).

19. See John C. Wood and Ronald N. Woods, eds., *Friedrich A. Hayek: Critical Assessment* (Routledge, 1991).

20. On this issue, see Steven Kelman, *Making Public Policy: A Hopeful View of American Government* (Basic Books, 1987), pp. 3–10.

21. Kenneth H. F. Dyson, *The State Tradition in Western Europe: A Study of an Idea and Institution* (Oxford University Press, 1980).

22. Bernard Bailyn, *The Ideological Origins of the American Revolution* (Harvard University Press, 1967).

23. On the difference between economists and anthropologists, see Lisa R. Peattie, "Economic Anthropology and Anthropological Economics," in Robert Hinshaw, ed., *Currents in Anthropology: Essays in Honor of Sol Tax* (Mouton, 1979), pp. 85–94.

24. For a nice elaboration of this point, see Michael S. McPherson, "The Social Scientist as Constructive Skeptic: On Hirschman's Role," in Alejandro Foxley, Michael S. McPherson, and Guillermo O'Donnell, eds., *Development, Democracy and the Art of Trespassing: Essays in Honor of Albert O. Hirschman* (University of Notre Dame Press, 1986), pp. 305–15.

25. Albert O. Hirschman, "Policymaking and Policy Analysis in Latin America—A Return Journey," in Hirschman, *Essays in Trespassing: Economics to Politics and Beyond* (Cambridge University Press, 1981), pp. 142–66.

26. See Foxley and others, eds., *Development, Democracy and the Art of Trespassing*.

Chapter 8

1. D. C. Minassian and V. Mehra, "3.8 Million Blinded by Cataract Each Year: Projections from the First Epidemiological Study of Incidence of Cataract Blindness in India," *British Journal of Ophthalmology*, vol. 74 (1990), p. 342.

2. Bradford H. Gray, "World Blindness and the Medical Profession: Conflicting Medical Cultures and the Ethical Dilemmas of Helping," *Milbank Quarterly*, vol. 70, no. 3 (1992), p. 535.

3. Minassian and Mehra, "3.8 Million Blinded," p. 341.

4. Lawrence B. Brilliant and others, *The Epidemiology of Blindness in Nepal: Report of the 1981 Nepal Blindness Survey* (Chelsea, Mich.: Seva Foundation, 1988), p. 220.

5. World Bank, *Trends in Developing Economies, 1990* (Washington, 1990), p.

383; Population Reference Bureau, *1993 World Population Data Sheet* (Washington, 1993); and World Bank, *World Development Report 1992* (Oxford University Press, 1992), pp. 218, 280.

6. See the Background and Acknowledgments in Brilliant and others, *Epidemiology of Blindness in Nepal*, for a full list of the individuals and organizations from many nations who carried out the survey.

7. Ibid, p. 175.

8. The absence of any direct measures of incidence requires estimations based on prevalence data combined with educated guesses. The 22,000 figure can be considered only a very rough approximation.

9. Albert O. Hirschman, *Development Projects Observed* (Brookings, 1967), p. 75.

10. Ibid., p. 77.

11. Albert O. Hirschman, *A Bias for Hope: Essays on Development and Latin America* (Yale University Press, 1971), pp. 26–37.

12. Hirschman, *Development Projects Observed*.

13. Elliot Marseille, "What Does It Really Cost to Deliver Cataract Surgery in Nepal," Seva Foundation, Chelsea, Mich., 1989.

14. The increase in surgical caseload in Lumbini and elsewhere began before the introduction of IOLs; other programs, most notably that of the German eye hospital, also had large increases in caseload before they, too, began using lenses in 1989; and many other factors are likely to have contributed to the increases. These include more sophisticated outreach and publicity including a national radio program on eye care; more ophthalmologists and ophthalmic assistants; and more and better equipment.

Chapter 9

For supporting this research, the authors thank the Massachusetts Institute of Technology, the Ceará State Institute of Planning (IPLANCE), Antônio Cláudio Ferreira Lima, Antônio Rocha Magalhães, and Ciro Gomes. For helpful suggestions on an earlier version, many thanks go to Rose Batt, Susan Eckstein, Albert Hirschman, Kris Heggenhougen, and Hubert Schmitz. None of these persons or institutions is responsible for, or necessarily agrees with, the opinions and interpretations expressed here.

1. Albert O. Hirschman, *The Strategy of Economic Development* (Yale University Press, 1958), pp. 64–65.

2. Hirschman's warnings can be found in the following works: *Journeys toward Progress: Studies of Economic Policy-Making in Latin America* (New York: Twentieth Century Fund, 1963), pp. 244–45; "Policymaking and Policy Analysis in Latin America—A Return Journey," in Hirschman, *Essays in Trespassing: Economics to Politics and Beyond* (Cambridge University Press, 1981), pp. 142–66; and "Underdevelopment, Obstacles to the Perception of Change, and Leadership," in Hirschman, *A Bias for Hope: Essays on Development and Latin America* (Yale University Press, 1971), pp. 328–41.

3. Seminal works in this field were Anne Krueger, "The Political Economy of the Rent-Seeking Society," *American Economic Review,* vol. 64 (June 1974), pp. 291–303; William A. Niskanen, *Bureaucracy and Representative Government* (Chicago: Aldine, 1971); and Gordon Tullock, *The Politics of Bureaucracy* (Washington, Public Affairs Press, 1965). For reference to more recent works, as well as a critique of this literature, see Merilee S. Grindle, "The New Political Economy: Positive Economics and Negative Politics," in Gerald M. Meier, ed., *Politics and Policy Making in Developing Countries: Perspectives on the New Political Economy* (San Francisco: ICS, 1991), pp. 39–67. With respect mainly to developing countries, see also Paul Starr, "The Meaning of Privatization," *Yale Law and Policy Review,* vol. 6 (1988), pp. 6–41; and Steven Kelman, "Why Public Ideas Matter," in Robert B. Reich, ed., *The Power of Public Ideas* (Ballinger, 1988), pp. 31–54.

4. A recent example can be found in an article on the government of the Northeast's smallest state, Alagôas: James Brooke, "Even Brazil Is Shocked: State Is One Family's Fief," *New York Times,* November 12, 1993, p. A3. That state was also home of the first Brazilian president to be impeached (for corruption in 1992), who was governor of the state before becoming president.

5. Each of these cases became a master's thesis in the Department of Urban Studies and Planning at the Massachusetts Institute of Technology.

6. For a discussion of the themes as they manifested themselves across several of the cases, see Judith Tendler, "Good Government in the Tropics," book manuscript, MIT, Department of Urban Studies and Planning, January 1994.

7. Sara Beth Freedheim, "Why Fewer Bells Toll in Ceará: Success of a Community Health Worker Program in Ceará, Brazil," master's thesis, Massachusetts Institute of Technology, June 1993, p. 6.

8. The only exception was Fortaleza, which, as the state's capital and most populous city (1.5 million inhabitants), already had health services.

9. James Brooke, "Brazilian State Leads Way in Saving Children," *New York Times,* May 14, 1993, p. A1.

10. Michael Lipsky was one of the first to point out the important determining character of the unsupervised worker-client relationship in these large bureaucracies, which he named "street-level bureaucracies." See *Street-Level Bureaucracy: Dilemmas of the Individual in Public Services* (New York: Russell Sage Foundation, 1980). James Q. Wilson did the same with respect to policing, in *Varieties of Police Behavior: The Management of Law and Order in Eight Communities* (Harvard University Press, 1978).

11. A former finance minister of Venezuela attributes the low quality of delivery of social services in his country in large part to these kinds of problems. In the area of health, he notes that materials and medical equipment— "from beds to x-ray machines"—periodically disappeared from hospitals and had to be completely replaced every few years. As a result, "massive overstocking [was required] to guarantee the minimum necessary supply of medicines." See Moises Naim, *Paper Tigers and Minotaurs: The Politics of Venezuela's Economic Reforms* (Carnegie Endowment for International Peace, 1993), p. 81.

12. For an excellent recent review of this literature, see Eileen Appelbaum

and Rosemary Batt, *The New American Workplace: Transforming Work Systems in the United States* (Cornell University Industrial and Labor Relations Press, 1994).

13. For the U.S. case, see David Levine and Susan Helper, "A Quality Policy for America," Organizational Behavior and Industrial Relations Working Paper OBIR-61 (University of California-Berkeley, Haas School of Business, 1993); David Osborne and Ted Gaebler, *Reinventing Government: How the Entrepreneurial Spirit Is Transforming the Public Sector* (Reading, Mass.: Addison-Wesley, 1992); Colin Campbell and B. Guy Peters, *Organizing Governance, Governing Organization* (University of Pittsburgh Press, 1988); and Michael Barzelay, *Breaking through Bureaucracy: A New Vision for Managing in Government* (University of California Press, 1992). For the European case, see Anne Marie Berg, "Excellence in Government—A Case Study of Well Performing Government Agencies in Norway," paper prepared for the seminar "Concepts and Methods of Quality Awards in the Public Sector," Post Graduate School of Administrative Sciences, Speyer, Germany, October 21–22, 1993; Robin Murray, "Introduction" and "Towards a Flexible State," in Robin Murray, ed., *New Forms of Public Administration, IDS [Institute of Development Studies] Bulletin,* vol. 23 (October 1992), pp. 1–5, 78–88; and Robin Murray, "Well Performing Administration— International Experiences," paper prepared for a conference on excellence in government, Oslo, June 6, 1993.

14. On trust, see Charles F. Sabel, "Studied Trust: Building New Forms of Cooperation in a Volatile Economy," in Frank Pyke and Werner Sengenberger, eds., *Industrial Districts and Local Economy Regeneration* (Geneva: International Institute of Labor Studies, 1992), pp. 215–50, and the literature cited therein.

15. See, for example, the proposal to the Clinton administration along these lines in Levine and Helper, "A Quality Policy for America"; or some of the recommendations made by Osborne and Gaebler in their study of innovations in local and state government, *Reinventing Government.*

16. For the latter figure, See William McGreevey, *Brazil Public Spending on Social Programs: Issues and Options,* Report 7086-BR (World Bank, 1988). The existing system, of course, is heavily biased toward curative care, which is by definition more costly than preventive health.

17. This varied from one municipality to the next, with some assuming costs for transportation (bicycles, canoes, donkeys) and others providing additional funds for nutritional supplements, meals for training sessions and other meetings, and chlorine for cholera campaigns.

18. Each backpack contained oral rehydration packets, antiseptic cream, iodine, gauze, cotton, adhesive tape, thermometer, soap, comb, scissors to cut hair and fingernails, a measuring tape to monitor babies and pregnant women, growth and immunization charts for children under the age of five, and a card to record health information about the households.

19. For discussions of resistance to the use of paraprofessionals, see Thomas Marchione, "Evaluating Primary Health Care and Nutrition Programs in the Context of National Development," *Social Science and Medicine,* vol. 19, no. 3 (1984), pp. 225–35; George E. Cumper and Patrick Vaughan, "Community Health Aids at the Crossroads," *World Health Forum,* vol. 6, no. 4 (1985), pp. 5–7;

World Health Organization, "Strengthening the Performance of Community Health Workers in Primary Health Care," WHO Technical Report, JC:X05, 780, 1989, pp. 1–46; and Gill Walt and others, *Community Health Workers in National Programmes: Just Another Pair of Hands?* (Milton Keynes, England, and Philadelphia: Open University Press, 1990).

20. For an excellent and typically negative picture of unhappy or self-seeking government bureaucrats in a similar rural health program in Nepal, see Jean-Marion Aitken, "Conflict or Complicity? Different 'Cultures' within a [Health] Bureaucracy in Nepal," Liverpool School of Tropical Medicine, 1992. Also in Nepal, see Judith Justice, *Policies, Plans and People: Culture and Health Development in Nepal* (University of California Press, 1986), and the literature cited therein for other countries.

21. Although the wage for agricultural day labor was half the minimum, agricultural workers often earned an additional income in kind, depending on their informal arrangements with their employers.

22. For a study of the Brazilian National Development Bank (Banco Nacional de Desenvolvimento), and the importance of the protection of the technocrats, see Eliza Jane Willis, "The Politicized Bureaucracy: Regimes and Presidents in Brazilian Development," Ph.D. dissertation, Boston College, 1990.

23. For a similar argument with respect to the importance of protection of technocrats by politicians—albeit with respect to macroeconomic policy reforms—see Merilee Grindle, "Challenging the State: Crisis and Innovation in Latin America and Africa," forthcoming, 1994; and Merilee Grindle and Francisco E. Thoumi, "Muddling toward Adjustment: The Political Economy of Economic Policy Change in Ecuador," in Robert H. Bates and Anne O. Krueger, eds., *Political and Economic Interactions in Economic Policy Reform* (Oxford: Basil Blackwell, 1993), pp. 123–78.

24. Freedheim, "Why Fewer Bells Toll in Ceará."

25. See, for example, Patrick Vaughan and Gill Walt, "Implementing Primary Health Care: Some Problems of Creating National Programmes," *Tropical Doctor* (July 1984), pp. 108–12; Gill Walt, "CHW's: Are National Programs in Crisis?" *Health Policy and Planning*, vol. 3, no. 1 (1988) pp. 1–21; Lucy Gilson and others, "National Community Health Worker Programs: How Can They Be Strengthened?" *Journal of Public Health Policy*, vol. 10 (Winter 1989), pp. 528–326; and World Health Organization, "Strengthening the Performance of Community Health Workers," pp. 1–46.

26. Walt and others, *Community Health Workers in National Programmes.*

27. For other reasons why the typical resistance from professionals to such programs was less than usual in this case, see Freedheim, "Why Fewer Bells Toll in Ceará."

28. Judith Tendler, *New Lessons from Old Projects: The Workings of Rural Development in Northeast Brazil*, A World Bank Operations Evaluations Study (World Bank, 1993).

29. At the same time, the state government was radically pruning its payrolls of "phantom workers" in trying to cope with its severe deficit. Like most

governments of the period, it was leery about bringing on any new large group of workers like this in a way that would imply legal responsibility to give them tenure. Because Brazil's labor courts had been tending to judge worker complaints of unjust firing in favor of workers, however, state officials said they knew that their precautions in hiring the health agents at arm's length would protect them for no more than three or four years. After this "grace period," they expected that these contracts, and the length of service accumulated by some of the agents, would be interpreted as conferring some kind of de facto security. Interestingly, they did not necessarily worry about what would happen when such challenges started to occur, because they felt that if the program was successful, they *would* want to upgrade the status and training of the agents anyway. At the time of this research, the expected pressures had already started to mount, with agents organizing to demand greater job security and fringe benefits and with discussions among the program's managers about how to proceed to the next phase being held.

30. Fay Haussman, "Ceará Keeps Promise to Children," *First Call for Children*, vol. 4 (October–December, 1993), p. 7.

31. See, for example, Paul Osterman and Rosemary Batt, "Employer-Centered Training for International Competitiveness: Lessons from State Programs," *Journal of Policy Analysis and Management*, vol. 12, no. 3 (1993), pp. 456–77. They say that this problem appears more in small than large firms, and hence recommend that public training programs focus special attention on developing programs with small firms. For a review of the U.S. experience with preventive health and other community programs in the 1960s, when, as in Ceará, large numbers of untrained workers from the community were hired in the name of "maximum feasible participation," see Michael Lipsky and Morris Lounds, "Citizen Participation and Health Care: Problems of Government-Induced Participation," *Journal of Health Politics, Policy and Law*, vol. 1 (Spring 1976), pp. 86–111. They cite the eventual frustration by these workers, and hostility to the very programs that hired them because of their inability to rise up in their organizations or to obtain equivalent jobs elsewhere.

32. See, for example, Peter Underwood and Zdenka Underwood, "New Spells for Old: Expectations and Realities of Western Medicine in a Remote Tribal Society in Yemen," in N. F. Stanley and R. A. Joske, eds., *Changing Disease Patterns and Human Behavior* (London and New York: Academic Press, 1981), pp. 272–97; Robert H. Bannerman, John Burto, and Ch'en Wen-Chien, eds., *Traditional Medicine and Health Care Coverage: A Reader for Health Administrators and Practitioners* (Geneva: World Health Organization, 1983); Harald Kristian Heggenhougen, *Community Health Workers: The Tanzania Experience* (Oxford University Press, 1987); and Harald Kristian Heggenhougen and Lucy Gilson, "Perceptions of Efficacy and the Use of Traditional Medicine, with Examples from Tanzania," unpublished paper (1992). Also, for WHO estimates indicating that traditional medicine is the primary health service for up to 80 percent of the population in rural areas of many countries, see Harold Kristian Heg-

genhougen and Lucy Shore, "Cultural Components of Behavioral Epidemiology: Implications for Primary Health Care," *Social Science and Medicine*, vol. 22, no. 11 (1986), pp. 1235–45.

33. Gustavo Maia Gomes, Carlos Osório, and Jose Ferreira Irmão, *Recessão e desemprêgo nas regiões brasileiras* (Recession and unemployment in the Brazilian regions) (Recife, Pernambuco: Federal University of Pernambuco, Postgraduate Program in Economics, 1985). The authors also note the influence in this hiring of the 1979–83 drought years and the emergency employment programs triggered by the drought.

34. See, for example, Paul Bowden, "The Administration of Regional Development," *Journal of Administration Overseas*, vol. 18 (1979) pp. 193–201; Dennis A. Rondinelli, "Administration of Integrated Rural Development Policy: The Politics of Agrarian Reform in Developing Countries," *World Politics*, vol. 31 (April 1979), pp. 389–416; Arturo Escobar, "Decentralization and Community Participation in Nutrition Planning," *Decentralization and Development Review*, University of California, Berkeley (Spring 1981), pp. 8–10. For a bibliography on decentralization and development, see Commonwealth Secretariat, *Decentralization for Development: A Select Annotated Bibliography* (London: Marlborough House, 1983).

35. Freedheim, "Why Fewer Bells Toll in Ceará."

36. Ibid.

37. Elinor Ostrom, "A Public Choice Approach to Metropolitan Institutions: Structure, Incentives and Performance," *Social Science Journal*, vol. 20 (1983), pp. 79–96.

38. With respect to agricultural and business extension, see Tendler, *New Lessons from Old Projects*.

39. Peter A. Berman, Davidson R. Gwatkin, and Susan E. Berger, "Community-Based Health Workers: Head Start or False Start Towards Health for All?" World Bank Technical Paper, Population Health and Nutrition Department (World Bank, 1986).

40. See, for example, Harald Kristian Heggenhougen, "Will Primary Health Care Efforts Be Allowed to Succeed?" *Social Science and Medicine*, vol. 19, no. 2 (1984), pp. 217–24; and Heggenhougen, *Community Health Workers*. See also John W. Thomas, "Employment Creating Public Works Programs: Observations on Policy and Social Dimensions in Employment in Developing Nations," in Edgar O. Edwards, *Employment in Developing Nations: Report on a Ford Foundation Study* (Columbia University Press, 1974), pp. 279–311. Thomas describes a remarkably analogous case of "creep" in the wrong direction within programs intended to go against the prevailing ways of doing things. In an article on labor-intensive public works programs in South Asia, he shows how capital-intensive approaches tend, through time, to edge out labor-intensive ones. As in the health case, this "creep"—which he calls "mutation"—is the result of a greater taste for the "wrong" approaches on the part of powerful actors on the scene—in this case, the engineering professionals in government and design and construction firms.

41. See, for example, Berman, Gwatkin and Berger, "Community-Based Health Workers."

42. The literature on the participatory and empowering aspects of health programs is reviewed in Lynn M. Morgan, *Community Participation in Health: The Politics of Primary Health Care in Costa Rica* (Cambridge University Press, 1993), chap. 1. It should be noted that the planning process for the health program, and the selection of the agents and the supervising nurses, did not involve "participation" of the community, although health agents and other community members might have influenced the program's direction once it was started.

43. As with the health agents, the work environment of agricultural extension workers changed radically when they were faced with an epidemic of crop disease or pests. Often threatening the agricultural economy of a whole region—its income, employment, and tax base—the epidemics would mobilize high-level concern and support across the public sector. With respect to Indian agricultural extension workers during the emergency period of Indira Gandhi's government, see Mick Moore, "Institutional Development, the World Bank, and India's New Agricultural Extension Programme," *Journal of Development Studies*, vol. 20 (July 1984), pp. 303–17. With respect to the southern United States, Egypt, and Northeast Brazil, see Tendler, *New Lessons from Old Projects.*

44. Tendler, "Good Government in the Tropics."

Chapter 10

1. Albert O. Hirschman, *Development Projects Observed* (Brookings, 1967), is an evaluation classic. Based on a worldwide tour of World Bank–financed projects, it has long been an inspiration to project officers, not only because it validates their day-to-day experience, but also because it reflects a preference for cooperative learning over doctrinal haranguing.

2. See Gerald M. Meier and Dudley Seers, eds., *Pioneers in Development* (Oxford University Press, 1984). This work includes Hirschman's "A Dissenter's Confession: The Strategy of Economic Development Revisited" (pp. 87–111).

3. Michael Scriven, *Hard-Won Lessons in Program Evaluation*, New Directions for Program Evaluation, no. 58 (Summer 1993), p. 9.

4. Albert O. Hirschman, *Rival Views of Market Society and Other Recent Essays* (Harvard University Press, 1992), p. 158.

5. Albert O. Hirschman, *Journeys toward Progress: Studies of Economic Policy-Making in Latin America* (Doubleday, 1965), p. 11.

6. Scriven, *Hard-Won Lessons*, pp. 15–16, 37.

7. The Bank considers an operation to be satisfactory when it has fulfilled most of the main objectives and is expected to produce a positive development result. A 10 percent economic return threshold is normally used. World Bank,

Operations Evaluation Department, *1992 Evaluation Results* (Washington, 1992), pp. 86, 167.

8. Ibid., pp. 86–87, 181.

9. World Bank, Operations Evaluation Department, *Agriculture Extension and Research in India*, Précis 5 (April 1991).

10. Judith Tendler, *New Lessons from Old Projects: The Workings of Rural Development in Northeast Brazil* (World Bank, 1993).

11. World Bank, Operations Evaluation Department, *Bank Support for Flood Control in Bangladesh*, Précis 12 (June 1991).

12. Christine Kessides, *Institutional Options for the Provision of Infrastructure*, World Bank Discussion Paper 212 (September 1993).

13. Bradford Morse and Thomas Berger, *Sardar Sarovar, The Report of the Independent Review* (Ottawa, Canada: Resource Futures International, 1992).

14. World Bank, Operations Evaluation Department, *Community Development in Columbia*, Précis (forthcoming).

15. World Bank, *Getting Results, The World Bank's Agenda for Improving Development Effectiveness* (Washington, 1993), p. 13.

16. World Bank, Operations Evaluation Department, *Adjustment in Sub-Saharan Africa*, Précis 53 (October 1993).

17. World Bank, Operations Evaluation Department, *Involuntary Resettlement*, Précis 52 (June 1993).

18. Albert O. Hirschman, *The Strategy of Economic Development* (Yale University Press, 1958), p. 5.

19. World Bank, *1992 Evaluation Results*, p. 142.

20. Hirschman's most recent book analyzes the rhetoric used by reactionaries to resist the new agenda. See Albert O. Hirschman, *The Rhetoric of Reaction: Perversity, Futility, Jeopardy* (Belknap Press, 1991).

21. For a promising approach, see John H. Johnson and Sulaiman S. Wasty, *Borrower Ownership of Adjustment Programs and the Political Economy of Reform*, World Bank Discussion Paper 199 (May 1993).

22. World Bank, Operations Evaluation Department, "Area Development Projects," *Lessons and Practices*, no. 3 (September 1993).

23. "But, chiefly, do not let us overestimate the importance of the economic problem, or sacrifice to its supposed necessities other matters of greater and more permanent significance. It should be a matter for specialists—like dentistry. If economists would manage to get themselves thought of as humble, competent people, on a level with dentists, that would be splendid!" J. M. Keynes, *Essays in Persuasion* (Harcourt, Brace, 1932), p. 373.

Chapter 11

In writing this essay I benefited immeasurably from many conversations with Zhiyuan Cui, Richard Doner, David Friedman, Mark Granovetter, John Griffin, Gary Herrigel, Horst Kern, Toshihiro Nishiguchi, Hikari Nohara, Michael Piore, Tom Sample, Richard Samuels, Judith Tendler, Meenu Tewari, Harrison White, and Jonathan Zeitlin. Research for this project was financed in part by the Program for the Study of Germany and Europe at the Center for European Studies at Harvard University. This essay is an edited version of a chapter that appeared in Neil J. Smelser and Richard Swedberg, eds., *The Handbook of Economic Sociology* (Russell Sage Foundation and Princeton University Press, 1994).

1. On contracts and hierarchies as alternative forms of economic governance, see Oliver E. Williamson, *Markets and Hierarchies: Analysis and Anti-Trust Implications* (Free Press, 1975), and "Comparative Economic Organization: The Analysis of Discrete Structural Alternatives," *Administrative Science Quarterly*, vol. 36 (June 1991), pp. 269–96. In these writings Williamson introduces a third, trust- or norm-based form of governance—the relational contract—as regulating exchanges where the parties rely on one another more directly than is consistent with standard contracting but not so much as, in his view, to justify coordination by hierarchy. For extended discussion and criticism of this category from the point of view developed in this chapter, see Charles F. Sabel, "Constitutional Ordering in Historical Context," in Fritz W. Scharpf, ed., *Games in Hierarchies and Networks* (Westview Press, 1993), pp. 65–124, especially pp. 70–80. On principal-agent problems, see Sanford Grossman and Oliver Hart, "The Costs and Benefits of Ownership: A Theory of Vertical and Lateral Integration," *Journal of Political Economy*, vol. 94 (August 1986), pp. 691–719; and Bengt Holmstrom and Paul Milgrom, "Multi-Task Principal-Agent Analyses: Incentive Contracts, Asset Ownership, and Job Design," *Journal of Law, Economics and Organization*, vol. 7 (Special Issue 1991), pp. 24–52.

2. Ronald Dore, "Goodwill and the Spirit of Market Capitalism," *British Journal of Sociology*, vol. 34 (December 1983), pp. 459–82.

3. David M. Kreps, "Corporate Culture and Economic Theory," in James E. Alt and Kenneth A. Shepsle, eds., *Perspectives on Positive Political Economy* (Cambridge University Press, 1990), pp. 90–143.

4. Chalmers A. Johnson, *MITI and the Japanese Miracle: The Growth of Industrial Policy, 1925-1975* (Stanford University Press, 1982).

5. Albert O. Hirschman, "The Rise and Decline of Development Economics," in Hirschman, *Essays in Trespassing: Economics to Politics and Beyond* (Cambridge University Press, 1981), pp. 1–24.

6. John Maynard Keynes, *The General Theory of Employment, Interest, and Money* (Harcourt, Brace, and Jovanovich, [1936] 1980); Alexander Gerschenkron, *Economic Backwardness in Historical Perspective* (Harvard University Press, 1962); W. Arthur Lewis, "Economic Development with Unlimited Supplies of Labor," *Manchester School of Economic and Social Studies*, vol. 22 (1954), pp. 139–91; and W. Arthur Lewis, *The Theory of Economic Growth* (London: Allen and Unwin, 1955).

7. Bela Balassa, "Trade Policies in Developing Countries," *American Economic Review*, vol. 61 (May 1971, *Papers and Proceedings, 1970*), pp. 178–87; and Ian M. D. Little, Tibor Scitovsky, and Maurice Scott, *Industry and Trade*

in Some Developing Countries: A Comparative Study (Oxford University Press, 1970).

8. Fernando Henrique Cardoso and Enzo Faletto, *Dependency and Development in Latin America,* trans. Marjory Mattingly Urquidi (University of California Press, 1979); Andre Gunder Frank, *Capitalism and Underdevelopment in Latin America* (New York: Monthly Review Press, 1967); and Folker Frobel, Jurgen Heinrichs, and Otto Kreye, *The New International Division of Labor* (Cambridge University Press, 1980).

9. Neoclassical views of competitive growth assume that factors of production—labor or stocks of physical capital—eventually have diminishing returns: for large stocks of capital, the greater the stock, the smaller the increase in output from an increment of capital. This suggests that the returns to investments would be greater in developing economies with small capital stocks than in advanced economies with large ones. Given perfect mobility of factors, the developing economies should attract investment, in time causing their growth rates to converge with those in the advanced ones. But apart from the well-known Asian exceptions, most other economies that started the postwar period poor have become even poorer.

As formulated by Romer and others, the new growth theory accounts for this discrepancy by introducing knowledge in the form of, say, semiconductor designs or chemical processes as a type of capital with increasing returns. See Elhanan Helpman, "Endogenous Macroeconomic Growth Theory," *European Economic Review,* vol. 36 (April 1992), pp. 237–67; Robert E. Lucas, "On the Mechanics of Economic Development," *Journal of Monetary Economics,* vol. 22 (July 1988), pp. 3–42; Paul M. Romer, "Increasing Returns and Long-run Growth," *Journal of Political Economy,* vol. 94 (October 1986), pp. 1002–37; Paul M. Romer, "Human Capital and Growth: Theory and Evidence," NBER Working Paper 3173 (Cambridge, Mass.: National Bureau of Economic Research, 1989); and Paul M. Romer, "Are Nonconvexities Important for Understanding Growth?" *American Economic Review,* vol. 80 (May 1990), pp. 97–103. More precisely, knowledge is said to be a nonrival form of property. Nonrivalry means that the same knowledge can be used simultaneously at an unlimited number of sites, or, equivalently, that copies of the original are (for the owner) essentially free. This implies increasing returns. The price of the first turbine-blade factory includes design costs; the second uses exactly the same combination of labor, capital, and knowledge but costs less to build because the design can simply be reused. Doubling the inputs produces a disproportionately large increase in output—the reverse of the standard neoclassical case. Given such nonrival inputs, returns on investment need not decrease when the capital stock becomes large, nor will developing economies with small capital stocks automatically profit from the exhaustion of investment opportunities in the advanced economies.

But distinguishing knowledge as a type of input creates as much confusion as it resolves. In the new theory as in the old, growth rates are associated with factor stocks; only the direction of the influence has, in an important case, changed. Yet why assume a direct relation between a stock of knowledge in the form of current plans and designs and future growth rates? Not the stock of knowledge but how it is used seems likely to shape how fast an economy grows, and how rapidly it can acquire new knowledge. Otherwise it is hard to explain how the Soviet-type economies could have fallen so far behind the advanced capitalist ones, how the United States could have fallen back as compared with Japan, or why certain developing countries have been able to absorb and refine technology so rapidly. This chapter can be understood as an effort to indicate some of the institutions that can make knowledge an engine of growth. Naturally it would be possible to take the institutions of learning by monitoring, or some better specification of the mechanisms of growth, and treat *them* as the relevant stock of inputs for assessing growth rates. But as will become clear in the body of the text, the notion of economic agency advanced here is so at odds with neoclassical assumptions that the result would be intractably syncretic.

10. The new theory of international trade, like the new growth theory, reaches novel results within the general neoclassical framework by assuming increasing returns to investments in certain kinds of knowledge. See Paul R. Krugman, "Endogenous Innovation, International Trade and Growth," in Paul R. Krugman, ed., *Rethinking International Trade* (MIT Press, 1990), pp. 165–182; Paul R. Krugman, *Geography and Trade* (MIT Press, 1991); and Luis A. Rivera-Batiz and Paul M. Romer, "International Trade with Endogenous Technological Change," NBER Working Paper 3594 (Cambridge, Mass.: National Bureau for Economic Research, 1991). In the new trade theory the first firms to enter broad markets where mass production allows economies of scale or narrow markets where close relations between producers and users are a precondition for further development of the product can enjoy such increasing returns. These first movers enjoy potentially insuperable advantages over late comers. Protection in the new trade theory can therefore be used to allow domestic producers to learn how to cut costs sufficiently to compete on world markets with first movers.

11. Marcus J. Fleming, "External Economies and the Doctrine of Balanced Growth," *Economic Journal*, vol. 65 (June 1955), pp. 241–56; Ragnar Nurkse, "The Conflict Between 'Balanced Growth' and International Specialization," in Gerald M. Meier, ed., *Leading Issues in Economic Development*, 4th ed. (Oxford: Oxford University Press, 1984), pp. 373–76; and Paul N. Rosenstein-Rodan, "Problems of Industrialization of Eastern and South-Eastern Europe," *Economic Journal*, vol. 53 (June–September 1943), pp. 202–11.

12. Albert O. Hirschman, *The Strategy of Economic Development* (Yale University Press, 1958); and Paul Streeten, "Unbalanced Growth," *Oxford Economic Papers*, vol. 2 (June 1959), pp. 167–90.

13. Michael A. Cusumano, *The Japanese Automobile Industry: Technology and Management at Nissan and Toyota* (Harvard University, Council on East Asian Studies, 1985).

14. Masahiko Aoki, *Information, Incentives, and Bargaining in the Japanese Economy* (Cambridge University Press, 1988).

15. In the following characterization of Japanese production methods in general and subcontracting in its various stages of development, I rely on

Toshihiro Nishiguchi, *Strategic Industrial Sourcing: The Japanese Advantage* (Oxford University Press, 1994); Taiichi Ohno, *The Toyota Production System: Beyond Large-Scale Production* (Cambridge, Mass.: Productivity Press, 1988); Michael J. Smitka, *Competitive Ties: Subcontracting in the Japanese Automobile Industry* (Columbia University Press, 1991); and Shigeo Shingo, *A Study of the Toyota Production System from an Industrial Engineering Viewpoint*, trans. Andrew P. Dillon (Cambridge, Mass.: Productivity Press, 1989), as well as discussions with Bruce Hamilton, vice-president, operations, United Electric Control, Watertown, Mass., and David Nelson, vice-president, purchasing, Honda of America Manufacturing, Inc., Marysville, Ohio.

16. See Rebecca M. Henderson and Kim B. Clark, "Architectural Innovation: The Reconfiguration of Existing Product Technologies and the Failure of Established Firms," *Administrative Science Quarterly*, vol. 35 (March 1990), pp. 9–30.

17. The following draws on discussions with managers from Yamazaki Mazak and Mori-Seiki, both leading Japanese machine-tool firms, on June 8 and June 11, 1992, respectively. I would like to thank Professor Hikari Nohara of the Faculty of Law, Hiroshima University, for making these discussions possible.

18. W. Carl Kester, "Governance, Contracting, and Investment Time Horizons," Working Paper 92-003 (Harvard Business School, 1993).

19. Nishiguchi, *Strategic Industrial Sourcing;* and Smitka, *Competitive Ties.*

20. A good overview of the rational choice literature on talk is David Austin-Smith, "Strategic Models of Talk in Political Decision Making," *International Political Science Review*, vol. 13 (January 1992), pp. 45–58.

21. David Friedman, *The Misunderstood Miracle: Industrial Development and Political Change in Japan* (Cornell University Press, 1988); and Nishiguchi, *Strategic Industrial Sourcing.*

22. J. Mark Ramseyer, "Legal Rules in Repeated Deals: Banking in the Shadow of Defection in Japan," *Journal of Legal Studies*, vol. 20 (January 1991), pp. 91–117.

23. J. Bradford De Long, "Did J. P. Morgan's Men Add Value? An Economist's Perspective on Financial Capitalism," in Peter Temin, ed., *Inside the Business Enterprise: Historical Perspectives on the Use of Information* (University of Chicago Press, 1991), pp. 205–36.

24. Ramseyer, "Legal Rules in Repeated Deals."

25. Masahiko Aoki, "Toward an Economic Model of the Japanese Firm," *Journal of Economic Literature*, vol. 28 (March 1990), pp. 1–27.

26. For an interesting discussion on the difficulties of applying standard ideas of property to Japanese firms, see W. Mark Fruin and Toshihiro Nishiguchi, "Supplying the Toyota Production System: Intercorporate Organizational Evolution and Supplier Subsystems," in Bruce Kogut, ed., *Country Competitiveness: Technology and the Organizing of Work* (Oxford University Press, 1993), pp. 225–46; and Nishiguchi, *Strategic Industrial Sourcing.* Also see Hajime Miyazaki, "Employeeism, Corporate Governance, and the J-Firm," *Journal of Comparative Economics*, vol. 17 (June 1993), pp. 443–69.

27. For the current standoff between neoliberal and "structural" or strong-state views about the role of public authorities in economic development, see Rhys Jenkins, "(Re-)interpreting Brazil and South Korea," in Tom Hewitt, Hazel Johnson, and Dave Wield, eds., *Industrialization and Development* (Oxford University Press, 1992), pp. 167–98, especially pp. 196–97.

28. The formative accounts of German financial capitalism are Jakob Reisser, *Zur Entwicklungsgeschichte der deutschen Grossbanken mit besonderer Rücksicht auf die Konzentrationsbestrebungen* (The German great banks and their concentration) (Jena: Fischer Verlag, 1906); and Rudolf Hilferding, *Finance Capital: A Study of the Latest Phase of Capitalist Development*, trans. Morris Watnick and Sam Gordon (Boston: Routledge & Kegan Paul, 1981). For a discussion of the breakdown today of such systems of monitoring by bank owners, see Charles F. Sabel, John R. Griffin, and Richard E. Deeg, "Making Money Talk: Towards a New Debtor-Creditor Relation in German Banking," in John C. Coffee, Ronald J. Gilson, and Louis Lownstein, eds., *Relational Investing* (Oxford University Press, forthcoming).

29. Ann O. Krueger, "The Political Economy of the Rent-Seeking Society," *American Economic Review*, vol. 64 (June 1974), pp. 291–303; Deepak Lal, *The Poverty of "Development Economics"* (London: Institute of Economic Affairs, 1983); and Ian M. D. Little, *Economic Development: Theory, Policy, and International Relations* (Basic Books, 1982).

30. To avoid confusion at the risk of creating it: the term *developmental association* is like Johnson's term *developmental state* in that it attributes potentially benign formative powers to an entity that in standard economic accounts cannot have such. Johnson, *MITI and the Japanese Miracle*. But the developmental state uses incentives to get firms to act as they would want to act if they knew what the central authorities know. Developmental associations use incentives to get member firms to acquire the information they need to know how to act.

31. I am being a little unfair to the private-interest government argument—but only a little. Writers in this school, such as Schmitter and Streeck, have occasionally observed that the interests of associations and their members can be mutually defining. Wolfgang Streeck and Philippe C. Schmitter, eds., *Private Interest Government: Beyond Market and State* (London: Sage Publications Ltd., 1985). But the concern with interest (inter)mediation typically overshadows concern for interest generation.

32. See Jean L. Cohen, "Strategy or Identity: New Theoretical Paradigms and Contemporary Social Movements," *Social Research*, vol. 52 (Winter 1985), pp. 663–716.

33. Johnson, *MITI and the Japanese Miracle*. A more sophisticated variant of the strong-state view argues that the Japanese state and firms simply learned the lesson of the new trade theory before their competitors and acted in concert accordingly. Laura D'Andrea Tyson and John Zysman, "Developmental Strategy and Production Innovation in Japan," in Chalmers Johnson, Laura D'Andrea Tyson, and John Zysman, eds., *Politics and Productivity: The Real Story of Why Japan Works* (Ballinger, 1989), pp. 59–140.

34. Friedman, *Misunderstood Miracle.*

35. Richard J. Samuels, *The Business of the Japanese State: Energy Markets in Comparative and Historical Perspective* (Cornell University Press, 1987).

36. Teiichiro Fujita, "Local Trade Associations (*Dogyo Kumiai*) in Prewar Japan," in Hiroaki Yamazaki and Matao Miyamoto, eds., *Trade Associations in Business History* (University of Tokyo Press, 1988), pp. 87–113, especially pp. 88–98.

37. For example, the Kobe Trade Association, formed in 1900, "inspected brushes for export, investigated opportunities for obtaining financial credit, and distributed information on overseas markets." William Miles Fletcher, *The Japanese Business Community and National Trade Policy, 1920–1942* (University of North Carolina Press, 1989), p. 23. For the argument that cooperative inspection was the main function of these associations, see Hideaki Miyajima, "Comment," in Yamazaki and Miyamoto, eds., *Trade Associations in Business History,* pp. 114–19.

38. Keijiro Otsuka, Gustav Ranis, and Gary Saxonhouse, *Comparative Technology Choice in Development: The Indian and Japanese Cotton Textile Industries* (London: Macmillan, 1988), pp. 87–88.

39. Tetsuji Okazaki, "Import Substitution and Competitiveness in the Prewar Japanese Iron and Steel Industry," in Etsuo Abe and Yoshitaka Suzuki, eds., *Changing Patterns of International Rivalry: Some Lessons from the Steel Industry* (University of Tokyo Press, 1991), pp. 166–90, especially pp. 177–87.

40. Fujita, "Local Trade Associations," pp. 105–08; and Miyajima, "Comment," pp. 113–14.

41. Fletcher, *Japanese Business Community and National Trade Policy,* pp. 92–95.

42. Friedman, *Misunderstood Miracle,* pp. 187–95.

43. Jonah D. Levy and Richard J. Samuels, "Institutions and Innovation: Research Collaboration as Technology Strategy in Japan," Working Paper MITJSTP 89-02 (Massachusetts Institute of Technology, Department of Political Science, 1989), especially pp. 30–37, pp. 58–73.

44. Gerald Jiro Hane, "Research and Development Consortia in Innovation in Japan," Working Paper MITJP 92-07 (Massachusetts Institute of Technology, Japan Program, 1992).

45. Gary Herrigel, "The Case of the West German Machine-Tool Industry," in Peter Katzenstein, ed., *Industry and Politics in West Germany: Toward the Third Republic* (Cornell University Press, 1989), pp. 185–220.

46. Jürgen Häusler, Hans-Willy Hohn, and Susanne Lütz, "The Architecture of an R&D Collaboration," in Fritz W. Scharpf, ed., *Games in Hierarchies and Networks* (Westview Press, 1993), pp. 211–250; and Susanne Lütz, *Die Steuerung industrieller Forschungskooperation: Funktionsweise und Erfolgsbedingungen des staatlichen Förderinstrumentes Verbundforschung* (Guiding cooperation in industrial research: the functioning and preconditions of the research consortium as a policy instrument) (New York: Campus, 1993).

47. Alice H. Amsden, *Asia's Next Giant: South Korea and Late Industrialization* (Oxford University Press, 1989); and Robert Wade, *Governing the Market: Eco-*

nomic Theory and the Role of Government in East Asian Industrialization (Princeton University Press, 1990).

48. On the current reappraisal of the role in developing countries of associations of the sort discussed here, see Richard F. Doner, *Driving a Bargain: Automobile Industrialization and Japanese Firms in Southeast Asia* (University of California Press, 1991); Richard F. Doner, "Limits of State Strength: Toward an Institutionalist View of Economic Development," *World Politics*, vol. 44 (April 1992), pp. 398–431; and Peter Evans, "The State as Problem and Solution: Predation, Embedded Autonomy and Adjustment," in Stephan Haggard and Robert Kaufman, eds., *The Politics of Economic Adjustment: International Constraints, Distributive Politics, and the State* (Princeton University Press, 1992), pp. 139–81.

49. Cheng-Tian Kuo, "Economic Regimes and National Performance in the World Economy: Taiwan and the Philippines," vol. 1, Ph.D. dissertation, University of Chicago, 1990, pp. 99–122.

50. On the *chaebol's* strong-arm insistence that the "strong" state allow them to orchestrate entry into heavy industry, see Byung-Sun Choi, "Institutionalizing a Liberal Economic Order in Korea: The Strategic Management of Economic Change," Ph.D. dissertation, Harvard University, John F. Kennedy School, 1987, especially p. 133; and for evidence that trade associations played an important role alongside the *chaebol* in forming government policy, see ibid., p. 215 fn. 22. I have not, however, found an account of what that role was.

51. Monica Alves Amorim, "Lessons on Demand: Order and Progress for Small Firms in Ceará, Brazil," master's thesis, Massachusetts Institute of Technology, 1993.

52. Emile Durkheim, *The Division of Labor in Society*, trans. W. D. Halls (Free Press, 1984); and Herbert Spencer, *The Principles of Sociology* (Westport, Conn.: Greenwood Press, 1975).

53. Emile Durkheim, *Professional Ethics and Civic Morals*, trans. Cornelia Brookfield (New York: Routledge, 1992).

54. Mark Granovetter, "Economic Action and Social Structure: The Problem of Embeddedness," *American Journal of Sociology*, vol. 91 (November 1985), pp. 481–510.

55. Excellent criticisms of classical social theory that arrive at this result are Pierre Bourdieu, *Outline of a Theory of Practice*, trans. Richard Nice (Cambridge University Press, 1977); and Roberto Mangabeira Unger, *Politics, a Work in Constructive Social Theory* (Cambridge University Press, 1987). I take a different route because of the centrality of the idea of discussion to my argument; but the paths cross.

56. For contrasting views of how such reflexive choices actually occur, see Amartya K. Sen, "Rational Fools: A Critique of the Behavioral Foundations of Economic Theory," in Henry Harris, ed., *Scientific Models and Man* (Oxford University Press, 1979), pp. 317–44 (the self as choosing among various preference orderings); and Marvin Minsky, *The Society of Mind* (Simon and Schuster, 1986) (the self as the result of exchanges among its constitutive faculties).

57. Donald Davidson, "On the Very Idea of a Conceptual Scheme," in John

Rajchman and Cornel West, eds., *Post-Analytic Philosophy* (Columbia University Press, 1985), pp. 5–20; and Donald Davidson, "A Coherence Theory of Truth and Knowledge," in Ernest LePore, ed., *Truth and Interpretation: Perspectives on the Philosophy of Donald Davidson* (Oxford: Basil Blackwell, 1986), pp. 307–19.

58. Karl Popper, "Normal Science and Its Dangers"; Imre Lakatos, "Falsification and the Methodology of Scientific Research Programmes"; and Paul Feyerabend, "Consolations for the Specialist," all in Imre Lakatos and Alan Musgrave, eds., *Criticism and the Growth of Knowledge: Proceedings of the International Colloquium in the Philosophy of Science, London, 1965, Vol. 4* (Cambridge University Press, 1970), pp. 51–58, 91–196, 197–230.

59. Contrast this view with Kuhn's distinction between "normal" science dominated by "puzzle solvers" with no inkling of radically different understandings of the world and "revolutions" dominated by "philosophers" absorbed to obsession by their own alternative to orthodoxy. Thomas S. Kuhn, *The Structure of Scientific Revolutions*, 2d ed. (University of Chicago Press, 1970).

60. Feyerabend, "Consolations for the Specialist."

61. Bruce A. Ackerman, *We the People*, vol. 1: *Foundations* (Harvard University Press, 1991); and Frank Michelman, "Law's Republic," *Yale Law Journal*, vol. 97 (July 1988), pp. 1493–1537. Contrast this view with the idea of the constitution as a device for purifying particular interests into a general will (Jean Jacques Rousseau, *The Social Contract*, trans. Charles M. Sherover [Harper and Row, (1772) 1984]), and the idea of the constitution as a master contract setting general conditions under which all private agreements become self-interpreting (Russell Hardin, "Why a Constitution?" in Bernard Grofman and Donald Wittman, eds., *The Federalist Papers and the New Institutionalism* [New York: Agathon Press, 1989], pp. 100–20).

62. Jürgen Habermas, "Erläuterungen zum Begriff des kommunikativen Handelns" (Commentary on the concept of communicative action) in Jürgen Habermas, ed., *Vorstudien und Ergänzungen zur Theorie das kommunikativen Handelns* (Preliminaries and supplements to the theory of communicative action) (Frankfurt am Main: Suhrkamp, 1984), pp. 571–605.

63. Jürgen Habermas, *Faktizität und Geltung: Beiträge zur Diskurstheorie des Rechts und des demokratischen Rechtsstaats* (Facticity and validity: contributions to a discursive theory of law and the democratic rechtsstaat) (Frankfurt am Main: Suhrkamp, 1992).

64. Gunther Teubner, "Ist das Recht auf Konsens angewiesen? Zur sozialen Akzeptanz des modernen Richterrechts" (Does law depend on consensus? On the social acceptance of modern judge-made law), in Hans Joachim Giegel, ed., *Kommunikation und Konsens in modernen Gesellschaften* (Communication and consensus in modern society) (Frankfurt am Main: Suhrkamp, 1992), pp. 197–211.

65. Richard Rorty, *Philosophy and the Mirror of Nature* (Princeton University Press, 1979).

66. For a criticism of Habermas on these lines, see Paul Ricoeur, *Oneself as Another*, trans. Kathleen Blamey (University of Chicago Press, 1992). For an

argument that the distinction between communicative and strategic action reflects a German intellectual tradition of seeing the truth as revealed in words, not deeds, see Rainer Döbert, "Konsenstheorie als deutsche Ideologie" (Consensus theory as German ideology), in Giegel, ed., *Kommunikation und Konsens*, pp. 276–309.

67. Karin Knorr-Cetina and Klaus Amann, "Konzensprozesse in der Wissenschaft" (Consensual processes in science), in Giegel, ed., *Kommunikation und Konsens*, pp. 212–35, especially p. 216.

68. Richard Rorty, "Pragmatism, Davidson and Truth," in LePore, ed., *Truth and Interpretation*, pp. 333–55. The pragmatists' influence on Habermas is ambiguous. He refers to Peirce in elaborating the notion of purified, "universalizable" truth, but to Mead in tracing language as the medium that allows creation of sociable selves. On Peirce, see Habermas, *Faktizität und Geltung*, and on Mead, Jürgen Habermas, "Individuierung durchVergesellschaftung: Zu G. H. Meads Theorie der Subjektivität" (Individuation through socialization: on G. H. Mead's theory of subjectivity), in Jürgen Habermas, ed., *Nachmetaphysisches Denken* (Postmetaphysical thinking) (Frankfurt am Main: Suhrkamp, 1992), pp. 187–242.

69. See, for example, George Herbert Mead, "Industrial Education, the Working Man, and the School," *The Elementary School Teacher*, vol. 9 (1909), pp. 369–83; and City Club of Chicago, *A Report on Vocational Training in Chicago and in Other Cities* (1912).

70. John Dewey, *The Public and its Problems* (New York: H. Holt, 1927), p. 69.

71. Nishiguchi, *Strategic Industrial Sourcing;* and Mari Sako, *Prices, Quality and Trust: Inter-Firm Relations in Britain and Japan* (Cambridge University Press, 1992).

72. Elinor Ostrom, *Governing the Commons: The Evolution of Institutions for Collective Action* (Cambridge University Press, 1990); and Elinor Ostrom, "Rational Choice Theory and Institutional Analysis: Toward Complementarity," *American Political Science Review*, vol. 85 (March 1991), pp. 237–43.

73. Elinor Ostrom, "Community and the Endogenous Solution of Commons Problems," *Journal of Theoretical Politics*, vol. 4 (July 1992), pp. 343–51, and *Crafting Institutions for Self-Governing Irrigation Systems* (San Francisco: Institute for Contemporary Studies Press, 1992).

Notes to Chapter 12

I am very grateful to Harry Frankfurt for detailed critical comments.

1. See my two articles, "The Search for Paradigms as a Hindrance to Understanding," *World Politics*, vol. 22 (April 1970), pp. 329–43, also in *A Bias for Hope: Essays on Development and Latin America* (Yale University Press, 1971), pp. 342–60; and "Against Parsimony: Three Easy Ways of Complicating Some Categories of Economic Discourse," in *Economics and Philosophy*, vol. 1 (April 1985), pp. 7–21, also in *Rival Views of Market Society and Other Recent Essays* (Viking, 1986; paperback edition, Harvard University Press, 1992), pp. 142–62.

2. *National Power and the Structure of Foreign Trade* (University of California Press, 1945); and *The Rhetoric of Reaction: Perversity, Futility, Jeopardy* (Cambridge, Mass.: Belknap Press, 1991).

3. *The Strategy of Economic Development* (Yale University Press, 1958).

4. See "The Changing Tolerance for Income Inequality in the Course of Economic Development," *Quarterly Journal of Economics*, vol. 87 (November 1973), pp. 544–65, with a mathematical appendix by Michael Rothschild; republished (without the appendix) in my collection, *Essays in Trespassing: Economics to Politics and Beyond* (Cambridge University Press, 1981), pp. 39–58.

5. *Exit, Voice, and Loyalty: Responses to Decline in Firms, Organizations, and States* (Harvard University Press, 1970).

6. Michael S. McPherson, "The Social Scientist as Constructive Skeptic: On Hirschman's Role," in Alejandro Foxley, Michael S. McPherson, and Guillermo O'Donnell, eds., *Development, Democracy, and the Art of Trespassing: Essays in Honor of Albert O. Hirschman* (University of Notre Dame Press, 1986), pp. 305–16.

7. "Beyond Asymmetry: Critical Notes on Myself as a Young Man and on Some Other Old Friends," *International Organization*, vol. 32 (Winter 1978), pp. 45–50, republished in *Essays in Trespassing*, pp. 27–33.

8. *Essays in Trespassing*, p. 30.

9. See my paper, "*The Rhetoric of Reaction*—Two Years Later," *Government and Opposition*, vol. 28 (Summer 1993), pp. 292–314. I have argued along somewhat similar lines in "The Case against One Thing at a Time," *World Development*, vol. 18 (August 1990), pp. 1119–22.

10. "Exit, Voice, and the Fate of the German Democratic Republic: An Essay in Conceptual History," *World Politics*, vol. 45 (January 1993), pp. 173–202.

11. Ibid., p. 178.

12. "*The Rhetoric of Reaction*—Two Years Later," pp. 292–93.

13. Ibid., pp. 302–07.

14. Ibid., p. 149.

15. "Exit, Voice, and the Fate of the German Democratic Republic," p. 202.

16. Gaston Bachelard, *La psychanalyse du feu* (Paris: Gallimard, 1949), p. 164.

17. Ray Monk, *Ludwig Wittgenstein: The Duty of Genius* (Penguin Books, 1990), p. 467.

Notes to Appendix A

These discussions were edited by Lloyd Rodwin. Jean Riesman made the tape transcription and prepared the first draft of the summaries for the Hirschman Seminar Minutes. Alex Walter substituted for Jean Riesman on the first drafts of the summaries of the Picciotto and Marseille discussions.

1. In a note to Lloyd Rodwin (September 8, 1994), Lisa Peattie suggested that "the discussions, like discussions in general, touched on, rather than really engaging, the central issues. One of these is surely the relationship between

saying and doing. This is inadequately rendered as the relationship between theory and practice, as shown by the way in which the question is raised as to whether Hirschman's stuff is theory or not. There are various forms of saying, among them 'lore,' 'epigrammatic one-liners,' 'powerful generalizations,' 'theories,' 'concepts,' 'pieces of advice.' The relationship between these various sorts of saying and various sorts of practice cannot be determined without inquiring as to the institutional settings of both saying and practicing: for example, national planning bodies, implementing agencies, the World Bank as lending body, the World Bank as producer of reports (sayings), the academic profession of economics. Congruence between sayings and doings may be the result of doers following sayers or of sayers bringing their statements into line with observed practices of doing or of similar forces operating on both. For an example of the latter: A meeting was arranged between Keynes and Roosevelt on the basis that they would find their views on what to do about the depression mutually congenial. It didn't work. Roosevelt had come to his pump-priming out of improvisational politics. He said of Keynes, 'I thought he was an economist but he seemed to be a mathematician.'"

Notes to Appendix B

This appendix was edited by Lloyd Rodwin. Jean Riesman prepared the tape transcription and the summaries for the Hirschman Seminar Minutes.

1. "Through the years, a man peoples a space with images of provinces, kingdoms, mountains, bays, ships, islands, fishes, rooms, tools, stars, horses, and people. Shortly before his death, he discovers that the patient labyrinth of lines traces the image of his own face." Cited in Jorgé Luis Borges, *A Personal Anthology* (Grove Press, 1967), p. 203.

Faculty Participants

David Barkin teaches international economics and rural development at Universidad Autonoma Metropolitana in Mexico City. He was awarded the National Prize in Political Economy in Mexico for his book, *Inflation and Democracy: The Mexican Case*. Member of the National Research Council of Mexico and a fellow of the Academy for Scientific Research, he participated in one session of the Hirschman seminar in his capacity as a senior fellow at the Lincoln Institute of Land Policy.

Robert C. Einsweiler, director of research for the Lincoln Institute of Land Policy, was a professor in the Humphrey Institute of Public Affairs at the University of Minnesota (1979–91), and is former president of the American Institute of Planners and the American Planning Association. His books include *Urban Growth Management Systems* (with Robert H. Freilich and others), 1976; *Strategic Planning: Opportunities and Threats for Planners*, 1988; and *Shared Power* (with colleague John Bryson), 1992.

Sara Freedheim received her MCP degree in May 1992 from MIT. The title of her thesis is: "Why Fewer Bells Toll in Ceará: Success of a Community Health Worker Program in Ceará, Brazil." She is now a consultant for the Technical Department in the Latin American Caribbean Region of the World Bank.

Albert Hirschman was born in 1915 in Berlin, left Germany in 1933, and studied economics in Paris, London, and at the University of Tri-

355

este, where he received his doctorate in 1938. After serving in the French army in 1939–40 and then with the International Rescue Committee in Marseilles, he emigrated to the United States in 1941. Following two years at the University of California (Berkeley) and three years in the U.S. Army, he joined the Federal Reserve Board in 1946, where he worked on the financial problems of postwar reconstruction of Western Europe. From 1952 to 1956 he lived in Bogota, Colombia, first as financial adviser to the National Planning Board and then as a private consultant. In 1956 Hirschman went to Yale University and then taught at Columbia (1958–64) and Harvard (1964–74). Since 1974 he has been professor of social science at the Institute for Advanced Study in Princeton, New Jersey (emeritus since 1985).

Hirschman's books include *National Power and the Structure of Foreign Trade*, 1945 and 1980; *The Strategy of Economic Development*, 1958; *Journeys toward Progress*, 1963; *Development Projects Observed*, 1967; *Exit, Voice and Loyalty*, 1970; *A Bias for Hope: Essays on Development and Latin America*, 1971; *The Passions and the Interests*, 1977; *Essays in Trespassing: Economics to Politics and Beyond*, 1981; *Shifting Involvements*, 1982; *Rival Views of Market Society and Other Recent Essays*, 1986; paperback edition with new introduction, 1992; *The Rhetoric of Reaction*, 1991; and *A Propensity to Self-Subversion: Essays*, 1995.

Paul R. Krugman, until recently professor of economics at MIT, is now professor of economics at Stanford University. His most recently published books include *Peddling Prosperity*, 1994; *The Age of Diminished Expectations*, 1992; *Currencies and Crises*, 1992; *Geography and Trade*, 1991; and *Rethinking International Trade*, 1990.

Elliot Marseille, currently a Ph.D. candidate in health policy at the School of Public Health at the University of California at Berkeley, was program director with the Seva Foundation's nationwide eye care program in Nepal, 1984–89.

Lisa Redfield Peattie, professor emeritus and senior lecturer in the Department of Urban Studies and Planning at MIT, has done research on housing and planning programs in Boston, Lima, Cairo, and Ciudad Guayana, Venezuela, and on small enterprises in Colombia and China. She is the author of *The View from the Barrio, Thinking About Development, Making Work* (with William Ronco), *Women's Claims: An*

Essay in Political Economy (with Martin Rein), and *Planning: Rethinking Ciudad Guayana.*

Robert Picciotto was raised in Lebanon and educated in France. He studied mathematics and statistics at the Sorbonne and obtained his aeronautical engineering degree from the Ecole Nationale Superieure de l'Aéronautique. A graduate of the Woodrow Wilson School of Public and International Affairs, Princeton University, Picciotto is currently director general, Operations Evaluation in the World Bank, a vice presidential position he assumed after handling corporate planning and budgeting responsibilities from 1987 to 1992. He is the author of several sector and project studies and of articles on topics ranging from agriculture research evaluation to the myths and dilemmas of participatory development.

Michael Piore, David W. Skinner Professor of Economics and Management at MIT, has been a consultant to various international organizanions, U.S. government agencies, and private business organizations. His most recent books include *The Second Industrial Divide* (with Charles Sabel), 1984; *Dualism and Discontinuity in Industrial Society* (with Suzanne Berger), 1980; and *Birds of Passage: Migrant Labor and Industrial Societies,* 1979.

Karen R. Polenske is professor of regional political economy and planning in the Department of Urban Studies and Planning at MIT, vice-president of the International Input-Output Association, and a council member of the North American Regional Science Association. She has published six books, the latest of which is *Chinese Economic Planning and Input-Output Analysis.*

Martin Rein is professor of social policy at MIT. His most recent books are *Work, Age and Social Security* (with Tony Atkinson), 1992; *Frame Reflection: Toward the Evolution of Intractable Policy Controversies* (with Donald Schön), 1992; and *Time for Retirement* (with Martin Kohli), 1991.

Jesse C. Ribot is a MacArthur fellow at the Harvard Center for Population and Development and a former lecturer in the Developing Areas Group of the Department of Urban Studies and Planning at MIT. His recent books include *L'Arbre Nourricier en Pays Sahelien* (with Anne Ber-

358   Faculty Participants

geret) and *Climate Variability and Change in the Semi-Arid Tropics: Vulnerability and Policy Response,* of which he is chief editor.

Lloyd Rodwin, Ford International Professor Emeritus at MIT, was a cofounder of the Joint Center for Urban Studies of MIT and Harvard University (1959–69); also director of the Guayana, Venezuela, planning and research program of the Joint Center (1959–64), head of the Department of Urban Studies and Planning (1969–73), and president of the Regional Science Association (1986–87). His books include *The British New Towns Policy,* 1956; *Housing and Economic Progress,* 1961; *Nations and Cities,* 1970; and *Cities and City Planning,* 1981. He has also edited or coedited books on the future metropolis; planning urban growth and regional development; shelter, settlement, and development; images and themes of the city in social sciences; and industrial change and regional economic transformation in Europe and the United States.

Emma Rothschild is director of the Centre for History and Economics and a fellow of Kings College, Cambridge. She is also chair of the Research Council of the Common Security Forum and a member of the Faculty of the Center for Population and Development Studies at Harvard University. A graduate of Oxford University (1967), she was associate professor of science, technology and society at MIT from 1978 to 1988, where she is now a fellow at the Sloan School of Management. A member of the Royal Commission on Environmental Pollution (United Kingdom) since 1986, she has written extensively on the environment, defense and economic policy, and also on economic history and the history of economic thought.

Charles Sabel is the Ford International Professor of Social Science in the Department of Political Science and the Program in Science, Technology and Society at MIT. His books include *Work and Politics,* 1982; and *The Second Industrial Divide: Possibilities of Prosperity* (with Michael J. Piore).

Bishwapriya Sanyal is an associate professor of urban and regional planning at MIT. He has worked as a development consultant with the World Bank, the United Nations Development Program, the United Nations Center for Human Settlements, the International Labor Office,

USAID, and the Ford Foundation. His most recent book is *Breaking the Boundaries: One World Approach to Planning Education* (ed.), 1990, and he is currently working on a second book entitled "Sailing Against the Wind: A Treatise in Support of Poor Countries' Bureaucrats."

Donald A. Schön was a Ford Professor of Urban Studies and Education at MIT from 1972 to July 1990 and chair of MIT's Department of Urban Studies and Planning from 1990 to 1992. He is currently Ford Professor Emeritus and senior lecturer in that department and in the Department of Architecture. In 1970 he delivered the Reith lectures on the BBC. His books include *The Displacement of Concepts*, 1963; *Technology and Change*, 1966; *Beyond the Stable State*, 1971; *Theory in Practice: Increasing Professional Effectiveness*, 1974; and *Organizational Learning: A Theory of Action Perspective*, 1978 (both with Chris Argyris); *The Reflective Practitioner*, 1983; *Educating the Reflective Practitioner*, 1987; and *Frame Reflection: Toward the Resolution of Intractable Policy Controversies* (with Martin Rein), 1994.

Lance Taylor, currently a member of the Graduate Faculty Department of Economics at the New School for Social Research in New York City, was formerly professor in the Departments of Economics and Urban Studies and Planning at MIT. A development economist, he has worked as a visiting scholar or consultant in about twenty-five countries, most recently including India, Nicaragua, and South Africa. His two most recent books are *Varieties of Stabilization Experience*, 1988; and *Income Distribution, Inflation, and Growth*, 1991. He has also published over ninety papers.

Judith Tendler is a development economist and professor of political economy in the Department of Urban Studies and Planning at MIT. She has carried out extensive evaluation research on programs in the government and nongovernment sectors, particularly in Brazil and other Latin American countries. Her publications include *Inside Foreign Aid* and *Electric Power in Brazil: Entrepreneurship in the Public Sector*, and *New Lessons From Old Projects: The Workings of Rural Development in Northeast Brazil*. She has just completed a manuscript entitled "Good Government in the Tropics."

Other Participants

Graduate Students
Paola Perez-Aleman
Matthias Beck
Anuradha Joshi
David Laws
Xiannuan Lin
Lynn McCormick
Marisela Montoliu Munoz
Lourdes Paragan

Meenu Tewari
Karen Umemoto
Alex Walters

Seminar Coordinator
Jean Riesman

Postdoctoral Fellow
Christie Baxter

Acknowledgments

Professors Bishwapriya Sanyal and Donald A. Schön conceived the idea of a faculty seminar rethinking the experience of development, using as a starting point the ideas of Albert O. Hirschman. Lisa Peattie, Karen R. Polenske, Martin Rein, Lloyd Rodwin, Lance Taylor and Judith Tendler—together with Sanyal and Schön—attended all or most of the sessions. So did Robert Einsweiler of the Lincoln Institute. Other faculty at MIT and elsewhere, who attended one or more sessions, were David Barkin, Paul R. Krugman, Michael Piore, Emma Rothschild, and Charles F. Sabel. Albert Hirschman agreed to lead the final session and discussion. He also reviewed the manuscript and contributed many perceptive suggestions.

Robert Picciotto—after learning belatedly about our activities—expressed interest in participation, which we very much welcomed. And it was Albert Hirschman who called our attention to Elliot Marseille's paper. We held a special seminar in the fall of 1993 to discuss these two papers. Still other participants for one or more sessions were two friends of Hirschman   Luca Mendolesi and Nicoletta Stame.

Twelve graduate students and a postdoctoral fellow were invited to attend the sessions. Those who made observations or raised questions that are included in appendix A include Paola Perez-Aleman, David Laws, Lynn McCormick, Meenu Tewari, Jean Riesman, Karen Umemoto, and Alex Walters.

Rodwin coordinated these activities, and Jean Riesman served as his research and administrative assistant. She arranged—with exceptional imagination and efficiency—for reprints, an annotated bibliography of Hirschman's articles, resumes of the seminar, and presentations and discussions, and attended to other matters relating to the conduct of the seminar. Alex Walters did the same for the special session involving Elliot Marseille and Robert Picciotto. Their gracious assistance was most helpful.

We want to express our appreciation and thanks to the United Nations Center for Research and Development—and to Hidehiko Sazanami—who arranged to defray the cost of selected papers of the seminar participants and for a special seminar that was held in Nagoya, Japan, in the spring of 1994 on "Learning In and About Development." Peattie, Rodwin, Sanyal, and Schön participated in those sessions.

We also want to record and express our thanks to the Lincoln Institute and to Robert Einsweiler, its research director, for a grant that helped to defray the administrative costs of the enterprise; Myron Wiener, former director of MIT's Center for International Studies, for a grant to defray some of the costs of editing; Alice E. Ingerson, director of publications, Lincoln Institute; Nancy D. Davidson, acquisitions editor, Brookings Institution; Robert L. Faherty, director of publications, Brookings; and Amartya Sen, Raymond Vernon, and John Friedmann for exceptionally helpful suggestions. We also thank Venka Macintyre for editing the manuscript, Laura Kelly for verifying its factual content, and Robert Elwood for preparing the index.

Not least, we are indebted to Rolf R. Engler, administrative officer of the Department of Urban Studies and Planning at MIT, for his customary efficient and gracious assistance.

Lloyd Rodwin
Donald A. Schön

Index

Agricultural development, 215–16
Airport construction, 125, 295
Allais, Maurice, 112
Antidevelopment movements, 125–26, 129
Aoki, Masahiko, 241, 251
Aurobindo, Sri, 151
Auto industry, 33; inventory management, 239–40

Bailyn, Bernard, 140
Balanced-growth model, 42
Bangladesh, 216–17
Bateson, Gregory, 78
Bauman, Zygmunt, 121, 123
Benor, Daniel, 215
Bias for hope, 7, 21–23; in absence of theory, 137–38; balance in, 176–77; basis for, 131–33, 141, 142–43; historical analysis in, 139; political context, 132–33; tradition of, in economics, 131–32
Bias for Hope, A, 22–23, 176
Big Push model, 41–42, 52–57, 139, 293
Bloom, Alan, 135
Bourne, Randolph, 138
Boycotts, 126–29
Brazil, 16, 23, 81, 82; developmental associations, 263–65; development successes in, 178–79
Brazilian health care intervention, 26–29; basis for success, 183–84, 206–07; community relations, 205–06; curative care, 202–04; design, 182–83; hiring process, 184–87, 193–95, 199; job enlargement, 201–02, 204–06; monitoring of workers, 187–89; organizational structure, 197–201; outcomes, 26, 178–80; popular perception of public sector workers, 195–96; preventive care, 203–04, 205; professional supervision, 190–93; publicity, 189–90; significance of, 207–09; worker commitment in, 180–81, 184
Brilliant, Larry, 156, 157, 170, 173, 174
Bureaucracies, 124
Burke, Kenneth, 5

Camus, Albert, 283
Cardoso, Fernando Henrique, 279
Chenery, Hollis, 62, 63
Chile, 16, 81, 82, 227
China, 65
Circular causation, 46–47
Coase, R. H., 104
Cognitive style: contractarian approach, 268; Hirschman's, 21–22, 23, 210–11; as impediment to development, 69–70; interpretation in market-oriented approaches, 6; learning by doing, 16, 76–78, 82, 137; loss of popular faith in rationality, 20–21; passion versus reason, 120; in program evaluation, 26, 29–30; self-subversion, 281–82
Colombia, 16, 65, 81, 221
Complementarity, 70; versus substitution, 12, 61
Condorcet, M. J. A. N., 103, 107–09, 111,113, 115–16
Contractual relationships: construction of meaning in, 268; interpretation of noncompliance, 248–49; in Japan, 34, 246–47; limits of, 266; subcontracting practices in Japan, 242–44; in unbalanced growth environment, 247–48
Crisis management: as development project outcome factor, 214; social learning in, 82
Crozier, Michael, 124

Decentralization, of development, 229; of government, 197, 200–01; of industrial organizations, 235, 239
Dependencia thesis, 279
Developmental associations: in Brazil, 263–65; in disequilibrium learning, 255–56; international trends, 261–63; in Japan, 256–61; role of, 255
Development economics: balanced versus unbalanced growth, 237–39; Big Push model, 41–42, 52–57, 139; concept of progress in, 19–20; disequilibrium processes in, 12, 23, 60, 70–71, 238; high development theory,

39–43, 45–47; human rationality as factor
in, 124–25, 130; ideological basis of development planning, 122–23; and institutions,
226; market-oriented theory in, 6; modeling techniques and, 5, 10–11, 35, 40, 45,
47, 52–57, 62–63; participants in project design, 228–29; pessimism in practitioners,
133–35, 176–77; policymaking and, 64–65;
and public sector performance, 181; role of
state in, 61; social learning in, 14–15, 35,
137–38; trends, 5–6, 22–23, 39–43, 52, 57,
115–17, 143–44, 236–37
Development Projects Observed, 16, 30, 32,
83, 210, 213, 221
Dewey, John, 137, 138, 271
Disequilibrium: development as, 12, 23, 60,
70–71, 239; inflation as, 12, 60; in manufacturing practice, 33–34; social learning in,
15, 23, 70–71, 239; state intervention and
learning in, 252–56
Duesenberry, James, 13
Durkheim, Emile, 120, 266, 267
Dyson, Kenneth, 140

Ecology movement, 125, 128–29
Economic behavior: boycotts, 126–29; conceptual trends, 18–19, 109–14; economic
man concept, 7, 17–19, 100; game-
theoretic orientation, 233; in Hirschman's
thought, 17–18, 99–100, 141–42; individual differences in, 100; rationality in, 122;
self-interest in, 103–09; as sociable behavior, 235–36, 265–68. *See also* Economics
and economic theory
Economics and economic theory: complexity
of psychological factors in, 102, 109–12,
113–14; as discipline versus profession, 12,
36; evolution of development economics
in, 42; implications of social learning theory, 90–95; interdisciplinary studies in,
13–14; policymaking and, 11; social context of, 7–8, 13, 19–20; trends, 12–13, 22–
23, 65–66, 236–37. *See also* Development
economics; Economic behavior
Economies of scale, 10, 11–12, 41, 42, 236;
forward and backward linkages in, 43; modeling of, 43, 45–48
Ecuador, 31, 214
Ekstein, Modris, 123
Evaluation, of development: current trends,
65–66, 225–29; disappointment concept in,
213, 217–19; hiding hand and, 219–25; policymaking and, 212–13, 222–23; techniques of, 8, 211; visibility concept in,
213–17; versus research, 211; World Bank,
8, 16, 29–32

Exit, Voice, and Loyalty, 72, 118, 300; Hirschman on, 278, 280
Eye care programs: India cataract project,
148–53, 172–73; intraocular lens procedure for cataracts, 25–26, 149–50, 152–53,
167–75; Nepal project, 23–26, 154–75

Feedback processes, 41; in social learning,
73–74
Feyerabend, Paul, 269
Fishlow, Albert, 22–23
Fleming, J. M., 42, 46
Folger coffee, 127–28
Forward and backward linkages, 12, 42; con-
ceptual evolution, 47, 63; current applica-
tions, 59–60; definition, 42–43; Hirschman
on, 279–80
Frank, André Gunder, 279
Fultz, Dave, 11, 49
Fundraising, for Nepal blindness program,
24–25, 162–63, 164, 168
Fussell, Paul, 123

Game theory, 33, 34, 112; and economic co-
operation, 233–35, 249–50; Japanese indus-
trial style and, 246
General Electric, 127
Germany, 261, 262, 280
Gerschenkron, Alexander, 101, 236
Grandmont, J.-M., 112
Grasset, Nicole, 154–55, 156, 159, 162–63
Great Britain, 17–18, 307

Habermas, Jürgen, 270, 271
Health care. *See* Brazilian health care intervention; Eye care programs
Helvétius, 107, 108
Herder, J. G., 110–11, 113
Hiding hand, 24, 25, 31, 32, 84, 140; in Colombian community intervention, 221; evaluation and, 219–25; in Nepal blindness program, 160–64, 165, 301–02, 304
Hirschman, Albert O.; balanced-growth
model of development, 42; bias for hope,
22–23, 131–33, 136–38, 142–44, 176–77;
cognitive style, 21–22, 23, 210–11; concept
of diversity, 99–103; concept of linkages,
42–43, 279–80; cross-disciplinary approach,
13–14, 141–42; on decline of development
economics, 236–37; on *dependencia* thesis,
279; economic modeling and, 10–11, 40,
51, 285–86; evaluation methodology, 30–
31, 32, 211–13, 226, 228, 229–30; on German Democratic Republic, 280; historical
context, 118–19, 138–40; on human motivation, 120; influence of, 10, 12, 36, 59,